The
UNITED STATES
CONSTITUTION

The Smithsonian Institution gratefully acknowledges the generous financial support from Times Mirror, the Annie Laurie Aitken Charitable Trust, and the U.S. Congress, which made the "Constitutional Roots, Rights, and Responsibilities" international symposium possible in 1987.

Additional support for aspects of the symposium program, also gratefully acknowledged, came from:

    Gannett Foundation/Gannett Co., Inc.
    Ford Foundation
    The Lawyers Co-operative Publishing Company/Bancroft-
      Whitney
    Charles E. Culpeper Foundation, Inc.
    Beazley Foundation
    Charles F. Kettering Foundation
    Siemens Capital Corporation
    Merrill Lynch
    American Federation of Labor–Congress of Industrial
      Organizations
    Joseph H. Hazen Foundation
    United States Information Agency
    Institute for Psychiatry and Foreign Affairs
    A. Smith Bowman Distillery, Inc.
    Barrick W. Groom
    The Dillon Fund
    Saul Poliak

The
UNITED STATES
CONSTITUTION

Roots, Rights, and Responsibilities

...

Edited by A. E. Dick Howard

Smithsonian Institution Press

Washington and London

Editor: Jan McInroy
Production Editor: Duke Johns
Designer: Kathleen Sims

Library of Congress
Cataloging-in-Publication Data

The United States Constitution : roots, rights, and responsibilities/
  edited by A. E. Dick Howard.
    p. cm.
  Papers originally presented at the Ninth International
Smithsonian Symposium, Charlottesville, Va., and Washington,
D.C., May 1987.
  Includes bibliographical references.
  ISBN 1-56098-120-2 (alk. paper)
  1. United States—Constitutional law—Congresses.
2. United States—Constitutional history—Congresses. 3. Civil
rights—United States—Congresses. I. Howard, A. E. Dick.
  II. International Smithsonian Symposium
(9th : 1987 : Charlottesville, Va., and Washington, D.C.)
KF4550.A2U55 1992
342.73'029—dc20 [347.30229]   91-23703

British Library Cataloguing-in-Publication Data is available

Manufactured in the United States of America
99 98 97 96 95 94 93 92   5 4 3 2 1

⊗The paper used in this publication meets the minimum requirements of the American National Standard for Permanence
of Paper for Printed Library Materials Z39.48-1984

CONTENTS

CONTENTS

Contents

CONTENTS

Contents

Foreword

We are likely to agree that, at a symposium of this kind, very few wholly new ideas about the Constitution will emerge. But points will be sharpened, nuances will find new light and shading, and, as at Philadelphia two hundred years ago, we will all come away wiser for having heard other points of view, especially those of the guests from other countries who will perceive what we overlook. It is always useful to see ourselves through other eyes.

You may be sure I will not add anything that you have not heard or read, but an anniversary is an occasion to remember things well known but taken for granted. I have no speech or address; I would like simply to recall with you a few small parts of one of the greatest stories in the history of freedom, a story with few parallels other than the sources from which we drew both our organic law and our common law.

To understand our Constitution and our constitutional system, we must begin with a realization of how difficult it was for those fifty-five delegates at Philadelphia to produce it. They created a structure that had never before been tried on a national scale, and they did it in the face of widespread opposition to a central government that would diminish some of the powers of the states. They did not invent all these concepts. They drew on ancient wisdom and the more recent thinking of France, England, and the Scottish Enlightenment. Besides creating enforceable new rights between 1787 and 1791, they laid the basis for a common market on which our prosperity rested.

There were important cohesive factors, to be sure. One was the common language. Another was that the colonists or their immediate ancestors had come here seeking greater religious and political freedom and new opportunities. Yet another was that they had shared in the hardships of the long war for independence. Most of them probably came here because any change would give them a better life. But the common language, the new freedom, and shared hardships could not offset the powerful historic reality of the differing interests and concerns these people had—some economic, some social, some political.

Such manufacture as there was in the colonies took place largely in New England. While a great proportion of all the people were engaged in food production, the states of the South depended on agriculture, and agriculture in turn depended largely on the evil institution of slavery. And below the surface—but not far below—the abolitionists of the North and the dominant economic interests of the South were irresistible forces waiting to clash. At Philadelphia the inevitable decision was postponed, not to be made until three-quarters of a century later in a bloody civil war that destroyed countless lives and vast wealth. The agonizing problem of slavery was not fully brushed under the rug in 1787. While the delegates were debating in Philadelphia, the Continental Congress enacted the Northwest Ordinance, outlawing slavery in the new western lands.

The widespread dispersion of the American population created its own set of difficulties, in terms of both travel and communication. Philadelphia was four days from Mount Vernon by carriage. Boston and Savannah were weeks of travel apart, whether one moved by land or by sea. Communication could not be speedier than travel by horsepower or by sailing vessel. In short, Americans did not know each other very well, and that made them distrustful of any distant government that put power in the hands of people they did not know.

Once the Declaration of Independence had been signed and the American Revolution begun, this distrust of government prevented the former colonies from forming a strong, workable central government. They fought the Revolution under a loose confederation—a "firm league of friendship," they called it—that was little more than a multilateral treaty, more like the NATO of our day than a true nation. The members of that "firm league of friendship" described themselves as separate, independent, sovereign states.

The inadequacy of this Confederation emerged clearly during the war. Washington and his officers—who included Alexander Hamilton and young John Marshall—well knew that the terrible privation, the needless deaths from malnutrition and freezing that Washington's troops suffered throughout the war and especially at Valley Forge, only a few miles from where the delegates later met, were the result of the Confederation's weakness. Washington and other leaders had to beg and cajole the states just to get money and supplies sufficient to carry on the war.

Given the lack of a strong central authority to levy and collect taxes and raise armies, it is a wonder the Revolution was successful, and therefore that there was any occasion to convene the meeting in Philadelphia. It was Washington's leadership and the fact that George III had to keep his powder dry to deal with France, Spain, or Holland that gave us victory.

It soon became clear that the Articles of Confederation were even less adequate during peacetime than during war. As a result, soon after the surrender of Cornwallis at Yorktown, the Confederation—as has been true of all victorious wartime alliances—began literally to fall apart. States that had suffered much in the war were resentful of those that had shirked and failed to contribute their share. When the delegates met, one state had been in default of its "dues" for five years.

Under the Confederation, states were free to act as they pleased in matters of trade, and the Continental Congress was virtually impotent. Each of the thirteen states could set up trade barriers, and they began to do so once the war was over.

New York, for example, imposed duties on goods bound for Connecticut and New Jersey through New York harbors. This act enriched New York but enraged New Jersey and Connecticut, whose sea trade depended in large measure on the use of New York shipping facilities. When the Continental Congress failed to do anything about it, the New Jersey legislature voted to withhold its financial support from the Confederation. One congressman, Nathaniel Gorham of Massachusetts, feared that New Jersey and Connecticut would join forces in marching on New York, and, he said, "bloodshed would very quickly be the consequence." Other states with good ports—Pennsylvania,

Massachusetts, and South Carolina—treated their less fortunate neighbors in much the same way that New York treated Connecticut and New Jersey.

States were also free to issue their own currency, which impeded the development of commerce by increasing the costs of trade. The states seemed almost to compete with each other to see which could issue the most paper currency; much of the state-issued money was eventually worth next to nothing. Bankers and merchants had to keep an eye on as many as twelve different state currencies. A healthy commerce could never develop when not one but thirteen "yen versus dollar" kinds of problems arose daily.

Other economic differences led to political strife. States whose western lands extended to the Mississippi River, for example, wanted greater military protection from the Spanish. States with no western lands, on the other hand, were afraid that war with Spain would bring the Spanish Armada, which would threaten cities on the coast. And when, in 1785, Massachusetts, Rhode Island, and New Hampshire passed laws restricting British trade in their ports in an attempt to force the British to permit them to reopen trade with the West Indies, Connecticut, seeking more trade for itself, promptly undercut the other states by announcing that British ships would be welcomed in its ports. That very wise observer James Madison remarked, "Most of our political evils may be traced to our commercial ones."

The Continental Congress was also unable to resolve conflicting claims to frontier lands. Connecticut, for example, had claimed land in part of what is now Pennsylvania. It had even sent settlers there, who ended up fighting with Pennsylvania troops before the dispute was resolved. And settlers in the wilderness of northern New York had seceded and formed a separate state, in the area we now know as Vermont.

The weaknesses of the Confederation were perhaps most evident in the areas of foreign relations. The Continental Congress could not force the states to abide by the treaties it made. The states refused to repay debts owed to British creditors, as required by the Treaty of Paris—an issue not formally resolved until a Supreme Court case in 1796. Several states entered treaties with American Indian tribes that were in conflict with those entered by the Continental Congress. We remember that England used such state maneuvers as an excuse for failing to dismantle its forts on the Great Lakes, as required by the Treaty of Paris. The weakness in foreign policy matters was further evidenced by the inability to protect American shipping interests against the Barbary pirates—to whom we paid great sums in gold to ransom hostages.

These difficulties convinced Washington, Madison, Marshall, and Hamilton that the government under the Articles of Confederation was what we would call today a paper tiger. To continue that structure would not only inhibit our development as a nation and encourage parochial rivalries, it would also tempt the great powers to exploit our internal conflicts and rivalries.

But convincing the states of the need for a stronger central government was no easy task. In the eighteenth century and, indeed, well into the nineteenth, many people thought of themselves as Virginians or New Yorkers first and Americans second. They regarded themselves as allies—*allies*—of other states. During the Revolution, when New Jersey troops reporting for duty at Valley Forge were asked to swear allegiance to the United States, the soldiers at first refused, saying, "New Jersey is our country."

Quite aside from their loyalty to their own states, the American people in 1787 had a great and understandable fear of central governments, stemming from their experience with the distant, strong, insensitive central government in London, from which they had just fought a war to escape. Patrick Henry, for example, was so opposed to the idea of a stronger central government that he would later refuse even to be a delegate to Philadelphia, saying, "Methinks I smell a rat." The "rat" was the Constitution that emerged. He knew, of course, what Washington, Madison, and Hamilton wanted.

But the fallings-out among the thirteen victorious allies began to get very serious in about 1785. A quarrel arose between Virginia and Maryland over the use of the Potomac River and the Chesapeake Bay. It was a serious dispute, the kind of boundary conflict over which wars have often been fought in Europe and other parts of the world. In an effort to resolve the conflict, both states appointed commissioners. When they failed to reach an agreement, George Washington invited them to Mount Vernon, where they were able—no doubt with some gentle nudging—to resolve their differences.

James Madison and others then persuaded the Virginia legislature to invite all the states to send representatives to a general meeting in Annapolis, Maryland, in September 1786, to discuss commercial matters. Delegates from only five states showed up. Hamilton and Madison, however, persuaded those who attended to adopt a resolution reciting the existence of a grave crisis and noting the futility of considering commercial problems without also addressing the underlying political issues. The Annapolis resolution, sent to all the states and the Continental Congress, proposed that the states send representatives to a convention, to be held at Philadelphia in May 1787, to consider these basic problems.

The Virginia legislature approved the idea of a convention and placed George Washington at the head of its delegation. Six other state legislatures followed suit in short order. The Continental Congress, however, initially tabled the proposal and refused to endorse the idea.

About the time of the Annapolis Convention, an uprising now known as Shays' Rebellion broke out in western Massachusetts. It began as a series of protests by indebted farmers who wanted paper money and more favorable foreclosure and bankruptcy laws. On September 26, 1786, an armed band led by Daniel Shays defeated the state militia and obliged some state courts to adjourn. During December 1786 and January 1787, Shays gathered a large force and attempted to seize the federal arsenal at Springfield, but he and his men were ultimately routed by General Benjamin Lincoln. This was not merely protest; blood was shed.

Needless to say, Shays' Rebellion made a tremendous impression on the rest of the country at a time when many of the states were still deciding whether to send delegates to Philadelphia and when the Continental Congress was still deciding whether to endorse that meeting. George Washington summarized the sentiments of many of his countrymen by expressing disgust that the country, having just won a difficult war, could not keep order in peacetime: Shays' Rebellion, he said, "exhibit[s] a melancholy proof of what our trans-Atlantic foe has predicted; and of another thing perhaps, which is still more to be regretted, and is yet more unaccountable, that mankind when left to themselves are unfit for their own Government. I am mortified beyond expression when I view the clouds that have spread over the brightest morn that ever dawned upon any Country. . . . To be more exposed in the eyes of the world, and more contemptible than we already are, is hardly possible." Mr. Shays had helped persuade some that changes were needed.

Finally, on February 21, 1787, the Continental Congress, with some reluctance, officially invited the thirteen states to send delegates to Philadelphia. Although Washington, Hamilton, Madison, and others had urged calling a true constitutional convention, the Continental Congress—many of whose members shared Patrick Henry's fears—refused to endorse the idea fully. Its resolution was explicit: The meeting was to be called "for the *sole* and express purpose of *revising* the Articles of Confederation." There was no hint of drafting a new Constitution. Patrick Henry's "rat" worried many people.

This, then, was the setting two hundred years ago today as Washington, Madison, and Hamilton waited for a quorum of states' delegates to arrive in Philadelphia. Bad weather and overflowing streams caused delay. Washington had expressed doubts about even going to the meeting. He had said: "I do not conceive we can long exist as a nation without having lodged somewhere a power which will pervade the whole Union in as energetic a manner as the authority of the state governments extends over the several states."

But four and a half days by carriage put him in Philadelphia. While they waited, Washington, Madison, Hamilton, Mason, and others quietly went forward with plans for a more comprehensive convention, which finally produced a constitution. They created a national government sufficiently strong to deal with the pressing problems that the Confederation had been unable to resolve.

Was their document perfect? Of course not. The barons who forced King John to agree to Magna Carta at Runnymede did not solve all the problems that existed in 1215, nor did we solve all the problems that existed in 1787, or even in 1791. Human institutions have long gestation periods and often agonizing birth pains. But that Constitution set up a structure of government that has permitted our nation to achieve a kind of freedom and prosperity unprecedented in human history.

Jefferson, writing from Paris, with all his reservations about the absence of a Bill of Rights, called the Constitution the work of "demigods." It unleashed the latent energies of millions of people as never before in all of history. It enabled this small band of Americans to lay the foundations of a world power in less than a century and a half. That is what we celebrate.

Warren E. Burger
Chairman, Commission on the Bicentennial of the Constitution
Chief Justice of the United States, 1969–1986

Introduction

There is something about a centenary—or its multiples—that invites musings upon the lessons of history. National leaders, historians, poets, playwrights, official and unofficial bodies, and others take the occasion of a great event's anniversary to spin yarns, make speeches, and have parades. National virtues are celebrated, God's bounty is acknowledged, moral teachings are unfolded, aspirations and hopes are aired.

Each generation brings its own insights to such anniversaries. English notions about the defeat, in 1588, of the Spanish Armada offer a case in point. For centuries the armada has been a central motif in popular definitions of the English character. Whig history represented the English victory over Spain as being the triumph of liberty over despotism. Song and verse hailed Sir Francis Drake's sangfroid— legend has him playing at bowls on the eve of the battle—and the pluck of the English sailors facing, like David, a Spanish Goliath. Austin Dobson's verse told of King Philip's "army of heathenish names," then declared, "But we had bold Neptune to back us / And where are the galleons of Spain?"

The year 1988 brought the inevitable retrospective as to how, four hundred years later, the drama of 1588 should be viewed. Books appeared in numbers seemingly as dense as the ships of Spain. But this time the mythmaking of earlier anniversaries gave way to more sober reflections. Oxford University Press brought forth an account—by a Spanish-surnamed don at St. Antony's College—concluding that the traditional view of the 1588 encounter was based on "a pride of achievement unjustified by the facts."[1]

The closing decades of the twentieth century brought a series of bicentennial occasions. Americans marked the bicentenary of Independence in 1976, of the Constitution's drafting in 1987, and of the submission of the Bill of Rights to the states by Congress in 1989. France invited the world, in 1989, to consider the legacy of the Declaration of the Rights of Man and the Citizen.

Government, naturally enough, wished to accentuate the positive. Of France's 1989 celebrations, Alexander Cockburn commented: "The French Government seems to have decided to remember a revolution occurring between 1789 and 1792; Mirabeau, Danton, and the Girondins who, with a little touch-up here and there, can be made to look like decent moderate Socialists of the late Twentieth Century. Robespierre, Saint-Just, and the great Committee of Public Safety, who presided over the Terror, saved the revolution, and have not been invited."[2]

The thrust of France's Bicentenaire was decidedly upbeat. The official mission published a handsome eighty-four-page "Programme" cataloging commemorative events, not only in France but throughout the world. The organizers' theme is reflected in Mirabeau's declaration, made to the National Assembly in 1789 and quoted on the cover of the "Programme": "Montrons au monde la superbe perspective de la France, l'ensemble de ses besoins, de ses ressources, de ses droits, de ses esperances."[3] In 1989, as in 1789, France wanted the world to look to Paris for inspiration.

What of the United States Constitution? It is now in its third century, and one may properly assume that as that document has seen periodic anniversaries pass, Americans have sought to take its measure and gauge its meaning.

There were, of course, fetes on the occasion of states' ratification of the Constitution. When the Massachusetts convention gave its approval to the Constitution, on February 6, 1788, a local newspaper reported that "a large concourse of spectators testified their satisfaction by repeated huzzas."[4] The next day, church bells were rung all day. The day after that, the Committee of Tradesmen organized a parade in which bakers, hatters, mast-makers, seamen, bookbinders, and others marched.[5]

Not everyone, of course, approved the outcome of the contest over ratification. (Virginia ratified 89–79, and in New York the vote was even closer.) After Pennsylvania, on December 12, 1787, became the second state to ratify the Constitution, in Carlisle a riot disrupted the celebration. As the organizers of the planned event began to light a bonfire, they were threatened and set upon by armed protesters. "Having accomplished their pre-meditated designs of preventing the public rejoicing," members of the mob proceeded to burn copies of the Constitution.[6] Supporters of ratification gathered the next day, lit their bonfire, and enjoyed supper at a local tavern. Although the dinner was, it was reported, an "evening with the most perfect harmony, good humor, and conviviality," outside in the streets protesters burned effigies of James Wilson and Thomas M'Kean (ardent supporters of the Constitution).[7]

The Constitution's semicentennial was marked not on the anniversary of the document's signing but on April 30, 1839, the fiftieth anniversary of the inauguration of George Washington as president of the United States. The New-York Historical Society organized a public oration and dinner, selecting as the orator President John Quincy Adams. After the singing of an ode (composed for the occasion by William Cullen Bryant), President Adams held forth for two hours. It is recorded that "by the extraordinary ability, learning, and eloquence which it displayed," the president's address "fully sustained the most sanguine anticipations of the friends of the distinguished orator."[8]

The nation's semicentennial—as opposed to that of the Constitution—had begun some years earlier. On the eve of the nation's celebration of the fiftieth birthday of the Declaration of Independence (1826), Americans welcomed the Marquis de Lafayette. His tour, which took him to twenty-four states, was a triumph, its high point coming when he and Thomas Jefferson, both advanced in years, met at Monticello. On July 4, 1826, in a coincidence so extraordinary that many observers thought it divinely ordained, both Jefferson and John Adams died. By the time John Quincy Adams orated on the Constitution's semicentennial, the founders' generation had passed from the scene. In 1839, although sectional differences had surfaced (notably at the Hartford Convention in 1814 and in the nullification controversy centering upon South Carolina), the clash of arms still lay more than two decades in the future. As of 1839, President Adams could declare, "[T]hanks to this Constitution . . . these are the halcyon days of our existence. . . ." But Adams had a word of warning: Americans would be in for "sharp and bitter times" should they ever "betray, renounce, or abandon the self-evident principles upon which our Union was formed, our Independence declared, and our Constitution established, by our forefathers of former days."[9]

In 1887 Philadelphia undertook to celebrate the Constitution's centenary with all the fervor and spectacle that one might expect of America's gilded age. On September 15, the Industrial Parade included 300 floats, 12,000 men, 3,000 horses, and 150 bands. Some of the floats' themes focused on education and civic progress. The *Brooklyn Eagle* reported on the exhibit of the Indian Industrial School at Carlisle, Pennsylvania: "In the neat uniforms of their schools, trim and tidy as any boys in any grammar-school in the land, marching steady as soldiers, with the free, easy stride born of the prairies, each dark-skinned brave armed with a slate, marched these dusky warriors from Carlisle and Hampton and Lincoln Institute. It was grand, it was inspiring, it was sublime, it was Christian."[10]

Organizing a "Colored People's Display" caused the centennial committee some difficulties. The first float (of three) represented a plantation in the days of slavery, but, as the organizing committee's secretary noted, the committee "had failed to find colored people, even with the offer of a liberal pecuniary reward, willing to go on the float as slaves." (The secretary appears to have been surprised by this fact.) Another float in the series (labeled "Industry") showed artisans and craftsmen at their tasks. Again, however, the committee's secretary lamented that the float had fallen short of the committee's hopes to make a presentation of "physical, intellectual, and moral advance within the past century as would have astonished and delighted the well-wishers of their race."[11]

The celebrants of 1887 obviously saw a link between the blessings of the Constitution and the nation's material and industrial progress. Manufacturers and tradesmen were eager to use the Industrial Parade to show their wares and talents. The Remington Standard Type-Writer Company produced a float on which, at one end, a man dressed in the manner of 1787 wrote with a quill pen. (Whether he was working on a draft of the Constitution, the account of the parade does not say.) At the other end of the float, a businessman dictated to a typist, who produced words at the rate of sixty to seventy-five per minute. The organizing committee's secretary noted that the Remington Company was selling from 1,500 to 2,000 machines a month; he concluded, with evident pride, "It will, therefore, be seen that the business of this firm alone amounts to considerably more than one million dollars per year."[12]

The opportunity to put allegory at the service of commerce was not overlooked. Philadelphia's Lager Beer Brewing Association undertook one of the parade's most popular entries. One of that organization's floats carried a Gothic temple, in which the goddess Hebe offered nectar to King Gambrinus, who refused the offer, "preferring beer instead." A banner proclaimed, "Beer, Staff of Life." Another float, more elaborate still, represented "Wine, Woman, and Song." On the float, seated on luxurious chairs and divans, were Minnesingers, "who rendered homage to woman in verse and song." It is reported that this spectacle excited "universal applause among the spectators."[13]

Achievements great and small, useful and peculiar, were celebrated in Philadelphia's parade. The Pennsylvania Railroad, in a series of floats, traced the history of transportation—pack mules, canal boats, railroad cars. Borax Soap loaded two hundred boxes of its "improved soap" on a float, while Mr. Charles A. Glass exhibited his newly invented device for turning music leaves. There seemed to be a preoccupation with size: One float carried "the largest photograph in the world" (the centennial buildings of 1876), another displayed "the largest crayon in oil in the world" (which, for a proper view, had to be seen from two hundred feet away), and William John Christy exhibited "the largest bass-viol in the world." The motif of the parade might well have been summed up in the Philadelphia Wire Works motto: "What cannot be done in Philadelphia cannot be done elsewhere."[14]

After such displays of invention and enterprise, it was probably necessary for the centennial commission's chairman to remind the audience, at the concluding ceremonies in Independence Square, "The one object of this celebration has been to demonstrate and quicken the reverence and love of the American people of all orders for their national Constitution."[15] It was quite a ceremony. John Philip Sousa conducted the Marine Band. A chorus of two thousand boys from the city's public schools sang "The March of the Men of Columbia," and a chorus of three hundred men rendered Schiller's "Appeal to Truth," as set to music by Mendelssohn.[16]

President Grover Cleveland, who made brief remarks, saw in the Constitution's strength the evidence of divine blessing: "[T]o us is delivered this ark of the people's covenant, and to us is given the duty to shield it from impious hands."[17] Justice Samuel T. Miller, who gave the principal oration, celebrated an Anglo-Saxon veneration for law as the basis for the Constitution. He yielded to no man in his "admiration and love for the Constitution of the United States," but he added the admonition that "no amount of wisdom in a constitution can produce wise government unless there is a suitable response in the spirit of the people."[18]

If the Constitution's centenary was marked by piety and lofty rhetoric—mixed with civic pride and optimism—the sesquicentennial anniversary invited far different responses. For many people, 1937 was a year of apprehension and concern. Americans were still wrestling with the burdens inflicted by the Great Depression. Storm clouds were gathering in Europe. The Constitution itself—President Cleveland's "ark of the covenant"—was viewed through the lens of new and pressing crises. The "Nine Old Men" were using the power of judicial review to thwart President Roosevelt's New Deal, and FDR responded with his proposal, hotly debated, to "pack" the Court.

Roosevelt's Secretary of Agriculture, Henry A. Wallace, wrote a book titled *Whose Constitution?* Wallace invited 1936 to "shake hands with 1787," to recognize that the framers of the Constitution "were amazingly resourceful and daring in establishing a national mechanism with which to deal with their national problem."[19] Wallace's thesis, of course, was that a "living Constitution" provided ample basis for the New Deal. Phillips Bradley commented, "Liberty Leaguers will be enraged by the clarity and cogency of his arguments; for the rest of us, it provides an intelligible platform for economic as well as for political democracy."[20]

Edward S. Corwin, perhaps the country's leading constitutional scholar, was especially critical of the uses being made of the Constitution at its sesquicentenary. Reviewing principal chapters in the Constitution's uses and interpretation, Corwin saw the document as having passed through three phases, as (1) a source of national power, (2) an object of popular worship, and (3) in Corwin's time, "a protection of certain minority interests seeking escape from national power"—that is, "the *negative* instrument of certain special interests, not the *positive* instrument of a government of the people." Thus the Constitution as symbol parted company with the Constitution as instrument, the symbol of the many becoming the instrument of the few.[21]

Constitution Day—September 17, 1937—was quite different from the date marked fifty years earlier. On that date in 1937, opponents to the Court-packing plan addressed a rally in Chicago stadium.[22] Justice Hugo L. Black's alleged ties with the Ku Klux Klan made front-page news on Constitution Day. In Philadelphia, a justice of the Pennsylvania Supreme Court included in his oration the comment "No man with prejudice in his heart against any race or religion has ever sat on the Supreme Court of the United States. May that proud record never be broken."[23] There were, in 1937 as in 1887, public ceremonies. In Philadelphia, rain forced the cancellation of a military parade featuring 1,500 marchers from the thirteen original states, but Boston's Constitution Day parade sufficiently impressed the local press that it declared, "As a spectacle, the parade was enough to indicate to the visitors from Mars that the Constitution has been a great success."[24]

As Americans prepared to mark the Constitution's bicentennial year, there were ample reasons to mull over the ever more obvious place of the Constitution in the life of the nation and its people. Under Chief Justice Earl Warren, the Supreme Court, bent on reform, had undertaken to desegregate American schools, to require that legislatures be based on a principle of one person, one vote, and to nationalize state criminal procedure by interpreting the Fourteenth Amendment as "incorporating" most of the provisions of the Bill of Rights. Even after President Richard M. Nixon appointed four justices to the Court, the tribunal during Chief Justice Warren E. Burger's years found yet more work for the Constitution to do—sharply limiting state power to impose capital punishment, vastly expanding the notion of a constitutional right to privacy (including a woman's right to an abortion), and ordering Nixon to turn over the Watergate tapes, resulting in the president's resignation. By 1987, never had "judicial activism" and "judicial restraint" been more widely debated.

After his retirement as chief justice, in 1986, Warren Burger took on the task of chairing the Commission on the Bicentennial of the United States Constitution. Burger saw the bicentennial as an apt occasion for a national "history and civics lesson." He hoped to avoid such hoopla as having Elvis Presley imitators in the official program. The private sector brought forth the inevitable bicentennial pens, place mats, puzzles, ashtrays, and comic books. Public celebrations, as befits an age nurtured on hype and hoopla, tended to the spectacular. In New York, Citicorp's skyscraper lit up like the flag, while in Washington President Reagan played host as red, white, and blue balloons floated up in front of the Capitol. Philadelphia updated its idea of what a parade should look like. Radio City Music Hall Productions choreographed a thirty-block parade, including fifty CPAs marching in formation, carrying briefcases and chanting, "We don't care for rock and roll, we're gonna find a tax loophole."[25]

The bicentennial era had, of course, its more serious and cerebral side. Supreme Court Justice Thurgood Marshall stirred hot debate when, in remarks to a bar group, he took sharp issue with the basic premise of the commemorative undertakings:

> Nor do I find the wisdom, foresight, and sense of justice exhibited by the Framers particularly profound. To the contrary, the government they devised was defective from the start, requiring several amendments, a civil war, and momentous social transformation to attain the system of constitutional government, and its respect for the individual freedoms and human rights, we enjoy as fundamental today. When contemporary Americans cite "The Constitution," they invoke a concept that is vastly different from what the Framers barely began to construct two centuries ago.[26]

Other observers took issue with Justice Marshall, including William Bradford Reynolds, who declared, "Notwithstanding its very serious flaws, the Constitution in its original form constituted the greatest advance for human liberty in the entire history of mankind, then or since."[27]

What of scholarship during the bicentennial era? An article in the *Chronicle of Higher Education* announced a general verdict that, on the cerebral side, the bicentennial had been an "intellectual bust."[28] Critics complained that, despite a wealth of fellowships, grants, and conferences, constitutional scholarship during the bicentennial period had been, in general, lethargic. Peter S. Onuf, however, has written, "I challenge these prematurely pessimistic assessments."[29] Certainly important works have appeared. These include Leonard Levy's exceptionally valuable four-volume *Encyclopedia of the American Constitution*, Merrill Jensen's useful *Documentary History of the Ratification of the*

Constitution, and Michael Kammen's brisk *A Machine That Would Go of Itself: The Constitution in American Culture.*[30]

One of the earmarks of the Constitution's bicentenary was the series of academic conferences held on university campuses and elsewhere. It is hard to imagine that a more distinguished group of scholars gathered than those who came together, in May 1987, at the invitation of the Smithsonian Institution and the University of Virginia. Entitled "Constitutional Roots, Rights, and Responsibilities," the symposium opened in the Rotunda of Mr. Jefferson's University.

The Supreme Court was represented by Chief Justice Burger, who made remarks at the opening dinner, and Justice William J. Brennan, Jr. From Great Britain came dignitaries such as the Lord High Chancellor, Lord Hailsham, and scholars such as Edinburgh's Neil MacCormick. From other nations came, to give but examples, Robert Badinter, the president of France's Counseil Constitutionnel; Ernst Benda, of the University of Freiburg; and Marcelo Fernan, a justice of the Supreme Court of the Philippines. The Americans present were a who's who of constitutional scholarship, representing such disciplines as law, history, and political science, and prepared to embark upon spirited dialogue as to the Constitution and its powerful ideas.

The present volume flows from the papers presented at the Smithsonian's symposium. They represent, viewed from one perspective, a series of snapshots of the issues that scholars and public figures in the closing years of the twentieth century find worth debate and inquiry. But taken together they are far more than simply a photograph album of the issues of the moment. The reader who pursues these essays will find in them the enduring questions of constitutional government. There are papers that, written for one generation, remain worth the attention of posterity. I predict that the browser in a library in 2037—the 250th anniversary of the Constitution—who comes across this volume will find its questions still pertinent, its essays still worth the reading.

As the Constitution begins its third century, events in other lands have presented a bicentennial pageant that no planner of American conferences or other events could have predicted. In the streets of Berlin and Budapest, of Prague and Warsaw, we have seen the yearning for freedom bring about one of the rare moments in human existence that can—like the revolutionary eras in the 1770s and in 1848—be pronounced genuinely historic. As they fashion the means of self-government, the people of Eastern Europe understand the relevance of the American experience. Polish novelist Jerzy Kosinski has said, "In every Pole, there is a little Thomas Jefferson." The ideas of the American founding travel well, because the framers knew, with Condorcet, of the "common core of human happiness"—the aspirations that transcend national boundaries.

The United States Constitution has prospered, in good measure, because of the special fortune showered upon Americans—an abundant land, relative freedom from foreign invasion, a climate of enterprise, a belief in divine providence. But there is more to the Constitution than simply the American experience. Just as Magna Carta is a symbol understood by those who are not English, so the United States Constitution speaks to those in continents far from this one. It is appropriate, therefore, to dedicate this volume not only to the inspired drafters who met at Philadelphia but also to brave and committed people, whatever their land and tongue, who have made the phrase "We the People" an international birthright.

A. E. Dick Howard
Chairman, Ninth International Smithsonian Symposium
Charlottesville, Virginia
and Washington, D.C.

Notes

1. Felipe Fernandez-Armesto, *The Spanish Armada: The Experience of War in 1588* (Oxford: Oxford University Press, 1988), v.

2. "Tête à Tête," *Interview* 19, no. 3 (March 1989): 84.

3. Mission du Bicentenaire de la Révolution Française et de la Déclaration des Droits de l'Homme et du Citoyen, *Le Programme: Introduction, Les Grands Moments, Les Grandes Manifestations, France, Le Monde* (Paris, 1989).

4. *Boston Gazette and County Journal*, February 11, 1788.

5. Ibid.

6. *American Mercury*, January 27, 1788, 2.

7. Ibid.

8. William Cullen Bryant, *Great Were the Hearts and Strong the Minds* (New York, 1839), 124.

9. Ibid., 126–27.

10. Hampton L. Carson, ed., *History of the Celebration of the One Hundredth Anniversary of the Promulgation of the Constitution of the United States* (Philadelphia: J. B. Lippincott, 1889), 2:42.

11. Ibid., 70–71.

12. Ibid., 38.

13. Ibid., 89–90.

14. Ibid., 118, 145, 151–53, 156.

15. Ibid., 255.

16. Ibid., 252–53, 259.

17. Ibid., 262.

18. Ibid., 288.

19. Henry A. Wallace, *Whose Constitution?* (New York: Reynal and Hitchcock, 1936), 90.

20. Book Review, *Social Education* (March 1937): 214.

21. Edward S. Corwin, "The Constitution as Instrument and as Symbol," *American Political Science Review* 30, no. 6 (December 1936): 1080, 1082.

22. *Washington Post*, September 17, 1937, 1.

23. *New York Times*, September 17, 1937, 13.

24. *New York Times*, September 18, 1937, 1; *Boston Daily Globe*, September 18, 1937, 1.

25. *Newsweek*, September 28, 1987, 83.

26. Thurgood Marshall, "The Constitution's Bicentennial: Commemorating the Wrong Document?" *Vanderbilt Law Review* 40 (1987): 1338.

27. Ibid., 1346.

28. *Chronicle of Higher Education*, March 4, 1987, 6.

29. *William and Mary Quarterly* 46, no. 2 (April 1989): 342.

30. Leonard W. Levy, Kenneth L. Karst, and Dennis J. Mahoney, eds., *Encyclopedia of the American Constitution* (New York: Macmillan, 1986); Merrill Jensen, ed., *Documentary History of the Ratification of the Constitution* (Madison, Wis.: State Historical Society of Wisconsin, 1976–   ); Michael Kammen, *A Machine That Would Go of Itself: The Constitution in American Culture* (New York: Knopf, 1986).

PART I

*Roots: The Old and New World
Origins of American
Constitutionalism*

CHAPTER I

The State Constitutions as Analogy and Precedent

The American Experience with Constituent Power before 1787

•••••

WILLI PAUL ADAMS

The same train of ideas which belonged to the relation of the
Citizens to their State Govts. were applicable to their relations to
the Genl. Govt., and in forming the latter, we ought to proceed
by abstracting as much as possible from the idea of State Govts.
—James Wilson, 1787

The state constitutions' profound influence on the drafting of the federal Constitution and on the ratification debates was taken for granted
by contemporaries. That influence took various shapes and forms,
ranging from explicit institutional precedent and reasoning by analogy
to negative examples of what to avoid. Whether in a positive or a
negative sense, the state constitutions were natural points of reference
in the constitutional debates of 1787–88 because they were the constitutions that Americans knew best. When, for example, Alexander
Hamilton set out to persuade his fellow New Yorkers of the advantages
of the draft Constitution of 1787, he did not fail to point out to them
"the analogy of the proposed government to your own State constitution." "It is remarkable," he wrote, "that the resemblance of the plan of
the convention to the act which organizes the government of this State
holds, not less with regard to many of the supposed defects than to the
real excellences of the former." He mentioned specifics: "Among the
pretended defects are the reeligibility of the executive, the want of a
[governor's/president's] council, the omission of a provision respect-

3

ing the liberty of the press."[1] Historiography, to date, does not adequately reflect the state constitutions' importance to the framers and to the public(s) whose consent was needed to turn their draft into a living Constitution. The reason may be that nationally minded historians have been so taken by the Federalists' victory in 1788 and so mindful of the harsh criticism, voiced in the Philadelphia Convention, of such state policies as prodebtor paper money legislation, that they have underestimated the indebtedness of the federal Constitution to its predecessors in the states.[2]

But the better we understand these connections, the more clearly we recognize the extent of the continuity between the values and institutions of 1776 and those of 1789. Neglect of these continuities has led to the exaggerated claim that "modern" politics began in Philadelphia in the summer of 1787.[3] In fact, the modern politics of American constitution making began in the spring of 1776, with the public debate triggered by Thomas Paine's scathing critique of British monarchy and his call for separation. As independence became a publicly acknowledged and openly debated goal, the central issue of American politics—second in importance only to the war effort—was how to put republican government into practice in a large and regionally diversified territory. After the decision for independence was made, there was no alternative to the establishment of republican state constitutions. Their drafting demanded answers to core questions of modern politics: how to reconcile individual freedom with the Republic's "common good" and stable and efficient government; how to have a multitude of free and equal citizens living in dispersed communities draft and agree on a set of constitutional ground rules—in the absence of a more or less enlightened monarch to "give" them one. The answers—an effective and fair system of representation, regulated by a written, amendable constitution and a catalog of inalienable fundamental rights, drafted by a constitutional convention and agreed upon by more or less "popular" ratification—were first given in the states between 1776 and 1780.[4] A continuous process of learning, communication, and adjustment among the same political elites, not a quantum jump, breakthrough, or revolutionary exchange of leadership, led from Virginia's revolutionary convention codifying a set of fundamental rights in June 1776 to federal protection of such rights in 1791.

By 1787, the idea of republican government had thus acquired a body in the shape of the state constitutions, especially those (of Massachusetts and New York, for example) with provisions for a bicameral legislature and an independent executive and judiciary. (The shape of the Confederation, by comparison, was obviously more the result of political circumstance than of conscious constitution making.) By contrast, British limited monarchy and other European forms of government mentioned repeatedly in the federal Convention, ranging from Sparta to the Swiss cantons, served a different function. They were a foil, not a model, a backdrop for highlighting American distinctiveness. The president of the United States, clearly, was not a downgraded monarch for four years but a governor writ large. The U.S. Senate was not a chamber of lords representing no one but themselves for six years but a cross between a governor's council and a Confederation-type representation of state interests. The U.S. House of Representatives was not a parliament of "virtual" representatives of the nation who did not even have to live in their highly unequal, sometimes "bought" constituencies and who could be tempted by executive patronage; instead, it was a transposed state house of representatives, each member of which clearly identified his own interests as those of the voters in his carefully defined district.[5]

Instances of Reasoning by Analogy in 1787

The state-nation analogy was invoked at the Philadelphia Convention, for instance, in the tense debate over the composition of the Senate. Nathaniel Gorham of Massachusetts accepted the small states' argument that the Senate need not be composed according to population size because, among other things, the hypothetical sixteen senators of a large state like Virginia were more likely to vote together and hence exert more influence than the sixteen senatorial votes that might be mustered by several small states combined. This observation, Gorham added, applied "not only to States but to Counties and other districts of the same State"; his home state's constitution also did not provide for the larger electoral districts to be represented in the state senate in strict numerical proportion. "And experience he thought had shewn the provision to be expedient."[6]

One of Gorham's opponents, James Wilson of Pennsylvania, insisted on proportional representation in the U.S. Senate as well as in the House. Both state and national governments, Wilson argued, "were derived from the people—both meant for the people—both therefore ought to be regulated on the same principles. The same train of ideas which belonged to the relation of the Citizens to their State Govts. were applicable to their relations to the Genl. Govt. and in forming the latter, we ought to proceed, by abstracting as much as possible from the idea of State Govts."[7]

Gouverneur Morris of New York pleaded for U.S. senators to be elected for life because state senators had shown themselves to be insufficiently independent of the state houses of representatives. When he argued against ratification of the U.S. Constitution by the state legislatures, Morris drew another parallel between states and nation: "In case of an appeal to the people of the U.S., the supreme authority, the federal compact may be altered by *a majority of them*; in like manner as the Constitution of a particular State may be altered by a majority of the people of the State."[8]

When the time finally came to compromise, Elbridge Gerry of Massachusetts once more explicitly drew on state experience: "We must make concessions on both sides. Without these the constitutions of the several States would never have been formed."[9]

Institutional Precedents: President, Impeachment, and Senate

The presidency, combining the functions of head of state and head of the government, was endowed with unique features. It is true that "even if the Philadelphia delegates built Article II by analogy with their experience of state governorships, they had additional and different prerogatives in mind. . . . [T]he new chief magistrate would in international affairs have responsibilities on another level from that of gubernatorial business."[10] Nevertheless, the structural characteristics of the office, including its peculiar relation to the bicameral congress, so different from that of a prime minister's connection with a parliament, did not have to be drafted onto a tabula rasa in 1787; it was developed from a small-scale blueprint.

The early state constitutions experimented with presidents elected by the council they chaired and whose consent they needed for most important executive decisions. The South Carolina Constitution of March 1776, for example, granted the president one traditional executive role, that of commander-in-chief, but denied him anything resembling a related prerogative: "The president and commander-in-chief shall have no power to make war or peace, or enter into any final treaty, without the consent of the general assembly and legislative council." Similarly, Virginia's governor, elected by separate vote in both houses, was to act "with the advice" of a council of state appointed by both chambers. Pennsylvania's controversial unicameral system nevertheless clearly distinguished the legislative from "the supreme executive power" to be wielded by a president elected jointly by the House of Representatives and the council he had to work with.[11]

The New York Constitution of 1777 was the first one to have the governor elected by direct popular vote. Instead of the power to veto legislation, he was given the right to join the supreme court judges and the chancellor in a novel "council to revise," whose duty it was to determine the constitutionality of new laws—a precedent followed by no other state nor (after some discussion) on the federal level. Once during each legislative session the New York governor was to present a report on "the condition of the State" and suggest legislative action—a precedent for the constitutionally prescribed State of the Union message.[12] "There is no need to cross the Atlantic to find a working model of the American presidency," concluded historian Charles Thach. "That it was the New York governorship is evident enough. . . . It afforded the only American example of government by a constitution actually controlling the departments of government and at the same time a completely independent and very energetic and active chief magistrate."[13]

The governor of Massachusetts, like his New York colleague, was elected directly by the qualified voters. Contrary to John Adams's draft constitution, the governor's veto could be overridden by a two-thirds majority in the House and the Senate. The Massachusetts governor also had to work with an advisory executive council elected by the legislature, in particular to prevent favoritism in appointing judges and military and administrative officers.[14]

Calls for "vigour," "secrecy," and "dispatch" in the executive were prompted long before 1787 by the necessities of war. The striking fact was not that the governor's term of office was brief, typically one year (except for the three years allowed in Delaware and New York), or that usually only three consecutive terms were permitted, but how soon, after the bitter struggles against royal governors, considerable executive power was again invested in a one-man institution.[15] The republican executive's power was checked, however, by a council not of his own making, whose task it was "to advise the Governor in the execution of his office," as the North Carolina Constitution typically phrased it.[16]

The president of the United States, the Philadelphia Convention decided, should not be surrounded by an executive council of this nature. (But the same Convention also thought there was no need for a federal Bill of Rights.) Nevertheless, it decided to adapt several of the executive council's advisory and supervisory functions to the federal level and simply assigned them to the Senate. For George Mason, the omission of a full-fledged federal executive council was reason enough not to sign the draft constitution he had done so much to help shape; the author of Virginia's Bill of Rights considered the projected one-person presidency "a thing unknown in any safe and regular Government" and anticipated the president's isolation and uncontrolled private influence by "Minions and Favourites." Mason maintained that "had a constitutional Council been formed (as was proposed) of six Members; vizt. two from the Eastern, two from the Middle, and two from the Southern States, to be appointed by Vote of the States in the House of Representatives, with the same Duration and Rotation of Office as the Senate, the Executive would always have had safe and proper Information and Advice."[17]

Impeachment, another check on the federal executive (and on other misbehaving officeholders), *was* introduced following state precedent and British antecedents. New York's impeachment procedure depended on the clear division of labor between the House of Representatives, which alone was authorized to initiate impeachment, and the Senate, which would sit together with the judges of the supreme court and the chancellor as a novel "court for the trial of impeachment."[18]

By 1787, the prescription of a functional separation and combination of powers had come to include a subdivided legislative branch. Hence replacement of the unicameral Confederation congress by a two-chamber legislature was almost a foregone conclusion as soon as establishment of a "regular" sort of government on the federal level became the majority's intention. Pennsylvania's one-chamber legislature, copied by Georgia and the would-be state of Vermont, had been opposed from the beginning as lacking stability.[19]

The Virginia Constitution of June 1776 was the first one to proclaim the principle of the institutional separation of powers: "The legislative, executive and judiciary departments shall be separate and distinct, so that neither exercise the powers properly belonging to the other: nor shall any person exercise the power of more than one of them, at the same time." Virginia's also was the first constitution to have the senators elected directly by the counties, making them independent of the House of Delegates.[20]

Distribution of senate seats by territorial unit instead of population size was also no new idea in 1787. Strict construction of Whig constitutional theory would have required state senatorial election districts of equal amounts of property, real as well as personal; putting such districts on a map, however, was an impossible task. Several states, therefore, simply used existing counties as geographic units to be represented. North Carolina, for instance, allotted one senator per county, regardless of size and population. But Virginia, New York, and Massachusetts did take the trouble to create special senatorial election districts based on the number of freeholders (New York) or on tax revenue (Massachusetts). Maryland had a unique electoral college, made up of two delegates from each county, plus one delegate each from Annapolis and Baltimore, elected by the qualified voters and called "electors." The electors were to assemble and ballot for nine senators from the west bank and six from the east bank of the Potomac.[21]

The state senate, it soon became clear, would not represent special and regionally calibrated property interests but would be an additional, smaller, all-purpose legislative chamber, based not on representation proportional to the number of voters but roughly on territory or corporation. The senators' term of office was slightly longer than that of the representatives: two years in South Carolina, three years in Delaware, four years in Virginia and New York, five years in Maryland, and one year in all the other states.[22]

Public discussion of "equal representation" that accompanied constitution making in most states included, in New England, insistence on the integrity of the corporation of the town, a principle that was thought to require at least one seat in the legislature, no matter how small the town's population. In short, the materials, the thought categories for the Great Compromise between the large and the small states were available by 1787; they had to be applied creatively to a new situation, but they did not have to be created ex nihilo.

Procedural Precedents: From Constituent Power to Constitutional Convention and Ratification

Precisely how to apply the principle of popular sovereignty to constitution writing had been an open question in 1776; thanks to the states' experiments, it no longer was in 1787. The first step in clarifying the issue was to distinguish between the traditional delegated authority of a parliament to legislate and the newly activated fundamental "constituent power" of "the people," needed to legitimate the ground rules for legislation in the form of a written constitution. That distinction was first articulated and elevated to a political demand by town meetings in Massachusetts and mechanics' associations in New York and Philadelphia, not by gentleman pamphleteers or established political leaders. In response, the combination of a specially elected constitution-drafting convention with "popular" ratification had been successfully practiced in Massachusetts.

British precedence was of little help, save for providing the term "convention." The irregular, quasi-parliamentary assemblies that in 1660 and 1688–89 had bridged the hiatus between constitutionally settled epochs were called "convention parliament" in recognition of their exceptional composition and assumed (others said usurped) powers, which went far beyond routine legislation.[23] This precedent was explicitly referred to in an anonymous call for electing a convention in Philadelphia in May 1776: "When the tyrant James the Second, King of Britain, abdicated the government, that is, ran away therefrom, or rather, was driven away by the just indignation of the people, the situation of England was like what America is *now*; and in that state a Convention was chosen, to settle the new or reformed plan of government, before any Parliament could presume to sit."[24]

The same situation, distrust in the Pennsylvania Assembly's anti-independence majority, prompted the following striking dialogue in the *Pennsylvania Journal* of May 22, 1776:

Q. Who ought to form a new Constitution?
A. The people.
Q. Should the officers of the old constitution be entrusted with the power of the making [*sic*] a new one when it becomes necessary?
A. No. Bodies of men have the same selfish attachments as individuals, and they will be claiming powers and prerogatives inconsistent with the liberties of the people.

The anonymous radical thinker, perhaps well read in the history of Athenian democracy, took the idea one step further. Making a constitution, he declared—with an ironic smile, one suspects—was "so high and sacred a trust, that the man who was thought worthy to frame it should be forbid ever to degrade himself by holding any office whatever."[25]

In the following weeks, the Philadelphia Committee of Inspection and the equally revolutionary county committees simply set a date for electing a Provincial Convention and extended the right to vote and the right to be candidates for the convention to adult militia members. Voting was to be limited, however, to men willing to take a pro-Independence loyalty oath. On July 8, 1776, for the first time in modern history, at least a substantial (even if politically preselected) proportion of an adult population had the rare opportunity of "choosing Deputies to form a Government," as one call to the polls phrased it.[26]

Pennsylvania's constitutional convention, the first one to take place in any of the thirteen states, took up its deliberations on July 15, 1776. It spoke of itself as "a Convention to form a Government under the authority of the people."[27] It drafted and immediately enacted both the declaration of rights and the form of government, to be effective instantly, as of September 27, 1776.[28]

Popular ratification was first demanded by proud Massachusetts towns, jealous of their traditional ways of self-government. Aware of the towns' jealousy, the Massachusetts House of Representatives, before instructing its delegates to the Continental Congress to vote for Independence, asked for the towns' vote on May 10, 1776.[29] When the next important step was to be taken, the towns, not surprisingly, insisted on being asked again. The frontier town of Pittsfield had been pushing for a new constitution for months. On May 26, 1776, the town meeting sent yet another set of resolutions to the representatives sitting at Watertown. When George III broke his contract, Pittsfield argued, the colonies reverted to "a state of Nature" and were no longer bound by previous constitutional arrangements:

> [T]he first step to be taken by a people in such a state for the Enjoyment or Restoration of Civil Government amongst them, is the formation of a fundamental Constitution as the Basis & ground work of Legislation. . . . The Approbation of the Majority of the people of this fundamental Constitution is absolutely necessary to give Life & being to it. . . . Then & not 'till then is the foundation laid for

Legislation. . . . A Representative Body may form, but cannot impose said fundamental Constitution upon a people. They being but
servants of the people cannot be greater than their Masters, & must
be responsible to them. If this fundamental Constitution is above the
whole Legislature, the Legislature cannot certainly make it, it must
be the Approbation of the Majority which gives Life & being to it.[30]

The House of Representatives, occupied with organizing a war, had
hoped for a simpler solution, and on September 17 asked the towns
"whether they will give their Consent, that the present House of Representatives . . . together with the Council if they consent, in One
Body with the House, and by equal Voice, should consult, agree on,
and enact . . . a Constitution . . . if they would direct that the same be
made Public for the Inspection and Perusal of the Inhabitants, before
the Ratification thereof by the Assembly." In recognition of the fundamental character of this question, the House recommended that the
town meetings' voting on the answer be open to all adult, free men,
regardless of their status as taxpayers or property owners.[31]

The October town meeting returns triggered by this request contained demands by the towns of Lexington, Norton, and, less clearly
so, Concord, for the two-step procedure of drafting by special constitutional convention and ratifying by town meeting vote. The simpler
method suggested by the House, Lexington replied on October 21,
"gives us to expect a Publication of the proposed Form of Government,
for the Perusal of the Inhabitants, before the Ratification of the Same,
yet it does not appear from thence, that there is any just Provision made
for the Inhabitants, as Towns, or Societies, to express their approbation, or the Contrary."[32]

Concord, on the same day, emphasized the first part of the de-
mand: "It appears to this Town highly necessary & Expedient that a
Convention, or Congress be immediatly Chosen, to form & establish
a Constitution. . . . When the Convention, or Congress have formed a
Constitution they adjourn for a Short time, and Publish their Proposed
Constitution for the Inspection & Remarks of the Inhabitents of this
State."[33] The vast majority of the town meeting returns of October
1776, however, seem to have accepted the simple plan proposed by the
House (seventy-four out of the surviving ninety-seven returns did so);
the historic calls for a special constitutional convention by Pittsfield,
Lexington, Concord, Norton, and a few other Massachusetts towns
were ignored by the House.[34]

On June 15, 1777, a newly elected Massachusetts House of Representatives and Council declared themselves to be a constitutional convention. Before the election, they had announced their intention to begin drafting a constitution and now felt authorized to proceed. In February 1778 they submitted their draft to the towns for approval; in this they met at least the second half of the Lexington demands. So it was in March 1778 that, for the first time in modern constitutional history, the free, adult, male citizens of a state had the opportunity to accept or reject the constitution that organized their polity. They rejected, by a vote of 9,972 to 2,083, giving such reasons as the allegedly unfair distribution of the seats of the House of Representatives, the lack of a declaration of rights, the disqualification of Negroes, Indians, and mulattoes as voters, and the high property qualifications for male Euro-American voters.[35]

The House and the Council decided to start over again, and now they also accepted the first part of the Lexington demands. They asked the towns whether they still wanted a new constitution and whether they were ready to authorize their representatives in the next legislature to call "a State Convention, for the sole Purpose of forming a new Constitution." The circular letter reminded the towns that this question was to be answered only by those "duly qualified to vote for Representatives."[36] With almost a three-to-one margin in favor, a date for electing delegates to the convention was set, and on September 1, 1779, the first freely elected convention "for the sole Purpose of forming a new Constitution" met in Cambridge. The result of its labors, an elaborate declaration of rights as well as form of government, carefully drafted by John Adams, occupied the town meetings in the spring of 1780. Faithful to the convention's recommendation, the towns did not simply vote yes or no on the constitution as a whole, but tallied votes for each article separately and drafted alternative and additional clauses and amendments. These returns, of which 181 survived, produced logical snarls that the tellers of the convention found impossible to untangle. The same article that one town overwhelmingly accepted as submitted would be accepted by another with certain changes or omissions that made it unacceptable to the first town. After two weeks of frantically tallying votes article by article and recognizing that statistically meaningful evaluation was impossible, the convention resorted to the logic of Baron Munchhausen, who saved himself and his horse from drowning in a swamp by pulling hard at his pigtail. The question was put whether members were convinced that each article had been agreed to, as submitted, by at least two-thirds of those voting. Most delegates professed that they were convinced, and on October 25, 1780, the Massachusetts Constitution went into effect. Today (albeit much amended) it is the oldest written constitution, in the modern sense of the word, still in effect.[37] This unsettling experience with conditional ratification of individual articles of a constitution may very well have strengthened the Federalists' vehement opposition to conditional ratification eight years later.

Eleven of the states put a total of thirteen constitutions into effect before 1787. (New Hampshire and South Carolina replaced their pre-Independence constitutions, and two states kept their charters: Connecticut until 1818, Rhode Island until 1842.) Of the eleven, only Massachusetts and New Hampshire (whose second constitution of 1784 copied that of Massachusetts in text and procedure) drafted theirs in a constitutional convention proper and had them ratified by the sovereign, the people.[38] But contemporaries soon recognized this as the model to follow in the future because it put republican political theory most convincingly into practice. When in 1788 Edmund Randolph spoke before the Virginia ratifying convention in favor of adding a Bill of Rights to the federal Constitution, he played down the protective force of Virginia's own Bill of Rights with the procedural argument that it "is of no validity, because . . . it is not formed on due authority"; it had, indeed, not been properly ratified according to the standards developed by 1780.[39]

Procedural Precedent: Amending Constitutions

Those who were convinced, with David Hume, "that politics may be reduced to a science" had good reason to regard the institutionalizing or "constitutionalizing" of the constitutional ground rules as statesmanship's ultimate achievement.[40] The amending clauses in the state constitutions document that achievement.[41] In essence, they required that the two steps of drafting and ratifying that had brought about the constitutional text to begin with be respected and repeated in the amending process. It is therefore not surprising that the same towns and groups that called for popular ratification demanded amending procedures, and for the same reasons: the desire for regulated, peaceful change by majority vote and the lack of trust in a legislature's power to change its own ground rules.

The pre-Independence constitutions of New Hampshire, South Carolina, and Virginia still ignored the amending question altogether. New Jersey permitted the legislature to change constitutional provisions but introduced the distinction between changeable and permanent clauses: The legislature was not to touch the right to trial by jury or the rules governing its own composition, term of office, and powers. (No Long Parliament or Septennial Act in New Jersey!) Delaware followed New Jersey's solution, added the whole text of the declaration of rights to the list of "untouchable" clauses, and permitted amendment of the rest of a special majority of five-sevenths of the House of Representatives and seven senators.[42] North Carolina also exempted the Bill of Rights from the scope of legislative action.[43]

The Pennsylvania Constitution of September 1776 was the first explicitly to reject British parliamentary practice by declaring, "[T]he legislature . . . shall have no power to add to, alter, abolish, or infringe any part of this constitution." The Pennsylvania solution for amending, although in accord with republican theory, was too mechanistic and cumbersome to become a model for the other states, except for the territory of Vermont. Every seven years, two delegates of each county and city were to meet as the Council of Censors to determine whether there was "an absolute necessity of amending any article of the constitution." On their recommendation, a constitutional convention had to be called within two years.[44]

Maryland also addressed the issue creatively, bridging British parliamentary and American popular sovereignty: The constitutional amendments could be voted by two-thirds of both chambers of the legislature, but would take effect only after confirmation by a two-thirds majority of the next newly elected House and Senate.[45] Georgia, otherwise much taken with the Pennsylvania example, invented yet a different method, so practical and theoretically sound that it provided the structural precedent for the solution adopted for the whole country in 1787: Whenever the majority of the counties petitioned the legislature, a constitutional convention had to be called.[46]

The town meeting of Lexington, Massachusetts, rejected the 1778 draft constitution of that state, in part because it lacked an amending procedure and thus left open the possibility that the legislature might follow bad British parliamentary precedent and decide to amend on its own. Lexington insisted on continued involvement of the electorate in future adjustments of the constitution as "an happy Means, under Providence, of preventing popular Commotions, Mobs, Bloodshed and Civil War; which, too frequently, have been the Consequences of the want of such an Opening, which they might have legally and constitutionally improved."[47] On the same occasion the town meeting of Roxbury, Massachusetts, used Machiavellian language to justify its demand for a mandatory constitutional convention at a set date, for example, in 1795. Such a procedure would be one way to ascertain "that the people might recur to the first principles in a Regular Way, without hazarding a Revolution in the Government."[48]

The towns' demands for an amending procedure proved stronger than John Adams's draft constitution, which, like Virginia's and New York's, had ignored the question. The convention added an article enjoining the legislature to ask the towns in fifteen years whether they wanted a constitutional convention. If two-thirds of those voting in the whole state so chose, a convention would be held.[49]

The state constitutions that regulated amending experimented with two procedures: (1) permitting the legislature to vote changes that might be corrected after the next election (South Carolina, New Jersey, Delaware, Maryland) and (2) calling a constitutional convention on the recommendation of a special committee (Pennsylvania, Vermont) or at the request of electoral units such as towns (Massachusetts, New Hampshire) or counties (Georgia). The convention's proposals were to be submitted, presumably, to the same form of popular ratification used when the constitution was originally established. Thus the ground was laid for including in the federal Constitution an amending procedure more practical than the unanimity rule in the Articles of Confederation. In addition, several procedural details worked out in the states became part of Article V: exempting certain clauses from amendment; providing for the alternative of legislative (federal) or local (state) initiative in the amending process; and giving an option of two routes to ratification, one through state legislatures (the structural equivalents of the town meetings), the other through special conventions.

The *Oxford English Dictionary* wrongly attributes the first known usage of the term "constituent power," defined as "the power to frame or alter a political constitution," to post–1789 translation from the French *pouvoir constituant*.[50] In reality, American state constitution makers not only exercised constituent power, they also named what they did. "Constituent power" was used in precisely the sense of the *OED*'s definition at least as early as 1777 by the radical New York doctor and political activist Thomas Young, then living in exile in Philadelphia. Young was active as the secretary of the Whig Society and supported the movement for Vermont statehood. He advised a delegation of the Green Mountain secessionists to justify their right to a constitution, in the face of opposition from New York and New Hampshire, by way of a unilateral declaration of independence of a border-area population. Young encouraged them to adopt the Pennsylvania Constitution he had helped draft, and on April 11, 1777, published an open letter in Philadelphia, *To the Inhabitants of Vermont, A Free and Independent State, Bounding on the River Connecticut and Lake Champlain.* In it he distinguished between the "supreme delegate power" of elected representatives and the "supreme constituent power" of the settlers: "They are the supreme constituent power, and of course their immediate Representatives are the supreme delegate power; and as soon as the delegate power gets too far out of hands of the constituent power, a tyranny is in some degree established."[51] In other words, what right did the legislatures of New York and New Hampshire, and the Continental Congress, wielding mere delegated power, have to prevent their superiors, the people of a certain area, from creating a new, self-governing polity?

The question fundamental to the process that we now call nation building was not, of course, to be answered in such theoretical terms as sovereignty, constituent power, and majority rule; rather, it was to be answered in terms of political power. The point here is that in the public debate accompanying that process in 1776 and the following decade, the idea basic to modern constitutionalism, that of the constituent power resting in a (largely) territorially defined "people," was successfully employed and unequivocally named.

Enlightenment Ideals and Original Intent

American constitution makers were not guided by a detailed ideological manifesto or a programmatic blueprint such as James Harrington's account of a republican utopia (*Oceana*, 1656). Trial and error and

political compromise for the sake of national unity shaped their decisions. National unity was clearly recognized as a precondition for
security and commercial development. For the American founding
generation, organizing stable republican government did not mean
preserving idyllic stagnation in virtuous isolation; it meant organizing
the political base from which to enter into the competition already in
full force among the national and colonial economies bordering on the
North Atlantic.

To the surprise of skeptical observers at European courts, the
constitutional system put in place between 1776 and 1791 proved
workable for seven decades of breathtaking expansion and economic,
social, and cultural change before it broke down and had to be preserved by force of arms in a war of national unification. There was to
be no "de-constituent" power to secede. If the founders' structural
concept of national government was indeed shaped to a considerable
degree by that of the state governments, then President Abraham
Lincoln's conviction of the indissoluble nature of the Union was quite
in agreement with the inner logic of American nation building since
Independence. Secession from the Union, from that perspective, was
as inadmissible as secession from an existing state by unilateral declaration of independence, as was demonstrated by the Vermont experience:
Only the consent of New Hampshire and New York brought the
fourteenth state into the Union.

Furthermore, if the relationship between state and national constitution making was as close as is here argued, those who today search
for the framers' "original intent" need to broaden their vision and look
beyond the text proposed on September 17, 1787, and considerably
amended in 1791. If they wish to understand what shaped the framers'
intentions, they need to look back to 1776 and that generation's experience with state constitution making. They will find in that trying
decade an openness to the lessons of experience, as well as the courage
to build on historical precedent in the light of present necessity.

Notes

The author expresses his gratitude for the detailed critique of the
manuscript that he received from John P. Reid and Knud Krakau.

1. *The Federalist*, ed. Jacob E. Cooke (Middletown, Conn.: Wesleyan University Press, 1961), no. 85.

2. Even Forrest McDonald's *Novus Ordo Seclorum: The Intellectual Origins of the Constitution* (Lawrence, Kan.: University Press of Kansas, 1985), one of the few monographs that report in detail on the state constitutions' role as the most important practical expression of the American founders' political ideas before 1787, stops short of a full evaluation of their meaning for the constitutional changes of 1787–88. The question itself is, of course, not new; see James H. Robinson, "The Original and Derived Features of the Constitution," *Annals of the American Academy of Political and Social Science* 1 (1890–91): 203–43.

3. This seems to be the interpretative message of Gordon S. Wood, *The Creation of the American Republic, 1776–1787* (Chapel Hill: University of North Carolina Press, 1969).

4. See Willi Paul Adams, *The First American Constitutions: Republican Ideology and the Making of the State Constitutions in the Revolutionary Era*, trans. Robert and Rita Kimber (Chapel Hill: University of North Carolina Press, 1980). The present article builds on the documentation presented in that monograph.

5. See J. R. Pole, *Political Representation in England and the Origins of the American Republic* (London: Macmillan, 1966).

6. Max Farrand, ed., *The Records of the Federal Convention of 1787*, 2d ed. (rev. ed., 1937; reprint, New Haven: Yale University Press, 1966), 1:404–5.

7. Ibid., 1:405–6.

8. Ibid., 2:92.

9. Ibid., 1:515.

10. Marcus Cunliffe, "The Invention of the Presidency," in *The Great Ideas Today: 1987* (Chicago: Encyclopedia Brittanica, 1987), 212. Cunliffe convincingly sketches the ambivalent attitude of American republicans between 1776 and 1829 toward monarchical traces in the presidency.

11. Francis N. Thorpe, ed., *Federal and State Constitutions* (Washington, D.C.: Government Printing Office, 1909), 3247, 3255, 3813, 3084.

12. Ibid., 2628–36.

13. Charles C. Thach, Jr., *The Creation of the Presidency, 1775–1789: A Study in Constitutional History* (1923; reprint, with an introduction by Herbert J. Storing, Baltimore: Johns Hopkins University Press, 1969), 176.

14. Thorpe, *Constitutions*, 1901.

15. Table with governors' terms of office in Adams, *First American Constitutions*, 245.

16. Thorpe, *Constitutions*, 2791.

17. George Mason, "Objections to the Constitution of Government Formed by the Convention," in *The Complete Anti-Federalist*, ed. Herbert J. Storing (Chicago: University of Chicago Press, 1981), 2:12.

18. Thorpe, *Constitutions*, 3086–87.

19. Jackson Turner Main, *The Sovereign States, 1775–1783* (New York: New Viewpoints, 1973), chap. 5.

20. Thorpe, *Constitutions*, 3816.

21. Ibid., 3816 (Virginia), 2632 (New York), 1895–96 (Massachusetts), 1693–94 (Maryland).

22. Table of rotation stipulations in Adams, *First American Constitutions*, 308–9.

23. John Alexander Jameson, *The Constitutional Convention: Its History, Power, and Modes of Proceeding* (1908; reprint, Cambridge: Cambridge University Press, 1963), 283–84. "Conventions" had been banned in Ireland as criminal acts. See John Phillip Reid, *In a Defiant Stance: The Conditions of Law in Massachusetts Bay, the Irish Comparison, and the Coming of the American Revolution* (State College, Pa.: Pennsylvania State University Press, 1978).

24. *The Alarm, or An Address to the People of Pennsylvania* (Philadelphia, May 19, 1776; Evans no. 14642), 3.

25. *Pennsylvania Journal*, May 22, 1776. On the American debate about the meaning of "constitution" after 1775, see Wood, *Creation of the American Republic*, chap. 7.

26. Peter Force, ed., *American Archives*, 4th ser. (Washington, D.C.: Government Printing Office, 1837–53), 6:962.

27. Ibid.

28. Ibid., 6:965–66.

29. *A Journal of the Honorable House of Representatives of the Colony of Massachusetts Bay* (Watertown [?], 1776), 276.

30. Robert J. Taylor, ed., *Massachusetts, Colony to Commonwealth: Documents on the Formation of Its Constitution, 1775–1780* (Chapel Hill: University of North Carolina Press, 1961), 27–28.

31. Ibid., 41.

32. Oscar Handlin and Mary F. Handlin, eds., *The Popular Sources of Political Authority: Documents on the Massachusetts Constitutions of 1780* (Cambridge: Belknap Press of Harvard University Press, 1966), 150.

33. Taylor, *Colony to Commonwealth*, 45–46.

34. Ibid., 44, 47; Handlin and Handlin, *Popular Sources of Political Authority*, 105, 125, 169.

35. Taylor, *Colony to Commonwealth*, 59–89.

36. Ibid., 116.

37. See the detailed account by Samuel E. Morison, "The Struggle over the Adoption of the Constitution of Massachusetts," *Proceedings of the Massachusetts Historical Society* 50 (1916–17): 353–411.

38. Walter F. Dodd, "The First State Constitutional Conventions, 1776–1783," *American Political Science Review* 2 (1908): 545–61; Adams, *First American Constitutions*, chap. 3.

39. *Papers of George Mason*, ed. Robert A. Rutland (Chapel Hill: University of North Carolina Press, 1970), 1:291.

40. Douglass Adair, "'That Politics May Be Reduced to a Science': David Hume, James Madison, and the Tenth Federalist," in *Fame and the Founding Fathers: Essays by Douglass Adair*, ed. Trevor Colburn (New York: Norton, 1974), 93–106. (First published: *Huntington Library Quarterly* 20 [1957]: 343–60.) Gerald Stourzh, in his *Fundamental Laws and Individual Rights in the Eighteenth-Century Constitution* (Claremont, Calif.: The Claremont Institute for the Study of Statesmanship and Political Philosophy, 1984), defines "constitutionalizing" as "a process whereby certain imperatives or prohibitions become part of a higher law in the technical sense that it cannot be abrogated or changed by normal legislative procedure" (12).

41. Charles Borgeaud, *Adoption and Amendment of Constitutions in Europe and America*, trans. Charles D. Hazen (New York: Macmillan, 1895); Walter F. Dodd, *The Revision and Amendment of State Constitutions* (Baltimore: Johns Hopkins University Press, 1910).

42. Thorpe, *Constitutions*, 2454, 3813, 2598, 568. Benjamin F. Wright, *Consensus and Continuity, 1776–1787* (Boston: Boston University Press, 1958), 11, considers the Delaware amending clause the first one since William Penn's Frame of Government of Pennsylvania spelled out an amending procedure in 1682; see Thorpe, *Constitutions*, 3059.

43. Thorpe, *Constitutions*, 2749.

44. Ibid., 3085, 3091–92. Cf. Lewis H. Meader, "The Council of Censors," *Pennsylvania Magazine of History and Biography* 22, no. 3 (1898): 265–300.

45. Thorpe, *Constitutions*, 1701.

46. Ibid., 785.

47. Taylor, *Colony to Commonwealth*, 67–68.

48. Handlin and Handlin, *Popular Sources of Political Authority*, 793.

49. Thorpe, *Constitutions*, 1911.

50. *Oxford English Dictionary*, 1933 ed., s.v. "constituent."

51. Thomas Young, *To the Inhabitants of Vermont, a Free and Independent State, Bounding on the River Connecticut and Lake Champlain*, bound together with the broadside *In Congress, May 15, 1776* (Philadelphia, 1777). On further context, see Matt Bushnell Jones, *Vermont in the Making, 1750–1777*

(Cambridge: Harvard University Press, 1939); Nathaniel Hendricks, "A New Look at the Ratification of the Vermont Constitution of 1777," *Vermont History* 34 (1966): 136–40; Egan Zweig, *Die Lehre vom Pouvoir Constituant* (Tübingen: J. C. B. Mohr, 1909).

CHAPTER 2

The Origins of American Constitutionalism

.....

JACK P. GREENE

Within the English-speaking world, the idea that English political society had a *constitution* seems to have only gradually taken shape during the late Middle Ages and the early modern era. Even as late as the American Revolution, English political and legal thinkers had difficulty defining precisely what the English constitution was, and they used the term in an inclusive way to refer to several analytically separable, if related, phenomena. The phrase "British constitution," declared the political writer Robert Robinson in the early 1780s, was "expressive first of a natural constitution of rights native and inherent in all the inhabitants of this kingdom and in all mankind—next a body of laws peculiar to this kingdom, declaratory of these natural rights— and lastly, of a form of making and executing these laws."[1]

Of course, many of the most fundamental principles associated with the idea of the English constitution were incorporated within various great state papers, including especially Magna Carta (1215), the Petition of Right (1628), and the Declaration of Rights (1689). But the constitution, according to emerging English conceptions, was never thought of in modern—that is, later American—terms as a single inclusive written document. Rather, it was conceived of as an accumulation of *customary* practices, long-standing legal procedures and principles, and basic individual rights that had slowly taken shape over the centuries, not just in the courts and legislative chambers in the capital

23

but also in the various administrative and judicial institutions in the local communities. It was an accumulation of concepts and practices, moreover, that expressed the fundamental rules by which the polity was "constituted" and on which it operated. These concepts and practices in turn depended for their authority upon their prescriptive character and their widespread acceptance by local populations as appropriate and just.

Basic to the emerging English idea of a constitution was the concept of *limitation*. In an unlimited government, the will of the sovereign was absolute. By contrast, a constitutional government was one in which the will of the sovereign as well as the scope of authority exercised by the basic political institutions responsible for carrying out the sovereign's commands were limited by the constitution. The most important constitutional limitations upon the power of the sovereign were the two principles of the rule of law and consent. According to the principle of the rule of law, all people, including the monarch, were equally subject to and protected by the laws of the realm and the basic processes and procedures that those laws expressed. In turn, laws consisted not only of legislative enactments but also of the myriad of judicial decisions and practices, again both national and local, that made up the English common law.

The principle of consent entailed the idea that citizens could not be subjected to any laws or taxes not first approved by themselves through either long-standing acquiescence or the medium of their elected representatives in the House of Commons. Although it had long been claimed by the House of Commons as part of the "ancient constitution" of the realm, this principle, along with most of the other important constitutional rights of English citizens, was finally secured only after a long series of bitter constitutional struggles during the seventeenth century.

During the sixteenth century, English monarchs had exercised extraordinary power, one historian having characterized the government of Henry VIII as a "royal dictatorship." During the first eight decades of the seventeenth century, Parliament had sought, with modest success, to diminish the relative authority of the Crown by appeals to fundamental law and customary restraints on arbitrary power. From the early 1640s on, as Corinne C. Weston has shown, radical advocates of the expansion of parliamentary power had invoked the coordination principle in lawmaking in an effort to redefine "relationships between the king and the two houses of Parliament by elevating the two houses at the expense of the king." A "theory of shared legal sovereignty by which the two houses became the predominant partners in lawmaking," this doctrine held that sovereignty rested not in the king alone but in the king-in-Parliament. [2]

But the diminution of the king's power within England during the seventeenth century was relatively minor compared to that which took place in the wake of the Glorious Revolution of 1688. As a result of that revolution, the principle of coordination was enshrined as the new constitutional orthodoxy. As Jennifer Carter has observed, England now "had a monarch depending on a parliamentary title, and a constitution based on [parliamentary] law." "The two salient features of the post-Revolution constitution were, first, that however much it was disguised a parliamentary monarchy had replaced a divine right monarchy; and, secondly, that since 1689 the monarch had learned somehow to live with Parliament."

Carter has emphasized also, however, that these developments were by no means a "foregone conclusion" at the time of the Glorious Revolution. Only gradually over the next half century did Parliament grow from what Edmund Burke called "a mere representative of the people, and a guardian of popular privileges for its own constituents . . . into a mighty sovereign," from a body that was not simply "a control on the crown on its own behalf" to one that, as Burke put it, "communicated a sort of strength to the royal authority." As several historians recently have pointed out, however, the "concept of a sovereign parliament" had not been "reasonably foreseeable in 1689," was largely "a development of the mid-eighteenth century," and was only just beginning to harden into an orthodoxy during the 1760s, on the eve of the American Revolution. [3]

Before the Glorious Revolution, the English constitution had been very largely a *customary* constitution. That is, it was based for the most part not upon codified statutes or other written documents but upon custom—unwritten but widely accepted law—and the slow accretion of precedents favorable to the rights of the citizenry. During the half century following the Glorious Revolution, however, people began to think of Parliament's role within the English polity as omnipotent, and the British constitution came to be seen—within Britain—as virtually identical with Parliament itself. As a result, parliamentary statutes gradually thereafter came to be thought of as having primacy over custom, and the constitution became in essence whatever Parliament said it was. This was the prevailing conception of the British constitution within Great Britain at the time of the American Revolution.

How these great constitutional changes within Britain affected Britain's overseas possessions in Ireland and America was never explicitly worked out before the American Revolution. Indeed, from the beginnings of English colonization in the early seventeenth century, there was considerable confusion over precisely what the constitutional status of the colonies was. By the early seventeenth century, the English had had extensive experience in dealing with areas that, though parts of the monarch's dominions, were physically attached to the realm of England. These included several French possessions (which by 1600 had long since passed out of the monarch's control), the Channel Islands of Guernsey and Jersey, Wales, Ireland, and the Isle of Man.

Most of the dominions of this medieval empire had come to the monarchy through inheritance, but two—Wales and Ireland—had been acquired by conquest. Each was adjacent to or reasonably close to England, well peopled with non-English inhabitants, and possessed of its own peculiar socioeconomic, legal, and political traditions that differed from, and were to varying extents independent of, those of England. Of them all, only Wales had been fully incorporated into the realm of England, and then not until 1536. The rest were a series of small satellite states bound together by their mutual connection with the monarchy and its advisers, either in the conciliar parliaments of the Middle Ages or in the Privy Council under the Tudors. With the accession of James I in 1603, Scotland came into this loose association of political entities, although before the Act of Union in 1707 it was explicitly and formally independent of the realm—as opposed to the monarchy—of England.[4]

England's colonies in the New World differed from these old dominions in many respects. First, they were three thousand miles away. Second, although all but one or two island colonies had significant native populations at the time of initial settlement, population density was low relative to the most fully occupied areas of Europe. Much of the land was uncultivated and therefore, according to contemporary European theory, "waste," available for colonization. The natives were both pagan and, the English thought, culturally less advanced than most Europeans. Showing very little interest in absorbing the natives, the English preferred to displace them through physical expulsion, purchase of their lands, or both. Thus, unlike the monarch's dominions on the eastern side of the Atlantic, those in America were to an important degree composed of emigrants from the British Isles and their descendants, new settler populations in places from which the old populations had been or soon would be almost entirely removed. The very newness of these societies—the absence of long-settled traditions, institutions, and patterns of social relations—constituted a third important distinction between them and the various components of the English monarchy's medieval empire.

The new plantations of English and Scots established in Ireland under the first two Stuarts were in several respects similar to the American colonies. But they differed in two important ways. First, they were established in territories conquered from a people that were numerous, Christian, and, by European standards, civilized. Second, the English and Scottish immigrants and their increase became a majority in only a few localities and thus had to live in the midst of a numerically superior and often hostile native population.[5] To be sure, a few of the American colonies had, like Ireland, also been conquered. Previously settled by colonists from rival European societies, Jamaica had been wrested from the Spanish in 1655, New York from the Dutch in 1664, and Nova Scotia and half of St. Christopher from the French in 1713. Except in Jamaica, from which all of the Spanish settlers fled following the English conquest, many of the old inhabitants of these colonies chose to remain and live under English governance. In contrast to the situation in Ireland, however, incoming immigrants from the British Isles quickly became a majority and eventually established their political and cultural predominance over the earlier inhabitants.

If the American colonies differed in many ways from the monarch's more ancient dominions in the British Isles and Europe, they were also somewhat different from most other colonies with which contemporaries were familiar. Colonization had, of course, been a familiar phenomenon in antiquity. As early modern Europeans understood the earliest colonies, those of Greece had been autonomous settlements in previously unoccupied lands by surplus population from Greece itself, and those of Rome, as one eighteenth-century commentator remarked, had been "planted among vanquished nations to over-awe and hold them in subjection."[6] The plantation in Ireland bore some strong resemblance to the Roman prototype, as did, many English people believed, the contemporary Spanish colonies in Mexico,

Peru, and elsewhere in Hispanic America. Similarly, some of the Anglo-American colonies were initially conceived and, at least to some extent, actually functioned for a time along the lines of the garrison settlements on the English frontiers and in Ireland.[7]

But observers early recognized that the colonies in America were unlike either of these ancient models. Unlike the Greeks, they did not have de jure autonomy; unlike the Romans, they were not primarily concerned with "keep[ing] conquered Countries in Subjection." Rather, like most of the early modern European colonies in America, they were groups of people who, with the authorization of the monarch, settled in vacant or lightly occupied places for the specific purposes of cultivating the land and promoting trade "for the good of themselves and that [of the] state they belong[ed] to." Thus, "intended to increase the Wealth and Power of the[ir] native Kingdom," these "Colonies of Commerce," people gradually came to perceive, were an entirely "new species of colonizing, of modern date, and differing essentially from every other species of colonizing that is known."[8]

There is some evidence that in the early days of colonization metropolitan officials hoped that the colonies might eventually be incorporated into the realm of England in the manner of Wales.[9] But they soon recognized that distance made such a goal unfeasible, with the result that the American colonies, like the monarchy's older non-English territories, soon came to be thought of *not* as "Part of the Realm of England" but as "Separate and Distinct Dominions." In this conception, each colony was thus a separate corporate entity, a body politic authorized by the Crown, with jurisdiction over a well-defined territory and its own distinctive institutions, laws, customs, and, eventually, history and identity—all of which reflected its peculiar "Circumstances . . . in respect of its Soil, Situation, Inhabitants, and Commerce."[10]

Separateness did not, of course, mean independence. The colonies might indeed be "distinct" dominions and not actually part of the English realm. Nevertheless, virtually all English officials agreed that they were also "dependent" dominions. The officials were much less certain about the further constitutional questions of in what ways and to what extent the colonies were dependent and how much autonomy or independence such dependent institutions might enjoy.[11]

The basic objectives of the English in establishing colonies dictated that these questions would not be easily resolved. The American colonies were "first planted on *Commercial Views*" with trade and profit as "their first principle." To obtain these goals at minimal cost to itself and the nation, the monarchy encouraged private adventurers—either organized into chartered companies or acting as lords proprietors—to sponsor colonies by granting them exclusive title to vast areas of land and "sundrie verie large immunities and privileges," including extensive self-governing powers and, in many cases, special economic concessions. Such arrangements were similar to those used earlier in the expansion of England into the Celtic fringe, where the monarchy had granted local magnates in places such as Chester and Durham a large measure of autonomy in return for their continuing fealty. Lacking the fiscal resources to undertake such territorial expansion on their own, English monarchs had no other means by which to establish the legitimacy of their claims to both new territories and the allegiance of the inhabitants of those territories.[12]

But the colonies differed from English border areas in three important respects. First, they were far more distant. Second, they did not have settled native populations that could be easily mobilized to achieve the objectives of the colonizers. Third, the new, predominantly English settlers brought with them English traditions of law and governance, which put a high premium upon individual and local corporate liberties and autonomy, especially upon the traditional English constitutional principles of limited government and consent. Tudor England, as Kenneth R. Andrews has remarked, was "a largely self-governing society—under the crown," and the "increase in governance" through the establishment of many "new local institutions that tied the counties [more closely] to the center" during the century following the accession of Elizabeth does not seem to have seriously dampened "the fierce, full-hearted localism" that both supported and encouraged those local self-governing tendencies.

One important consequence of this deeply etched "characteristic of early modern English society" was what Andrews refers to as a powerful "tendency towards self-government in the emergent empire." At the same time that the sponsors of the several colonial enterprises invariably proved to be both "particularly jealous of" their "autonomy and resistant to royal interference," they found that they could not recruit settlers for such distant and unfamiliar areas in numbers sufficient to meet their objectives without generous guarantees of self-governing rights and concessions in the form of access to land and, occasionally, temporary exemption from taxation and other public obligations.[13]

Mostly settled at the same time as the great constitutional struggles of the seventeenth century, England's colonies in Ireland and America thus inherited the seventeenth-century English constitutional traditions of limited government, consent, and local control. Accordingly, long before John Locke's elegant formulation of the theory of emigration in his *Two Treatises of Government,* colonial leaders had developed the view that English people had a right to migrate to a new country, to take their constitutional rights as Englishmen with them into the new political entities they founded overseas, and to establish local institutions and adopt local customs to secure those rights to themselves and their posterity.

From the colonists' point of view, the Crown seemed to have recognized the legitimacy of this theory by granting them royal charters that not only empowered them to establish governments over a specific territory but also confirmed their entitlement to all the traditional rights, privileges, and immunities of Englishmen. In the few cases in which groups of people settled without such a charter—the Plymouth Colony being the earliest example—the settlers themselves often adopted written "plantation covenants," in which they pledged their mutual cooperation in establishing a government modeled along the lines of the one they had left behind.

American constitutional historians have emphasized the centrality of these charters and covenants in early American constitutional development and have traced to them the beginnings of the subsequent American attachment to written constitutions. But the early settlers seem never to have thought of their colonial constitutions as being wholly or even principally contained within these documents. Rather, they regarded the charters *not* as the *principal* component of their several constitutions but, as in the case of Magna Carta itself, as *mere* legal confirmations by the English Crown of their entitlement to rights they already possessed by virtue of their birthright as English people. In any case, the Crown subsequently revoked, withdrew, purchased, or amended the charters of most of the colonies. By 1750, the only colonies that still had charters were Maryland, Connecticut, Rhode Island, Pennsylvania, and Massachusetts. Indeed, like the English constitution before the Glorious Revolution, the several colonial constitutions were, from the start, primarily *unwritten customary constitutions* that developed slowly over time through a series of precedents that functioned to protect and extend the colonists' inherited rights as Englishmen.

Notwithstanding the provisions in the early charters, English officials were never willing to admit in their fullest extent the colonists' claims to enjoy all the rights of the English constitution. For that reason, the exact nature of those constitutions rapidly became the main point of contention between Crown and colonies in much the same way that the nature of the *English* constitution had been at the heart of the struggles between Crown and Parliament in seventeenth-century England. The many contests that everywhere developed over this issue revolved around two principal questions: whether the colonists were entitled to all the benefits of the laws of England and whether the representative assemblies that were established early in the history of every colony to make laws for the local populations enjoyed the same status in the colonial constitutions as the House of Commons did in the English constitution.

Crown officials never accepted the colonists' demands for explicit statutory guarantees of their rights to the benefits of English laws. Nevertheless, through the extensive use of English legal precedents and statutes by colonial judges, the colonists seem eventually to have managed to secure those benefits through custom, usage, and practice. Although most of the empirical research necessary to nail down this point and to show fully the precise extent and character of the transfer of English law to the colonies remains to be done, the diminution of demands for explicit guarantees of English laws in the colonies during the first three decades of the eighteenth century strongly suggests that provincial and local courts had by that time effectively established the customary rights of the colonists in this broad area.

In much the same way, the colonial assemblies succeeded in establishing their strident and often reiterated claims to constitutional authority within their respective jurisdictions equivalent to that of the House of Commons in Britain. Although Crown officials consistently recognized the assemblies' authority to pass laws, they always insisted that the assemblies were subordinate institutions much like the governing bodies of English corporations and without the full rights and privileges of the English Parliament. Because they controlled the power of the purse, however, and because the Crown's colonial governors found it impossible to govern effectively without their consent, the colonial assemblies slowly managed to obtain in practice the authority that Crown officials denied them in theory.

As the English House of Commons had itself done during the seventeenth century, the colonial assemblies by the middle of the eighteenth century had thus managed, through precedent and custom, to establish their authority and status as local parliaments, as the most important institutions in the colonial constitutions and the primary guardians of the colonists' inherited rights as Englishmen. These rights included especially the right not to be subjected to any taxes or laws relating to their internal affairs without the consent of their representatives in assembly.

Custom carried enormous authority within the British constitutional tradition. The British constitution was itself based as much upon custom as upon statute law. Both the common law and Parliament itself derived authority from the force of custom. As J. G. A. Pocock has noted, however, with the rise of the doctrine of parliamentary supremacy during the seven or eight decades after the Glorious Revolution, "the concept of custom, and of English institutions as founded on custom," received less and less emphasis until it was revived by Edmund Burke during the last quarter of the eighteenth century. Yet, even in Britain, custom continued to be accorded considerable weight in the courts, in local legal and social relations, and in the works of some political and legal writers, including especially the Cambridge legal theorist Thomas Rutherforth. That the colonies had been settled long enough to claim their liberties and privileges by custom was denied by most British authorities. Yet from very early on, colonists had defended their rights to government by consent on the basis not just of English custom but of their own custom as well.[14]

At least at the provincial level, then, constitutional development within the colonies was thoroughly within the mainstream and largely a mere extension of English constitutional traditions of the seventeenth century. No less than their English counterparts, colonial legislators, lawyers, judges, and citizens displayed an obsessive concern with constitutional rights, including especially those associated with the principles of consent and due process. Their constitutions, like the seventeenth-century English constitutions, were largely customary. Indeed, the broad similarities arising out of the common Englishness of their emerging constitutional traditions are the only things that make it possible even to talk about a *colonial*—but not without anachronism an *American* colonial—as well as specific Virginia, South Carolina, New York, or Jamaican constitutional traditions. Yet, specific provincial circumstances, experiences, and traditions made possible manifold and important variations among the several constitutions of individual provinces in the early modern colonial world. Indeed, the very range of these variations has made it very difficult for constitutional historians to discover a general colonial constitutional tradition that can be easily related to later American national constitutional history.

In recent years, a growing cadre of scholars has suggested that in resisting parliamentary authority during the 1760s and 1770s, the American colonists were "reject[ing] the results of" the Glorious Revolution and placing themselves outside of the British constitutional tradition. But there are major difficulties with this argument. The ascendancy of Parliament within Britain and the eventual triumph of the doctrine of parliamentary omnipotence during the mid-eighteenth century may have been the most important results of the Glorious Revolution, but they were by no means the only ones. Within Britain, as Jennifer Carter has pointed out, another consequence of the revolution was "a distinct, though not complete, withdrawal of central authority from . . . local affairs."

Earlier in the seventeenth century, Charles I had undertaken an extensive effort to exert the authority of the central government over county and local affairs in both the civil and the religious realms, and, although this effort was interrupted during the Civil War, the later Stuarts resumed it after the Restoration. "Perhaps nothing done in the 1680s by Charles II and James II," Carter has noted, "caused so much reaction against them as their interference with local privilege and the accustomed pattern of existing hierarchies—in counties, in corporations, or in university colleges." At least in the short run, the revolution effectively put an end to this effort and thereby created the conditions necessary for "the typical eighteenth-century situation of gentry and aristocratic independence in the localities." Within Britain, the localities, along with the people who dominated them, enjoyed much less interference from the central government than they had at any time under the Stuart monarchy. During the eighty years following the Glorious Revolution, Britain seems to have experienced a significant redistribution of power to the localities as English, Welsh, and (after 1707) Scottish counties became what Edward Shils would refer to as "pockets of approximate independence."[15]

The preoccupation of historians with the rise of Parliament and the establishment of a constitution of parliamentary supremacy in the wake of the Glorious Revolution has thus drawn attention away from the important extent to which the Glorious Revolution also represented a reassertion of the authority of *local* magistracies, whose pervasive jurisdiction over many of the constitutive elements of the English polity had never been stronger than it was during the eighteenth century. Notwithstanding the alleged supremacy of Parliament in the eighteenth-century British constitution, these local magistracies, historians are coming increasingly to realize, continued to exert widespread authority over a large range of constitutional matters, including especially issues concerning due process of law, while the foundations of that authority continued, like the basis of the authority of Parliament itself before the Glorious Revolution, to be based to a significant degree upon custom, usage, and prescription as sanctioned by local consent and enforced by a broad group of citizens who, serving as jurors and administrative and judicial officials, gave English local government a participatory character that often astonished foreign observers.

The same development was evident in Britain's more distant peripheries in Ireland and America. As each of these overseas entities developed its own peculiarly local constitutional tradition, the localities in each of them played a significant role in the creation and perpetuation of those traditions. Perhaps to a greater extent even than in contemporary Britain, the constitutional order in the several colonies was throughout the colonial period at once local, consensual, participatory, lay-directed, and customary. This diffusion and localization of authority ensured that, in contrast to contemporary continental monarchies, Britain's expanding nation-state and overseas empire would not be founded on methods of centralization and absolutism.

In both Ireland and the American colonies, the growth of parliamentary power during the eighteenth century epitomized this development. Before the Glorious Revolution, the Irish Parliament had convened only rarely. Beginning in 1692, it both met regularly and developed a vigorous "spirit of independence."[16] The same happened in the American colonies. Hence, in terms of the constitutional development of the British Empire as a whole, perhaps the most important results of the Glorious Revolution over the following eighty years were the localization of authority and the growth of parliamentary institutions, not just within Britain itself but throughout the overseas British Empire. Just as the growth of parliamentary power after 1689 had changed the constitution of Britain in fundamental ways, so also had similar developments in Ireland and the colonies altered the constitutions there.

Throughout the British Empire, constitutions were basically customary. That is, they were all the products of evolving usage. By the early 1760s, the unformulated and unasked question was whether, in the process of changing the constitutions of their respective political jurisdictions, the several legislatures and judicial systems of the empire were also changing the constitution of the whole to which they all belonged. Without as yet having formulated a coherent and fully articulated sense of empire, the British political nation had not, before the 1760s, developed any explicit sense of an imperial constitution. Yet the absence of the concept did not mean that an imperial constitution did not exist or was not being slowly formed through the same evolutionary process that was shaping and reshaping the constitutions of the several entities that composed the British Empire.

As Burke would subsequently remark, during the eighteenth century an imperial constitution had gradually emerged out of "mere neglect; possibly from the natural operation of things, which left to themselves, generally fall into their proper order." In this constitution, as Andrew C. McLaughlin, the doyen of American constitutional historians, pointed out half a century ago, the metropolitan government exercised general powers and the Irish and American colonial governments exerted de facto and virtually exclusive jurisdiction over all matters of purely local concern.[17]

Thus, according to the practice of the extended polity of the British Empire as it had developed during the three-quarters of a century following the Glorious Revolution, there were three separate kinds of constitutions. First, there was a British constitution for the central state and its immediate dependencies, including Cornwall, Wales, and, after 1707, Scotland. Second, there were separate provincial constitutions for Ireland and for each of the colonies in America. Third, there was an as-yet-undefined, even unacknowledged, imperial constitution—the constitution of the British Empire—according to the practice of which authority was distributed in an as-yet-uncodified and not very clearly understood way between the center and the peripheries, with Parliament exercising power over general concerns and the local legislatures handling local affairs within their respective jurisdictions.

That the American colonists would not readily subscribe to the emerging British doctrine of parliamentary omnipotence could easily be surmised from the direction of their own constitutional development between 1660 and 1760. Their view of the constitution was developmental in the sense that they saw their own constitutions and, by implication, the constitution of the empire as moving in the same direction as had the British constitution in the wake of the Glorious Revolution: that is, toward increasing limitations upon prerogative power and greater security for individual and corporate rights under the protection of a strong legislature. According to this view, further gains in the direction of still-greater limitations and security could yet be achieved, but those already made could not—constitutionally—be lost. From this perspective, any effort to impose the principle of unlimited parliamentary authority upon the colonies was bound to appear to the colonists as retrogressive and unacceptable. Because they had for so long exercised exclusive jurisdiction over their own internal affairs, while the British Parliament had limited its interference in colonial matters to regulating trade and other aspects of the external economic life of the colonies and the general welfare of the empire, the colonial legislatures thus protested vigorously that Parliament's effort to tax them for revenue by the Stamp Act in 1765 was a violation of their inherited and customary constitutional right not to be taxed except by their own local representatives.

For the next ten years, the colonists engaged in a prolonged effort to wrest from British authorities explicit guarantees of these constitutional rights. They repeatedly pointed out that over the previous 150 years the British Empire had developed an unwritten customary constitution that was quite distinct from either the British constitution or the specific constitutions of the several colonies. According to this developing imperial constitution, they contended, the empire was organized in a federal way with legislative authority distributed among many local legislatures, with the British Parliament retaining unlimited jurisdiction only over matters of specific concern to Great Britain itself and general concern to the empire as a whole. They argued that these customary constitutional developments limited the authority of the British Parliament in the colonial sphere. In the colonists' view, Parliament was subordinate to—and could not act contrary to—this unwritten imperial constitution.

But the widespread commitment in Britain to the emerging doctrine of parliamentary supremacy meant that few people there could consider the possibility that there might be any limitations upon parliamentary authority. The impasse over this question eventually drove thirteen of the continental colonies to seek independence. Throughout the colonial period, their constitutions had been composed almost entirely of uncodified and unratified custom and inheritance. Enormously frustrated between 1765 and 1775 by their inability to obtain any recognition from the British government of the validity and scope of these unwritten constitutions, they quickly moved in 1776 to give their constitutions explicit and concrete form by writing them down. Two colonies, Connecticut and Rhode Island, simply adapted their colonial charters to this purpose. Between 1776 and 1781, each of the other eleven revolting colonies adopted new written constitutions. By the end of the American Revolution the tradition of written constitutions, a marked departure from both the colonies' English inheritance and their own earlier colonial experience, had been firmly established in American political life.

Contrary to the work of many recent historians, this analysis of constitutional development in Britain and America before the establishment of the American nation assumes that, so far from being authoritative, pronouncements from the centers of early modern extended polities like the British Empire acquired constitutional legitimacy for the whole only through implicit or explicit ratification by the peripheries. Had Britain had the requisite coercive resources, which it did not, it presumably could have enforced the views of the center in all the peripheral areas of the empire. To have secured obedience through force, however, would have constituted an admission of the absence or breakdown of authority, which, as most contemporary political thinkers in the British-American world were acutely aware, was always a function of opinion.

In practice, then, political and constitutional arrangements within the extended polity of the early modern British Empire were founded upon the consent of its many constituent components. That is, local sanction from the peripheries was essential to endow any position of the center with constitutional authority—and vice versa. Constitutional customs and doctrines could emanate from either the center or the peripheries, but they could not attain full constitutional authority outside the area of emanation—or for the empire as a whole—until they had been accepted by all parties to which they might apply.

Both in its origins and in its results, the American Revolution provides a classic illustration of the truth of these observations. Between 1765 and 1775, the center simply could not secure colonial consent to its emerging view of the constitutional structure of the empire without resorting to force, and when, after nearly eight years of war, its will and resources proved inadequate to that task, it had no alternative but to permit the former colonies to go their own independent ways. With this experience behind them, political leaders of the United States in the 1770s and 1780s automatically understood that no new center for the American Union could be constituted without the formal and explicit consent of the several entities that composed that Union.

In conclusion, it might be said that the fixation of modern historians upon the concept of the nation as the most significant unit of historical discourse and their focus almost exclusively upon the national stage and the development and functioning of national institutions has not been entirely salutary. One of the important results of the new appreciation of the local dimensions of constitutional development in eighteenth-century Britain has been to facilitate the emergence of a broader and richer conception of the nature and content of not just colonial but later American constitutional history. For there is no reason to suppose that the vigorous flow of these local streams of constitutional development was immediately stemmed in the United States by the superimposition of a national constitutional system during the final decades of the eighteenth century, or that the local customary foundations of that development were immediately overthrown by the establishment of explicit written constitutions. What may be suspected is that more attention to the *local* context of constitutional development after the establishment of the American nation—with "local" being conceived of as applying both to states and to localities within states—will reveal significant continuities between pre- and postnational constitutional history that will greatly enrich our appreciation of the dimensions of that subject and thereby help us to identify more fully the relevance of colonial history to the history of the nation.

Notes

1. Robert Robinson, *A Political Catechism*, 3d ed. (London, 1784), 38, as quoted by John Phillip Reid, *Constitutional History of the American Revolution: The Authority of Rights* (Madison: University of Wisconsin Press, 1986), 6.

2. A. F. McC. Madden, "1066, 1776, and All That: The Relevance of English Medieval Experience of 'Empire' to Later Imperial Constitutional Issues," in *Perspectives of Empire,* ed. John E. Flint and Glyndwr Williams (London: Longman, 1973), 9, 24; Corinne C. Weston, "Co-ordination—A Radicalising Principle in Stuart Politics," in *The Origins of Anglo-American Radicalism,* ed. Margaret Jacob and James Jacob (London: George Allen and Unwin, 1984), 85, 89.

3. Jennifer Carter, "The Revolution and the Constitution," in *Britain after the Glorious Revolution, 1689–1714,* ed. Geoffrey Holmes (London: Macmillan; New York: St. Martin's, 1969), 39, 40, 47, 55; Edmund Burke, "Letter to the Sheriffs of Bristol on the Affairs of America, 1777," in *The Works of Edmund Burke* (London, 1808), 3:188; H. T. Dickinson, "The Eighteenth-Century Debate on the Sovereignty of Parliament," *Transactions of the Royal Historical Society,* 5th ser., 26 (1976): 189; Barbara A. Black, "The Constitution of Empire: The Case for the Colonists," *University of Pennsylvania Law Review* 124 (1976): 1157, 1210–11; H. T. Dickinson, "The Eighteenth-Century Debate on the 'Glorious Revolution,'" *History* 61 (1976): 28, 33, 39.

4. The best discussion of England's medieval empire and the relationship among its various parts is Madden, "1066, 1776, and All That," 9–16. On the Welsh experience, see B. E. Howells, "Society in Early Modern Wales," in *The Satellite State in the 17th and 18th Centuries,* ed. Stale Dyrvik, Knut Mykland, and Jan Oldervoll (Bergen, Norway: Universitetsforlaget, 1979), 80–98.

5. On the Elizabethan and Jacobean plantations in Ireland, see a series of articles by Nicholas P. Canny: "The Ideology of English Colonization: From Ireland to America," *William and Mary Quarterly,* 3d ser., 30 (1973): 575–98; "Dominant Minorities: English Settlers in Ireland and Virginia, 1550–1650," in *Minorities in History,* ed. A. C. Hepburn (London: St. Martin, 1978), 51–69; and "The Permissive Frontier: The Problem of Social Control in English Settlements in Ireland and Virginia, 1550–1650," in *The Westward Enterprise: English Activities in Ireland, the Atlantic, and America, 1480–1650,* ed. K. R. Andrews, N. P. Canny, and P. E. H. Hair (Detroit: Wayne State University Press, 1979), 17–44.

6. See among many similar characterizations of Greek and Roman colo-

nization, Samuel Estwick, *A Letter to the Reverend Josiah Tucker, D.D.* (London, 1776), 92–93. The most extensive contemporary analysis of the bearing of the colonial experience in antiquity upon that of the early modern British is by James Abercromby, a Scottish lawyer and member of Parliament. See Jack P. Greene, Charles F. Mullett, and Edward C. Papenfuse, Jr., eds., *"Magna Charta for America": James Abercromby's "An Examination of the Acts of Parliament Relative to the Trade and the Government of our American Colonies" (1752) and De Jure et Gubernatione Coloniarum, or An Inquiry into the Nature, and the Rights of Colonies, Ancient and Modern" (1774)* (Philadelphia: American Philosophical Society, 1986).

7. See Stephen Saunders Webb, *The Governors-General: The English Army and the Definition of the Empire, 1569–1681* (Chapel Hill: University of North Carolina Press, 1979), which provides an extended discussion of the ways metropolitan experience with garrison government affected English official thought about the colonies.

8. John Trenchard and Thomas Gordon, *Cato's Letters* (London, 1724), 3:282–84; William Douglass, *Summary, Historical and Political, of the first Planting, progressive Improvements, and present State of the British Settlements in North-America* (1749; reprint, New York: Arno, 1972), 1:205–7; Malachy Postlethwayt, *The Universal Dictionary of Trade and Commerce* (London, 1757), 2:471; Estwick, *Letter to Josiah Tucker*, 92–93; and Anthony Stokes, *A View of the Constitution of the British Colonies* (London, 1783), 1–3, all contain contemporary discussion of the nature of colonies. An interesting short modern analysis is M. I. Finley, "Colonies—An Attempt at a Typology," *Transactions of the Royal Historical Society*, 5th ser., 26 (1976): 167–88.

9. William Lawson Grant and James Munro, eds., *Acts of the Privy Council of England, Colonial Series* (London: His Majesty's Stationery Office, 1908), 1:49. For the confusion over whether the colonies were "foreign" or "home," see the description of the House of Commons debate over whether Sir George Somers, admiral of the fleet that sailed for Virginia in May 1609, should lose his seat in Parliament for having left the realm, in Wilcomb E. Washburn, "Law and Authority in Colonial Virginia," in *Law and Authority in Colonial America*, ed. George Athan Billias (Barre, Mass.: Barre Publishers, 1965), 121.

10. William Smith, *Mr. Smith's Opinion Humbly Offered to the General Assembly of the Colony of New York* [New York, 1734], 17; James Knight, "The Natural, Moral, and Political History of Jamaica, and the Territories thereon depending," 2:112, in Long Papers, Additional Manuscripts, 12,419, British Library, London; Jeremiah Dummer, *A Defence of the New-England Charters* (London, 1726), 56; John Vaughan, *The Reports and Arguments of that Learned Judge Sir John Vaughan* (London, 1677), 401–2; Opinion of Sir Robert Henley

and Charles Yorke, May 18, 1757, in *Opinions of Eminent Lawyers on Various Points of English Jurisprudence Chiefly Concerning the Colonies, Fisheries, and Commerce of Great Britain*, ed. George Chalmers (1814; reprint, New York: Burt Franklin, 1971), 1:197–99.

11. Stokes, *View of the Constitution*, 12.

12. Grant and Munro, *Acts of the Privy Council of England, Colonial Series*, 1:48–49; "The Watchman, Letter IV," *Pennsylvania Journal and Weekly Advertiser* (Philadelphia), April 27, 1758; Michael Hechter, *Internal Colonialism: The Celtic Fringe in British National Development, 1536–1966* (Berkeley and Los Angeles: University of California Press, 1975), 62–63.

13. Kenneth R. Andrews, *Trade, Plunder, and Settlement: Maritime Enterprise and the Genesis of the British Empire, 1480–1630* (Cambridge: Cambridge University Press, 1984), 16–17; Mark A. Kishlansky, "Community and Continuity: A Review of Selected Works on English Local History," *William and Mary Quarterly*, 3d ser., 37 (1980): 139, 140, 146.

14. J. G. A. Pocock, *The Ancient Constitution and the Feudal Law: A Study of English Historical Thought in the Seventeenth Century* (Cambridge: Cambridge University Press, 1957), 30–38, 50–51, 170–78, 233–43; Thomas Rutherforth, *Institutes of Natural Law; being the Substance of a Course of Lectures on Grotius' de Jure Belli ad Pacis* (Cambridge, 1754–56).

15. Alison Gilbert Olson, "Parliament, Empire, and Parliamentary Law, 1776," in J. G. A. Pocock, ed., *Three British Revolutions: 1641, 1688, 1776* (Princeton: Princeton University Press, 1980), 289; Carter, "Revolution and the Constitution," 53; T. H. Breen, *Puritans and Adventurers: Change and Persistence in Early America* (New York: Oxford University Press, 1980), 4–24; Edward Shils, *Center and Periphery: Essays in Microsociology* (Chicago: University of Chicago Press, 1975), 10. See also Norma Landau, *The Justices of the Peace, 1673–1760* (Berkeley and Los Angeles: University of California Press, 1984), on the continuing independence of county elites in regard to the internal affairs of the counties, and E. P. Thompson, "The Grid of Inheritance: A Comment," in *Family and Inheritance: Rural Society in Western Europe, 1200–1800*, ed. Jack Goody, Joan Thisk, and E. P. Thompson (Cambridge: Cambridge University Press, 1976), 328–60, on the "tenacity and force of local custom" in determining patterns of social and legal relations in English local society.

16. James Camlin Beckett, "The Irish Parliament in the Eighteenth Century," *Belfast National History and Philosophical Society Proceedings*, 2d ser., 4 (1955): 18–20.

17. John Phillip Reid, "In Accordance with Usage: The Authority of Custom, the Stamp Act Debate, and the Coming of the American Revolution," *Fordham Law Review* 45 (1976): 335, 341; Richard Koebner, *Empire*

(Cambridge: Cambridge University Press, 1961), 61–193; Burke, "Letters to the Sheriffs of Bristol," in *Works*, 3:190; Andrew C. McLaughlin, *The Foundations of American Constitutionalism* (New York: New York University Press, 1932), 138.

CHAPTER 3

The Idea of a Written
Constitution in the Thought
of the Founders

The Organization of Consent
. . . . .

MERRILL D. PETERSON

"Constitutionalism," Walton H. Hamilton informed us in 1931, "is the name given to the trust which men repose in the power of words engrossed on parchment to keep a government in order."[1] That definition, I think, might even have raised a knowing smile on James Madison's face. The idea of a written constitution as the means of giving supremacy and permanence to the fundamental law was an American invention of the Revolutionary era. Apart from the Cromwellian aberration, there was no precedent for it in English experience, and, of course, the glory of the English constitution was coming to be associated with a degree of parliamentary freedom and flexibility that was incompatible with a written frame of government. In 1861 Walter Bagehot expressed the Englishman's astonishment that the Union should break up over arguments drawn from "the limited clauses of an old State-paper"—arguments more befitting lawyers than statesmen. His countryman James Bryce was no less astonished a generation later, after the revolution in the Union produced by the Civil War, by the strange American fascination with "an unchangeable law." "How can a country whose very name suggests to us movement and progress," Bryce asked, "be governed by a system and under an instrument which remains the same from year to year and from century to century?"[2]

This great conundrum pertained to the federal Constitution, although Bryce understood very well that the idea of a written frame of

43

government had its immediate source in the state constitutions. Quite beyond the necessity that gave rise to them, these instruments were framed more out of devotion than hostility to the English constitution, the best parts of which, it was believed, might be preserved by overcoming the deficiency of its unwritten form. Regardless of conservative intent, however, the American experience with constitution making led to radical new ideas and made manifest a national genius for innovation and improvement in "the science of politics." It was from the state constitutions that Europe learned to admire American republicanism. It was from them that the American people learned to treat their constitutions, in Thomas Paine's words, as "the political bible of the State."[3] And it was against the background of the state constitutions—the good with the bad—that the framers worked in the Convention at Philadelphia.

The American founders embraced the theory of a written constitution, with its promise of making the restraints on government fixed and certain and durable, because of their fundamental commitment to the principle enunciated in the Declaration of Independence that governments derive their just powers from "the consent of the governed." All authority being derived from the people, government being founded in compact and instituted for the good of the whole, faithful adherence to the terms of the compact became the first obligation of rulers. According to a recent study, the word "consent" appears 127 times in the state constitutions before 1800.[4] It was used with reference not only to the just grounds of government but also to popular voice and participation in the workings of government. The word, with the concept, was pervasive. The founders' idea of a constitution may be discerned in their effort to implement and give organization to the principle of "the consent of the governed."

Several ideas were basic to the organization of consent. The first was constituent sovereignty, with its vehicle, the constitutional convention. Eleven of the thirteen newly "free and independent states" framed constitutions during the Revolutionary War; most of them proceeded to revise and improve those documents after the peace. It was axiomatic in this process that, to cite the first article of the Maryland Declaration of Rights, "all government of right originates from the people, is founded in compact only, and instituted solely for the good of the whole."[5] Yet none of the first state constitutions, not excepting Maryland's, was framed by a convention founded on the consent of the people other than as it might be represented in a Revolutionary legislature. No theory or model of a constitutional convention existed in 1776. It came about gradually through trial and error. As finally realized, this new institution involved three main elements: first, the popular election of delegates to a convention specifically authorized to frame a constitution; second, the convention's deliberate choice of a frame of government reduced to written form; and third, the consent (or dissent) of the people to the proposed constitution through a process of ratification. Thus developed, this marvelous invention became, as Andrew C. McLaughlin once said, "America's basic institution."[6]

The institution rested on a distinction, unknown to English theory and practice, between the constitution-making authority and the lawmaking authority. As James Wilson, the Pennsylvania founder, observed, "[T]he idea of a constitution limiting and superintending the operations of legislative authority, seems not to have been accurately understood in Britain. . . . To control the powers and conduct of the legislature by an overruling constitution was an improvement in the science and practice of government reserved to the American States."[7] Thomas Paine boldly articulated the key distinction: "A constitution is a thing *antecedent* to a government, and a government is only the creature of a constitution. The constitution of a country is not the act of its government, but of the people constituting a government."[8] But this was in *The Rights of Man,* not in *Common Sense.* The distinction was little understood among the founders in 1776, yet it was essential to emerging American constitutionalism.

Two illustrations, one drawn from Virginia, the other from Massachusetts, may help to define this development. The Virginia Constitution of June 29, 1776, was adopted by the Revolutionary convention sitting at Williamsburg. Thomas Jefferson, stuck in Philadelphia with the task of drafting the Declaration of Independence when he would rather have been in Williamsburg, frantically forwarded his own plan of government. It had little influence on the plan adopted, however, and Jefferson at once became the Virginia Constitution's severest critic. In part, this was because he thought it too conservative in its provisions. But—more significant in the present context—he also thought that it failed to meet the critical test of republican legitimacy. The convention, so-called, that adopted it was the Revolutionary

45

successor of the House of Burgesses, elected in April to perform the ordinary business of government. With what authority, then, could it frame a supreme law binding on government itself? Jefferson was not being frivolous; he was groping toward the conception of constituent sovereignty embodied in an appropriate convention. He actually proposed a form of popular ratification in his draft constitution, as well as provision for future amendment with the consent of the governed, both unprecedented in the constitution making of 1776. When peace came in 1783, Jefferson drafted a new constitution for consideration by a legitimate convention. In this effort he was joined by James Madison. But no convention occurred or would occur during Jefferson's lifetime, despite his continuing criticism of the Virginia Constitution—or perhaps because of it.[9]

The outcome in Massachusetts was entirely different; indeed, it foreshadowed the future. There the initial decision of the patriot leaders to resume the old charter as the frame of government met with opposition from various sources, most interestingly from the "Berkshire Constitutionalists," in the western part of the state. They argued that dissolution of the British connection had thrown the people into "a state of Nature," that a new civil covenant was the essential "Basis and ground work of legislation," and that approval by the majority of the people was required "to give Life and being to it."[10] The general assembly itself undertook to frame a constitution, even in the face of widespread objection that this effort violated the fundamental idea of a constitution as a law superior to, and unalterable by, the legislature. That instrument was overwhelmingly rejected when referred to the people for approval. Finally, in 1779, the legislature authorized election of a special convention to frame a constitution. This document, mainly from the hand and mind of John Adams, was approved in town meetings across the state in 1780. And so the Massachusetts Constitution of 1780 was the first to give finished form to the theory and practice of constituent sovereignty.

The extension of the theory to the national government was fairly straightforward, at least as straightforward as things were allowed to be under "the *composite* constitution" (Bagehot's term) of the United States. The Articles of Confederation were framed by the Congress and ratified by the thirteen state legislatures. Obviously, then, the instrument was liable to the same objections as state constitutions framed by legislative bodies and introduced without popular approval. Such objections were seldom voiced, however, because republicanism was identified with the state governments. There was no equivalent theory of republicanism for the general government of the Union. As one developed in the 1780s, it was inspired less by considerations of popular sovereignty than by considerations of more vigorous national government, which, some believed, would flow from the fountain of popular consent. As Alexander Hamilton maintained in *The Federalist*, the fact that the Confederation rested on no other foundation than the consent of the several state legislatures, any one of which might repeal what it had earlier approved and thereby sink the government, was a terrible infirmity. Madison went into the Convention convinced that the new system should be "ratified by the authority of the people"; the Virginia Plan provided for it and Article VII of the Constitution secured it. No more radical decision was made in the federal Convention than that of August 31 to send the proposed Constitution to conventions of the people in the several states. It was "a revolutionary step," indeed, in Charles Warren's opinion, the only one in the Convention. Hamilton forcefully stated the rationale for it: "The fabric of American empire ought to rest on the solid basis of THE CONSENT OF THE PEOPLE. The streams of national power ought to flow immediately from the pure, original fountain of all legitimate authority."[11]

The adoption in most states of declarations of rights made manifest the second crucial component of the organization of consent. Since a government founded on consent implied the voluntary surrender of certain liberties for the common good, it was the business of a constitution to mark the limits of what was surrendered and to secure what liberties were retained. In making this discrimination, constitution makers were defining the res publica, not only the powers and purposes included therein but, more important, the liberties excluded and guaranteed to the individual. Such liberties might be named in the body of the constitution; increasingly, however, they were set down in a separate bill of rights, which was presumably safe from alteration or amendment.

In bills of rights the states attempted to codify those natural and inalienable rights for which American independence had been declared. There was, of course, some discrepancy in the contents of these documents. Several ran into statements of the general principles of government; one of these—Maryland's—was forty-two articles in length. Some made claim to curious natural rights, for instance the right to navigate the Mississippi River, claimed by Tennessee in 1796. Yet, for all their differences, these documents reveal a broad consensus on both rights and principles. The Virginia Declaration of Rights of June 12, 1776, became the model, copied almost verbatim in several states and clearly influential in others. The preamble states that these rights, reduced to sixteen articles, "pertain to [the people] and their posterity, as the basis and foundation of government." Article I, the most basic, reads as follows:

> That all men are by nature equally free and independent, and have certain inherent rights, of which, when they enter into a state of society, they cannot by any compact deprive or divest their posterity; namely, the enjoyment of life and liberty, with the means of acquiring and possessing property, and pursuing and obtaining happiness and safety.

Jefferson, it is worth recalling, had this document in hand when he drafted the Declaration of Independence. He chose to make a broader assertion of human equality: "that all men are created equal." And his more felicitous phrasing of the inalienable rights as "life, liberty, and the pursuit of happiness" enabled him to withhold the mantle of protection from unnatural forms of property such as slaves as well as to set forth an encompassing liberal ideal.

The celebration of "the pursuit of happiness" not simply as an end, which it had attained in Enlightenment thought, but as an inalienable right, worked toward contracting the sphere of civil authority and expanding the sphere of individual freedom. The most remarkable instance of this development was the establishment of the dual principles of religious freedom and separation of church and state. Although religious freedom was a commonly declared right in the new states, most of them maintained religious tests, tax support for Christian ministers, or other civil entanglements with religion. The Virginia Statute for Religious Freedom, enacted in 1786 after a decade-long struggle, set a bold new course centered on the idea that religion is exclusively a private concern. Through James Madison the same idea was carried into the First Amendment of the United States Constitution. The last remnant of state-supported religion disappeared in Massachusetts in 1833. This development, in its larger implications, eroded older notions of government formed around a common core of moral and spiritual values, leaving it only with the secular value of freedom itself.

A bill of rights, while at first an option of a state constitution, rapidly became a requirement. The proffered Massachusetts Constitution of 1778 was rejected, in part, because it omitted a bill of rights. The error was rectified in 1780. Given the widespread sentiment favorable to bills of rights, the deliberate rejection of such a charter by the framers of the United States Constitution was surprising. In their defense, the Federalists offered a number of plausible arguments. The clamor for rights and liberties mistook the issue, they said. The danger to the nation came not from abuses of power but from abuses of freedom. The very state governments that boasted bills of rights ran roughshod over individual liberties. To Madison this was damning evidence against the effectiveness of parchment guarantees. Historically, as in England, charters of rights were granted by kings to the people—by rulers to the ruled. What relevance did they have to government founded on the sovereignty of the people themselves? Even conceding their usefulness in the states, where legislatures might legislate unless powers were withheld or rights reserved to the people, such an instrument had no application to the general government limited to the exercise of delegated powers. "For why declare that things shall not be done which there is no power to do?" Hamilton asked in the 84th *Federalist*. "Why, for instance, should it be said that the liberty of the press shall not be restrained, when no power is given by which restrictions may be imposed?" (The definitive answer to that question, though Hamilton might not have admitted it, came a decade later when Congress enacted the Sedition Law.) But the Anti-Federalists had the better of the argument. In the end, of course, Madison himself was persuaded, partly by Jefferson's rhetoric, that a Bill of Rights should be added to the Constitution. For whatever its defects, Madison acknowledged, a Bill of Rights was potentially a valuable accessory of republican government. "The political truths declared in that solemn manner acquire by degrees the character of fundamental maxims of free Government, and as they become incorporated with the national sentiment, counteract the impulses of interest and passion."[12]

Although "the consent of the governed" expressed itself first and primarily in the making of constitutions, it had reference as well to a third element in the organization of consent—the practice of republican government through a system of representation. The founders were well versed in theories of representation, for, in a sense, the Revolution was fought over them. Republican government was assumed to be representative government because the people did not, and could not, act collectively. Except that both were popular, it bore little resemblance to ancient democracy. The representation of the people by deputies of their own election, according to Madison, was one of the "wholly new discoveries" in the "science of politics" that gave hope to the friends of free government. It overcame the objection of Montesquieu and other theorists that a republican government was suitable only for a small territory. Madison, as we know, stood Montesquieu on his head, maintaining in the 9th and 13th *Federalist* papers that "extensive republics" were actually advantageous: first, to control "the violence of faction" and second, "to refine and enlarge the public views."

The great issues of representation—Who should share in it? How popular should it be? How should accountability to the people be secured?—were fought out in the states. Political rights had always been associated with the possession of property, particularly landed property; and so *persons* and *property* were usually joined in debates over representation. John Adams, while conceding that in the absence of traditional orders and estates no basis existed in this country upon which to rear aristocratic representation, nevertheless sought their faded equivalent through the special representation of property. Something like the balanced government of his idealized English model might thus be established in America.

Most of the state constitutions liberalized the suffrage. In Pennsylvania and several other states the ancient freehold requirement was replaced by a simple taxpaying requirement. Yet it was not until Vermont and Kentucky entered the Union in 1791–92 that any of the states boasted universal adult male (or adult white male) suffrage. The Virginia Constitution continued the colonial freehold suffrage. Jefferson had proposed going to a reduced property or simple taxpaying qualification and, in any event, would have turned every adult citizen into a freeholder by the grant of fifty acres of land. The disparity between liberal theory and conservative practice was perhaps nowhere better illustrated than in the Virginia Constitution. For although the freehold requirement withheld the franchise from as many as two-thirds of Virginia's adult white males, at least on Jefferson's reckoning, the Declaration of Rights said that the election of representatives ought to be free, "that all men having sufficient evidence of permanent common interest with and attachment to the community have the right of suffrage" and cannot be taxed or otherwise bound "without their own consent or that of their representatives."[13] With a view to ensuring representation of property as well as persons, two of the state constitutions, those of New York and North Carolina, provided for a dual suffrage, that is, setting different eligibility requirements for participation in elections of representatives to the lower and upper houses of the legislature. Another means of reaching the same object was by setting different eligibility requirements for the representatives themselves. Madison favored arrangements of this kind. For he believed, as he said repeatedly, that there were two classes of rights, those of persons and those of property, and both should be secured in the constitution of government. On this point, certainly, he and Jefferson were at odds.

Equally important to the character of representation was its apportionment. The most democratic advance came in Pennsylvania. Its radical constitution of 1776 concentrated all legislative power in a single house, which ruled out the differentiation of persons and property, and it adopted a simple numerical system of apportioning representatives. "In this concept," J. R. Pole has said, "it was not the business of a system of representation to prescribe patterns or formations or to predetermine the character of politics; the system was conceived as existing to find any such formations among the people and to translate them into decisions and policies."[14] This was revolutionary. Jefferson had the same goal in Virginia. Representation, at least in the lower house, would be proportioned to the number of voters in the various counties and boroughs. But the Virginians adhered to the traditional county-unit system of representation, which gave the least-populous county the same representation as the most-populous and proved grossly unfair to the western parts of the state. The system withstood Jefferson's assault under the banner of equal voice and participation in government and endured with little change until 1851. The Massachusetts Constitution of 1780 also fell short of democratic standards. Representation in the lower house, being based on townships, was unequal; and membership in the upper house, the senate, was proportioned to the amount of taxes paid in the several senatorial districts, which was Adams's way of achieving something like a balance of persons and property.

There is no analogue to the debate over representation in the federal Convention. To be sure, the Great Compromise itself was about representation, but the question at issue was the distribution of power in the federal system rather than representation in republican theory. Except for the provision that each of the states elect two United States senators, the Convention adopted a hands-off attitude toward suffrage and representation. The apportionment of representatives, the rule of suffrage with respect to them, the mode of appointment of presidential electors—on these matters the Constitution was silent. Curiously, the determination of the political community of the United States was left to subordinate authorities. The Anti-Federalists raised no objection. They concentrated their criticism on the small size of the House of Representatives—only sixty-five at the start—which, they said, gave only a shadow of representation and must normally lead to the choice of the rich and famous, in large electoral districts, to the exclusion of ordinary citizens. Madison pooh-poohed the objection in *The Federalist*, but upon entering the first Congress he admitted its justice and proposed, unsuccessfully, to enlarge the House by one of the series of amendments that would become the Bill of Rights.[15]

The fourth major element in the organization of consent was the separation of powers. The theory of separation of powers was mixed up with the older theory of balanced government; disentangling them was, in fact, one of the solid achievements of American republicanism between 1776 and 1787. Separation of powers was important to consent because it introduced internal checks and balances that worked to secure the liberty of the people and the equilibrium of the Constitution. In the view of the distinguished constitutional historian of a previous generation, Charles H. McIlwain, the founders conflated the new theory of separation of powers, taken from the mind of Montesquieu, with the limitation of powers that belonged to English constitutionalism. "The limiting of government is not the weakening of it," McIlwain wrote indignantly in 1940. Indeed, the enfeeblement resulting from checks and balances, far from guaranteeing constitutional government, was more likely to cause its overthrow. Twentieth-century democratic thinkers concurred in this criticism of checks and balances and made it part of their attack on the Constitution as a counterrevolution against the democracy of the Revolutionary era.[16] Today, of course, we recognize that separation of powers was more than a product of Montesquieu's imagination, and also that the Anti-Federalists, rather than opposing it, wanted even more rigid separation than the Constitution provided.

Most of the new state constitutions bowed ceremoniously to the principle of separation of powers. Thus Virginia's typically declared, "The legislative, executive, and judiciary departments, shall be separate and distinct, so that neither exercise the Powers properly belonging to the others; nor shall any person exercise the powers of more than one of them at the same time."[17] The Essex Result, the report of a county convention in Massachusetts against the tendered constitution of 1778, made one of the strongest statements of the theory. Any combination of the three powers in the same persons, whether few or many, was pronounced despotic. The influence of the Essex Result was reflected in Article XXX of the Massachusetts Declaration of Rights: "In the government of this Commonwealth the legislative department shall never exercise the executive and judicial powers, or either of them: The executive shall never exercise the legislative and judicial powers, or either of them: The judicial shall never exercise the legislative and executive powers, or either of them: To the end it may be a government of laws and not of men."[18] This is often attributed to John Adams; in fact, Article XXX was one of several articles of the Massachusetts Constitution that he did not write, nor could he have done so in the light of his own theory of balanced government that required a tripartite legislative power embodying the one, the few, and the many. The democratic lower house would be offset by an aristocratic senate, while the chief magistrate, vested with an absolute negative, would be the presiding genius—a kind of patriot king—over the whole. The one fatal error of the Massachusetts Constitution, in Adams's opinion, was the substitution of a merely suspensive veto for the absolute veto proposed in his plan.

The movement toward a functional theory of separation of powers coincided with what Gordon Wood has called "the disembodiment of government from society."[19] It is well illustrated by gradual abandonment of the effort to found the two branches of a consistently republican legislature on different principles or classes of society. The last important experiment of that sort was Adams's Massachusetts Constitution, which, as earlier noted, apportioned representation in the upper house to the taxable wealth of the constituencies, while basing representation in the lower on population. Nothing was more striking in the early American constitutions than the degradation of the executive.

Monarchy, as an element of a balanced constitution, was virtually eliminated. Typically the governor was elected by the legislature for an annual term, with limited or no reeligibility, stripped of a negative power, and shackled by a privy council. There were exceptions—for instance, New York—where the governor was elected for a three-year term by the people qualified to vote for senators. By 1787, certainly, the tendency was toward strengthening the gubernatorial office, and this was reinforced by the example of a strong executive in the United States Constitution. There was little theoretical background for the judiciary as an independent power. The judiciary had no place in balanced government theory, and even Montesquieu had been inexact about its role. But the judiciary soon claimed its place, aided and abetted by the idea of a written constitution as supreme law embodying the sovereignty of the people. Judicial review was the result. As early as 1786, in the landmark case of *Trevett v. Weeden*, Rhode Island's high court held that it was the unique function of American courts of justice to enforce constitutional limitations on legislative bodies. The argument would be brilliantly completed, for the United States Constitution, in Hamilton's 78th *Federalist* paper.

In the eyes of the framers at Philadelphia, separation of powers had been honored more in theory than in practice. The very existence of the federal Convention was, in fact, owing to the violence and instability attendant on the failure of that theory in the state governments dominated by the popular branches of the legislatures. "What led to the appointment of this convention?" one delegate asked. And he answered, "The corruption and mutability of the Legislative Councils of the States."[20] Madison, after reviewing the constitutional assertions of the theory, concluded, "[I]n no instance has a competent provision been made for maintaining in practice the separation delineated on paper" (*The Federalist*, no. 47). Obviously something more was required, and Madison sought it in the new federal system. He did not return to antiquated ideas of balanced government along the lines Adams seemed to be proposing in his *Defense of the American Constitutions*. In advocating the constitution of the senate, which invited those ideas, Madison chose to emphasize its value as a salutary check on legislative obliquities. "It doubles the security of the people, by requiring the concurrence of two distinct bodies in schemes of usurpation or perfidy, where the ambition or corruption of one would otherwise be sufficient."[21] Nor did Madison go for a pure theory of separation of powers. He offered, instead, a theory of checks and balances under which each branch would have a partial agency in, or control over, the acts of the others, thereby allowing each to protect itself and maintain the stability of the whole. In the great 51st *Federalist* paper, Madison described his system of "a compound republic." The federal division of powers was part of it, of course, as was the multiplicity of interests in the society. But nothing was more important than the contrivance of checks and balances within "the interior structure" of the general government. Neither the virtue of rulers nor the force of law could be relied upon to keep the government in order. "Ambition must be made to counteract ambition. The interest of the man must be connected with the constitutional rights of the place. . . . In framing a government which is to be administered by men over men, the great difficulty lies in this: you must first enable the government to control the governed; and in the next place oblige it to control itself. A dependence on the people is, no doubt, the primary control on the government; but experience has taught mankind the necessity of auxiliary precautions." The principal "auxiliary" was the policy of opposite and rival interests built into the Constitution. John Taylor later summed up the whole passage from Adams's classical republicanism to Madison's system of checks and balances when he wrote, "Our policy divides power and unites the nation in one interest; Mr. Adams divides the nation into several interests and unites power."[22]

One of the purposes of a written constitution was to give greater permanence to the supreme law. In the words of a Pennsylvania pamphlet in 1776, "Men entrusted with the formation of civil constitutions should remember they are PAINTING FOR ETERNITY."[23] Yet there could be no permanence without change; and quite aside from the need to accommodate constitutions to the changing exigencies of human affairs, there was the question of how future generations might exercise their right of consent to the supreme law. At the outset, certainly, the founders had no clear conception of formal constitutional change. None of the Cromwellian constitutions made provision for revision and change. The only American colonial charter to do so was Pennsylvania's. The idea had no place in the history of political theory. The contractual tradition from John Locke was a blank on the subject. While the government is in being, according to Locke, the legislature is the supreme power; and from a despotic legislature, or executive, the people have no appeal but to heaven. Their sovereignty comes into play only after the government is dissolved—only by return to the state of nature. In this William Blackstone, whose *Commentaries* was so familiar to the founders, concurred. Parliament was supreme. Blackstone could not conceive of a law ruling over it; and if tyranny ensued, the people might resume, as in 1688, "those inherent powers of society, which no climate, no time, no constitution, no contract, can ever destroy or diminish."[24] In the classical republican tradition running through the dissenting English Whigs, whose writings the founders knew well, change was precisely the thing to be avoided. Change was more or less synonymous with decline. In their origins governments were pure, imbued with first principles; as time passed, they fell prey to corruption and decay, though such perils might be arrested by a properly contrived balance of principles and powers. Algernon Sidney, in his *Discourses on Government,* employed the metaphor of the aging human body to describe the degeneration of constitutions and said that they "must perish unless they are timely renewed and reduced to their first principles."[25] George Mason gave immortal statement to this idea in Article XV of the Virginia Declaration of Rights: "That no free government, or the blessings of liberty, can be preserved to any people, but by . . . frequent recurrence to fundamental principles."

Insofar as we can speak of a conception of constitutional change during the Revolution, this was it; and how this recurrence might be carried out was even less well understood than how governments might be founded on the consent of the governed. Of the eleven original state constitutions, nine contained no provision for amendment, seven no provision for change by way of a convention, and five neither. In the only two with an amendment provision—those of Maryland and Delaware—amendment was by the legislature only. The Pennsylvania Constitution offered a model provision. "In order that the freedom of the commonwealth may be preserved inviolate forever," this article declared, "there shall be chosen in 1783, and every seventh year thereafter, two citizens from each city and county to form a Council of Censors to meet and inquire whether the constitution has been preserved, or where and how it has been violated; and if in the judgment of the Council corrective amendments are indicated, it may call a convention to be elected by the people for the purpose of acting on such amendments." (It was assumed that the convention's authority was limited to action on specific amendments.) New Hampshire and Vermont adopted this provision. And while it had a short life in the other two states, it lasted in Vermont until 1870. The purpose, clearly, was not to innovate or improve upon the constitution but, rather, to preserve it inviolate forever.

The idea of progressive constitutional change, together with the participation of the people in the process, was a gradual development. In this matter, as in so many others, Jefferson led the way. His draft constitution of 1776 included a provision for amendment by the legislature with the approval of two-thirds of the counties all voting on the same day. This was unprecedented; an amendment process with popular ratification had no parallel in the first constitutions. In his proposed constitution of 1783 Jefferson sought periodic change through conventions authorized by any two branches of the government and elected by the people. James Wilson expressed similar ideas, though they remained very much the minority view. Samuel Williams, the Vermont historian, brilliantly set forth the modern rationale of constitutional change in 1794. In an improving age, he said, every government must look to its own improvement. "And no policy would appear more puerile or contemptible to the people of America, than an attempt to bind posterity to our forms, or to confine them to our degree of knowledge and improvement: The aim is altogether the reverse, to make provision for the perpetual improvement and progress of the government itself."[26]

Article V of the United States Constitution—the amendment article—represented an attempt, as Madison remarked, to guard equally against "that extreme facility [of amendment], which would render the Constitution too mutable; and that extreme difficulty, which might perpetuate its discovered faults." Madison himself was no friend of frequent constitutional change. In *The Federalist* he criticized the Pennsylvania Council of Censors for actually contributing to the instability and impermanence it was intended to check; and, astonishingly, he entered a rebuttal against the proposition of his good friend Jefferson, United States Minister to France, to "new model" government periodically. Madison underscored the twin dangers of "disturbing the public tranquility" by too frequent appeals to the people and depriving the government of "that veneration which time bestows on every thing, and without which perhaps the wisest and freest government would not possess the requisite stability" (*The Federalist*, nos. 43, 49).

Whatever may have been the intent of the framers with respect to Article V, it proved extremely difficult to implement in practice. Excluding the Bill of Rights, which is properly considered part of the original Constitution, the American people have adopted only sixteen amendments in two centuries of incredible change punctuated by a civil war; and, of course, the part of the article authorizing conventions has been dormant. The Constitution has been accommodated to the changing crises of American affairs by construction and usage, especially by the agency of judicial review, which had no place in the original frame of government. A constitution ordained and established by "We the People" has become the property of lawyers and judges. The theory of consent has atrophied. The principle of real and active consent in the making and remaking of the fundamental law, though it survives tenuously in American state government, has been displaced by the principle of passive or "implied" consent. While that may have little bearing on the vitality of consent in other contexts, as in the everyday responsiveness of government to public opinion, it suggests that the American Constitution has evolved, willy-nilly, into something almost as malleable and mutable as the English constitution. Bagehot and Bryce, could they return among us, would surely pay more attention to the *living* constitution than to the one engraved on parchment and enshrined in the nation's capital. And who can doubt that they would smile complacently on this historical development?

Notes

1. "Constitutionalism," in the *Encyclopaedia of the Social Sciences*, ed. Edwin R. A. Seligman et al. (New York: Macmillan, 1930), 4:255.

2. *Bagehot's Historical Essays*, ed. Norman St. John–Stevas (New York: New York University Press, 1966), 349; James Bryce, *The American Commonwealth*, 2d ed. (London: Macmillan, 1891), 1:350.

3. *The Complete Writings of Thomas Paine*, ed. Philip S. Foyer (New York: Citadel Press, 1945), 1:378.

4. Donald S. Lutz, *Popular Consent and Popular Control* (Baton Rouge: Louisiana State University Press, 1980), 47, 49.

5. The state constitutions, to which frequent reference is made, are conveniently assembled in *The Federal and State Constitutions, Colonial Charters, and Other Organic Laws of the United States*, ed. Ben P. Poore (Washington, D.C.: Government Printing Office, 1878).

6. Andrew C. McLaughlin, *The Foundations of American Constitutionalism* (New York: New York University Press, 1932), 95.

7. Quoted in Bryce, *American Commonwealth*, 1:351.

8. *Writings of Paine*, 1:278.

9. For Jefferson's drafts and the Virginia Constitution of 1776, see *The Papers of Thomas Jefferson*, ed. Julian P. Boyd et al. (Princeton: Princeton University Press, 1950–), 1:329–86.

10. The Pittsfield Petitions of 29 May 1776, in *The Popular Sources of Political Authority: Documents on the Massachusetts Constitutions of 1780*, ed. Oscar Handlin and Mary F. Handlin (Cambridge: Belknap Press of Harvard University Press, 1966), 90.

11. *The Federalist*, ed. Jacob E. Cooke (Middletown, Conn.: Wesleyan University Press, 1961), no. 22 (subsequent references to the *Federalist* papers are to this edition; citations in the text are given according to number); James Madison to Edmund Randolph, April 8, 1787, *The Papers of James Madison*, ed. Robert A. Rutland (vols. 1–10 at Chicago: University of Chicago Press; vols. 11–15 at Charlottesville: University Press of Virginia, 1962–77), 9:369–70; Charles Warren, *The Making of the Constitution* (Boston: Little, Brown, 1937), 224.

12. James Madison to Thomas Jefferson, October 17, 1788, *Madison Papers*, 9:298–99. See also Martin Diamond's use of this passage in "Ethics and Politics: The American Way," in *The Moral Foundations of the American Republic*, ed. Robert H. Horwitz (Charlottesville: University Press of Virginia, 1977), 71.

13. *Jefferson Papers*, 1:379, 358, 362.

14. J. R. Pole, *Political Representation in England and the Origins of the American Republic* (London: Macmillan, 1966), 276.

15. *The Federalist*, no. 57; *Madison Papers*, 12:207.

16. Charles H. McIlwain, *Constitutionalism Ancient and Modern* (Ithaca: Cornell University Press, 1940), 144–47; J. Allen Smith, *The Spirit of American Government* (New York: Macmillan, 1907), chap. 6.

17. *Jefferson Papers*, 1:379.

18. Robert J. Taylor, ed., *Massachusetts, Colony to Commonwealth: Documents on the Formation of Its Constitution, 1775–1780* (Chapel Hill: University of North Carolina Press, 1961), 79, 131.

19. Gordon S. Wood, *The Creation of the American Republic, 1776–1787* (Chapel Hill: University of North Carolina Press, 1969), 608.

20. Warren, *Making of the Constitution*, 166.

21. *The Federalist*, no. 51.

22. John Taylor, *An Inquiry into the Principles and Policy of the Government of the United States* (Fredericksburg, Va.: Green and Cady, 1814), 88.

23. *Pamphlets of the American Revolution*, ed. Bernard Bailyn (Cambridge: Belknap Press of Harvard University Press, 1965), 1:105.

24. William Blackstone, *Commentaries on the Laws of England*, 8th ed.

(Oxford: Clarendon Press, 1778), 1:245. For Locke's views, see chaps. 13, 14, and 19 of his *Second Treatise*.

25. Algernon Sidney, *Discourses Concerning Government* (Edinburgh: G. Hamilton and J. Balfour, 1750), 1:210, 267.

26. *American Political Writing during the Founding Era, 1760–1805*, ed. Charles S. Huneman and Donald S. Lutz (Indianapolis: Liberty Press, 1983), 965–66.

CHAPTER 4

Capitalism, Liberalism, and the United States Constitution

•••••

JOYCE APPLEBY

We are well aware that the past is over, never to be experienced again save through our imaginative reconstructions from the detritus of history that we call evidence. What is less obvious is how those reconstructions are made more difficult by our knowledge of subsequent events. When we see certain events in one age connect with later ones while others die stillborn, we often concentrate on the former to the neglect of the latter, using the legerdemain of rhetoric to create "processes" and "developments." Our 20/20 hindsight reveals the future to have shaped the past, rather than vice versa. Nowhere is this logical absurdity more evident than in writings about the economic impact of the United States Constitution. In part this distortion has happened because our two modes for analyzing the dramatic transformation of the American economy in the nineteenth and twentieth centuries—classical liberal and Marxist—overdetermine the outcome. The movement from an agricultural economy to the modern industrial era has acquired for us the force of inevitability.

It is against this tendency that I shall present an economic interpretation of the Constitution. I will put forward three propositions that deal with its impact upon capitalism and liberalism in the late eighteenth century. First, I will argue that the economic components of the Constitution represent a solution to a problem the framers faced, not in light of their future expectations but because of their traditional political assumptions, their sensibilities rooted in the past. The Constitution they drafted was an imaginative response to a new situation, specifically, the sudden disappearance of deference among ordinary Americans in the years following Independence. My second proposition is that the liberal order made possible by the ratification of the Constitution involved a fundamental reworking of venerable ways of thinking about time and nature. In constructing a frame of government, the founders helped propel the United States into the modern world, but they were dealing with prospects, not actualities. Finally I will make the claim that the American ideal of a nation dedicated to freedom for independent white men did not emerge in the form we know it until Thomas Jefferson triumphed in the election of 1800. To put a finer point on this last proposition: While it could be argued that the Constitution provided the political framework for capitalism, it was Jeffersonian republicanism that joined capitalism and liberalism to a particular interpretation of the Constitution, thereby changing the fate of all three.

We are so familiar with the characterization of the 1780s as a time of crisis—it comes to us labeled "the critical period"—that we forget that the designation is not a fact but an interpretation, a particular reading of Confederation politics that stems from the Federalists themselves, especially the writers of the *Federalist* papers. Many things about contemporary politics bothered these men: the indifference to the terms of the Treaty of Paris, reluctance to pay prewar debts, confiscation of Loyalist property, interstate trade wars. Problematic too were a whole host of measures favoring the debtor interest that predominated in most of the state legislatures: paper money issues, insolvency laws, legal tender acts, and moratoriums for tax payments. Such populist legislation required organized majorities, and herein lay the real cause of the Federalists' alarm. The challenge to the political ascendancy of the gentry went much deeper than group interest; it struck at the foundations of their political world, the undergirding assumptions in their conceptual universe.

The political thinking of the framers began with social categories formed in Europe. In the seventeenth century successive groups of colonists had institutionalized various Old World notions of what constituted a well-ordered society. Calvin's Geneva was stamped upon the Puritan commonwealth in New England. Parliamentarian ideals about the landed gentry's leadership fired the imagination of Chesapeake planters. Arriving in America at the end of the seventeenth century, the Whig founders of Pennsylvania brought with them a receptivity to commercial expansion and religious toleration, giving to the middle colonies a less antiquated model of government, one that was to be led by the meritorious. All of these variants of the good society reflected as well the aftereffects of England's century of revolution: a suspicion of autocratic power, a capacity for concerted action among different social groups, and a new reverence for fundamental law. The gentry leaders of Revolutionary America also assumed that the world was divided between the many, who enjoyed civil liberties—and, if minimally propertied, the privilege of voting—and the few, who legislated, administered, and adjudicated for the whole. Like other established practices, this one had been challenged by the cumulative effects of commercial growth during the eighteenth century. General prosperity, progressive scientific inquiries, the extension of literacy, and the proliferation of published material all worked to enlarge the domain of shared social life while eroding the critical distinction between the few and the many.

Although members of an elite group, the framers were Americans, not Europeans. Their political texts emerged from a social situation dramatically different from their own. Even those among them who aspired to form an American aristocracy were implicated in social changes that favored meritocracy and middle-class values. In the century preceding the federal Convention, the meaning of landed property had undergone a profound change. Once principally regarded as the material underpinning for a specific social order, property had become an economic concept, a resource for producing marketable goods. By contrast, in the classical republican political view that was popular among these eighteenth-century gentlemen, property figured as a social category. As J. G. A. Pocock has suggested, property anchored the individual in the structure of power and virtue and liberated him to practice these as activities.[1] Property—enough to render one financially independent—enabled men to rise above petty, private concerns and identify their interests with those of the commonwealth. Yet in America, land had always had the characteristics of a commodity; owning property anchored one less to the structure of power than to the free-floating system of market bargains that animated the Atlantic trade world. American experience taught that property was not fixed but fluid; participation in the market created interdependence, not

independence; and attention to one's affairs was essential to the maintenance of one's estate. Property rights in England preserved an existing
convergence of economic and political power; property rights in America protected individuals' access to resources that were themselves un-
dergoing changes subversive to the existing distribution of power.

Equally distinctive in America was the widespread ownership of
property. The overwhelming majority of adult white men owned land
or could expect to in their mature years. Indeed, the absence of a class
of desperate, landless men helps explain the remarkable phenomenon
of a revolution led by the gentry. In vain did English authorities
inveigh against the dangers of propertied men courting rebellion. The
material basis for a hierarchical society had never existed in the colonies, except in the South, where legalized, physical intimidation sub-
dued an African work force. The language of classical republicanism,
thus, lacked a correspondence in social reality. Ordinary men acting on
their own initiatives in the market lost their character as social mutes.
The English lexicon of property found an awkward American analogue
in land, an accessible resource. Not only could men of wealth not cut
off the economic opportunities of their social inferiors but they also had
to compete with them in the marketplace. The Old World economic
equation in which the control of choice property forced the poor onto
marginal land was actually reversed after 1783; the cultivation of new
acreage made old land marginal.

By the time of the Revolution, tendencies latent in this situation
became manifest. The deferential attitudes that flourished when few
demands were made upon the deferring changed to contentious asser-
tiveness under the multiple pressures of securing Independence. As
religious sentiments gravitated to the poles of evangelical enthusiasm
and skeptical rationalism, churches ceased to promote obedience. From
the 1770s onward, the exigencies of financing and fighting the war
breached the isolation that had enabled many communities to impose
conformity upon their members. With the adoption of new state constitutions, power shifted toward the center, socially, politically, and
geographically. Western areas in most states acquired equal representation in the legislatures at the very time that the state constitutions
concentrated power in the legislative branch of government. Simultaneously, the social composition of those legislatures changed as ordinary men began electing their own to office. Even worse, from the
perspective of the Revolutionary elite, these new men pursued legisla-

tive goals of their own—the easy-money, debtor-favoring laws that the Federalists looked upon as a scandal. These events disclosed the dangers of democratic self-government and created the perception of crisis that led to the designation of the Confederation era as the "critical period" in American history.

This then was the predicament facing the framers. In the midst of trying to solve the many post-Revolutionary political problems, the electorate within the states stopped accepting the social direction of the elite. Yet most of the state constitutions had placed the full scope of public power in the hands of the majorities, who were electing representatives to the all-powerful legislatures. Gathered in Philadelphia to consider this situation, the framers faced a problem both practical and philosophical. Much as they might have liked to erect a national government along classical or modern British lines, they lacked the requisite social materials. Popular attitudes no longer reflected the politically relevant distinction between the few and the many. Their own political careers had been studded with repeated proof that ordinary white men in America were not humbled by their social deficiencies. What they saw as an excess of democracy was interpreted by ordinary men as the fulfillment of their natural right to civil participation. Gentlemen could no longer count on the balance between the few and the many to stabilize government.

The founders exercised the authority of the meritorious, but their society now lacked the authoritarian institutions, both political and religious, that had long operated to bring the ignorant many under the guidance of the enlightened few. It was the absence of this solution that constituted the political problem for the framers of the Constitution. Their awareness of the situation is evident in the debates. The secrecy of the deliberations at Philadelphia eliminated political cant, making it all the more striking that the debaters openly recognized their dependence upon popular support. Never before had the many been so little patronized by the few as during that summer of 1787. To be sure, the speakers often said that the people had been misled by the Pied Pipers of paper money, or they ascribed demagogic causes to legislative outcomes that they disliked, but the power of ordinary American voters can be inferred quite accurately from the framers' frequent statements to the effect that they had to construct a national government out of the real materials of American life, not from the attractive alternatives of old political philosophies. A national government removed from popular will (such as Alexander Hamilton described) was out of the question. So too was James Madison's proposal to invest Congress with the power to veto legislation passed by the states.

Rather than construct a strong central government, the drafters of the Constitution chose an opposite course of action: They limited the scope of formal power at both the national and the state levels. This was the liberal solution to the problem posed by classical republican ideas. The powers of Congress enumerated in Article I, Section 8 represented a stunning novelty in political construction. Section 10 of that same article went on to curb the legislative scope of state governments. Specifically, it took away those very powers that popular majorities had wielded to the consternation of the elite: the power to coin money, make anything but gold and silver legal tender, lay duties, or impair contracts.

In the end, the framers worked out a solution that enlisted the support of ordinary voters against the entrenched interests of state politicians like George Clinton and Patrick Henry. Their constitutional plan limited the power of citizens acting as a corporate body, that is, through representatives in their legislatures, but it guaranteed their rights as individuals pursuing their personal interests. While it is important that the Constitution created a national citizenry along with a national government, it is equally significant that it limited the traditional powers associated with government. Moreover, in devising a substitute for the English balance of commons and lords, the Constitution relied upon self-interest rather than virtue. Madison recognized that in order to prevent a concentration of powers in the new government, elected officials must be given the means of repelling intrusions from other officials: "Ambition must be made to counteract ambition. The interest of the man must be connected with the constitutional rights of the place."[2] This was an innovation, not a tried and true recourse. Hence the full range of possible developments, implicit in this method, was necessarily unknown, indeed was unknowable, in 1787.

Far more important than the hobbled national government that the framers brought into existence was the national market that they perfected. Simultaneously that market was opened to the initiatives of all white males and closed to the intrusion of legislative majorities in the states. This extensive national market became the arena for the free exercise of talents and resources. And because the Constitution also

defined who was in the constituent body, the market was closed to
women and slaves, who thereby escaped the liberating thrust of the
Convention's work. It is of course this outcome that has led subsequent
observers to emphasize the connection between capitalism and the Constitution. In his classic formulation of an economic interpretation of the
Constitution, Charles Beard wrote back into the past the profound
conflicts between owners and laborers in the industries of early-
twentieth-century America. It was precisely because those conflicts
were not implicit in the economic structure of the new nation that
Federalists and Anti-Federalists split along regional rather than class
lines. Where commerce predominated, enthusiasm for the new frame
of government ran high, as evident among mechanics as among merchants. Madison had substituted ambition for virtue not in order to
empower future economic interests but rather to introduce a balancing
mechanism to make good the loss of the social categories of the few and
the many.

The Constitution's influence on the economic development of the
United States has been distorted in most scholarly writing on the
subject. Subsequent developments have been transformed into motives,
and the compatibility between the Constitution and capitalism has been
converted into a necessary condition of continued economic growth in
the United States. It would take an ingenious counterfactual study of
economic life under an enduring Confederation to measure with any
precision the difference that the Constitution made. We are writing
proleptic history when we impute to the framers a knowledge of the
correspondence between industrial capitalism and the Constitution.
When we do that, we are not only ascribing to them a prescience they
could not have possessed but we are also neglecting critical issues in
their own understanding of politics.

Where Beard's formulation makes the Constitutional Convention
an act in anticipation of the relentless dynamic of nascent capitalism, I
would argue that it was the imaginative construction of men who reflected their own times. They chose to constrict a public sphere that
they could not be sure of controlling, which meant expanding the private realm that they occupied as undifferentiated individuals. Beard's
view that the Constitution shifted political power onto a national plane
dominated by a moneyed elite obscures the far more historically significant fact that the Constitution actually limited the areas of authority

long monopolized by elites. To reorient society away from political to personal incentives was above all to eschew coercion in favor of cooperation.

At Philadelphia, Montesquieu's influential "small republic" theory was abandoned in favor of empowering a large but limited government congenial to economic growth. It is this decision that marks a clean break with the older libertarian tradition emanating from English commonwealth writers. American leaders had adopted a fresh social prospectus in which liberty from restraint was translated into a new freedom of action.

In my second proposition I said that the liberal social order promoted by the ratification of the Constitution involved a reworking of traditional ideas about time and nature. In classical republican thought, time appeared as contingency, and change brought on frightening cycles of degeneration. The accrued wisdom of human experience was valued because it suggested ways of averting the downward spirals in an inevitable cycle. In contrast to this pessimistic view, some eighteenth-century thinkers had come to consider time as part of a linear progression that reversed the age-old relation of past to present and future. The framers reflected this more modern notion of the future as fundamentally different from the past, drawing upon the powerful new concepts of process, development, and progress. The conviction that the future would be different because of the ongoing processes of change rendered knowledge of the past interesting but not very relevant. In this spirit Jefferson had dismissed concern about the loss of some of Aristotle's writings. In this new notion of development, an orderliness was imputed to human affairs that undercut older worries about human willfulness and passion. When human beings were viewed as rational agents, their condition no longer appeared intractable. Human nature—an eighteenth-century term—became the proper subject of investigation. This new attitude, more than any particular cluster of beliefs, gave the era its pivotal character, the past being darkened as much by the brilliance of the eighteenth century as by the preceding ignorance. Alexander Hamilton exemplified this confident approach to the knotty problem of political organization when he claimed in the introductory *Federalist* paper that Americans were "to decide the important question, whether societies of men are really capable or not of establishing good government from reflection and choice" rather than having it imposed, as in the past, by accident and force.[3]

What emerged from these new conceptions of time as process, of human conduct as orderly, and of social systems as rational was a dramatic reversal of attitudes toward society and government. Both classical and Christian political theory had viewed the state of nature in the unkind light that Hobbes made famous. Life without government would be solitary, poor, nasty, brutish, and short. Government, both civil and ecclesiastical, offered a haven from the heartless war of all against all. In contrast to these views the new "science of politics" hailed by the Federalists built on the radical distinction between society and government that Thomas Paine had drawn in *Common Sense*: "Society is produced by our wants, and government by our wickedness; the former promotes our happiness *positively* by uniting our affections, the latter *negatively* by restraining our vices."[4] This invidious comparison between society and government is suffused with moral implications. No economist himself, Paine had little to say about utility maximization and profit motives. Instead he found in the emerging free-market economy an empirical demonstration that a society of equals could function harmoniously without the overweening power of priests, kings, and patriarchs. Here again, a backward look at economic choices obscures their significance to eighteenth-century men and women. The reformers' goal was to detach the economic domain of voluntary interaction from the world of privilege and attach it instead to the sociability that Scottish moral philosophy had found in human nature.

In choosing to limit the formal powers of government, the framers, far less given to visionary zeal than Paine was, nonetheless wedded American political philosophy to a belief in the natural ordering capacity of free men. In this view human nature could not be blamed for the dreaded classical corruptions of tyranny, oligarchy, and anarchy. Rather, government itself was held accountable because it gave to men the institutional means for oppression. Thus the public realm that had once provided the means for men to realize their human potential became, with this dramatic reversal, the area of high risk for human frailty. Disarmed, men could live cooperatively because their competitive urges would be deflected to the realms of commerce and culture. The framers practiced what Samuel Johnson had preached when he said that men were never so innocently engaged as when they were busy making money. They might lament the fact that virtuous men could not be counted upon to lead the commonwealth, but that loss was mitigated by the possibility that the commonwealth, reconceived as an area of voluntary interaction, offered an alternative domain for human endeavor that did not require the exercise of virtue.

Capitalism in the context of these hopes was not merely an economic system; it was an area for human striving untainted by the corruptions of power and the restraints of authority. In an area of protected free association men pursued happiness by choosing their own goals, they learned responsibility through the discipline of predictable consequences, and they were teased from sloth by the opportunity to seek self-improvement. The market had but recently been discovered as a new system where, as Adam Smith wrote, every man lives "by exchanging, or becomes in some measure a merchant, and the society itself grows to be what is properly a commercial society."[5] Observers of the market hailed its civilizing effect, its promotion of peaceable intercourse among nations, its proof that men, without the prompting of authorities, could exert themselves, make intelligent decisions, keep their word, plan for the future, and provide for their families. Here was a kind of materialism that touched on moral as well as practical concerns because individuals had to mobilize their will to attain their goals. It was the framers' genius to accept the cultural imperatives of their less distinguished countrymen. The benign and expansive character of the American economy with its owner-run farms and shops and its extraordinarily favorable ratio of natural resources to population had created an identity of interests among white men, and it was that upon which the framers built.

Within four years after the inauguration of George Washington, the American Indians of the upper Ohio River Valley had been decisively beaten in war, Eli Whitney had invented a machine that could cheaply process the short staple cotton grown throughout the South, and the French Revolution had plunged Europe into a general war that would continue intermittently for twenty-three years. Within the context of these events, a political movement arose that seized the liberating potential of the new constitutional order. It began with Thomas Jefferson's return from Paris to take up his duties as secretary of state. Appalled by the centralizing tendencies of Hamilton's fiscal program, the abandonment of limited government in the Federalists' broad construction of the Constitution, and the aristocratic tendencies of New

York society, Jefferson mounted a public opposition to Washington's administration that revealed the depths of the divisions among those nationalists who had written the Constitution. Successful in mobilizing ordinary voters "out of doors," Jefferson redirected the influence of the national government in public life and frustrated the centralizing tendencies of Federalist policies. When he entered the presidency in 1801, he dismantled Hamilton's program, purged the civil service of the Federalist elite, and led his party in Congress toward new goals. The size of the federal government was decreased, the funded debt paid off, access to land immeasurably expanded. More evocatively, Jefferson infused the nation with his understanding of the meaning of limited government, free inquiry, religious tolerance, and individual self-fulfillment in his "empire of liberty." Capturing the sympathy of thousands of ordinary voters, particularly in the mid-Atlantic and the South, Jefferson stripped the Constitution of its elitist potentiality. The triumphant Federalists of 1789 became the frustrated aristocrats of 1800 while his party of optimistic social engineers laid the political basis for an egalitarian, open society of free white men capable of improving themselves without the active intervention of government.

The liberal formula that the government governs best that governs least owed its empirical base to the American experience in the free-market economy that the Constitution so well protected. The widened scope of opportunity in the early nineteenth century engaged men's energies and confirmed their expectations about the blessings of liberty. The relationship between capitalism, an economic structure, and liberalism, a set of beliefs about what is true and good, merged as well, creating the deeply felt conviction that both owed their being to nature itself rather than to a conception of nature that was still being challenged when the framers met in Philadelphia. The distinction between fact and prescription has not been one that has interested most Americans in the intervening years. In the generation that followed the ratification of the Constitution, the novelty of ideas about time as process and about social integration as natural wore off. Repeatedly stated and confirmed by experience, the claim that freedom was a part of nature's plan for humankind sank into the substratum of unexamined assumptions. People forgot the traditional political prescriptions from which the framers disentangled themselves in 1787. After that, they lost their curiosity about a set of values that were now so self-evident as to require no explanation.

Liberalism began as a conception of politics that posited that people had natural rights and needed government principally to protect them. Less fully articulated was the notion that liberal ideals required a reconception of the economy as a nexus of market exchanges among individual bargainers whose private contracts could be enforced when necessary by the coercive arm of the state. The Declaration of Independence expressed with felicitous brevity the natural-rights philosophy. The United States Constitution secured the optimal operation of America's free-market economy. The Jeffersonian revolution determined which of several liberal orders would be instituted in the new nation. What might have persisted as a political philosophy and an economic doctrine became for Americans a description of reality. So easily did economic freedom and natural rights fuse in the American imagination that the relentless concentration of economic power under capitalism appeared as a correctable aberration in an otherwise harmonious social world.

The concepts of time as process and change as development that came to dominate political thought at the end of the eighteenth century have obscured what was specifically human and historically conditioned in the American fusion of constitutionalism, capitalism, and liberalism. Once a historical tradition has been accorded the status of a set of truths embedded in objective reality, that tradition has been liberated from human responsibility. Charles Beard's economic interpretation of the United States Constitution emphasized motives and modes of behavior that were themselves traceable to the nineteenth century. The framers helped bring this new world into existence; they were not themselves products of it. It is for us, the men and women of the twentieth century, to recover the contingency and design in the writing of the Constitution so that we may assume responsibility for a new relationship between its meaning and the forms of capitalism and liberalism it brought into being. Such, I think, is an economic interpretation of the Constitution that will empower us, its possessors, to act with the boldness and imagination of our founding generation.

Notes

1. J. G. A. Pocock, *The Machiavellian Moment* (Princeton: Princeton University Press, 1975), 391.

2. *The Federalist*, ed. Jacob E. Cooke (Middletown, Conn.: Wesleyan University Press, 1961), no. 51.

3. Ibid., no. 1.

4. Thomas Paine, *Common Sense* (Philadelphia, 1776), 1.

5. Adam Smith, *The Wealth of Nations*, ed. Edwin Cannan (London: Methuen, 1925), 1:24.

CHAPTER 5

The Revolutionary Constitutions
of Eighteenth-Century Europe

· · · · ·

R. R. PALMER

In the dozen years following the Philadelphia Convention in 1787, no fewer than fifteen constitutions were written and proclaimed in Europe, none of which lasted for more than four years. They were therefore ephemeral documents, but the ideas contained in them have been more lasting and are not altogether irrelevant to the two-hundred-year-old Constitution of the United States.

Let me begin by identifying the fifteen constitutions that I have in mind. The first in date was written in Belgium in December 1789 after a revolt against the Austrian emperor, and it set up an entity called the United States of Belgium, Les Etats-Unis belges.[1] The second was proclaimed in Poland in May 1791.[2] The third was the French Constitution put fully into effect in September 1791, though work on it had begun two years before, at the time of the fall of the Bastille.[3] Then in April 1792 war broke out between revolutionary France and monarchical Europe. All the remaining twelve constitutions were produced under circumstance of this continuing war. In France the short-lived constitution of 1791 was replaced by another in 1793 and still another in 1795.[4] Meanwhile the British, occupying the island of Corsica in 1794, and with the cooperation of certain Corsicans, promulgated a constitution for that island.[5] The French, however, proved victorious in the war, and their armies swept into Italy, the Dutch Netherlands, and Switzerland. In all these regions local patriots cooperated with the French to establish republics of a new kind—new because republics in an older sense, or states having no king, had been known in Europe since the founding of Venice a thousand years before. The constitutions of these new republics, written from 1796 to 1799, were all modeled on the French Constitution of 1795, or on the regime of the Directory in France. The new entities were known as the Sister Republics, sisters to la Grande Nation, as France was then called, at a time when the very word "nation" had a revolutionary impact. The Sister Republics were the Batavian, replacing the Old United Provinces of the Netherlands;[6] the Helvetic, replacing the old Swiss confederation;[7] and four republics in Italy: the Cisalpine in the former Austrian Lombardy; the Ligurian at Genoa; the Roman in the papal states; and the Neapolitan, replacing the old kingdom of Naples.[8] We may add a constitution that was secretly circulated but never proclaimed, worked out in detail on the French model by a revolutionary Greek patriot for a Hellenic Republic to replace the Ottoman Empire throughout the Balkans and Asia Minor.[9] If we consider that the Cisalpine Republic absorbed two predecessors with their constitutions, the Bolognese and the Cispadane, we reach the total of fifteen.

Obviously, I shall have little to say about most of them. All of them embody the idea of a written constitution, but three of them were less than revolutionary in any full sense of the word. The Belgian Constitution, which contained echoes of the American Articles of Confederation, simply asserted the independence of ten historic and neo-medieval provinces, without internal change, from an outside authority perceived as foreign. The Polish Constitution, while providing more liberties to the middle class of town dwellers than could be found elsewhere in Eastern Europe, was revolutionary in a limited sense, since it was devised mainly by the king of Poland himself and retained special advantages for the nobility. By the constitution of Corsica, during the British occupation, King George III of England became the king, with a British viceroy in residence, and with a Parliament composed of the Catholic bishops and some of the richest landowners on the island. These three least-revolutionary constitutions were also very short-lived. In Belgium the Austrians restored their authority within a year. In Poland, likewise within a year, the new constitution was destroyed by the intervention of Russia and Prussia and the Second Partition of Poland. In Corsica, when the Corsican-born Napoleon

Bonaparte began to win victories in north Italy, the British evacuated the island, and the regime collapsed.

We are left with the more strictly revolutionary constitutions: one for a constitutional monarchy in France from 1789 to 1792 and the others all designed for republics, for France in 1793 and 1795, and for the Sister Republics after 1795. None of them outlasted the year 1800. But the arrangements made thereafter by Napoleon, both for France and for his Grand Empire, while certainly not revolutionary, incorporated important features of the preceding constitutions, to which alone the following observations pertain. It may be added parenthetically that, as Belgium and the German Left Bank of the Rhine were annexed to France for twenty years after 1795, they shared in the general transformation that issued from the French Revolution.

What was revolutionary in these revolutionary constitutions? It was, first of all, the idea or fact of an explicit written document, drawn up at one time and place by persons outside the government, claiming to act in the name of a sovereign people. The point in the sovereignty of the people was precisely that the government was *not* sovereign, that it exercised only powers delegated to it by the people, through branches of government created and defined by the constitution. Formerly, the word "constitution," when used at all, had referred to an indefinite body of inherited traditions, liberties, and procedures, believed to be more fundamental than ordinary laws. Or it might designate some basic act issued by an existing authority, like the "constitutions of Clarendon" issued by Henry II of England in the twelfth century, or the Golden Bull of the Holy Roman Empire. In France, before 1750, the word "constitution" was most often used to mean a papal bull, *Unigenitus dei*, issued by the pope in 1713 to repress the heresies of Jansenism. After 1750 in France, however, the highest courts of justice, the *parlements*, began to use the word in a political sense, to mean various powers and liberties enjoyed by French subjects against arbitrary actions by the king and his ministers. This constitution, in the view of the *parlements*, was inherited from the remote past. In defending it, however, they used the very language of the coming Revolution, insisting on the rights of "citizens" and of the "nation." But this constitution, if it existed, was not codified or written down, so that some said that France had no constitution at all, and others that it needed a new one.

It was in 1776 and the following years, in the several states of

British America, in Virginia, Massachusetts, and nine others, that the first revolutionary constitutions appeared. They not only set up a new "frame of government," as several of them called it, consisting of executive, legislative, and judicial powers, but they prefaced this delegation of functions with an affirmation of the sovereignty of the people and a list of the "rights of man."

It was these American state constitutions, not the federal Constitution, that had an influence in Europe. In France they were translated and published several times, and as the French were already engaged in constitutional arguments they found much of interest in American examples, of which the very fact of an explicit written constitution was the most obvious. It will be recalled that when the French Estates General met at Versailles in May 1789, they did not limit themselves to dealing with the financial crisis and a few important reforms, as the king would have preferred. Instead, the Third Estate insisted on the need of a wholly new written constitution, swore the Oath of the Tennis Court never to disband until a constitution was written, and converted the Estates General into a National Assembly. As a first step the Assembly issued its Declaration of the Rights of Man and the Citizen in August 1789. I have always thought that this determination to have a written constitution, with a preliminary list of rights in a numbered series, is the point at which the influence of the American Revolution on the French conflict can be most clearly seen.

The French, in their Declaration of 1789, used the two key words that had become current in political discussion since the 1750s but were still absent (or virtually absent) from political discourse in America—the words "nation" and "citizen." Since in French the word *peuple* usually referred to the lower classes, the French put the locus of sovereignty in the "nation" instead, meaning by it all the inhabitants of the country without regard to social class. To quote the Declaration of 1789: "The principle of all sovereignty rests essentially in the Nation. No body, and no individual, may exercise authority that does not emanate from the Nation expressly." By "no body" they meant no court, magistracy, or governing group; by "no individual" they meant the king himself; and by "expressly" they meant explicitly stated in a constitution still to come. The word "citizen" meant that rights, though natural, did not arise in some supposed state of nature, distant in time and place, but were the product of membership in a properly organized civil community. This word "citizen" or *citoyen*—which we find as *cittadino* in Italy and as *Burger* among the Swiss and Dutch—was neither a neologism nor a cliché. It was loaded with meaning and became a hallmark of the revolutionary era. By sharing in the national sovereignty, citizens possessed power as well as rights. So when the French rewrote their constitution in 1793 and 1795, they attributed sovereignty to the "universality of the citizens," and this phrase was carried over into the Batavian, Helvetic, and Italian constitutions of the following years. The new sense of the word crept into American usage and became a point of distinction between American and British English. What Americans called a citizen continued in England to be a "subject," and the sovereign continued in ordinary parlance to be the king or, for lawyers, the king in Parliament.

Yet, though the asserted rights pertained to citizens, they were also "natural," the same everywhere, and regardless of history or circumstance. Persons had indeed possessed rights before 1776 or 1789, but in varying degree, depending on the political culture into which they were born, or on their social class or place of residence, or on past agreements made by particular groups with their rulers. Since 1791, rights are said to inhere in human nature itself. Rights are anterior to government, which is seen as a machine invented to secure them. They are also imprescriptible and inalienable; they cannot be lost by time or taken away by force; when denied, in fact, the denial is an injustice, a moral wrong. They pertain to individuals; the abstraction "man" refers to the whole human race, but it refers also to the human being without regard to group membership or affiliation. The French, accordingly, recognized the equal rights of free blacks in 1792 and abolished slavery in their colonies in 1794. To what extent "man" included women was obscured by ambiguities in the English and French languages; certain particular rights were to be exercised by men only, in the sense of adult males, but at least no one ever said that women possessed none of the rights of man. And we find the feminine *citoyenne* very common during the Revolution, when women were prominent in all the disturbances, demonstrations, and armed insurrections.

The French Declaration of 1789, like the American Declaration of Independence and several of the state constitutions, announced that "all men are born free and equal." It immediately added that social distinctions might exist if they were based on "common utility." The constitution of 1793 in France, written at the onset of the Reign of Terror and under pressure of popular upheaval, added the word "equality" to

79

the enumerated rights, and this has been taken to show that that particular constitution was more democratic than the others, as indeed it was. In the formula of 1793 the basic rights, called natural and imprescriptible, were those to "equality, liberty, security, and property." Equality is defined to mean that "all men are equal by nature and before the law." Security meant that each member of society should be protected "in his person, his rights, and his property." But the constitution of 1793 was no sooner proclaimed than it was suspended for the duration of the war, and it never went into effect. That the quoted phrases were not considered excessively radical is shown by their recurrence in the later republican constitutions (sometimes dismissed as merely bourgeois), those of the French Directory of 1795, and of the Cisalpine and several other Sister Republics. All declared "equality, liberty, security, and property" to be the basic rights.

All the republics were secular, dissociating the state from religion, in the sense that religion was irrelevant to citizenship. Thus Catholics and minority Protestants for the first time acquired equal rights with the Dutch Reformed in the Batavian Republic, Protestants in France and Italy, and Jews in all the new republics. By implication the same would have applied to Moslems and Buddhists if there had been any in Western Europe. In his constitution for a Hellenic Republic to replace the Ottoman Empire, the author put the matter explicitly. "The sovereign people," he said, "is composed of all inhabitants of the State, without distinction of religion or language: Hellenes, Albanians, Rumanians, Armenians, Turks, and any other race." Or again: "Christians and Turks are equals in the order of nature." Everywhere the "nation" was conceived of as a civic, not a religious or ethnic, community.

The more specific rights declared in Europe were much the same as those set out in the American state constitutions and the first ten amendments to the United States Constitution. They had been adumbrated in the American Declaration of Independence, in some of the protests of the French *parlements* under the Old Regime, and by writers during the Enlightenment in various parts of Europe. They included the rights to freedom of speech, assembly, and religion, freedom from arbitrary arrest and cruel punishments, the right to representative government, trial by jury, and access to public office without regard to birth or social status, according to individual virtues and talents.

Most of the republics from 1795 to 1799 issued declarations of duties as well as rights. It was the French and the Italians who did so; curiously enough, the Protestant Dutch and Swiss declined to follow the French model in this respect. To us the duties, as declared, seem a combination of the obvious and the sentimental. But in fact, to declare them had a practical purpose. Even in the first enthusiasms of 1789, when the French were discussing their first declaration of rights, there had been cautious spirits who warned against a publication of rights without attention to obligations. They were overruled in 1789, but their views prevailed in 1795. The listed obligations then included the duty of the citizen to obey the law and of the officeholder to be free from corruption and dedicated to the public interest, but they also announced that no one was a good citizen unless he was also a good husband, good father, good brother, and good son—here the male chauvinism of the time is most apparent. Although all the republics provided for a separation of church and state, five of their declarations actually incorporated the Golden Rule or Christian principle verbatim: "Do nothing to others that you would not wish done to yourself, and do for others all the good that you would wish to receive." In addition, the European constitutions, like those of several American states, included provision for a system of schools—if not as a right, then as a duty or function of government. And furthermore, since the continued existence of the revolutionary republics depended on the outcome of the war in Europe, several of them added the duty of military service. The problem everywhere was to produce a new kind of civic or national consciousness.

In Europe, as in the American states, the assertions of sovereignty and declarations of rights, or of rights and duties, served as a preamble to the constitution itself, which set up the organs of government. Here we note, excepting only in the abortive French Constitution of 1793, the acceptance of the doctrine of the separation of powers, meaning primarily a separation of the legislative, executive, and judicial functions, such as Montesquieu had favored half a century before. It might also mean a separation between the executive and a legislature divided into two chambers. Revolutionaries in Europe, however, while adhering to the principle, were unwilling or unable to put it effectively into practice. The French in their Declaration of 1789, Article XVI, announced that "any society in which the separation of powers is not determined has no constitution." But in their fear of despotism they granted only restricted powers to Louis XVI, who in any case disapproved of the constitution with which he was presented; and in their fear of nobility or any privileged class they created a legislative assembly in a single chamber. Then a few years later, under pressure of war and foreign invasion, with the fall of the monarchy and civil war in the provinces, and in the face of radical demands for a truly democratic society, the constitution of 1793, while calling for a universal male suffrage, envisaged no independent executive at all, but only a large council of rotating members, elected by the legislature for two-year terms. Even the legislature, in this plan, could not put a law into effect if a certain minority of voters opposed it in a general referendum.

Then in 1795, in what is called the Thermidorian reaction, the French again attempted a separation of powers to avoid both the dictatorship and the democracy associated with the Terror. They now created a bicameral legislature, with a weak executive board of five members, called a Directory, one of whom was elected each year by the two legislative chambers acting together. It was expressly forbidden for any director to be also a member of either legislative chamber. The lower chamber proposed legislation, which became law only when approved by the upper chamber. Otherwise the difference was chiefly one of age; the upper chamber was composed of slightly older men, usually over forty. They were called Anciens or "elders" in France, Seniori or "seniors" in the Cisalpine and Ligurian republics; in the Roman, Neapolitan, and Helvetic republics the upper chamber was called a Senate, as in the United States. The word "senate," of course, derives from the Latin *senex*, an old man. The same provision found its way even into the curious project for a Hellenic Republic that I have mentioned, whose Greek author explained the reason perhaps better than his Western European counterparts. Members of the lower house, he said, "being younger, are ingenious and energetic; those of the upper, being older, are more reflective and able to see into matters more deeply."

As for the judiciary, most judges were to be elected, though with provisions for secure tenure. It was widely agreed that judges must be independent, but never strong enough to encroach on the other two branches. As the French Constitution of 1795 expressed it: "Judges may not mix in the exercise of legislative power, nor make regulations, nor stop or suspend the execution of any law, nor call administrative officers before them by reason of their functions." All of the Sister Republics repeated this language almost exactly. There was reason for such precautions. Revolutionary republics could remember how the *parlements* in France, and similar bodies elsewhere, by their decrees and regulations, had often blocked the innovations desired by governments, which we now see as attempted reforms. Judicial review, one might say, was a feature of the Old Regime, of which European revolutionaries had seen enough. But under such circumstances, a firm distinction between constitutional and ordinary law would be hard to maintain.

The revolutionary republicans called their regimes "democratic," by which they were careful to specify a representative democracy, not the direct democracy demanded by more radical elements in 1794. It is my strong impression that there were far more self-declared democrats in Europe than in America in the 1790s. No need was seen for political parties. All the constitutions from 1795 to 1799 provided for local assemblies in which two or three hundred voters, qualified by a very extensive male suffrage, could meet to agree upon a person to send to an electoral or district assembly, at which members of the legislative body of the republic and other officials would be chosen. These electors, in the absence of political parties, had to find candidates, discuss their merits, and ascertain their opinions; the electors were therefore subject to a relatively high property qualification, in the not-unreasonable belief that ordinary voters, often illiterate and of limited experience, were unsuited for such a task. For membership in the legislative body no property qualification was required. All the republican constitutions specified that legislators should receive a salary. That itself was revolutionary at the time. The older idea was that it should be men with an independent income who took part in public life. Thus in the kingdom of Corsica during the British occupation, members of the parliament had to have an independent income from landed property of 6,000 lire, on the model of requirements for the House of Commons in England. Across the water in the Cisalpine Republic, inspired by the French, they received the same sum, 6,000 lire, as payment for public service. It was a further innovation that legislators should represent equal electoral districts, counting by population, and that their proceedings should be published.

All the republican constitutions, without exception, in France, Italy, Switzerland, and the Netherlands, began in Article I with a terse and resounding affirmation: "The Republic is One and Indivisible." Each then proceeded to what it called a division of the territory. This seeming contradiction reveals the most obvious and fundamental difference between Europe and America at the time. The American federal Constitution presupposed the continuing existence of the thirteen states. It was a rare and bold thinker, like Alexander Hamilton, who could imagine cutting up a large state like Virginia into a number of smaller ones of more equal size. The American state constitutions likewise accepted the continuing existence of counties and incorporated places. In the revolutionary constitutions of Europe all subordinate jurisdictions became creations of a central government, through which alone the sovereignty of the people was supposed to act. Thus the French, as early as 1790, in the constitutional monarchist phase of the revolution, divided the territory of France into eighty-three equal departments. Later, in annexing Belgium and the Left Bank of the Rhine, they simply added eight departments in Belgium and four in the Rhineland. The Batavian Republic transformed the old United Provinces into eight departments, the Helvetic Republic defined twenty-one cantons, and the Cisalpine Republic created eleven departments, later increased by expansion to twenty. The legislature in each case had the power at any time to suppress, create, divide, or combine the departments, or to redraw their boundaries. All the constitutions also provided for municipal government below the department level. One conservative writer, in 1798, warning against the spread of the French Revolution, saw the essence of it in a departmentalization, a municipalization, and, as he said, a Cisalpinization of all Europe.

In America the state and local governments were thought to be closer to the people, or more democratic, than a distant central authority. In Europe the opposite situation prevailed. It was in local institutions that the inequalities against which the revolutionary movement was directed were most firmly embedded. Power before the revolution reposed with provincial magnates, regional assemblies of estates, sovereign courts, lords of manors, wealthy landowners, seigneurial judges, ancestrally prominent families, burgomasters, guild masters, town councils, and urban patriciates that were usually, if not hereditary, at least self-perpetuating and oligarchic. All based their various and unequal rights on historical arguments, reinforced by an established religion.

Such conditions existed not only in the great French monarchy but also in the small, nonmonarchical states that formed an eastern fringe to France from Amsterdam to south Italy. The United Provinces before 1795 consisted of seven very unequal provinces, among which Holland enormously predominated, plus a conquered region that had no provincial status at all, with full civic rights everywhere only for members of the Dutch Reformed church. The old Swiss federation consisted of only thirteen cantons, together with allied districts, subject districts, and miscellaneous jurisdictions, in which German-speaking Protestants of Bern, Zurich, and Basel ruled over subordinate rural, usually Catholic, and in some cases French- or Italian-speaking subjects. North Italy, outside the small kingdom of Piedmont, was a composite of old-time republics, city-states, papal territories, and duchies, some of which were possessed or influenced by Austria.

In Europe it was therefore the democrats who insisted on having a homogeneous and unitary state, indivisible but divided into new departments approximately equal in population, and equal in having the same rights, duties, laws, law courts, liability to taxation, and public facilities for all inhabitants. The adversaries of the democrats were called federalists, because they objected to such unitary and centralizing authority, and they did in fact draw much of their strength from older local institutions of a kind that had originated in the Middle Ages. The word "federalism" took on opposite meanings on the two sides of the Atlantic in the 1790s. In America the Federalists were the party that favored a stronger central or national government. In Europe the "federalists" were those who resisted centralization. The Federalists in America were innovators; those in Europe were more fearful of change. In America democracy might grow out of what preceded; in Europe the most democratic spirits dreamed of wiping out the past.

European democracy became associated with memories of the Jacobinism of 1793 and the strong government of the Committee of Public Safety, which had been engaged simultaneously in a war with Europe, repression of internal rebellion, and a subordination of the demands for liberty to those for equality. In fact, after the fall of Robespierre, the European republics were mainly middle-class enterprises. But the conjunction of democracy with centralized power was very real, and it later worried Alexis de Tocqueville, who feared that democracy in Europe had an inherent and fatal tendency to despotism. Tocqueville believed democracy to be more successful in America because there it was uncentralized and rooted in local liberties. His analysis had insight, but not much prophecy in the sense of accurate prediction. Today it is not the democratic states of Europe that have become despotic or totalitarian. And in the United States the advance of democracy, in the sense of more equal rights for all citizens, has been brought about by a growing centralization of power, to which various local and historical liberties have had to yield. A republic "one and indivisible" in America is not wholly dissimilar to those attempted in Europe in the 1790s.

The European republics and their constitutions were indeed ephemeral, and for obvious reasons. They were all by-products of war, though embodying ideas that had germinated long before. They were more prospectuses than actual constitutions. They were plans, rather than buildings. They rested on no internal consensus; they were political documents, expressing the views of some persons against others who did not share them, and so at best they rested on foundations too shaky to support a viable constitutional system. They collapsed after a very short life, not by a triumph of the counterrevolution but at the hands of a man thrown up by the revolution itself, Napoleon Bonaparte, who preserved some of their features, partly by departmentalization and "Cisalpinization" and partly by his uniform law codes, in order to prevent a return of the Old Regime. And after Napoleon collapsed in his turn, ideas expressed in the revolutionary constitutions continued to animate the forces of liberalism and democracy in Europe, as indeed those of bureaucracy and strong government, and are still there today.

Notes

1. For the text of the Belgian Constitution of 1789, see Thomas K. Gorman, *America and Belgium: A Study of the Influence of the United States upon the Belgian Revolution of 1789–1790* (London: T. Fisher Unwin, 1925), 275–80. For further discussion, see my *Age of the Democratic Revolution: A Political History of Europe and America, 1760–1800*, 2 vols. (Princeton: Princeton University Press, 1959 and 1964), 1:350–57.

2. For the text of the Polish Constitution of 1791, in French, see Karol Lutostanski, *Les partages de la Pologne et la lutte pour l'indépendance* (Paris: Payot, 1918), 112–14. The constitution may be found in English in the *Annual Register, or a View of History, Politics and Literature for the Year 1791* (London: Annual Register, no date), appendix, 88–94, where the following pages also contain the text of the French Constitution of 1791. For a discus-

sion of the Polish Constitution, see Palmer, *Age of the Democratic Revolution*, 1:422–35.

3. For discussion of the initial constitutional debates through the year 1789, see Palmer, *Age of the Democratic Revolution*, 1:489–501.

4. For the texts and discussion of the French revolutionary constitutions, see Jacques Godechot, *Les constitutions de la France depuis 1789* (Paris: Garnier Flammarion, 1970), 21–140; Palmer, *Age of the Democratic Revolution*, 2:110 (constitution of 1793), and 2:214–16, 258 (constitution of 1795).

5. For the Corsican Constitution, see Alberto Aquarone et al., *Le costituzioni italiane* (Milan: Edizioni di Comunita, 1958), 715–20. For discussion, see Palmer, *Age of the Democratic Revolution*, 2:284–89.

6. For the text of the Batavian Constitution, in French, see D. R. C. Verhagen, *L'influence de la Revolution française sur la première constitution hollandaise du 23 avril 1798* (Utrecht: Kremink, 1949), 59–99. For discussion, see Palmer, *Age of the Democratic Revolution*, 2:192–204.

7. For the text of the Helvetic Constitution, in French, German, and Italian, see J. Strickler, *Achtensammlung aus der Zeit der Helvetischer Republik*, 12 vols. (Bern: Stampfliche Bucherei, 1886–1940), 1:567–603. For discussion, see Palmer, *Age of the Democratic Revolution*, 2:411–21.

8. For discussions of the constitution of the Cisalpine Republic, see Palmer, *Age of the Democratic Revolution*, 2:310–23; for that of the Roman Republic, 2:372–79; for that of the Neapolitan Republic, 2:384–86. For the texts of the Cisalpine, Ligurian, Roman, and Neapolitan constitutions, in Italian, see Aquarone et al., *Le costituzioni italiane*, 5–304. The texts of the Bolognese and Cispadane constitutions may be found here also. On the Sister Republics, see also Jacques Godechot, *La Grande Nation: L'expansion revolutionnaire de la France dans le monde de 1789 a 1799*, rev. ed. (Paris: Aubier Montagne, 1983), 331–57.

9. For discussion of the proposed constitution for a Hellenic Republic, see Palmer, *Age of the Democratic Revolution*, 2:347, 351–52. Its text may be found, in French and Greek, in A. Dascalekis, *Les oeuvres de Rhiges Velestinlis* (privately printed by A. Dascalekis in Paris, 1937), 74–125.

CHAPTER 6

British Reflections on the Bicentenary of the United States Constitution

.....

LORD HAILSHAM OF ST. MARYLEBONE

I must first of all examine my own credentials. I am a typical English-man; that is to say, I possess practically no English blood. I was born of an American mother, and her forebears and my father's were both predominantly Scots or Irish, mostly the former. Nevertheless, my education, my accent, my culture, and, above all, my loyalties, are English. It is, therefore, primarily as an Englishman that I come to congratulate you on the bicentenary of the Constitution of the United States.

Our own British constitution has, of course, gradually evolved out of centuries of history. That is not so much because we possess no single document we can call our constitution, with or without amend-ments. The differences between our constitution and yours are many. Your constitutional law is a separate body of jurisprudence, presided over by a specially created Supreme Court dedicated to its preservation and covert evolution and amendable only by a special procedure. Ours is only part of the general body of our law, principally customary in origin, amendable by Parliament exactly as any other part of our law, and enforced and developed by our ordinary courts, which also deal with everything from traffic regulations to the making of wills.

But there is yet a more subtle difference between the two: While your Constitution is a strictly legal document in most of its fundamen-tal aspects, our real constitution is not governed by law at all, but by convention. Over all acts of Parliament, for example, the queen has in law an absolute right of veto. That right has not been exercised for more than three hundred years and today could not constitutionally be exercised at all. Theoretically, the queen, like the president of the United States, could compose her cabinet of law professors, army officers, or anyone else. In practice, she is confined to members of Parliament. Of these, the lord chancellor must be, or be made, a member of the House of Lords, and the prime minister, the home secretary, the chancellor of the exchequer, and various other ministers, including the attorney general, must be members of, or immediately elected to, the House of Commons.

I will not labor the point. These are thoughts about the American, not the British, Constitution. Each is the product of history, and in your case the successful outcome of two single historical events, Independence and the Philadelphia Convention.

Your Constitution has emerged virtually unscathed after two hundred years. It enabled thirteen colonies of different sizes and interests, strung out along the eastern seaboard but all mainly of British origin, to grow into a single world power, rich in ethnic diversity, vast in numbers, unequaled in wealth and military resources, and occupying the entire breadth of the North American continent. It is indeed vain to commend this document's excellences. Nor is it profitable to point out its weaknesses, though I will later spend a little time doing just that. The real miracle is that it came into being at all, and just in time, in the interval between the Seven Years' War and the French Revolution, to prevent North America from becoming the plaything of European politics.

The alternative to the Constitution of 1787 and its appendant Bill of Rights would have been no constitution and no United States of America. There can be no doubt that the thirteen colonies would have fallen apart long before the Civil War had crystallized their latent mutual hostilities into the struggle against chattel slavery and the right of secession. European powers would certainly have been sought by some states as allies, on one side or the other or both, in the course of their struggles. What would have happened when the great influx of population took place from across the Atlantic can only be surmised. But it is fairly certain that no Statue of Liberty would have greeted them on their arrival in New York.

It is easy to see the English analogies that inspired the American founders. Nothing in the modern world more resembles the eighteenth-century House of Lords than the U.S. Senate, with its senators two to a state, curbing the power of the executive government, influencing foreign policy, and representing local interests of vastly varying kinds. There is no one at present enjoying prerogatives more similar to those of King William III of Orange after the abdication of King James II than the president of the United States. Congressional committees exercise much the same sort of power as the committees of both houses of Parliament that evolved during the struggle of Parliament against the Crown. With the partial exception of the Supreme Court, the American legal system replicates the old British system almost exactly, with the difference, to be expected in a country only partially settled, that here in America the two branches of the legal profession were fused. With the degree of exaggeration and paradox allowed to an educationist, I begin my lectures on the British constitution to American students with this proposition: The American Constitution is based on a monarchy with an elected king, the British on a republic with a hereditary president.

But this brings me to the most striking difference, apart from the obvious fact of federalism, that separates the British from the American constitutional system. In framing their Constitution, the founders inevitably looked to the past, and in particular to the victory of the Parliament over the Stuarts, as to a golden age, and regarded all its developments since the Hanoverian dynasty ascended the throne under the tutelage of Robert Walpole, as symptoms of decadence and even corruption. In that assessment they were greatly influenced by Montesquieu's *Esprit des Lois,* in which the checks and balances of the British system as Montesquieu perceived it in the 1720s are implicitly compared with the institutions of absolutist France, where the pendulum had swung in the opposite direction, in favor of the Sun King.

It was, of course, Montesquieu, rather than the framers, who thought that the distinctive characteristic that gave freedom to the British, or rather the English, as we called them at that time, was the division of powers among executive, legislative, and judiciary branches. In a way, of course, he was right. What Montesquieu failed to discern was that, although the king's days as the chief executive officer of the states were in fact numbered, his role as head of state, reigning but not ruling over the hearts of his subjects, was to endure during the next three hundred years. It was also not unnatural that, during the unreformed Parliaments of the eighteenth century, the cabinet system—the real growth point of the British constitution—remained undetected as such, or was even openly condemned as simply a corruption of representative government. It is here, of course, that the framers got the essence of the matter right. Henceforth, government of the people was also to be by and for the people on the basis of universal suffrage. But it is clear that the failure to establish a cabinet system within the body of Parliament, and the failure to distinguish between the functions of head of state and those of head of government, were the real points of divergence between the constitution of Britain and that of the United States. In this the framers were consciously looking back to an idealized past, while the British, totally unconsciously, were evolving slowly toward an absolutely unperceived future. It is idle to argue whether one system is better or worse than the other. Both are the product of history, and the characteristic institutions of the one can no more be grafted onto the other than can a pear or an apple be joined with a plum or a peach. It was as unthinkable that the framers should choose a Parliament and cabinet system on the British model as it would be for a British electorate to grant Margaret Thatcher the legal powers of the American president, the capacity to appoint ministers not forming an organic part of Parliament, or the authority to usurp the functions of the head of state in addition to those of prime minister.

When I come to the third of the great arms of government, I find my problem more difficult and more personal. One of the cases in which a written constitution is most admirable, and the separation of powers most important to the preservation of freedom, is in the administration of justice. The victory won in the struggle against the Stuarts is embodied in our own Bill of Rights and Act of Settlement. But these, as I have said, are only ordinary acts of Parliament, subject to amendment or repeal like any other act. With regard to the secure administration of justice, the separation of powers is nowhere more important, and nowhere less secure, than in a parliamentary democracy based on universal suffrage. Security in office was guaranteed by both acts of Parliament that I have mentioned. It is still part of our constitution. Yet, whenever I render a decision in a controversial case, the next day's mail invariably brings with it demands that, were they carried out, would be inconsistent with the principle of tenure for judges, or with the prohibition against cruel and unusual sentences, or simply with due process of law.

Here in America, thanks to your own Constitution, no such demands on the judiciary can legitimately be made either in the media or by individual congressmen, senators, or legal eccentrics. The Constitution, with its appendant Bill of Rights, is studied in every school, protected by even the most liberal of Supreme Courts, and amendable only by a process that normally increases rather than diminishes its protecting provisions. By contrast, the independence of the judiciary in the United Kingdom, where it is not always supported by public sentiment, depends on the courage, tenacity, and integrity of a single man or woman in the person of the lord chancellor, whose only protection consists in the fact that, by convention, he is not a member of the elected House but remains seated on an uncomfortable piece of furniture technically just outside the House of Lords. Hitherto these safeguards have been sufficient, and I trust they will remain so for centuries to come.

But in the two centuries since 1787 a great deal has come to pass. The Bible tells us that there is nothing new under the sun, yet I venture to think that in no other period of history has so much that is new intruded itself into our international relations, our culture, and our economic life. I have said that the true miracle of Philadelphia was that a Constitution emerged that proved so providentially adapted to take the strain not merely of two hundred years but of *those* two hundred years. What are the strains to which it will be subjected in the next two hundred? Or even the next fifty? When I was sent over to Yorktown in 1981 to celebrate the bicentennial of the British defeat there that virtually decided the outcome of the War of Independence, I ventured to say, in the presence of President Mitterand and President Reagan, that nothing is quite so humbling to the statesman as to contemplate the extent to which his predecessors acted in blissful ignorance of subsequent developments. Did General Cornwallis, surrendering at Yorktown, foresee that in two centuries' time Britain would have resumed its former stature as a relatively small island moored off the northwest coast of Europe? Would Thomas Jefferson, so much the apostle of rationalism, have perceived the advent of communism as the result of the Russian Revolution?

The answer to both questions must of course be no. But I know of no way to foretell the future save by examining the events of the recent past: two world wars, the emergence of the Soviet Union and the ascendancy of China and Japan, the Depression of the 1930s precipitated by the Wall Street crash of 1929, the wildly destructive properties of military technology (of which the arsenal of nuclear weapons is only one aspect), men on the moon and in space, air travel, and biological engineering, to name a few. Watching these developments has taken me from boyhood to manhood and through manhood to old age. They have not all been bad, these changes. They have been accompanied by a vast accumulation of wealth and, at least in the West, by a wider distribution of that wealth than was ever dreamed of by my own American great-great-grandfather, whose will I still possess. But, though not all bad, they are at least sufficiently alarming to lead me to make one or several observations about the future. The founders acted on the assumption, valid until 1900, plausible until 1917, but increasingly absurd after 1939, that the new nation could effectively isolate itself from world events. In practice, of course, isolation, far from being splendid, has ceased to be a possibility. Actually, it remained a dogma for too long. If it had been abandoned in 1914 or in 1939, many of the evils from which the world now suffers might well have been prevented.

International law is still based to a large extent on national sovereignty. In fact, it was the doctrine of national sovereignty more than any other factor that brought about the catastrophe of 1914. The dependence of national economies upon international economic movements brought about the Wall Street crash, the failure of the German banking system, the worldwide recession, and ultimately the rise of Hitler. The world is now an international society divided into two broad confederacies with an unstable Third World all too ready to play one off against the other. How the game will end I probably will never live to see, since I am already in my eightieth year. But the new international status of the United States seems certain to influence both its internal politics and its foreign policy. Whether American policy was wise to encourage and accelerate the liquidation of the British and other European imperial systems is a question I will leave to historians to determine. It has certainly not prevented the emergence of another and more compact imperial system between Berlin and the borders of China, a system that is not likely to break up within the foreseeable future. Whether we can cooperate in promoting the stability and prosperity of the Third World will be a challenge to the statesmanship and self-restraint of both sides in the dialogue for perhaps a century to come. While disarmament is intrinsically desirable for its own sake, those who see it as a cure for all ills should bear in mind that nations do not distrust one another because they are armed; they are armed because they already distrust one another. Before disarmament agreements can be meaningful, we need to build an atmosphere of trust between nations and to work together to maintain and improve that trust.

In reflecting thus, let us not forget the difficulty encountered by the delegates to the Philadelphia Convention and by the individual states in ratifying its work. Here were thirteen ex-colonies, speaking the same tongue, used to the same political institutions, just emerged from a successful war in which they fought side by side, and badly in need of a unified constitution. They labored long and with much dissension. The two largest, New York and Virginia, ratified with difficulty; the smallest, Rhode Island, only after much pressure from without and much heart-searching within. The moral of it is that we must not expect too much too soon. In the meantime, I would urge the American people not to undervalue the continuing influence of my own country, still the focus of a largely English-speaking and multiracial Commonwealth, a full partner in the new European community, an ally in NATO, and I hope always and immutably your friend in a world desperately in need of peace and stability, without which the future of humankind, in the light of the experience of this terrible twentieth century, can only be seen as in the direst jeopardy.

CHAPTER 7

Republicanism and Enlightenment Thought

Observations from Scotland

·····

NEIL MACCORMICK

The Enlightenment, that exceptional flowering of thought in the creative arts and in human, social, and natural sciences in eighteenth-century Europe and America (and wherever else European ideas were carried), has left innumerable traces and influences. Of its memorials, however, there is none more remarkable or durable than the Constitution whose bicentennial we are gathered to celebrate. What the Americans—you Americans—did in 1787 was found the first deliberately and formally constituted republic in human history. This was done by popular adoption of a Constitution giving permanent force, but also form and structure, to popular power.

The structure of the institutions then established, federal government and separation of powers, has survived in strikingly recognizable form to the present day. Of course, all human political arrangements—all durable ones, anyway—are subject to an inevitable and desirable process of interpretation and reinterpretation in changing times and circumstances. But the specific idea of a free and popular form of government—of a republic—implicit in that constitutional structure is a particularly American one. So is the achievement of sustaining it over two centuries. Nothing I say here is meant even marginally to qualify that, far less to gainsay it. My aim is to make some observations upon it from a specific point of view, that of an interest in the Scottish Enlightenment as one piece of the whole body of philosophical and political thought available to the American founders when they went to their nation-making labors before, at, and after Philadelphia.

It was not a merely capricious act whereby the organizers of this symposium gave me such a task. For of course American scholarship— I think here of the work of Douglass Adair, Caroline Robbins, Jack Greene, Garry Wills, and no doubt others whom I do not know as I should—has shown that James Madison and Alexander Hamilton owed special debts to David Hume.[1] James Wilson of Pennsylvania, an important figure in the Convention and in the subsequent debate on adoption of the Constitution, was a Scot by birth and education. The moral philosophy of Francis Hutcheson of Glasgow exercised particular influence in American education in the eighteenth century and was foundational for much of what we now call Scottish Enlightenment thought; one could even speculate that it was Hutcheson's particular reworking of the Lockean version of natural rights in a context of moral theory that was the most direct influence on those who drafted the Declaration of Independence.[2] Adam Smith's special contribution to political economy doubtless had not reached its full influence here or elsewhere as early as 1787; even so, like American independence, it was already eleven years old by then.[3]

However that may be, it appears that observations from Scotland may have some prima facie relevance to the search for the roots of American constitutional thought, provided one neither exaggerates their significance in relation to other streams of thought (English common law or French political theory, for example) nor underrates the sheer originality and boldness of the founders themselves or the vigor of American political thought as it must have been then.

Republicanism: Fletcher and Ferguson

My observations are in particular to be about republicanism; that is, about the very idea of a republic and the republican form of government but also about the spirit and the special virtues thought to be inherent in, required by, and best realizable through such a form of government. As this statement suggests, my idea of republicanism is at best a complex and clustered one,[4] at worst simply confused. We shall have to see which. A good first step is to ask why one should even suggest the existence of any particular linkage between personal virtues and political forms. The answer can be found in the critique offered by sundry eighteenth-century political thinkers of the tendency toward absolutism or despotism that they discerned in the kingdoms of their period. The case for limited or constitutional monarchy was commonly thought to be this: as *monarchy,* it enshrined sufficient authority to enable firm and expeditious dispatch of the business of state, and as *limited,* limited through laws and legislatures representative and partially democratic in form, it opened sufficient space for individual human liberty in one of the bewilderingly many senses of that phrase. It procured, in short, the best available balance of authority and freedom.

But why did liberty matter? Why, indeed, *does* it matter? One can answer such a question in at least three ways. One way is to assert a natural right to freedom. The trouble here is that everyone knows that civil society involves some departure from full natural right; the question is, how much? Another way is to appeal to private interest—to say that people like being free and can maximize their own good if free to pursue it. The problem here is to balance my freedom to pursue my interest against my need for certain protections from violence and misfortune, and to know what that balance should be. A third is to respond in terms of public good and civic virtue—to argue that free human beings best realize their humanity by acting as free members of a body politic and by identifying their good with its good. People best realize themselves in making their best possible contribution to the common good of a political community in which they have the opportunity for independent action. This view has its own difficulties, but it is the one I shall mainly consider here.

A favorite representative of the civic virtue case in Scotland during our period is Andrew Fletcher of Saltoun, "a Scotch gentleman of great parts and many virtues, but a most violent republican and extravagantly passionate," as Bishop Burnet described him.[5] His insistence, in the aftermath of the revolution of 1688–89, that the Scots Parliament should acquire and use the power to withhold public funds until the queen's government joined in enacting its laws, and even more his proposal that her ministers should be elected by and answerable to Parliament, exhibit his republicanism at the level of constitutional doctrine (and remind us that republicanism in the relevant sense does not preclude the possibility of favoring a hereditary headship of state). His vigorous opposition to the Articles of Union proposed by the Scottish and English commissioners for the constituting of a United Kingdom of Great Britain in 1707, subject to the required enabling legislation of the English and Scottish parliaments (which thereby abolished themselves), exhibits the other aspect of the theme. He foresaw that the incorporating form of union would remove from Scotland all independence of political initiative, depriving it of that theater of representative politics in which, he considered, civic virtue and the opportunity for dedication to the public good of one's community can alone be realized. He and others who pleaded in that debate for confederation rather than union, appealing to the good of part and whole alike, lost the vote, even if perhaps they won the argument. Some of what they argued has had lasting resonance in relation to the American constitutional debate.[6]

Such pleas were grounded in a view of Scottish constitutional history and the experience of Western European kingdoms, a view that goes back at least as far as the sixteenth-century humanist George Buchanan and his celebrated book *De Iure Regni Apud Scotos* (1579). That text asserted and argued for the right of the Scots to depose their chosen kings or—much to the point of the recent deposition of Mary Queen of Scots—queens, if ever they betrayed the trust consensually reposed in them by the people, thereby taking on the character of tyrants rather than that of lawful rulers. This conception of the liberty of the community, even subject to institutions of limited monarchy, is all-important to what I am calling the republican ideal. It is also important to John Locke's political and constitutional thought, as I have mentioned elsewhere. Thus it has a plain enough relevance to American constitutional roots. It is also important to the background of the greatest of Scots legal writings, Lord Stair's *Institutions of the Law of Scotland*. That book, which argues from the basis of a contractual theory of the state for a view of the private law of a civilized community as founded in personal freedom and aimed at the securing of "society, property and commerce," can in a way be read as a companion volume to the almost contemporary *Two Treatises of Government* by Locke.[7]

Some would doubtless correct me for ascribing Stair and Locke to the same intellectual tradition as Fletcher and his like. Stair and Locke, it might be argued, belong more to early or emergent liberalism than to the republican tradition, whether that be traced back to roots only in

Buchanan or (as would be more proper) to the theorists of the medieval Italian city-republics and their seventeenth-century revivals by thinkers such as James Harrington.[8] This is indeed an important point. Unquestionably, Stair and Locke stress something like the natural rights view of liberty as qualified also by the appeal to interest. Their idea is of law and government upholding natural liberty and fostering the conditions of general well-being through an established system of property and commerce. Here they foreshadow the economic liberalism of Adam Smith and his successors, rather than echoing the civic virtue theme of the republican tradition. Even so, the liberties they advocate are not dissimilar to the different strands of the various republican arguments. And even as late as Smith, the characteristic stoic and republican virtue of self-command remains an important shot in the liberal locker.[9]

However that may be, we can certainly find a difference between Fletcher and Stair or, rather, Stair's personal and political descendants,[10] in respect of the union debate in the opening decade of the eighteenth century. For Fletcher and his like, the incorporation of Scotland into an essentially English Great Britain meant its end as a theater of civic virtue. It meant the spiriting away of leading figures to a distant capital and the consequent impoverishment not only of local talent and ability but of local economic strength as well. The real argument on the other side was for peace, free trade, and the firmer preservation both in Scotland and in England of the individual, religious, and political liberties of the revolution settlement of 1688–89. Here, perhaps, we may ascribe a difference of political preference directly to the opposition of values between republicanism and proto-liberalism. At least, one can discern deeply held differences in perspective as to what counts as the flourishing and well-being of individuals and communities.

This dispute involves, even if it is not reducible to, a difference of opinion on the optimal size of a free society. Fletcher wanted to keep political communities manageably small and to build a regard for the public good upon the sense of loyalty to community, which the ancient tradition of small polities fosters. Against him, it was argued that the enlarged theater created for the pursuit of commercial advantage outweighed the advantages he claimed for his preferred outcome and that, in any event, loyalties could as well be transferred to the new union as kept narrowly to the old kingdom. The counterargument, that a federation could procure the commercial advantages without the other losses, hardly got off the ground once it was clear that the English were not interested in that alternative.

The theory of smallness as favorable to liberty continued as a theme of republican thought into the high period of the Enlightenment, certainly in Scotland. Its classic representative is Adam Ferguson, professor of moral philosophy in Edinburgh and, as the author of *An Essay on the History of Civil Society* (1767), one of the founders of sociology. In that work, Ferguson returns again and again to the theme of the liberty enjoyed in the Greek and Italian civic republics of antiquity and to the personal and communal virtues that arose from the intense identification that polities of that kind fostered between individual and community. There, he argued, was none of the servility or dependence such as arises in the courts of absolute monarchs or in lesser cases of patronage and clientage. Citizens made independent contributions to the commonweal out of their own commitment to it and their own judgment of what it required.[11]

Whereas critics of republicanism were usually apt to argue that small republics are always internally factious and externally warlike, Ferguson turned these arguments upside down. The problem of faction he regarded as grossly exaggerated. The good emerges not from bland consensus but, like truth, from the vigorous dissensus of passionate debate. The end should not be the extinguishment of faction but the securing of pluralism and overall equilibrium among factions. It is from the tension among vigorously held and hard-won contentions that a real conception of and regard for public good emerges. Such a spirit is also essential to the preservation of individual and political liberty. Only the insistence on one's right to put forward one's own view or that of one's party could guarantee the preservation of personal freedom and freedom of public action. Liberty resides more in civic spirit than in laws, however admirably framed. Here one finds a striking antinomianism, an outspoken mistrust of laws as alone sufficient (if even necessary) to the preservation of liberty. To become dependent on a specialized class of lawyers and judges who are the only ones able to find their way through the thickets of legal enactment or entrenchment of rights is, says Ferguson, a poor kind of freedom, for it substitutes one kind of dependency for another. It is worse indeed if one's freedom and estate depend on the whims of a despot rather than on the labyrinths of legal interpretation as conducted by experts, but neither is the optimal condition of humanity.[12]

As with internal faction, so too with external enmities. Peace at any price is not the goal. After all, says Ferguson, it is in warfare that some of the finer traits of human nature come into their own. Here are found courage and self-sacrifice for one's friends, here the virtues of patriotism and the exaltation of public over private good. Moreover, even in times of peace, the spirit of emulation and rivalry that characterizes small republics in relation to each other is more apt to call forth ingenuity and inventiveness than is soporific peace over extensive kingdoms. So even if it is true that republican liberties require small states rather than large empires, that is no disadvantage. The creation of extensive empires, necessarily involving strong central power, is inimical to the higher forms of human good.[13]

These higher forms of good are by no means to be defined in economic or materialist terms. It is not by loafing around, enjoying the fruits of materialistic enterprise, that humans find their good or even their happiness. To be human is to be active. No sooner is work over than play begins, and the favored forms of play are yet more violent and active than most forms of work. This point may, of course, suggest a certain detachment on Ferguson's part from the praises his contemporaries were wont to heap upon the emergence of a commercial society out of earlier and more barbarous epochs. Ferguson was perhaps the first to notice the fiction of the Hobbesian state of nature as a supposed representation of some presocial condition of humanity. It is the commercial form of society, Ferguson notes, that encourages humans to see each other in instrumental terms rather than as ends in themselves. The solitariness of human beings is at its greatest not in the most primitive but rather in the most advanced forms of human society. The problem for commercial societies is to sustain social solidarity and public spirit. And here they face special difficulties, given the ways in which their economic forms lead persons to relate to one another.[14]

It is certainly not difficult to find in Ferguson's advocacy of these views a precursor of certain aspects of Jeffersonian republicanism. The regard for an upright class of independent yeoman farmers, the mistrust of commerce and commercialism, the cool view of lawyers as a class are all opinions that a Virginian republican might warmly endorse. The thesis that "the right of the people to keep and bear arms shall not be infringed" is one that we can readily imagine striking a chord in the breast of a Ferguson. (Again, though, it is worth remarking that Fletcher of Saltoun was one of the more vigorous earlier advocates of the view that the collapse of the old feudal militia was a prerequisite for the rise of royal absolutism. He is among the more persuasive of the late-seventeenth-century advocates of the restoration of liberty through reestablishment of a militia as the chief national defense force.)[15]

Hume on Free Government

Hitherto I have risked being carried away on a tide of Fergusonian rhetoric, forgetting that his is a somewhat isolated voice during his period in Scotland—indeed, in Britain and Europe. His greatest influence came later, in Germany. If the republican ideal has a place in mainstream thought, it assumes there a more muted and qualified form. The standard view of it is as a part, rather than the whole, of political virtue. The point, as David Hume puts it in one of his essays,[16] is "that liberty is the perfection of civil society; but still authority must be acknowledged essential to its very existence." As I remarked earlier, an abundance of contemporary support is to be found for the view that some form of mixed constitution—monarchy qualified with elements of aristocracy and democracy—seems best adapted to securing the necessary balance in civil society. Such a structure provides the way to achieve adequate authority to give stability and security to government and at the same time to guard against incursions into liberty.

My usage is here perhaps somewhat confused, for Hume and his like are apt to regard Great Britain as a commonwealth or, in contemporary terms, a republic. The point was that it was not a pure republic, but a mixed form of government in which "the republican part of the government prevails, though with a great mixture of monarchy."[17] So Hume can in his way be considered a republican at least as to some strands in his thought, albeit not a "very violent" one along the lines of Fletcher or even Ferguson. Above all, the antinomianism we noted in Ferguson is wholly lacking from Hume—indeed, entirely anathema to him. For Hume is one of the early prophets of what we have come to call the rule of law, which he saw as an absolute prerequisite of free government. It is in the nature of a free government, says Hume, that it governs always and only by general and equal laws.[18] Such laws can always be clearly known to all the members of a government of divided branches and separated powers, and equally to all the subjects of the government. This arrangement leaves people free to lead independent lives in the knowledge that no broad and arbitrary powers can be suddenly invoked against them.

A part of the reason for mixed government's being a feature of constitutions like that of the British is precisely that it combines monarchical with republican (representatively democratic) elements. The appointment of judges and other magistrates may lie in the monarch's hands. But that gives the elective branch of government reason to exhibit a great jealousy as to potential abuses of power by the magistracy. That branch, says Hume, "is obliged, for its own preservation, to maintain a watchful jealousy over the magistrates, to remove all discretionary powers, and to secure everyone's life and future by general and inflexible laws. No action must be deemed a crime but what the law has plainly determined to be such; no crime must be imputed to a man but from a legal proof before his judges; and even those judges must be his fellow-subjects, who are obliged, by their own interest, to have a watchful eye over the encroachments and violence of the ministers."[19]

As well as being a rather good, if precocious, summary of what one might mean by "due process of law," these arguments link up with the theory that Hume puts forward both in his *Treatise* and in his *Enquiry* concerning the idea of justice in human societies.[20] Justice, he argues, is not so much a natural as an artificial virtue, in the sense that it presupposes and depends upon human artifices and conventions, namely those laws under which individuals' rights to property and to contractual services are secured and which provide for cognition and punishment of invasions of such rights, or of rights to personal and physical freedom from molestation. Such laws grow up on grounds of the necessities of human existence and remain justified by the general good they procure in human communities. But their utility depends on their inflexible observance. A regime that allowed discretionary decision making on the basis of the best outcome of each individual decision would defeat the ends of justice rather than serve them to a higher perfection. So the idea of restricting government to the implementation of "general and equal" or "general and inflexible" laws is built into the very foundations of the Humean enterprise.[21] Adam Smith, we may note, has a somewhat different analysis of justice, which he derives from our sympathy with resentment felt by those whose interests are infringed, as that sympathy comes to be standardized in terms of the reactions of an ideal impartial spectator. But the administration of justice through positive laws and the judicial organs of a community falls, for Smith, to be analyzed in the terms set out by Hume, provided it is recognized that at least some of the rights we thus administer are natural rights.[22]

For Hume, as for all liberal-minded thinkers of the Enlightenment, the great source of reflections on the idea of a free government, and on the way in which liberty has come to be so extensively enjoyed in Great Britain, is Montesquieu. From him, of course, as more remotely from Locke, comes the idea of the importance of a separation of powers. This idea is certainly, for Hume, definitive of the conception of the government "which, in common appellation, receives the appellation of free," since it is that government that "admits of a partition of power among several members."[23] This "partition" does not entail weak government but is rather a source of strength. Why it secures freedom as well as strength follows from the argument we considered already, having "several members, whose united authority is no less, or is commonly greater, than that of any monarch; but who, in the usual course of administration, must act by general and equal laws, that are previously known to all the members, and to all their subjects."[24] Such an arrangement, as we saw, gives one branch of government reason to remain jealously watchful to forestall forays into discretionary power by ministers and magistrates. Were it not so, the society would lapse into a condition that we might pointedly describe in the words of Adam Ferguson, a condition "in which the subject is told, that he has no rights; that he cannot possess any property, nor fill any station, independent of the momentary will of his prince."[25]

I deliberately refer here to Ferguson, for although his line differs from Hume's, it retains key points in common. It is in the subject's independence from discretionary powers and "momentary will" that political or civil liberty consists. Where government secures this independence, it is free government. And while it takes laws to bring this liberty about, according to Hume, these laws by themselves are not sufficient. As much as Ferguson, Hume insists on the need for an appropriate spirit toward, as well as of, those laws: that of jealous vigilance lest they be encroached upon. Where such a spirit prevails, there will be, as Americans would rightly say nowadays, adequate checks and balances among the various branches of government. This way of talking is not, however, a radically new one. Hume put forward the same point in terms of "checks and controls," which he took to be at their most effectual and "regular in operation" in "pure republics, where the authority is distributed among several assemblies or senates."[26] Indeed, as he says, a "republican and free government would be an obvious absurdity, if the particular checks and controls, provided by the constitution, had really no influence, and made it not the interest, even of bad men, to act for the public good."[27]

These are words that a present-day citizen of the United Kingdom may ponder anxiously. An American, contemplating, let us say, the rigorous inquiries into the legality of support given to the Contra guerrillas in Nicaragua, might perhaps consider them with greater equanimity; among us in Britain, journalists who draw attention to ostensible branches of law on disclosure of information to Parliament find themselves the objects of search and seizure under the Official Secrets Act.

However that may be, I hope I have now said enough about Hume's ideas of free government to show two things. First, his ideas are perhaps less radically republican than those of predecessors such as Andrew Fletcher or contemporaries such as Adam Ferguson. But second, they remain essentially, if qualifiedly, republican in the senses we have identified; and in their careful attention to the institutional and legal structures of free governments, as well as the spirit required to sustain them, they settle some key points with precocious clarity. Accordingly, they could well have been of value, among available sources of guidance or inspiration, to the founders of this great Republic as they went about their momentous deliberations two centuries ago in Philadelphia.

Madison, Hamilton, and Hume's Perfect Commonwealth

In this final section, I wish to move from canvassing the possibility that Hume's essays on politics may have been an available source for the American founders to rehearsing the grounds long since established by

Douglass Adair for supposing them to have been an actual and influential source.[28] My route to this goal will be only slightly roundabout. It starts with Ferguson's advocacy of small republics and his belittlement of the problem of factionalism in democratic polities. We have already noted some of the republican virtues that Ferguson ascribed to small republics. Now, to the point that identification by an individual with the public interest may be easiest in small, close-knit communities, let us add the further and perhaps converse point that any selection or election of representatives also gains from the circumstances of relative intimacy in small communities. There, one knows the people one elects, and can truly judge their personal capabilities to discharge the representative role as one thinks it should be discharged. No wonder, then, if small republics are the best.

If any point of view in America in 1787 would have found a use for Ferguson's advocacy, it would surely have been that of the confederalists, if one can so name those who favored continued adherence to the Articles of Confederation of 1783 and who would have rejected the Madisonian proposals emanating from the Philadelphia Convention. The objections that Ferguson mounts to great empires with large territories, and their inevitable evolution into centralist monarchies, were the very arguments put forward against federation. And even if a supporter of federation such as Alexander Hamilton may have believed these factual predictions to be substantially true, he did not propound them as arguments for federation, whatever he privately thought. Moreover, this was all something like conventional wisdom at the time: Pure republics, it was thought, had to be small; and small pure republics were endemically subject to ferocious internal factionalism, be that their defect or their virtue.

This understanding of pure republics must have been a major stumbling block, both in the thought of those taking part at Philadelphia and in the ratification debates in the states afterward. Yet it was not in the end a decisive obstacle. Why not? Well, of course, because the founders went ahead undeterred and because the advocates of the new constitution won the ratification debates. To judge by the *Federalist* papers, they based a fair part of their case on an audacious challenge to the received wisdom. They argued that republican forms of government would be better secured in a large union of states than in a small republic or a set of small republics. They argued that the system of partly direct and partly indirect elections to federal offices and assemblies would secure protection against demagoguery or mob rule (by contrast with forms of direct democracy). They argued that the mischiefs of faction would be canceled out by the multiplicity of different interest groups and parties inevitably to be found in a large union. And they argued that such a union would necessarily, by its federal form, set all the "greater obstacles . . . to the concert and accomplishment of the secret wishes of an unjust and interested majority," as James Madison put the point. This line of reasoning is all stated with fine flourishes of rhetoric by Madison in the 10th *Federalist* paper.[29]

In that essay Madison also stresses the difference between simple democracy and a duly constituted republic, with carefully structured powers ascending from popular elections, but ascending through layers of indirect election and appointment subject to legislative advice and consent. James Wilson made a like point in his profoundly influential speech to the Pennsylvania Constitutional Convention during its crucial ratification debate. "A free government," he said, "has often been compared to a pyramid. This allusion is made with particular propriety in the system before you; it is laid on the broad base of the people; its powers gradually rise while they are confined, in proportion as they ascend, until the end in that most permanent of all forms. When you examine all its parts, they will invariably be found to preserve that essential mark of free government—a chain of connection with the people."[30] Republicanism of this stamp indeed seeks to secure popular sovereignty; but to constitute popular rule, it operates chiefly through enlightened representatives and carefully regulated and divided forms, with all appropriate checks and balances.

To illustrate the weight given to such points in the *Federalist* papers, even at the risk of overdoing direct quotations, I should like to add here a quotation from Alexander Hamilton in the 9th *Federalist*:

> To [the] catalogue of circumstances, that tend to the amelioration of popular systems of civil government, I shall venture, however novel it may appear to some, to add one more. . . . I mean the ENLARGEMENT of the ORBIT within which such systems are to resolve either in respect to the dimensions of a single State, or to the consolidation of several smaller States into one great confederacy. . . .
>
> The utility of confederacy, as well to suppress faction and to

guard the internal tranquillity of States, as to increase their external force and security, is in reality not a new idea.[31]

Nothing could be truer than this modest disclaimer of novelty on Hamilton's part. Indeed, the whole story had been told already by David Hume in his 1755 essay "The Idea of a Perfect Commonwealth."[32] Here is Hume:

> Though it is more difficult to form a republican government in an extensive country than in a city, there is more facility when once it is formed, of preserving it steady and uniform, without tumult and faction. . . . In a large government, which is formed with masterly skill, there is compass and room enough to refine the democracy, from the lower people who may be admitted into the first elections, or first concoction of the commonwealth, to the higher magistrates who direct all the movements. At the same time, the parts are so distant and remote, that it is very difficult, either by intrigue, prejudice or passion, to hurry them into any measures against the public interest.

The whole tone and tenor of Hume's argument for the possibility of a large-scale republic with extensive internal devolution of power to parishes or counties, and with direct elections at the lower levels but indirect elections above, is echoed and reechoed by Hamilton and Madison, especially in the 9th and 10th *Federalist* papers. It is perhaps no wonder that Hume prescribes Presbyterianism for his perfect commonwealth, for there we find a structure of representative and indirectly elective officeholding, with power devolved to parishes, all nicely matching the Humean polity. No doubt the direction of influence is really the other way. It would have been from reflection on the governance of the kirk that Hume would have gone on to work out his utopia by way of a perfect commonwealth.

Here, perhaps, you will pull me back to remind me that not only did such an establishment of Presbyterianism fail to take place under your Constitution, but that the First Amendment of 1791, the very first clause in the Bill of Rights, expressly prohibits any establishment of religion. On this point, let me speculate upon another possibility of Scottish influence. One thing the Anglo-Scottish Union of 1707 did prove was that it is possible to have a single constitution and a single, even unitary, union of states and parliaments without having to establish one religion for the whole united country. Fundamental to the British constitution agreed upon in 1707 was the stipulation for the continued establishment of separate established churches, with different forms of worship and of church government, in the two parts of the now-united kingdom. Thus was defused one grave obstacle to consensual union. Perhaps the model was found relevant eighty years later.

Be that as it may (and what I have just said is mere speculation), we can return to safer ground in considering Enlightenment thought in Scotland on the theme of republics, republican virtue, and republicanism and its possible relationship to and relevance for developments in America. Surely the relevance is established. And the textual evidence suggests an actual relationship—how close and how influential, I should not care to say. Whatever may be the truth of that, we can be certain of a different truth. Hume tells us that in "a large government, which is formed with masterly skill, there is compass and room enough to refine the democracy." That the American framers did act with masterly skill is not to be doubted; nor have their successors been unskilled in refining the democracy that the framers founded.

Notes

1. See, e.g., Douglass Greybill Adair, *Fame and the Founding Fathers,* ed. Trevor Colburn (New York: Norton, 1974); Caroline Robbins, *The Eighteenth-Century Commonwealthman* (Cambridge: Harvard University Press, 1959); Bernard Bailyn, *The Ideological Origins of the American Revolution* (Cambridge: Belknap Press of Harvard University Press, 1967); Garry Wills, *Inventing America: Jefferson's Declaration of Independence* (Garden City, N.Y.: Doubleday, 1978); and *Explaining America: The Federalist* (Garden City, N.Y.: Doubleday, 1981). For searching criticism of Wills's earlier work, see Ronald Hamowy, "Jefferson and the Scottish Enlightenment: A Critique of Garry Wills's *Inventing America: Jefferson's Declaration of Independence,*" *William and Mary Quarterly,* 3d ser., 36 (1979): 503–23.

2. See T. D. Campbell, "Francis Hutcheson: Father of the Scottish Enlightenment," in *The Origins and Nature of the Scottish Enlightenment,* ed. R. H. Campbell and Andrew S. Skinner (Edinburgh: John Donald, 1982), 167–68; Wills, *Inventing America,* passim. Hamowy's critique must be borne in mind, but it is sufficient to note that Hutcheson's work was widely known in America; I make no claim in favor of an exclusive or dominant Hutchesonian influence on the drafting of the Declaration of Independence.

3. See Adam Smith, *The Wealth of Nations* [1776], ed. R. H. Campbell, Andrew S. Skinner, and W. B. Todd (Oxford: Clarendon Press, 1976).

4. My particular intellectual debts for such clarity and accuracy as may be found in my notion of republicanism are to Professor Frank Michelman, for a series of seminars presented at a legal philosophy symposium organized by Professor Dick Bronaugh at the University of Western Ontario in June 1986; and to Professor Quentin Skinner, for a seminar presentation at Edinburgh University in May 1987. I owe a general debt to J. G. A. Pocock, most recently refreshed by a reading of his *Virtue, Commerce, and History* (Cambridge: Cambridge University Press, 1985), esp. chap. 7.

5. Quoted from David Daiches, *Andrew Fletcher of Saltoun: Selected Papers* (Edinburgh: Scottish Academic Press, 1979), vii, taken from Gilbert Burnet, *History of His Own Time* (London: T. Ward, 1725), 3:1046.

6. See, generally, Paul Henderson Scott, *1707: The Union of Scotland and England* (Edinburgh: W. and R. Chambers, 1979); A. Fletcher of Saltoun, *State of the Controversy betwixt United and Separate Parliaments,* ed. Paul Henderson Scott (Edinburgh: William Blackwood for the Saltire Society, 1982). In discussion of the events of 1787, I am most frequently struck by the sound of a dog not barking, that is, by the total failure of almost everyone to note that the process of union between Scotland and England, which constituted Great Britain as a single united kingdom for the first time, bears a strong analogy to that whereby the United States first constituted themselves as such. That is, commissioners from separate parliaments met and worked out Articles of Union, which were then taken back to their several parliaments for implementation or rejection. Upon the enactment of enabling acts (Acts of Union) of each of the parliaments, the articles took effect to create a new British Parliament as of May 1, 1707. The oddity is that this has never been acknowledged, by English lawyers and historians anyway, as the original constitution of the United Kingdom. But see Neil MacCormick, "Does the United Kingdom Have a Constitution? Reflections on *MacCormick v. Lord Advocate,*" *Northern Ireland Legal Quarterly* 29 (1978): 1–23.

7. These points are fully discussed in Neil MacCormick, "Law, Obligation, and Consent: Reflections on Stair and Locke," chap. 4 in MacCormick, *Legal Right and Social Democracy* (Oxford: Clarendon Press; New York: Oxford University Press, 1982), discussing James Dalrymple, 1st Viscount Stair, *The Institutions of the Law of Scotland* [1681], ed. David M. Walker (New Haven: University Press of Edinburgh and Yale, 1981); John Locke, *Two Treatises of Government* [1698], ed. Peter Laslett (Cambridge: Cambridge University Press, 1960); and George Buchanan, *De Iure Regni Apud Scotos* [1579], trans. by D. H. MacNeill as *The Art and Science of Government among the Scots* (Glasgow: William MacLellan, Ltd., 1964).

8. Fletcher is a firm admirer of James Harrington's *The Commonwealth of Oceania* (1656), for which see *The Political Works of James Harrington* (Cambridge and New York: Cambridge University Press, 1977); cf. Daiches,

Andrew Fletcher, 1–4. I am again indebted to Frank Michelman and Quentin Skinner, but most particularly to Pocock, *Virtue, Commerce, and History*, 230–31.

9. See Adam Smith, *The Theory of Moral Sentiments*, ed. D. D. Raphael and A. L. Macfie (Oxford: Clarendon Press, 1976), 6.3.237–62.

10. Stair himself died in 1695, but his son, the first Earl of Stair, was one of the champions of the Anglo-Scottish Union of 1705–7, and Stair the elder was of that camp politically. Cf. Scott, *1707: The Union of Scotland and England*.

11. See Adam Ferguson, *An Essay on the History of Civil Society* [1767], ed. Duncan Forbes (Edinburgh: Edinburgh University Press, 1966), 126–27, 146–61, 192, 247–52.

12. Ibid., 162–67, 263–64.

13. Ibid., 22–25, 101, 125–26, 198–99.

14. Ibid., 19.

15. See Andrew Fletcher of Saltoun in Daiches, *Andrew Fletcher*, 2–26.

16. David Hume, *Essays Moral, Political, and Literary* [1741, 1742] (Oxford: Oxford University Press, 1963), 1:39.

17. Ibid., 1:10.

18. Ibid., 1:39.

19. Ibid., 1:10.

20. Hume, *A Treatise of Human Nature*, ed. L. A. Selby-Bigge and P. H. Nidditch, 2d ed. (Oxford: Clarendon Press; New York: Oxford University Press, 1978), 477–572, esp. 477–83; *An Enquiry Concerning the Principles of Morals*, ed. L. A. Selby-Bigge and P. H. Nidditch, 3d ed. (Oxford: Clarendon Press, 1975), 183–204, 303–11.

21. Cf. David D. Raphael, "Justice and Utility (I)," chap. 10 of his *Justice and Liberty* (London: Athlone Press, 1980).

22. Cf. Raphael, *Justice and Liberty*; Knud Haakonssen, *The Science of a Legislator: The Natural Jurisprudence of David Hume and Adam Smith* (Cambridge and New York: Cambridge University Press, 1981), which I consider to be the best and most thorough account extant of Hume's and Smith's approaches to justice.

23. Hume, *Essays Moral, Political, and Literary*, 1:39.

24. Ibid.

25. Ferguson, *Essay on the History of Civil Society*, 71.

26. Hume, *Essays Moral, Political, and Literary*, 1:46.

27. Ibid., 1:14.

28. Adair, *Fame and the Founding Fathers*, 93–106; cf. Wills, *Explaining America*.

29. *The Federalist*, ed. Jacob E. Cooke (Middletown, Conn.: Wesleyan University Press, 1961), no. 10.

30. James Wilson, quoted in Alpheus Thomas Mason, ed., *Free Government in the Making*, 3d ed. (New York: Oxford University Press, 1965), 247.

31. *The Federalist*, no. 9.

32. Hume, *Essays Moral, Political, and Literary*, 2:514–15.

CHAPTER 8

Constitutional and Tribal Governance

·····

LADONNA HARRIS

Being asked to address this prestigious meeting has brought me face to face with one of my own Comanche traditions. I have achieved the age of an elder. I have lived long enough to remember many changes. In traditional times I would from now on carry a large staff signifying my right and my responsibility to think about and comment on the state of the community. It is in the spirit of that tradition that I make my comments.

The traditions of Native American oration also demand that I place myself in context before expressing myself so that you will know what kind of person is speaking.

I grew up on a rural farm in Cotton County, Oklahoma, with my maternal grandparents, speaking only Comanche until I entered school. My grandfather maintained his Comanche culture and religion. My grandmother became a devout Christian. Each respected the other. This environment of mutual respect influenced my interest in all people and produced an abiding belief that there is room in one's world for all traditions. The world will be a better place for all of us if each tradition and each person is able to participate fully in the political process.

My life's work has been to work with Indian tribes in attaining their political, social, educational, and economic aspirations and to articulate the contributions that Native American people have to make to United States and global society as a whole.

Part of what makes creating an accurate history of the United States difficult is that up until now the only people whose perceptions influenced that history were those who had access to the written word. In his book *The Forgotten Founders*,[1] Bruce Johansen coined the term "intellectual mercantilism." The book is about the influence that the Iroquois Confederacy had on the United States' founding fathers. In it Johansen notes that Europeans from the fifteenth century onward observed the indigenous people of the Americas and brought their observations back to Europe, and that these observations influenced the development of European philosophy, especially the "natural philosophy" of the Enlightenment.

It is commonly assumed that American democracy evolved out of European political systems or was inspired by European political thinkers. By reading, studying, and talking with others, however, I have learned how inaccurate that assumption is. Dr. Bruce Burton of Castleton College points out that the facts of the period suggest that the process of democratization that eventually transformed the political systems of the world actually had its origin in the United States, specifically in the American Revolution, which grew out of an intimate association with Native Americans.[2]

When Europeans arrived in America they found confederacies of indigenous people up and down the eastern seaboard. The English colonies had the most contact with the Iroquois. Both at the individual and the governmental levels, interaction between the colonists and the Iroquois was intense and usually peaceful. For 150 years before the writing of the United States Constitution, the colonists from Virginia to New England were repeatedly urged by the Iroquois to unite. Often the Iroquois refused to deal with individual colonies, insisting that they agree among themselves before negotiating with the Iroquois Confederacy. This kind of restriction constantly encouraged and often forced the colonies to cooperate with each other, an action that the British monarchy seldom condoned.

The Constitution of the League of Haudeenosaunee, the Iroquois Confederacy of first five, then six, nations, as recorded in wampum belts, is the oldest surviving democratic constitution on earth, and the Iroquois Confederacy governed by this constitution still continues today. Iroquois law guarantees the rights of women, ensures freedom of speech and religion, and prohibits the illegal search of homes. Political power is divided between the sexes and among various governmental units, and checks (including impeachment) were established so that this power could not be abusive. Thus, American democracy owes its distinctive character of noncoercive government, of debate, negotiation, and compromise, of persuasion and consent, of balance of power and federalism, to principles and structures of civil government that had already been established in North America when the Europeans first arrived.

In 1740 Cadwallader Colden wrote his *History Of The Five Nations*, the first account in English of the Iroquois League. Thomas Jefferson styled himself a "savage" philosopher. Benjamin Franklin attended the treaty negotiations with the Iroquois and published accounts of these negotiations between 1736 and 1762. Franklin copied parts of the Iroquois Constitution to formulate the Albany Plan of Union, which preceded the United States Constitution by thirty years.

Even the great English democratic theoretician John Locke was inspired by the political examples of the people of America. His theories of equality in a state of nature are rooted in American examples. In the 1683 "Letter To The Free Society Of Traders," Locke quoted Gabriel Sagard's *Histoire Du Canada* (1636) in reference to the Huron noncoercive, elective system of government, as well as William Penn's account of the Delaware Indians. However, although Locke provided a theory of democracy, he provided Europeans and Euro-Americans no actual structure of democratic government. Europeans viewed his writings as only theoretical. Thus, his work did not inspire revolutions in his own country or in any other. Democratic revolution occurred first in the colonies because the colonists' long intimacy with Indian governments provided them with actual structures of democratic union and representative self-rule.

All European democratic principles were based on devolution, where it is the central authority that *allows* certain functions to be carried out in the political units that make up the whole. We have to remember that even the democracy of the ancient Greeks required the labor of five thousand slaves to enable five hundred *men* to be "free." The basic European concept of sovereignty implies the existence of a sovereign.

During the nineteenth century there was a folk tradition about the American Indian origins of democratic thought. It is time to revisit this tradition and investigate the extensive Euro-American written documentation and the strong oral tradition among the Iroquois people through which the transfer of democratic concepts took place.[3]

It is ironic that democratic concepts and a federal structure were borrowed from the Iroquois in the eighteenth century, and yet, after the decimation of Indian populations by disease and the Indian wars of the nineteenth century, this gift and many others were repaid by confining Indians to reservations. In the 1930s the Indian Reorganization Act imposed constitutional government on Indian communities. Though many of the ideas in the United States' concept of constitutional government were Native American in origin, others were not. Consensual democracy was replaced by majority rule, a divisive concept totally foreign to Native American culture.

Voting for representatives is not part of any Native American political philosophy. We selected leaders through discussion and consensus. To match Euro-American assumptions, we have over and over again excluded traditional elites (including women). Now we are working to put our communities back together—men and women, young and old, "conservatives" and "progressives"—on a basis that meets today's needs in a way that Indians recognize.

The cement of cooperative societies is the contribution that each person, family, and clan makes to the group. The explicit understandings of all are required if the community (the governance structure, ceremonial cycle, and so on) is to function effectively. What is paid attention to is not who is in charge but who is responsible, not who is leading but whether the group is all moving in the same direction.

In her book *In a Different Voice*,[4] Carol Gilligan says that the most valued place in a hierarchy is at the top, and the most valued place in a network is at the center. However, if we try to view one of these systems through the lens of the other, what we see is always distorted. If we flatten out a hierarchy, what results very much resembles a network, and if we pull up the center of a network, we have, magically enough, created a hierarchy. What we need, therefore, is a paradigm that encompasses both of these constructs so as to include the efficiency of one and the nurturance of the other.

The emphasis among Native American communities is not on rights but on responsibilities. Fulfilling responsibilities guarantees individual rights. Thus, elders are *responsible* for listening to the people, all of them, each one of them. In general, Indians do not think in terms of hierarchies. All people—male and female, old and young—are considered to have equal value. As an ancient saying puts it, "Equal value—varying skills."

Native Americans think in terms of relationships, with each individual the center of her or his own three-dimensional spiderweb of relations. That relationship structure leads toward consensus. No one *tells* anyone else what to do. It is discussed. It may be suggested. In a well-organized cooperative community, each individual, clan, and society needs to make its contribution for the whole system to work. Thus everyone is vital and valued. For this the Euro-American world wants us to substitute majority rule, which begins by dividing the community.

The place of North America's more than seven hundred Indian communities in the federal political fabric is very complex. Approximately three hundred tribes are federally recognized. Other tribes have state recognition. Some have both, and still others are self-identified and struggling for official recognition. In addition, more than half of all Indians are urban Indians who no longer live in their ancestral communities.

The initial relationship between the now federally recognized Indian tribes and the emerging government of the United States took the form of a treaty between sovereign nations in the realm of international law. This relationship has subsequently evolved into a system whereby Congress legislates Native American policy, the judicial branch interprets it, the executive branch administers it, and the tribes implement it. Joyotpaul Chaudhuri has said that Native American law-and policy-making, thus, have become "a branch of Anglo-American thinking" that has had "little to do conceptually with American Indian custom, law, or methods of conflict resolution."[5]

In this context Vine Deloria has remarked that Indians have largely been a "detached third-party observer" to the process of policy formation that has often been a contest between Congress and the executive branch. Sometimes policy-making became a completely executive affair carried out by the Bureau of Indian Affairs in the Department of the Interior. Congressional initiatives were twisted to perform functions that the bureaucracy wanted.[6]

The first of the major markers in the history of the relationship between Indian nations and the federal government was the era of treaty making, initially with the eastern tribes, in which lands were ceded for services, mostly in education and health. In the 1830s came the era of removals, the most infamous of which was the Cherokee Trail of Tears. However, even Indian country as a sacrosanct area beyond the Mississippi River was ephemeral. Euro-American pressure on Indian lands resulted in wars between federal troops and the western tribes after the Civil War. When extermination did not work, a peace policy was formulated that instituted a military stalemate until the tribes' economic base (the buffalo) was destroyed.

A new round of treaty making ensued. The same "benefits" were then imposed on the western tribes (without their consultation) as had been requested by the mixed-blood leadership of the eastern tribes. But these warrior societies of the West saw sedentary life as a form of death. Thus began a long era of unilateral decision making by Euro-American "experts" on the needs of Indian people. In 1871 treaty making came to an end by act of Congress. Then came a period of Indian policy by executive order that continued until the 1930s. The most important event of this era was the General Allotment Act of 1880, which authorized the president to conduct negotiations with the tribes for the allotment of their land to individual Indians and the ceding of the surplus to the government for settlement. As Vine Deloria points out, the amendments to the act changed it from an "educative process whereby Indians could learn how to manage private property to an administrative problem in which the federal government was assumed to be the supervisor of how Indian property was to be used."[7]

The superintendents of Indian reservations were supreme during this paternalistic era, and the result was that 90 million acres of land passed from Indian into white hands. That was 64 percent of all the land held by Indians at the end of the treaty period.

In 1924 Congress passed the Indian Citizenship Act, after which Indians were regarded as citizens, not only of their tribes but of the United States and the states in which they resided as well. This arrangement entailed three different sets of rights. In 1928 came the Meriam Report, which was highly critical of the Interior Department's paternalistic administration and recommended the Indian use of Indian lands and the strengthening of Indian communities and cultures. Nineteen thirty-four brought the Indian Reorganization Act, which established or reestablished tribal governments. Although that was the first step in strengthening tribal governments to have been taken since the end of the Indian wars, it substituted majority-based Anglo-American law and nontraditional tribal councils having overly broad powers for the old consensual governance system, with the resultant alienation of the old elites. The act also created new tribes by recognizing two or more tribes on one reservation as a single tribe and recognizing the larger bands of a single tribe with their own reservation as separate tribes. In addition, the secretary of the interior retained substantial veto power over tribal council decisions. So, although on one level the act was a reaffirmation of the tribes, it was still a unilateral decision in which the tribes had no say in the policy formation process.

Then in the 1950s came the termination policy. From 1954 to 1962 Congress terminated federal supervision of more than one hundred tribes. This policy was supposedly an attempt to provide equal rights for Indians, but it was a severe blow to tribal sovereignty in that, for the terminated tribes, there was no longer a land base over which to assert jurisdiction. The result was a total disaster, in every case drastic social and economic problems for the tribes. Some tribes have managed, after long struggles, to reinstate themselves as federally recognized tribes. In 1968 President Lyndon B. Johnson inaugurated an era of Native American self-determination, which President Richard M. Nixon strongly supported, so much so that he asked Congress to formally repudiate the termination policy. Thus, in a hundred years federal policy had moved from *ex*termination to termination to *self-de*termination.

In the 1960s the poverty programs in education, health, and housing resulted in the transfer of substantial funds into Indian communities. In 1975 the Indian Self-Determination and Education Assistance Act gave tribes permission to assume contractual responsibility for administering their own federal service programs. However, these education, health, and housing programs also often undermined effective tribal governance, because their administrators often had more resources at their disposal than either the tribal councils or the traditional decision makers. In fact, a new class was created in rural Indian communities, that of federal grant/program administrators whose regular wages made them an instant moneyed class in the rural settings.

Ultimately, however, there is less to the Assistance Act than meets the eye. As Joyotpaul Chaudhuri notes, in Native American tribes,

> authority is circumscribed with bureaucratic necessities, the realities
> of the histories of tribal resources, and the vagaries of congressional

appropriations bills. Tribes must have administrative permission for engaging in contracts. Further, large numbers of tribes, particularly in Oklahoma, have already lost their tribal resources over which to exercise authority. Of course the southwestern tribes are in a different position from the Oklahoma tribes. However, ultimately the success of "self-determination" is tied in part to the resource allocation to specific Indian programs. If obligations to Indians are regarded as purely discretionary, appropriations bills will reflect the moods of the country and of Congress. The "self" in self-determination remains in large part non-Indian.[8]

During the Carter and Reagan administrations the cuts in the federal budget have disproportionately affected Indian governments, because they have no private-sector tax base and no alternative source of revenues, with the very meager exception of the bingo games that are conducted on reservations. Vine Deloria remarks that the congressional initiative "to provide rules and regulations under which tribes can conduct gambling enterprises on their reservations" perhaps forecasts "the concluding chapter in the Indian effort to remain as politically distinct communities."[9] So, although in 1831 Supreme Court chief justice John Marshall defined the tribal nations of the United States as "domestic dependent nations,"[10] and although, unlike all other ethnic groups in the country, Native American communities are units of government (like cities, counties, and states) in the United States federal system, it is only in the past decade that many tribal governments have redeveloped enough infrastructure and political skill to begin to reassert this role. This task is in fact one of the pivotal challenges to be faced by Native American communities before the end of the century.

As tribes have begun to exercise their governmental powers, they have been brought into conflict with state and local governments, non-Indian individuals and organizations affected by tribal law, and individual tribal members whose interests differ from those of the tribes. These disagreements have resulted in much litigation and legislation. At Americans for Indian Opportunity, we designed and carried out a three-year tribal governance project in which about one hundred tribes participated. As part of this project we undertook a series of regional workshops. One full day of the three-day workshop was devoted to resolving conflicts within Indian communities, between Indian communities, and with other jurisdictions and organizations.

As Joyotpaul Chaudhuri points out, these conflicts derive largely from differences in perspective on authority between Anglo- and Native American legal cultures. At least three conceptions of authority are available to either culture: (1) a monistic conception, in which authority is an indivisible entity, (2) a pluralistic conception of a decentralized authority, and (3) a contextual concept, where authority can still be absolute but in a limited context of specific legal relations.[11] So, correspondingly, can Indian policy be shaped in three ways: (1) through unilateral decision making, (2) through consent, and (3) through a culturally sensitive extended dialogue. The first, of course, has characterized Indian policy formation at least since Andrew Jackson's day. Such unilateral decision making was often masked as "consent," as in "consent or die." We at Americans for Indian Opportunity, however, were interested in creating the conditions under which culturally sensitive extended dialogues could take place. In 1986, we began working with the Center for Interactive Management at George Mason University to adapt an issues-management process to Indian communities. This process sees conflict and multiple points of view as opportunities for identifying problems. Participants in the process design a strategic plan of action for dealing with the now fully articulated issue through computer-assisted consensus-building techniques.

What is especially interesting to us is how well this very modern process resonates with traditional ways of consensus building in Native American communities. Everyone observes an order of speaking, each person speaks without interruption, all points of view are received respectfully by the group, and discussion continues until no one has anything else to say. It is also rather ironic to us that it is a Greek, Dr. Alexander Christakis, a member of the oldest of the Old World schools of democratic philosophical thought, who helped develop the process that promises to catapult traditional Native American consensus-building processes into the twenty-first century.

The struggle of tribes in the lower forty-eight states to define their role in the political fabric parallels the other great indigenous struggle of the end of this century, the retribalization of the Alaska Native Corporations. In the 1970s the Alaskan Land Claims Settlement transformed tribal cultural entities into corporate businesses. Unfortunately, corporate structure is not adequate to accommodate an entire culture in all its spiritual, social, and economic dimensions. Corporate structure is especially inadequate to encompass the needs of subsistence cultures where the majority of families still get 65 percent of their food directly from the land.

In 1991 the shares in the Alaska Native Corporations are to go public. It is certain that many shares will pass out of Native hands. When that happens, aboriginal right to the land will be lost. Without the land the cultures will be destroyed. It is very frustrating, but over and over again we have seen that simply transplanting subsistence people into the market economy works just about as well as would transplanting a New Yorker to the middle of the Arizona desert. Skills and conceptualizations in each system are completely different. The calculus of the subsistence economy includes the social and spiritual roles people play in the community as well as their economic roles.

New legislation is being introduced in Congress to amend the Claims Act with provisions that would prevent shares from leaving Native hands, reorganize the way the shares are held (by the community rather than by individuals), and reinstitute traditional tribal councils, not corporate boards, as governing bodies. The nexus of this problem is not only how to organize communal entrepreneurship in an individualistic business environment but how to create governmental institutions that reflect the realities of Alaska's village cultures and afford full participation in the United States federal system. Just as mainstream majoritarian governmental norms are inadequate for tribal society in the lower forty-eight states, so those norms are inadequate to the village-clan societies in Alaska. It is appropriate that these new governmental forms are emerging as we celebrate the bicentennial of the Constitution and of the federal system.

The world's indigenous peoples, those who continue to live or have lived in the recent past at a subsistence level, have experience in living memory of what it is like to live constrained in a finite but dynamic and ever-changing system. These people are *not* "barely surviving." They have mastered the constant negotiation required to live in a balanced way. Living closer to the earth than most of us do today, the indigenous people of the world maintain—many of them—a way of life that treats our planet with great respect and makes few demands on it. Out of respect for *their* individuality, and awareness that our technology may place too great a strain on the ecosystem, we do well to encourage and enable the perpetuation of these alternative human answers to the possibilities of life. Moreover, if these people are surviving in a global system that is able to nurture them, that reality shows us that we have developed a system capable of nurturing some of the world's most vulnerable people. But perhaps those of us addicted to technology are even more vulnerable.

Nurturing contemporary subsistence or near-subsistence societies requires great creativity in inventing different ways for small groups to be autonomous within larger systems, while remaining responsible to and mindful of the total system of autonomous units. The League of the Iroquois mentioned earlier demonstrates one way that such responsible but coordinated multiple autonomy can be created and managed. Such systems can provide patterns of governance for the remaining tribal regions of the world, which include much of Latin America, the Middle East, Africa, and parts of Asia. In South Africa after apartheid, for example, a way of governing that multitribal society will have to be invented.

We are in an emergent era. The old world of European hegemony is over, and the European experience is being evaluated from new perspectives. Indigenous affairs involve core issues of democratic theory, consent, international law, cultural survival, and civil rights, which could benefit from systematic thought. The Organization of American States is sponsoring activities in 1992 that will examine the encounter between the Old World and the New World five centuries after Columbus's voyage. The Aborigines of Australia marked their bicentennial of European contact (1988) with organizational struggles. On the agenda for both commemorations is the creation of a global network of indigenous peoples so that tribal perspectives will be more effectively represented in the global "multilogue" of the end of this millennium, a "multilogue" respectful of its many perspectives and mindful that each perspective is necessary to the adequate comprehension and function of the whole.

As the Iroquois understood, peace will come when the voices of the most vulnerable (of women and of the very young) are heard in the Great Council and when the elders hold as the highest criterion of decision making the effect that today's choices will have on our children, and theirs, and so on through "the seventh generation." The Iroquois have a metaphor for their constitution. It is the Great Tree of Peace, an eastern white pine, still standing at Onondaga, under which the Iroquois buried their implements of war. The Great Tree is a dynamic, growing, encompassing metaphor for the ability of this peaceful agreement to include all nations. The white pine is evergreen *because* it is ever-growing. Although the old brown inside needles regularly fall to the ground, fertilizing it, enabling the tree to grow, three generations of green needles always remain. A new generation comes with each year and the tree grows. This symbol of a peaceful agreement living and growing among nations is a precursor of the United Nations.

You can see how many of the things I have done in my life emerge from a lifelong and deepening understanding of Native American traditions. How a Comanche girl from Cotton County insists that the federal government honor its responsibility to its sovereign domestic nations, the Indian nations of the United States. How she travels the world from Mali to the Soviet Union to Central America to help build peace. All of what I do is simply a present manifestation of my culture's ancient traditions, which have taught me that, internationally as well as domestically, the voice of the smallest, weakest, and most vulnerable must be heard, that *all* people may live. It is when the United States Constitution walks squarely in the path of this ancient tradition that it is most influential in the world.

Notes

1. Bruce E. Johansen, *The Forgotten Founders* (Ipswich, Mass.: Gambit, 1982).

2. Bruce Burton, "League of the Haudeenosaunee: Iroquois Confederate Law and the Origins of the U.S. Constitution," *Northeast Indian Quarterly* 3 (Fall 1986): 4–9.

3. In order to resolve the issue of the origin of these concepts in some definitive way, so that we may understand *all* the roots of our American system, my organization, Americans for Indian Opportunity, has selected as our Crawford Memorial Fellow for 1987 a historian who has been working in this field for over a decade. Dr. Donald Grinde, a Yamasee, will do an extensive study of written and oral documentation of the Iroquois-constitutional relationship. This project has been recognized as an official Bicentennial Commission Project. At the end of this study we plan to make available the results, which should demonstrate conclusively from both Native and Euro-American points of view exactly what is the interrelationship between Iroquois political theory and the U.S. Constitution.

4. Carol Gilligan, *In a Different Voice* (Cambridge: Harvard University Press, 1982).

5. Joyotpaul Chaudhuri, "American Indian Policy: An Overview," in *American Indian Policy in the Twentieth Century,* ed. Vine Deloria, Jr. (Norman, Okla.: University of Oklahoma Press, 1985), 15.

6. Vine Deloria, Jr., "The Evolution of Federal Indian Policy Making," in *American Indian Policy,* 248.

7. Ibid., 247.

8. Chaudhuri, "American Indian Policy," 28–29.

9. Deloria, "Evolution of Federal Indian Policy Making," 248.

10. *Cherokee Nation v. Georgia,* 30 U.S. (1 Pet.) 1 (1831).

11. Chaudhuri, "American Indian Policy," 22–23.

CHAPTER 9

A New Constitution for a New Nation

.....

JUDITH N. SHKLAR

The title of this paper may seem paradoxical since it appears at the head of an essay that is supposed to discuss the influence of classical antiquity on the framing of the United States Constitution. It is meant, however, not to deny that the founders reflected frequently and deeply upon the political history of European antiquity, but rather to note that it was by considering that remote past that they came to realize fully how very novel their project was, and to give the motto Novus Ordo Seclorum its full impact.

We ought not to forget that every person who had a secondary education in the eighteenth century would have read some of the classical authors. Certainly he would know some Cicero and Plutarch, and he might also have read some of Tacitus's lurid historical writings. These, rather than the great Greek philosophers, were the favored authors of the time. All were readily available in translation, so that no great knowledge of the ancient languages was required to read them.[1] They formed the young minds of all sides of every controversy, of loyalists no less than patriots during the Revolution, and of Anti-Federalists just as much as of those who wrote the Constitution of 1787. The classical authors whom everyone read did not point in any one political direction; they were simply part of the common understanding of an age. Because they provided a familiar pool of illustrations during debates, they were an important vehicle for the self-understanding of the opposed parties in any controversy, but they served all sides equally well. Their influence was genuine but diffuse.

Nevertheless, modern constitutionalism, of which the United States Constitution is the first complete example, depends upon certain philosophical conceptions that had their origin in ancient Greece. The very idea of the rule of law depends on Aristotelian logic, that is, on syllogistic reasoning. There has to be a general rule, a specific case that falls under it, and a necessary conclusion. And while Aristotle knew perfectly well that forensic argument could rarely be so exact, the syllogism was for him and has remained the standard not only of the fairness of the law but also of its rationality. Both the civil and the criminal law of a city were rational only if they were logically deduced from the most basic rules of justice that distributed the burdens and benefits of society to its citizens and that corresponded to their deepest political beliefs.[2] So one might well say that Aristotelian logic was a necessary, though not a sufficient, condition for constitutional political theory, which must have the rule of law at its very center. For, whatever else it may be, it is not arbitrary government.

The second set of politically relevant ideas and examples that were derived from classical antiquity concerned republican government, since with a few minor exceptions most medieval and modern states were monarchies. Here Polybius (200?–118 B.C.) and Cicero, as well as general histories of Rome, were decidedly significant. From Polybius, the exiled Greek general who had contemplated his conquerors, the Romans, at their height, the American framers learned the theory of the mixed constitution. Aristotle had already explained that a polity in which both the rich and the poor with their different interests and ideologies ruled jointly might be more stable and less prone to injustice than most other regimes. Polybius had a more institutional version of the mixed regime. In the normal course of historical change, he argued, monarchies become tyrannies and are overthrown by virtuous aristocrats, who in time decay into oligarchs and are ousted by law-abiding democrats, who eventually fall into mob rule. Sooner or later a new monarch restores order, and the cycle, based on the permanent human passion for power and wealth, resumes. Only Rome had been able to halt this process by devising a division of powers among the aristocratic senate, the democratic popular assemblies, and the monarchical consuls and other magistrates. In Rome's version of the mixed constitution, each political class had a veto to prevent the others from straying from the path of public duty. It allowed republican government to endure and to frame good laws that made virtuous statesmen and citizens.[3] Not only was any sector of the political society forced to stay within the limits of its assigned sphere of authority but the special talents of each one were put to the service of the whole.

To be sure, the ideal of the mixed state did not remain a republican notion. Americans were most familiar with it in its English form as the combination of a monarch, lords, and commons. However, as very few of the framers thought a return to English government possible or even desirable, they looked to the history of republics for models. Ultimately, after much discussion, both the classical republics and mixed constitutions ceased to matter in 1787. John Adams had still managed to write the mixed republic into the constitution of Massachusetts, and he certainly was an ardent admirer of Polybius. But Adams, with his truly Puritan habit of seeing corruption and declension as the only constants of public life, was a relatively isolated intellectual figure.[4] In fact, the mixed constitution was laid to rest rather early on in the federal Convention when Charles Pinckney got up and said out loud what everyone knew, that there was nothing to mix in America, that rich and poor were too much alike to require separate institutional embodiments.[5] "We the People" had a very new meaning: It was neither the plebeians of Rome nor the commons of England; it was everyone.

Moreover, the energetic young men in Philadelphia had absorbed the history of the Revolution in a way that put them at an enormous distance from all of classical antiquity and even from Adams's last colonial generation. They thought that change was good, desirable, and necessary. It was a sign not of decay or corruption but of improvement and reform. Not cycles but steady progress summoned them to write a new constitution. They were, to be sure (as has often been noted), without illusions about human moral capacities, but they had a great deal of confidence in new knowledge and the institutions it could help them build. They certainly believed that political science had come a long way in the recent past. And when they talked of advances in the science of government they meant one author above all others: Montesquieu, whose *Spirit of the Laws* was a widely used college text and, apart from the Bible, the most frequently cited book in the year 1787.[6] From its pages they learned, among other things, that the functional separation of governmental powers was the primary way to avoid concentrations of political authority in too few hands and the way to achieve the real end of modern constitutional government: political stability without the oppression of individuals.

Indeed, even the idea of the rule of law—or the government of laws, not of men, as they then said—was a set of notions drawn from English theory and practice as it was expounded by Montesquieu and Blackstone after him, rather than from ancient philosophy. The rule of law was not, as it had been for Aristotle, the rule of reason guiding a city to justice; it was the protection of the rights of individual citizens against arbitrary governmental actions. For Aristotle the rule of law covered potentially every human activity, public or private. So also Cicero's notion of law as the expression of the consensus that ties a people into a city is remote from modern constitutional thinking. The latter is built on a distinction between public and private life and makes it the task of law to keep every public agent within the limits of his assigned sphere. Such a view of law could have no place in the classical ideal of government whose highest aim was to educate its members according to a shared ideal of human virtue and political rationality. In contrast, every member of the Convention of 1787 agreed that it was the chief aim of good government to protect the liberty and property of individual citizens. The modern rule of law assumes that only a re-stricted number of activities and relationships may be ruled at all, which puts a vast distance between it and ancient legal ideals. The wide circumference of the private realm, to which guaranteed religious free-dom is a testimony, was a response to a Christian sectarianism that is utterly remote from the creedal world of classical paganism. That in itself is enough to recall the limits of the law's reach in eighteenth-century constitutional thought. Limited government has its roots in the divided loyalties created by biblical religiosity and in denominational conflict, not in ancient philosophy. And one might well argue that without the Bill of Rights the spiritual objectives of the Constitution were incompletely stated. Its origins are to be found in England, not in classical antiquity.

The framers of the Constitution were, in fact, well aware that they owed a lot to English legal precedents and that this in itself made them relatively modern. Their favorite author, Montesquieu, had explained that quite clearly, for he had a very strong sense of the differences between modern and ancient politics. The invention of the compass had transformed Europe.[7] That instrument's symbolic power was not lost on Montesquieu. Not only did it mean new worlds, new wealth, and immense power, it also meant a different sense of direction and a wholly altered relationship to nature—in short, an unprecedented culture. It pointed into directions that men had never taken before. Politically that meant, among other things, a new idea of the best possible regime.

Of the two models of free government, the old Roman Republic and modern England, only the latter was still practically relevant. Comparisons between the two polities were, however, possible and even instructive. It is as a contrast and as the illumination that comes from the alien and remote that the classical republics could still serve political understanding. And not the least important lesson of their history was the course of their decline. Montesquieu feared despotism above all else, and one of his objects was to show that any form of government, even a republic, could become an irreversible disaster. Republican Rome had fallen into that state, and it was an awful example and warning.[8] What mattered most to Montesquieu's heirs, including Publius, was therefore his analysis of the strengths and weaknesses of republican governments. According to Montesquieu, republican governments could be democratic or aristocratic; that is, their citizens ruled and were ruled in turn, or they elected permanent magistrates. Religion was manipulative or insignificant. Republics were small, cohesive communities in which citizens were carefully selected for political membership, knew each other well, and felt an intense emotional commitment to each other and to their city. They were guided by unspoken rules that arose insensibly from their physical and moral development, rather than by consciously made laws, such as those that govern modern states. Indoctrination, early education, constant vigilance by censors and fellow citizens were indispensable to maintain the ancient cities. They could last only as long as they remained deeply traditional societies, wholly geared to public purposes in which every institution served to maintain the disciplined egalitarian and military structure of the community. While they were free states because every citizen was at liberty to rule as well as to be ruled, they were insecure because they were excessively demanding. The citizens became unruly, or military expansion destroyed their cohesiveness.[9]

At no time did Montesquieu suggest that republics of this kind could or should be restored in a wholly transformed modern world. They were significant only for purposes of comparison. The famous chapter on the English constitution in *The Spirit of the Laws* is in fact a comparison between England and Rome as two examples of free states. Both were systems in which the political classes could take part in governing without being controlled or repressed by the others. In England representation served "the general will" of the people far better than direct democracy could in a large country. The king and the House of Lords served freedom by dividing and balancing the power of the state. Consent was at the very heart of this regime, and so was personal freedom. Unlike the ancient republics, it was governed by deliberate legislation, not custom. The cornerstone of English freedom was a judiciary that was completely independent from other governing agents. It was impartial, aided in its justice by popular juries, and dedicated to one end: the security and freedom of every individual. It was on this capital point that England proved its superiority to Rome, where each one of the branches had some judicial power, such that judges were never wholly independent. To be sure, democratic republics wanted punishments to be fair, because the life of every citizen was precious, but their institutional means were not adequate to that end.[10] Without the separation of powers, Montesquieu's great invention, no republic could be truly free. It was his deepest belief that criminal law especially, but also civil law, must be withdrawn completely from the political arena if the life, liberty, and property of the individual are to be secure.[11]

The second new feature of a modern state was commerce, about which Rome knew nothing, but which was the benign object of English government. While there had been ancient commercial republics, they had not in Montesquieu's view pursued trade consistently. In Montesquieu's idealized account, commerce in the new European world was on its way to eliminating Machiavellian foreign policies and war. Commerce also reduced prejudice, refined manners, and promoted justice, frugality, economy, moderation, labor, prudence, tranquility, and order. These were not the Aristotelian virtues, but they were the democratic virtues of ordinary people. Moreover, according to Montesquieu, the character-building powers of commerce and the dynamics of the political system relieved the English of any need to cultivate self-restraint or ancient virtue in order to maintain their regime. They needed to be, and were, ready to pay high taxes and to sacrifice everything for their freedom, but that was all. Citizenship in a modern free state demanded only that one pursue one's interest with determination and speak out and reason, no matter how badly. Religion played no part in politics and in England seemed to have no place even in private life. The English were unexceptional men and excellent citizens, and they presented to Montesquieu the very model of what the modern state should be like.[12] The only probable alternative was despotism.

The absence of unity did not disturb Montesquieu. Even in the classical republics that was not what virtue meant. Real political harmony was perfectly compatible with dissension and disagreements of every kind. What passes for unity usually is despotic and amounts only to "dead bodies buried next to each other."[13] Nor did Montesquieu bewail the absence of great men. Unlike the ancient historians, he did not believe that these celebrated individuals had ever played a very significant part in social change. His historiography was exceptionally impersonal, a matter of deep causes and incremental change. Had Caesar not destroyed the enfeebled republic, Montesquieu believed, some other general would have.[14] Nothing could be more remote from classical political science. And much as they admired George Washington, the framers also followed the wisdom of the modern age and planned a political system that did not require great statesmen in order to succeed in its aims.

This was the political science that Madison and Hamilton had learned in their youth, and that is how Montesquieu came to be written into *The Federalist*. Publius took the remoteness of classical republics for granted, even though the Anti-Federalists did not. They were convinced, quoting Montesquieu as well, that only a small and cohesive society was fit for republican government, and they considered the states quite comparable, culturally and demographically, to the ancient cities. It was an illusion that Publius did not allow them to entertain for long. In fact, it was the misgovernment and irresponsibility of state governments that led to the Convention in the first place and inspired James Madison to develop a theory of the modern extended republic.[15] The second battle fought with rival examples from antiquity was about the success or failure of the ancient confederacies, which might serve as models for the new federal government. Montesquieu, who had pointed to the military advantages of these arrangements for the smaller republics, was again often and inconclusively quoted in the Convention.[16] One can hardly blame Benjamin Franklin, who fully recognized the irrelevance of this line of thought, for protesting during the Convention that these discussions were "a proof of the imperfection of the Human Understanding. . . . We have gone back to ancient history for models of Government, and examined the different forms of those Republics which having been formed with the seeds of their own dissolution now no longer exist. And we have viewed Modern States all round Europe, but find none of their Constitutions suitable to our circumstances."[17] He suggested that the Convention try prayer instead, which for Franklin amounted to an expression of despair. As intelligent as ever, even in old age, he had put his finger on the difficulty that the framers confronted: There were no precedents, no models, no examples to guide them in their utterly novel enterprise. It would have to be all their own invention. Apart from the inheritance of English law, they would be obliged to create federalism, representative democracy, and a separation of powers that did not, in fact, exist even in England, in spite of Montesquieu's idealized depiction of its institutions. As Publius knew, the framers had only their own brief experiences and the modern science of politics to direct them. There was nothing else.

In keeping with all these considerations, classical antiquity served Publius mostly as a negative example of all that could go wrong in republics. In this he was actually following local traditions. The image of Rome was not a particularly inspiring one for those who recalled not only the palmy days of the Republic but also the history of the Empire. Protestants had little use for anything that the name Rome might suggest, in any case. And had not Saint Augustine told them all there was to be said about the morals of the Republic when he reminded his fellow citizens that their revered ancestors had found glory in the rape of the Sabine women?[18] Was there anything to be added to Tacitus's account of the horrors of even the early Empire and his cynical hints that the Romans had never been all that different? Readers who were more secular might have come to agree with David Hume that there was no correlation between the personal virtue and the military success of the Romans; they were pretty degenerate even at the height of the Republic.[19] No one at the federal Convention who mined the history of the old republics for warnings was dismissed as being eccentric.

It is therefore not surprising that the very first three words of the Constitution are a declaration of political independence from the entire European past. "We the People" is a declaration of popular sovereignty that makes the consent of the citizens the sole legitimate ground of government. The implications of this momentous novelty are spelled out very clearly in *The Federalist*, which remains our best interpretation of the original Constitution. This was to be a republic based not on virtue but on the consent of people with diverse interests and a shared concern for life, liberty, and the security of property. It was to be governed not as a direct democracy but by elected representatives and by a federal government that bore only the faintest resemblance to the unsuccessful confederacies of ancient Greece. Intellectually, that meant a new political theory, based not on the sanctity of tradition but on the use of past experiences only as illustrations, or as data for framing general propositions about both good and ineffective political institutions. Even this use of the past was less important than reasoning from careful observations of current American and English political institutions and conduct. Eventually Madison was to say that even Montesquieu had only opened up the science of politics that America was now fast developing.[20] That was certainly part of his and Hamilton's enduring intellectual self-confidence, but it was also part of their awareness of the novelty of their enterprise. What could possibly be learned from old chronicles in a wholly new political scene? Their main use of such sources was negative. The only time Rome is mentioned with full approval in *The Federalist* is to demonstrate that two concurrent taxing authorities are compatible with achieving greatness. The power of both the states and the federal government to tax the same citizenry does not, therefore, have to lead to any dire consequences at all.[21] With that exception, the institutions of antiquity were treated as suggestions to be discarded or as examples of everything that was to be avoided.

The rejection of antiquity begins very early on. Unlike Montesquieu and most liberal political theorists, Publius did not think that commercial states were particularly peaceful. Commercial republics, he noted, pointing to Athens and to Carthage, were inclined to go to war. And they did so for no good reason. War is always an option. Pericles apparently dragged Athens into war in order to please a prostitute (*The Federalist*, no. 6). There was no need to dwell on the conduct of military republics, since they were completely irrelevant to the civilian ethos of America (no. 8). The message of antiquity was, however, clear. Unless the states accepted the proposed Constitution and united under it, they would sooner or later go to war against each other. That did not mean that in other respects the states and the proposed federal republic were not superior to other forms of government. They were genuine republics designed to preserve liberty and property (no. 36). The new, extended republic, unlike the little republics of antiquity, would, moreover, be able to protect the public against the local factions that might threaten freedom and property (nos. 45 and 85). It would have the strength to do so because it was overtly grounded in the consent of the entire American people, "the only legitimate fountain of power" (no. 49). They would not only ratify the Constitution but would go on to elect representatives who would hold well-defined office for a limited time. That was the real mark of republican rule in the modern era. Without a union this would be impossible, as the history of the ancient cities proved (nos. 22 and 39). "It is impossible to read the history of the petty republics of Greece and Italy," Publius remarked, "without feeling sensations of horror and disgust at the distractions with which they were continually agitated, and at the rapid succession of revolutions by which they were kept in a state of perpetual vibration between the extremes of tyranny and anarchy" (no. 9). If one remembered that these republics were far smaller than any of the American states, and if one accepted Montesquieu's argument that the ancient republics were possible only as long as they remained tiny, then there were only two choices for the American states. They must either become thirteen monarchies or unite into a modern extended republic, built on principles that were unknown to the ancients. The latter knew nothing of a self-correcting electoral system that was both energetic and free. Should the Constitution be rejected, the states would also become "little, jealous, clashing, tumultuous commonwealths, the wretched nurseries of unceasing discord, and the miserable objects of universal pity or contempt." A genuine confederate republic would avoid all that, for it would have the resources to quell any uprising in any of the states as well as to provide for the common defense (no. 9).

When one considers the scorn that Publius heaped upon the disorders endemic to the republics of antiquity, one might suppose that unity was his highest political aim—which would scarcely be compatible with his ardent championship of liberty. That, however, was not the case. It was his view that America could overcome the tension between freedom and unity, thanks to the practices of representative government, thus again demonstrating the advancement beyond the ancient republics, for although the Athenians had understood representation, they did not use it fully and so fell prey to personal tyrants (no. 63). There was far too much direct participation by the entire body of citizens in every branch of the government, especially in the popular assemblies of Athens. "Had every Athenian citizen been a Socrates, every Athenian assembly would still have been a mob." Such a crowd is bound to give way to unreasoning passions and is invariably manipulated by some wholly unprincipled leader (no. 55). In contrast to that lamentable spectacle, "is it not the glory of the people of America" that "they have not suffered a blind veneration for antiquity?" Though they have shown "a decent regard for the opinions of former times," they have now embarked upon "the experiment of an extended republic," and posterity will be grateful for the innovation. "Happily for America, happily we trust for the whole human race," they have rejected the past and "pursued a new and more noble course" (no. 14).

Representative government in an extended republic is such a vast improvement because, unlike classical democracy, it has a built-in protection against the ruinous conflicts of factions. Far from having to crush differences of interest or political and religious opinion, it encourages them to flourish. The greater the multiplicity of religious sects and of tangible interests, the more likely these groups are to form changing and flexible electoral coalitions, none of which has a motive for crushing the others (nos. 10 and 51). Bargaining replaces the tumult of popular assemblies, as order and freedom are reconciled in society generally. The representatives, moreover, can deliberate calmly, save the people from occasional follies, and still remain close enough to the electorate to maintain their trust. The electoral system creates a disposition in favor of liberty, and the separation of powers prevents the concentration of authority in too few hands. All that was possible only because of America's great political invention, the large republic governed by representatives of the people. The small republics of antiquity knew nothing of this, and even their leagues were inadequate to defend them. The one confederation that had had central institutions sufficiently strong to be at all effective went down in military defeat like all the others. Such were the costs of smallness, an awful warning to the states (nos. 17 and 18).

The specific institutions of the ancient city-states also failed to pass muster. Rome had so feeble an executive that it had to resort to dictators in moments of danger. The consuls who made up its plural executive were often at odds and would have been so more often if, as patricians, they had not been joined in fear of the people (nos. 69 and 70). And finally, worst of all, ancient politicians did not really know how to put a constitution together. They had to find individual legislators who were driven to violence and superstition to impose a basic law upon their republics. The men who together had written the proposed Constitution of the United States were in every way their intellectual and ethical superiors. They had managed to introduce stability and energy into a limited republican government designed for a free people (nos. 37 and 38). And they had done so by "quitting the dim light of historical research" and following "reason and good sense" (no. 70). Antiquity had very little to teach them, except to remind them of its many errors.

One might argue that Publius did not really understand himself or his debt to antiquity, but why should we accuse him of such obtuseness? He did not deny that there was much to be admired in the classical past, but, unlike the French radicals of his day, he did not have to look to it for an alternative to a hated monarchical and clerical regime. That was behind him, and he could look forward to a resolutely modern republic, because he was faced with new circumstances. Intellectually Publius followed Montesquieu to the last. The final papers of *The Federalist* echo his every thought on the necessity of an independent judiciary and the protection of the accused in criminal cases. And the Bill of Rights that completed the Constitution devotes many of its provisions to rendering the procedures of the criminal law compatible with individual security and freedom. Such individual rights make up the very goal of modern republican government, and there is nothing in antiquity that resembles it. The Bill of Rights created a legal system to protect the property and freedom of individuals, not to teach them civic and martial virtue. To have fully understood that and to have recognized that antiquity was too remote to copy, and its passage not worth regretting, was no mistake on the part of Publius. America had discovered the future. And if Publius too longed for fame, so have many other men who were far removed from Plutarch's heroes. Nothing suggests that he would have wanted to become the object of ancestor worship. The best tribute we can possibly pay him and his generation is to follow their example and to think not about our imaginary roots but about our responsibilities.

Notes

1. Richard M. Grummere, *The Colonial Mind and the Classical Tradition* (Cambridge: Harvard University Press, 1963).
2. *Nicomachean Ethics* 5, *Rhetoric* 1.1, 3.17–18.
3. Kurt von Fritz, *The Theory of the Mixed Constitution in Antiquity* (New York: Columbia University Press, 1954).
4. Gilbert Chinard, "Polybius and the American Constitution," *Journal of the History of Ideas* 1, no. 1 (1940): 38–58.
5. Max Farrand, ed., *The Records of the Federal Convention of 1787*, 2d ed. (rev. ed., 1937; reprint, New Haven: Yale University Press, 1966), 1:397–404.
6. Donald S. Lutz, "The Relative Influence of European Writers on Late Eighteenth-Century American Political Thought," *American Political Science Review* 78, no. 1 (1984): 189–97.
7. *The Spirit of the Laws*, trans. Thomas Nugent (New York: Hafner Press, 1949), 21:21.
8. That was the main burden of Montesquieu's pioneering history of Rome, *Considerations on the Causes of the Greatness of the Romans and their Decline*, trans. David Lowenthal (Ithaca: Cornell University Press, 1968).
9. Montesquieu, *Spirit*, 2:3, 3:3–4, 4:4–8, 5:2–7, 7:2–3, 8:2–5.
10. Ibid., bk. 11.
11. Ibid., bks. 6, 12, 26.
12. Ibid., 19:27.
13. Montesquieu, *Considerations*, 93–94.
14. Ibid., 102.
15. Charles F. Hobson, "The Negative on State Laws: James Madison, the Constitution, and the Crisis of Republican Government," *William and Mary Quarterly*, 3d ser., 36, no. 2 (1979): 215–35.
16. Montesquieu, *Spirit*, 9:1–3.
17. Farrand, *Records*, 1:450–51.
18. *The City of God* 2.17, 3.13.
19. David Hume, "That Politics May Be Reduced to a Science," in *Essays Moral, Political and Literary*, ed. T. H. Green and T. H. Grose (London: Longmans, Green, 1896), 1:106.
20. Gordon S. Wood, *The Creation of the American Republic, 1776–1787* (Chapel Hill: University of North Carolina Press, 1969), 612.
21. *The Federalist*, ed. Jacob E. Cooke (Middletown, Conn.: Wesleyan University Press, 1961), no. 34. Subsequent references to *The Federalist* are to this edition and are cited in the text according to number.

PART 2

*Rights: Constitutional Freedoms
and the Interpretations
That Generate
and Sustain Them*

CHAPTER 10

The Origin of Rights

Constitutionalism, the Stork, and the Democratic Dilemma

•••••

BURT NEUBORNE

Parents often respond in one of two ways to precocious questions from children about their origins. Either they avoid the issue entirely, assuring the questioner that he or she will understand someday, or they invent a legendary explanation. I am neither a child psychologist nor a legal philosopher, but, as a parent who has blundered through the origins issue, I confess to a sense of déjà vu when trying to think about where individual rights in a political democracy come from. I have a strong sense of wonder at the miracle of their existence, but I find it difficult to explain the process of creation.

Most attempts to probe the paradox of judicially enforceable individual rights (as opposed to what I will call "oughts") in a democracy seem to share the same difficulty. Either they finesse the origins issue completely by asserting the self-evident existence of individual rights as an inherent result of the nature of things or they invent legends— some of the most beautiful and ennobling legends in our culture—to explain the miracle. I propose to sketch the roots of the dilemma by summarizing the work of others who have cogently described the tension between a genuine commitment to majority rule and a genuine insistence that areas exist—we call them rights—that are off-limits to the will of the majority, even when that will is expressed with scrupulous fairness. Somewhat immodestly, I will then explain why I fear that the existing attempts to describe the origins of individual rights fall into one of the two "parental" categories: (1) assertions that questions about origins do not really matter, since rights exist in the nature of things, or (2) explanations of rights that share as a common theme the invention of a legendary skyhook from which to suspend them. Finally, I shall conclude by suggesting that rights may be thought of not only as freestanding substantive phenomena but also as the real-world consequences of a complex institutional interplay that acts to deflect error—both legally and factually—in favor of certain values by vesting power in an independent and insulated arbiter, often called a judge, whose duty it is to ensure that the requisite level of error deflection has been applied by a democratic decision-making body when it decides to encroach upon the value. So described, the process of defining and applying legal rights in a democracy bears a close resemblance to another significant check on popular decision making, the use of sophisticated error-deflection mechanisms together with judicially administered checks to impose a greater degree of control over the jury's power to find adjudicative facts, especially in a criminal case. Briefly —and simplistically—put, I believe, first, that we temper the jury's power to find adjudicative facts with a set of judicially enforced error-deflection mechanisms and control techniques that insulate certain values; and second, that a comparable error-deflection process operates to check the democratic power to find legislative facts and enact legal rules in derogation of significant values. It is in the breathing space created by that complex institutional interplay that I find the origins of rights.

A Sketch of the Democratic Dilemma

The ambivalence of democratic political theory about the origins and (dare I extend the metaphor?) the legitimacy of judicially enforced individual rights in a functioning political democracy is understandable. Once a society has expended the enormous energy needed to throw off autocratic forms of rule and to achieve a functioning political democracy (and as it continues to expend the substantial psychic and economic resources needed to operate a tolerably fair political democracy), little energy is left over to explain why a process deemed by the society to be morally and pragmatically superior to competing forms of government should be ignored in certain intensely controversial areas. To use

Ronald Dworkin's metaphor, why should a judgment reached through the operation of fairly applied democratic principles be subject to a judicial trump via the concept of an individual right?

No such dilemma exists in an autocratic regime, where the pronouncements of the state do not rest upon a degree of individual participation and shared decision making. Under autocratic regimes, the concept of an individual right is a crucial device in an attempt to check the assertion of authoritarian power. Indeed, it is precisely in those political systems that arrogate to an elite the power to decide what is best for everyone else and to enforce that decision with the power of the state that the concept of individual rights is most important as a checking mechanism. Unfortunately, it is also precisely in those regimes that no institutional structure exists to give the rights tangible meaning. Thus, in authoritarian regimes, the rights concept plays a significant role in marshaling the human spirit to resist oppression and may even temper the harshness of the government's behavior, either out of deference to competing values or out of fear of the power of rights to inspire popular resistance. But in such regimes, claims of individual rights are, at best, demoted to passionately held and heroically defended "oughts" whose origins never really matter precisely because they cannot act as trumps.

In a genuine political democracy, the issue is more complex. The outcome of the governmental process is entitled to a presumptive moral legitimacy that flows from its participatory and consensual character. Self-government means that you abide by the rules even when you do not like them, in part because you participated in making them. In return, self-government entitles you to expect that, tomorrow, your opponents will also abide by the rules if you win, whether or not they like them. In an authoritarian regime, the concept of rights is readily (if weakly) deployed to justify resistance to an outcome because the objectors in no way participated in the governing process and cannot expect their opponents to defer to their outcomes at some later date. In a genuine democracy, however, the concept of rights cannot be so readily deployed as a challenge to government action for two reasons: First, if the democratic process is working, the decision was in some meaningful way participatory; and second, the consequences of rights deployment in a modern political democracy are more dramatic. If a right is to be used to trump the fairly expressed will of the political majority, and not merely to persuade it, the source and nature of such a right must be better explained.

One possible response to the dilemma is to demote rights in a democracy to powerful oughts by removing the institutional ability to turn the right into an enforceable trump. If a person claiming a right has no way to enforce it, the right resembles the concept as it exists in an authoritarian regime. Decisions about whether or not to defer to the assertion of right will be made not by the governing elite but by the political majority. As such, the concept becomes a powerful form of argumentation that may or may not persuade the political majority that it ought to behave in a certain way. Lacking an institutional enforcement mechanism, such a weak version of rights merely places moral and political constraints on majority will; it cannot prevent the majority from acting according to its will. As in authoritarian settings, assertions of rights to democratic bodies may temper behavior—especially if the values protected by the "rights" are widely respected by the electorate—but such assertions cannot trump those rights.

Until relatively recently in most political democracies, rights were subject to ultimate definition and application by majoritarian bodies. As such, they were merely powerfully argued oughts. We learned, unfortunately, that majorities, confronted with mere oughts, can be as arbitrary and authoritarian as elites when it comes to dealing with weak and unpopular groups or subjects. We learned that political democracy, while infinitely preferable to authoritarian regimes of the left or the right, is not a perfect system. Even at its best, political democracy risks overvaluing the needs of the "ins" and undervaluing the interests of the "outs," especially when the outs are despised or feared. That sobering perception led to a gradual realization that the traditional view of rights as powerfully argued oughts was insufficient. In its place, we evolved an institutional apparatus that empowers a nonmajoritarian organ to overrule the popular will when, in its view, "rights" are being violated. Once we move, however, from rights as oughts to rights as trumps, the legitimacy of our institutional process requires some explanation of where the rights come from. When you create a right by elevating an ought to a must, some explanation is needed to justify the promotion and to guide the officials vested with responsibility for identifying and enforcing the right, especially when the must is directed to a political majority that does not agree with the ought.

The Origin of Rights

A Survey of the Origins of Rights in a Political Democracy

One set of explanations for where rights as musts come from bears a marked resemblance to parental attempts to finesse the origins question by asserting that origins really do not matter. Rights exist, so the argument goes, in the nature of things as an inherent attribute of human dignity and reason. Natural law philosophers have expended vast intellectual resources in seeking to demonstrate the necessary existence of rights, as a matter of either logic, intuition, or faith.

I find the natural law tradition, viewed as powerfully argued oughts, immensely valuable and, for me, almost wholly persuasive. I believe that the inherent dignity of the individual does compel the recognition of certain rights that no earthly power can erase. I am prepared to seek to persuade my neighbors that due respect for our species calls forth certain obligatory behavior from the community needed to respect what I characterize, for the purpose of powerful argumentation, as rights. If the natural law tradition is viewed as a powerful ought, I believe that it is among our great civilizing influences. If it is viewed as a trump, though, I have trouble with it; I cannot accept the persuasive power of any argument that purports to derive countermajoritarian musts from the essential nature of man or the essential nature of the universe. For one thing, no consensus exists within the natural law tradition as to the contents of the rights or what to do about conflicts between them. How, for example, would a natural law thinker resolve the tension between assertions of political and economic rights? Thus, while natural law explanations of rights erect sublime banners behind which I gladly march, they do not justify an institutional structure that licenses officials selected by a nondemocratic process to trump the fairly expressed views of the majority.

Since natural law does not satisfactorily explain the origin of rights enforceable against the majority, a number of alternative explanations have emerged, all of which seek to identify an external source of originating power that both authorizes and compels the non–democratically selected official to act to preserve the right. I fear that unfortunately the attempts to posit an external source of authority as the origin of rights share a common flaw: They depend on an internally generated skyhook from which the rights are suspended.

The most obvious example—divine law—unashamedly invokes a very nearly literal skyhook in the form of a supernatural presence who commands that the rights be respected. Without denigrating the majestic belief systems that have been codified in various distillations of divine law, no serious case can be made for recognizing the word of God as an authoritative message to enforcers of rights in a political democracy. Divine law differs from natural law as an attempt to explain the origin of rights (as opposed to oughts) only as to the source. Natural law derives rights from the essential nature of things; divine law posits an external, supernatural conferer of rights. Both are powerful attempts to translate oughts into musts, but neither provides a persuasive justification for requiring nonbelievers to accept either as necessarily preferable to the will of the majority.

By far the most popular attempt to construct a legend that explains and justifies rights is a resort to variations on the theme of constitutional positivism. Constitutional positivism seeks to solve the democratic dilemma by locating a command in a fundamental document that requires the nondemocratic official to protect the rights created by the document; in other words, the Constitution-as-stork. For me, none of the ambitious versions of constitutional positivism propounded in recent years is any more persuasive in explaining the origin of rights than is the stork in explaining the origin of babies.

The first variation, literalism, is touted as a complete resolution of the dilemma, since neither choice nor discretion is permitted to seep into the process. If natural and divine law explanations were too vague and too subjective to be credible, literal application of the Constitution could not be more precise and objective, except for one obvious flaw: The language of the Constitution resists a literal reading. One need not be a deconstructionist to recognize that language is often ambiguous and that the language of the rights provisions of the Constitution is much more ambiguous than most. Of what help is it to try to find the literal meaning of "due process of law" or "equal protection of the laws"? People who claim to be able to read the Constitution literally are simply using literalism as the skyhook from which to suspend their subjective vision of what they believe it ought to mean. Looked at that way, literalism is not so very different from divine or natural law as a vessel to transmute subjective oughts into allegedly objective musts.

The second version, original intentionalism, is not much better. It assumes that the open-ended language of the constitutional text can be reduced to a single correct meaning by determining the meaning its framers intended. Original-intent theory has been subjected to well-deserved and devastating criticism. The legendary quality of original intent is exemplified by its fixation on a mythic group—called "the founders"—whose intent is deemed binding. No way exists to decide who these "founders" are. The delegates in Philadelphia? All of them, or just the dominant figures? The ratifying legislators? Every state, or just the sophisticated ones? The citizens who voted in referenda? Newspaper editors who commented pro or con? The list could go on and on. It is hard enough to make sense of the concept of a collective intent of a given body of legislators who harbor differing individual intentions, motives, and purposes. But when you cannot even agree on whose collective intent counts, the task is impossible. Even if we could agree on whose intent counts, there simply is no conclusive historical evidence that permits us to know with certainty what a given body of people intended two hundred years ago, especially concerning issues that probably never occurred to them. Not surprisingly, bitter disagreement exists over what original intent consists of—assuming that it is even worth discovering. For example, it is possible, even plausible, to argue that the best expression of original intent was the founders' decision to use open-ended language in the Constitution, evidencing an intent to leave the document open for subsequent interpretation by later generations in the light of the needs of their day. As we shall see, such a theory of constitutional positivism comes very close to the expansive conception of judicial power advanced by Justice Brennan. If commitment to original intent can lead to views of judicial power as diverse as those of Ed Meese, former attorney general, and Justice William Brennan, it hardly qualifies as a serious candidate for a persuasive source of objective external command. Like literalism, original intent is really a skyhook from which to hang a subjective view of what rights ought to look like. It does not explain where rights really come from; it merely masks their real origin and provides a convenient forum for argumentation over what stage they ought to take.

The most sophisticated attempt to explain rights as a command generated by the founders is an effort to derive the founders' constructive intention. Constructive intention theory recognizes that it is impossible to locate and identify the founders' intent as a historical fact. Rather, it is frankly embraced as a fiction, with the judge enjoined to generate a constructive intent that its closest to the intent the founders probably would have had if they had been asked. As with originalist thinking, constructive intent is deeply flawed as a source of objective command. Most obviously, it fails to identify the point in time at which the constructive intent is to be generated. Should the fictive founder be asked what he would have intended as a political figure in 1789, or should he be asked what he would have thought if he were transposed into the modern world? If the answer is 1789, a legitimate rejoinder is, Why? Once we go to a constructive intent, why should the fictive founder be asked to confront a modern problem from the truncated vantage point of two hundred years ago? If the answer is the modern world, constructive intent begins to look a lot like Justice Brennan's theory. Asking what a hypothetical founder transposed forward in time two hundred years would probably think about an issue he did not consider hardly qualifies as a serious attempt to generate a credible objective external command. Claiming that the constructive intent of a hypothetical founder is an objective external command that requires the overturning of a majoritarian choice is transparently unpersuasive. It is just another skyhook for someone's conception of ought.

Finally, Justice Brennan appears to have borrowed aspects of originalism and constructive intent and welded them into a theory that views the open-textured phrases of the Constitution as an authorization, not a command, to reach a certain result. Viewing the founders' decision to use such phrases as powerful evidence of an intention to delegate interpretive authority forward in time, and treating the founders as if they were contemporary figures, he attempts to decide how such a "contemporary" founder should exercise the delegated authority to give precise, contemporary meaning to the inchoate rights embedded in the Constitution. Unlike other forms of constitutional positivism, Justice Brennan's theory does not deny the existence of choice. He frankly recognizes that contemporary construction is a skyhook from which contemporary judges hang their conception of what rights ought to look like in light of the known concerns of the founders, the limits of intellectually honest readings of the literal text, and our nontextual constitutional tradition.

Of the competing versions of constitutional positivism, I find Justice Brennan's approach much the best for two reasons. First, it's honest. It places responsibility for choice where it belongs, on the interpreter of the document, rather than pretending that a given interpretation is compelled by a nonexistent external command. Second, it's functional. It places the ultimate power to define and apply individual rights in a forum that is insulated from majority will and better suited to enunciating a principled description of the relationship between the individual and the political majority. It does not, however, solve the basic dilemma, since my belief that rights are best defined and enforced by insulated bureaucrats called judges, who are only loosely bound by text and general value guidance, is not universally shared. Admitting that you are using a skyhook is admirably honest, but it does not explain why you should—or must—be permitted to use one in the first place.

Nor, in my opinion, have four mighty attempts at providing serious external guidance to judges about how to exercise the interpretive power solved the problem.

John Hart Ely sought to cabin judicial discretion by linking it to democratic political theory. If, he argued, the democratic structure of the Constitution generates sufficiently precise guidelines to assist judges in exercising Justice Brennan's vision of interpretive power, we can have both democracy and rights without undue tension. Ely's work remains a persuasive post hoc rationale for much of the Warren Court's jurisprudence, but it does not completely solve the problem. On one level, his suggested guidelines are so abstract as to leave enormous scope for disagreement over whether a guideline calls for a particular judicial result. As with the various intent theories, Ely's approach often obscures the skyhook by giving the impression that a particular judicial interpretation is externally mandated rather than merely plausibly authorized. In short, it never breaks the very substantial number of ties that an intellectually honest judge will confront using Ely's guidelines as a compass. On another level, Ely's guidelines are quite narrow, providing no guidance or support for judicial protection of a number of what, to many, are highly significant rights. Since it really provides neither external guidance for the type of decisions it purports to justify nor justification for effective institutional protection of important values, it does not resolve the problem of origins.

Ronald Dworkin[1] seeks to minimize the severity of the problem by brilliantly arguing that externally imposed right answers do exist in hard cases, if only we are perceptive enough to be able to find them. He argues that thinking hard about principles, as opposed to utilitarian policies, will permit judges to evolve toward principled definitions of rights that are not merely desirable but objectively correct. Despite the power of his argument, Dworkin's thesis requires a skyhook as well. Unless one accepts his initial postulates concerning the meaning and significance of equality norms, the remainder of his elegant structure is not necessarily derivable. I happen to agree with his postulates. So, for me, Dworkin's work is both a solace and a challenge. But I am not at all certain that his view would have the same effect on persons who have a different opinion about whether equality or autonomy is *the* prime value.

Ultimately, it seems to me that the persuasive value of Dworkin's attempt at justifying judicial protection of rights depends upon the selection of a prime value to start his machine. Since his candidate for the prime value—equality—is widely shared and, in my opinion, much the best of the available candidates, I find his work persuasive. But it depends, first, on an agreement that there is *some* prime value to act as a principled starting point and, second, on a consensus about what that prime value is. Since reasonable people can and do disagree on both points, I fear that Dworkin's work cannot be more than a persuasive exposition of how things ought to be.

Richard Posner's work,[2] conversely, tries to persuade us that efficiency, not equality, is the prime value from which a principled view of judicial definition of rights should evolve. Since I reject Posner's prime value, I do not find his work helpful or persuasive. It does, however, bear an uncanny resemblance to Dworkin's when both are viewed as attempts to provide externally mandated, principled guidance to judges in hard cases about rights. Both derive complex systems of thought as guidelines to judges. But while each views his system as providing *the* right road, putting them side by side reveals that both Posner and Dworkin have described *a* right road, depending on which prime value you start with. I cannot accept either, viewed that way, as a definitive explanation of where rights come from.

Finally, while John Rawls's[3] extraordinary attempt to deduce the nature of rights and justice from an exercise in contractarian logic provides, for me, a remarkably persuasive justification for much of what I already believe, it is a quintessentially legendary account of the origins of rights. Rawls places the origins in a fictive contract that hypothetical ancestors would have entered into in a state of nature, if they had had the opportunity to do so. Rawls's fictive founders are not terribly different from those of Ed Meese, in that either set is used as the vehicle to project a vision of what rights ought to look like. I find Rawls's conception of the world infinitely preferable to Meese's, but the decisions made by Rawls's fictive founders are not the only possible—or even plausible—ones. As with Dworkin's theory, Rawls's construct depends upon the existence of equal treatment as *the* prime value. I sometimes think that much of the debate over rights is a massive set of variations on the question of whether equality or autonomy ought to take preference in working out the conceptions of rights. But simply shouting—or even elegantly constructing—an argument for one does not obliterate the other.

At bottom, therefore, I fear that the various exercises in constitutional positivism that seek to locate the origin of rights in an external command fail to persuade. If anything, they reinforce my suspicion that the true origin of rights lies far more with the official empowered to define and enforce them than with any external source. That suspicion leads me to a troublesome (but, for me at least, not difficult) choice. On one hand, a deep commitment to democratic decision making as a morally superior form of governance counsels that the majority should not be trumped unless the source of the trump can be located in an external command that is consistent with democratic political theory. Of the various candidates, only the literalism variant of constitutional positivism (supplemented by a dose of original intent when it can be known with real certainty) qualifies as a genuinely external command. But the consequences of literalism are appalling, going far beyond Ed Meese's view. Literalism virtually wipes out nonmajoritarian enforcement of individual rights. Under literalism, almost any plausible action of the majority must be upheld.

That perception drives me to consider the alternative, which is giving up on an external source of rights and vesting judges with power to make the rights up as they go along, guided by constitutional text, the general value orientations of the founders, our unwritten constitutional tradition, and the felt necessities of modern life. I cannot square such open-ended power with respect for democratic decision making. Moreover, except for the relatively recent past, little in the judicial history of this nation or in the behavior of judges around the world leads me to trust them with such extraordinary power. After all, the very first state statute declared unconstitutional by the United States Supreme Court was Pennsylvania's law authorizing the shelter of fugitive slaves from recapture. But if I am forced to choose between the extremes of a world in which the majority decides what rights mean and a world where rights are defined and enforced by insulated officials, my choice is a clear one. A world where rights have been demoted to oughts is a world where the weak will inevitably be treated unfairly. If forced to choose, therefore, I choose judicially evolved rights, even with the knowledge that their origins are democratically illegitimate.

An Institutional View of the Origins of Rights

Is it even necessary to confront the stark choice between rights and democratic political theory? In large part, the choice is forced upon us by our tendency to think about rights as though they were tangible things having an existence independent from the institutional structure that defines and applies them. I understand why we have tended to talk about rights that way. In authoritarian regimes—or in democratic regimes that lack institutional mechanisms for enforcing individual rights— the concept of a right can have no meaning unless it is linked to an intellectual structure that transcends the political system against which the right is deployed. That is why natural law and divine law systems are so important in organizing and carrying out resistance to authoritarian oppression. But the process of reifying rights and thinking about them as tangible phenomena has its price, part of which is the democratic dilemma. If we think about rights as having a tangible existence, the troublesome question of why democratic bodies are not as qualified as insulated judges to describe them cannot be avoided. As my response to the dilemma suggests, I am prepared to answer the question on a strictly functional basis by arguing that majorities cannot be trusted to describe the rights fairly. But that answer causes me a good deal of discomfort precisely because I do not believe that rights have an independent existence apart from the institutions that participate in their description and application. That belief forces me to concede enormous power to unelected officials, since, if forced to think about rights as things, I believe that the unelected officials generate the rights internally. At the same time, though, my skepticism about whether rights have an independent existence permits me to attempt an institutional explanation of the origins of rights that generates less tension with democratic political theory.

The Origin of Rights

Henry Hart was fond of asking his students what meaning a single would have if there were no such thing as baseball. We shook our heads at that one, but I think he was trying to warn us about the danger of divorcing legal concepts from the institutional structure that gives them meaning and existence. Bishop Berkeley argued that reality was contingent on perception. I need not question the existence of objective reality to suggest that, if a right falls in the forest with no institutional mechanism to respond to it, there never was any right to begin with. I believe that rights should be thought of as the real-world consequences of the interplay between institutions, not as things discovered or created by a particular set of officials.

We have one obvious example of my thesis in the way we think about the interplay between judge and jury in the area of adjudicative fact. Without engaging in hyperbole, one could call the institution of the jury an enormously important infusion of popular decision making into the legal process. It delegates to an organ with a democratic pedigree the power to enunciate the minor premise in many judicial syllogisms. Along with voting, the jury is one of the founts of democratic legitimacy. We accept, albeit reluctantly, the impossibility of being certain about the existence of most adjudicative facts. We recognize that, in most cases, jurors are confronted with a set of plausible choices and that, in most cases, there is more than one potentially correct choice. Our response to the notion of inherent jury choice is to erect a set of mechanisms designed to ensure that the jury's choice deflects error in favor of certain deeply felt values. By varying the degree of certainty required before a democratic organ (the jury) can exercise choice in derogation of a deeply held value, and by tightly controlling the nature of the evidence it may consider, we generate breathing space for certain values. It is that breathing space, conceived in the interstices of the interplay between institutions, that I call a right. The interplay between the jury's inherently open-ended choice of adjudicative fact and the judiciary's application of a set of error-deflection mechanisms designed to ensure that the jury resolves doubts in favor of a significant value, culminates in the enjoyment of an individual right.

I have described the process starkly and quite simplistically, but I believe that it provides a model for thinking more generally about rights. There is a parallel between the way courts impose on juries error deflection in favor of liberty and the way courts exercise judicial review over legislatures. Much judicial activity in defense of rights is really nothing more than the application of error-deflection rules to legislatures. These oblige the political majority to demonstrate varying levels of factual and legal certainty before acting in derogation of significant values embedded in our constitutional heritage. So viewed, a unity exists between the institutional checks placed on the democratic power centers of the jury and the legislature. Each is vested with enormous power of choice; but each is enjoined to exercise that choice pursuant to error-deflection mechanisms that require varying degrees of certainty before the choice is exercised in ways that impinge on values that permeate our constitutional tradition. And, in our system, the duty to assure compliance with the error-deflection rules is vested in unelected officials whose interaction with the democratic power center translates abstract values into real-world rights.

When a legislature decides to enact a rule that trenches on a value of constitutional dimension, it engages in a form of syllogistic reasoning. The major premise consists of the legislature's reading of the relevant constitutional text. Given the open texture of many of the most significant provisions of the Constitution, the legislature will often exercise substantial choice in selecting a reading that it perceives to be the preferable one. Since legislatures are, by definition, designed to reflect the will of the political majority, they should, quite naturally, adopt plausible readings of the constitutional text that most closely accord with advancing the interests of the majority. Of course, in those rare settings where only one literal reading of the text is possible, or in those more prevalent settings where the meaning of an ambiguous phrase has become fixed as part of our constitutional tradition, legislatures will feel bound to adopt that reading of the text, whether or not it accords with the majority's desires. But, in the bulk of cases, legislatures will be offered a genuine textual choice, much as juries have genuine choices among potential versions of adjudicative facts.

The legislature's minor premise consists of a characterization of the social justification for the enactment. Given the almost infinite variation in worldviews and perceptions that can and should flourish in a free society, the legislature's range of choices as to what some have called legislative or social facts is enormous. When a legislature finds the facts that underlie its enactments, the range of choice and of evidence is far broader than the choices available to juries; but the process of choosing legislative fact for the legislative syllogism is not fundamentally different from the choosing of adjudicative fact by a jury.

When an American judge protects individual rights, I believe that she or he does not enforce a tangible phenomenon with some substantive meaning, but rather applies error-deflection rules to assure a given level of certainty about the choices made by the legislature concerning its textual authority and factual justification. In the vast majority of settings, the lack of a significant constitutional value that is threatened by the legislature's action results in a permissive error-deflection standard for both jury and legislative choice: Could reasonable decision makers have believed that it is more likely than not that their choices were correct? The net result of such an institutional interplay is a right not to be subjected to arbitrary action by both sets of popular decision-making organs—the jury and the legislature. When, however, the popular decision-making organs act in derogation of a value deemed particularly significant, an array of error-deflection devices comes into play, ranging from a requirement of guilt beyond a reasonable doubt before incarceration to one of virtual certainty about the necessity of legislative action in derogation of free speech or equality values. The net result of such institutional interplay is the real-world enjoyment of significant values.

Thinking about rights as the endgame of error deflection does not, of course, fully resolve the democratic dilemma. The choice of those values in favor of which error should be deflected and the precise degree of error deflection are decisions that place pressure on democratic theory. There does, however, appear to be a real difference between telling the legislature that it cannot do something at all and telling it that it must be very sure of its major and minor premises before it acts in derogation of certain values. Placing varying burdens of justification on legislatures and varying burdens of persuasion on juries has the effect of shielding significant values from unnecessary derogation without wholly depriving the popular institutions of the power to act.

Consider two significant examples of the countermajoritarian enforcement of individual rights as exercises in error deflection. In *Brown v. Board of Education*,[4] the Supreme Court reversed *Plessy v. Ferguson*[5] and held that officially mandated racial segregation violated the individual rights of black citizens to equal protection of the laws. None of the conventional approaches to constitutional positivism yields an acceptable explanation of the origin of the rights enunciated in *Brown*. Literalism is of no help, original intent probably yields the "wrong" result, and constructive intent is utterly fictive. The Warren Court's use of contemporary construction reached the "right" result, but at the price of delegating enormous power to nonelected officials. Rather than approaching *Brown* as an attempt at a definition of a substantive right of equality, it is possible to view it as a failure by the majority to carry its burden of justification for a rule that impinged on the value of equality. The syllogism—both legislative and judicial—that underlies both *Plessy* and *Brown* consists of a major premise drawn from a consensus reading of the meaning of the equal protection clause and a choice between the two versions of legislative facts as possible minor premises:

Major Premise

No person may be harmed by the state because he or she is a member of a racial minority [without an overwhelming showing of societal need]*

Minor Premise (*Plessy*)

Separate but equal facilities do not inflict harm on racial minorities

Minor Premise (*Brown*)

Separate but equal facilities inflict harm on racial minorities

The legislature's and the judge's choice between the two possible minor premises is the critical event in the process. If the choice is left entirely free, the result can be *Plessy*. If, however, a burden of justification is placed on the choice, it would be virtually impossible for a legislature to carry it, especially if it were set at a significant level of error deflection.

In *Roe v. Wade*,[6] the Supreme Court trumped the will of the political majority and held that criminal statutes forbidding abortion violated an individual woman's right to decide whether to bear a child.

---

*The bracketed material carries less of a consensus, but it appears necessary to take into account cases like *Korematsu v. United States* (323 U.S. 214 [1942]). No attempt was made to defend segregation as necessary to serve an overwhelmingly important social need.

Constitutional positivism is of no help in analyzing *Roe*. Neither literalism nor original intent can be thought to support the decision. Constructive intent is somewhat more plausible, but hardly persuasive. Even contemporary construction is troublesome because it is difficult to locate the precise provision of the Constitution that generated the right enforced by the *Roe* decision. I find it more helpful to think of *Roe* as a failure by the majority to carry its burden of justification for a rule seriously impinging on both privacy and the ability of women to play an equal role in society. The syllogism that underlies criminal statutes banning abortion consists of a major premise enjoying universal acceptance and a choice between two versions of legislative facts as possible minor premises:

Major Premise

No person may take the life of another in the absence of an overwhelming justification

Minor Premise I	Minor Premise II
A fetus is a person	A fetus is not a person

As in *Brown*, the choice of the fact-based minor premise is the crucial event in deciding whether abortion may be banned. If the choice is left entirely free, legislatures are free to ban abortion. If, however, a burden of justification is placed on the legislative judgment because it impinges on significant values, it cannot be satisfied. Indeed, the attempt by the *Roe* decision to draw distinctions based on the age of the fetus is an attempt to fine-tune the result to reflect those settings where the existence of a "person" is thought to be so clear that a consensus exists on the point, and those settings where so much doubt exists that neither side could carry a burden of proof.

While obvious differences exist over who should bear the burden of justification in constitutional cases and how heavy that burden should be, questions about how doubts should be resolved appear less insoluble than questions about how substantive rights should be defined. It is, therefore, in the necessity of choice, the inevitability of uncertainty, and the desirability of error deflection that I seek the origins of rights in a political democracy.

Notes

1. See especially Ronald Dworkin, *Taking Rights Seriously* (Cambridge: Harvard University Press, 1977).

2. See Richard A. Posner, *The Economics of Justice* (Cambridge: Harvard University Press, 1981).

3. See John Rawls, *A Theory of Justice* (Cambridge: Belknap Press of Harvard University Press, 1971).

4. *Brown v. Board of Education,* 347 U.S. 483 (1954).

5. *Plessy v. Ferguson,* 163 U.S. 537 (1896).

6. *Roe v. Wade,* 410 U.S. 113 (1973).

CHAPTER II

Victims as Heroes

A Minority Perspective
on Constitutional Law

......

DERRICK BELL

"And whose constitutional law course are you planning to take?"
I asked a student back in the days before I began teaching the
subject.

"Oh, I am getting as much con law as I need from your
course in race, racism, and American law," she replied.

"Your plan is hardly prudent," I warned her. "There is a
great deal of doctrine in constitutional law not covered in my civil
rights course."

Her reply was respectful but firm. "I think you should take
another look at your course content."[1]

I have tried to follow my student's advice. Each time I teach constitutional law, I find new areas of the course that gain in meaning when
viewed from a minority perspective. This paper examines my student's
implication that American constitutional law is a subject compiled by
those with insufficient understanding of the role of race in the development of constitutional doctrine—itself a major insight into several
"nonracial" precedents. But this essay will also serve as a tentative first
step toward a further exploration of the black struggle's value to white
Americans.

Robert Starobin observed that a few historians do stress "the
centrality of institutions like slavery to long periods of American history, and . . . regard the Negro as a key to the meaning of the Ameri-

can experience."[2] That was in 1968. Four decades earlier, the Southern historian Ulrich B. Phillips had asserted that race and the determination to maintain white domination was, as he titled an article, "The Central Theme of Southern History."[3] Few persons today would admit, with Phillips's candor, to a similar—if more decorously veiled—commitment to the tenets of white superiority. But society's rigid adherence to many "racially neutral" policies that are damaging to blacks suggests that it is the candor, and not the commitment, that has disappeared. The centrality of the role of blacks in constitutional development reflects both this continuing, if unspoken, adherence to tenets of white supremacy and the unceasing efforts by blacks to gain real equality through reliance on law.[4]

It is therefore not simply a retaliatory racial chauvinism that explains my attraction to the idea that blacks are a key to understanding the Constitution. We can draw lessons from the unique complexity of the black experience in America, which, stripped of the emotional content of color, can teach us much about this country that would otherwise be either forgotten or ignored. We know, for example, that few major policy issues, domestic or foreign, lack a racial component. Usually, race is a secondary rather than a primary consideration. Only rarely does the racial concern escape subordination to "bottom line" economic and political concerns. Quite often, the racial component includes a challenge to policymakers to rise above the stronger pulls of their primary concerns. Unremarkably, this moral challenge is seldom accepted—unless, of course, its acceptance serves to cloak with a veneer of "racial justice" undertakings actually motivated by the more usual concerns of power and vested interest.

But how can we blacks know these things? Or, rather, if history is written by the victors, how can what we know as victims gain credence? Here is a major barrier for those consigned by race to bear the burdens of constitutional development rather than to share as its primary beneficiaries. For both constitutional history and the legal doctrine it has generated affirm far more often than they contest the spoils-based rules of writing history. And a still dishonored (if no longer despised) minority needs to be ever mindful that even the most established concepts of constitutional dogma may literally as well as figuratively reflect the victor's view.

Painfully aware of how the rules work, people of color were ready for the victor-sponsored constitutional chronology now being promulgated throughout the Republic to mark the bicentennial occasion. During the two-hundredth anniversary rituals, the glow cast by all the roman-candle rhetoric makes it difficult to see that those descended from America's slave class have retained their subordinate status. In part, this difficulty arises because so few citizens who are not black can even conceive, much less concede, that the plight of blacks today has any but the most tenuous connection with either their slave background or the continuing vitality of beliefs in white superiority, which, together with motives of profit and power, first bred slavery and later spawned the various forms of subordination that substituted for chains.

The nation's memory on matters of race, so predictably selective during ceremonial occasions, also exerts its distorting influence on American jurisprudence. Few of even the most meticulous interpreters of constitutional meaning are immune to the attraction of the rationalizations that so often take the place of honest confrontations with the nation's lamentable racial past, reflected to an appalling degree in its contemporary legacy.[5]

The challenge here is not to convince an understandably defensive society of what blacks view as the obvious connection between racism and the Constitution. It is rather to better our understanding of constitutional functioning through lessons drawn from black experience. The task is more difficult than it should be because of the determined isolation of racial precedent from the major stream of constitutional discussion. It is easy to miss the significance of the subordination of black rights to various property-related interests of whites. This tendency is so because so much of what we now call civil rights law is taught as the long and painful, but successful, struggle up from slavery by a race whose members' chances for success still remain, in fact, determined as much by their color as by their competence.[6] For most students, lawyers, judges, and all but a few legal scholars, civil rights law constitutes the predictable chronology of the winning of rights as shields against the ever-present enemy, racial prejudice, for which no one is either guilty or responsible except, perhaps, out-and-out bigots like Bull Connor, Governor Faubus, and the Ku Klux Klan. The commonly held view of civil rights as a long, unbroken line of precedents resulting in slow but steady progress is reassuring. But encouragement, while welcome, is not actuality. And too often, what is denominated progress has been a cyclical phenomenon in which legal rights are gained, then lost, then gained again in response to economic and political developments over which blacks exercise little or no control. Constitutional law has always been a part of, rather than an exception to, this cyclical phenomenon.

Because the dimensions of this phenomenon remain uncharted, we who advocate on behalf of the nation's colored peoples seem to be trapped in a giant, unseen gyroscope. Even our most powerful efforts are unable to divert it permanently from its preplanned equilibrium or to alter its orientation toward dominance for whites over blacks. The symbols change, and the society even accepts those symbols that we civil rights advocates have urged upon it, but our status remains fixed, its stability secured rather than undermined by the upward mobility of the precious few who too quickly are deemed to have "made it."

The universal potential of interpretive meaning within the particulars of the black experience is often lost in the woeful tendency to treat civil rights precedents as sui generis: the unjustified bellyaching of those unable or unwilling to compete like everyone else (the conservative view) or the appropriate demands for the removal of the persistent stigma of racial inferiority (the liberal view). In neither case are the political and economic impact and value of the continued subordination of blacks given much attention. Rather clearly, enabling blacks engaged in constitutional law scholarship to gain the academic equivalent of "victor" status will not be an easy task.

Race, Property, and the Constitution

Recently, a black student sought my help in his and several classmates' efforts to persuade a first-year property teacher to include a component on the significance of slavery to the development of American property law. The teacher, recalling past complaints when he offered a slaves-as-property course segment, was reluctant to assent to the students' request. I begged off intervening, citing the traditional discretion that faculty members exercise in regard to the content of their colleagues' courses.

Actually, the students have a point, although it is one more appropriately addressed to constitutional law scholars than to those who teach the first-year property course. For it was in the wearying negotiations that led to our Constitution that the framers' idealism regarding the worth of the individual collided with their more pressing, pragmatic concern for the protection of vested property and political status based on wealth. It was a dilemma that would arise repeatedly in our history and that would usually be resolved according to the framers' response to the slavery dispute. As if tacitly recognizing the impossibility, within a slave economy, of a government that would protect life, liberty, *and* property, they chose to protect property interests, even when that decision necessitated the legally sanctioned enslavement of roughly 20 percent of the population.[7]

Jurists, scholars, and others involved in giving contemporary meaning to constitutional provisions readily acknowledge the presence of racial considerations in the original structure of the document. All agree that the slavery compromises reached between delegates from Southern and Northern states became the sine qua non without which no federal government would have been possible.[8] Those compromises served to protect the property interests of slaveowners at the cost of freedom for blacks, and to leave in place an inherent contradiction that the nation's basic legal document still retains.

What if one supposed that the slavery compromises of 1787 were merely an unhappy decision made under the pressure of the crisis of events and influenced by then-prevailing beliefs that (1) slavery was on the decline and would soon disappear of its own accord and (2) Africans were a different and inferior breed of beings. In that case the loyalty to property interests, even when it meant retention of a slave system, would have been fathomable, if not fully forgivable, and certainly no less sad. But the slavery compromises were too extensive to be dismissed as an oversight. The insistence of Southern delegates on protection of their slave property was far too vigorous to suggest that the institution would soon be abandoned.[9] And the antislavery statements by slaves and white abolitionists alike were too forceful to suggest that the slavery compromises were the product of men who did not know the moral ramifications of what they did.[10]

The compromise of 1787 is much more than history. It is the original and still-definitive illustration of the ongoing struggle between individual rights reform and the maintenance of the socioeconomic status quo. As was the case in Philadelphia, some of the most dramatic of the encounters in the contest involve blacks and racial issues. And as happened in 1787, the resolutions of these encounters are more readily reached because of a shared sense of superiority that affords the differing white groups a basis for compromise that sacrifices the interests of blacks. It is not the case that, like slavery itself, the country could not have come into being without the race-based compromises placed in the Constitution. It is simply that—as it happened— the economic benefits of slavery and the political compromises of black rights were thought to be essential to the growth and development of the nation.

Controversy has surrounded the work of Charles Beard, but what survives of that work is its now-accepted finding that the men who gathered in Philadelphia represented, and were themselves, major property holders motivated by the danger to that property in a country teetering between anarchy and bankruptcy.[11] Their unhappy experience under the Articles of Confederation taught them that a strong, central government would be required to save the floundering experiment in nationhood. Given the still bitter memory of England, consent to such a government would not come easily, as many feared it would become the domestic equivalent of the hated English Crown. It was essential that the new governmental structure embody recognition of the individual's entitlement to what John Locke designated as the three basic rights of "life, liberty, and estate."[12]

The framers understood property as an extension of the individual. The social compact was largely designed to protect whatever distributions of wealth came about through the varying talents and efforts of the society's members. Faced with that imperative, and taunted by General Charles Cotesworth Pinckney of South Carolina that "property in slaves should not be exposed to danger under a government instituted for the protection of property,"[13] the framers—including those who opposed slavery—joined in sacrificing freedom for blacks in order to safeguard their own. From their viewpoint, that was no contradiction.[14] It was simply an unavoidable paradox that their compromises denied liberty to the class whose labors in bondage over more than a century had provided the wealth that built the colonies and paid for the Revolution.[15]

But paradox or not, the decision was foreordained, predictable, and possessed of compelling logical force for the framers. Even Gouverneur Morris, the Convention's most outspoken opponent of slavery, had understood that "life and liberty were generally said to be of more value, than property, [but] an accurate view of the matter would nevertheless prove that property was the main object of Society."[16] Chief Justice Roger B. Taney missed the point. It was not, as he proclaimed in *Dred Scott*,[17] that the Constitution's commitment to individual liberty was not intended for Africans, but that the constitutional injunctions went to those who owned property—a qualification that excluded many whites as well as most blacks.

The Protection of Property
in a Post-Revolutionary World

To the framers, the subordination of black rights in 1787 was acceptable, if not particularly welcome (as indicated by their celebrated refusal to "stain" the Constitution with the words "slave" or "slavery").[18] But at that time, Northerners as well as Southerners reaped the profits of slavery.[19] Only avid (and mostly ignored) abolitionists and unrepresented (and mostly mute) slaves could decry the compromise that the framers were too ashamed to admit having made. But by 1857 the economic battle lines had been drawn. The differences between planters and businessmen, obscured seventy years earlier by shared vulnerability to the same dangers, could no longer be settled by the involuntary sacrifice of black rights. Justice Taney's conclusion that blacks had no rights that whites were bound to respect—a view rather clearly reflecting the prevailing belief of his time, and of the framers—was shocking less because it sought formally to remove all blacks from the ambit of constitutional protection than because it attempted to place the Supreme Court on one side of the fiercely contested issues of economic and political power that were propelling the nation toward civil war.

But after the Civil War amendments had been enacted and then cast aside, constitutional jurisprudence, while condemning Taney's opinion regarding the rights of blacks vis-à-vis whites, nevertheless fell in line with his conclusion. For the next seventy years, the Civil War amendments stood as definitive illustrations of the vulnerability of even constitutional provisions intended to protect the basic rights of blacks when those rights were deemed a threat to the property and political interests of whites. With few exceptions, the Court's decisions in racial cases were marked by hostility and hypocrisy.[20]

During the same era, the constitutional protections initially promoted to shield former slaves were transformed into the major legal bulwarks for corporate growth and the exploitation of working-class whites. Consider *Lochner v. New York*,[21] where the Court refused to find that the state's police powers extended to protecting bakers against employers who required them to work more than ten hours per day and sixty hours per week in a physically dangerous environment. Such extension, the Court held, would interfere with the bakers' freedom of contract. Compare *Lochner* with *Plessy v. Ferguson*,[22] decided only eight years earlier, upholding the state's police power to segregate blacks on the basis of race, even though such segregation must, of necessity, interfere with the liberties of facilities' owners to use their property as they see fit. The Fourteenth Amendment, the Court insisted, did not guarantee "social equality" between the races.

Both opinions are quite similar in the Court's use of Fourteenth Amendment fictions: the economic "liberty" of bakers in *Lochner*, the political "equality" of blacks in *Plessy*. And both enabled results that protected existing property and political arrangements, while ignoring the disadvantages to the powerless attributable to those relationships. In both decisions, Justice Harlan railed in dissent against the majority's refusal to recognize what they all knew: the injustice of declaring the law's formal equality in a grossly unequal world.

In *Lochner*, Harlan was morally right, but he was out of step with the prevailing "liberty of contract" philosophy in suggesting that the state's authority to protect its citizens' health and safety was sufficient to justify a statute that he conceded may have had "its origin, in part, in the belief that employers and employees in such establishments were not upon an equal footing, and that the necessities of the latter often compelled them to submit to such exactions as unduly taxed their strength."[23] He did not—as Justice Holmes did in his dissent—directly attack the Court's adoption of the laissez-faire economic philosophy that underlay the *Lochner*-era cases. In *Plessy*, though, Harlan urged—this time in line with that philosophy—that the state's segregation laws violated Fourteenth Amendment prohibitions by interfering with the personal liberty of citizens. He predicted, accurately enough, that segregation laws would signal the subordination by race of all blacks and would "permit the seeds of race hate to be planted under the sanction of law."[24] But as in *Lochner*, Harlan, while addressing the human injustices with great and articulate vigor, was unable to come to grips with the majority's view that "liberty" was a property-related right and that the state's segregation laws, far from interfering with liberty, were extending it to include the right not to associate in public places with blacks.

In his dissent, Harlan wrote: "Our Constitution is color-blind, and neither knows nor tolerates classes among citizens."[25] That now famous platitude was even more of a fiction than those upon which the majority relied. Moreover, it was a wholly inadequate response to a Court majority claiming its readiness to defend blacks' entitlement to "legal equality" under the law. In challenging the segregation law, the majority viewed blacks as seeking a constitutional guarantee of "social as distinguished from political equality."[26] And the Court was quite certain that the Fourteenth Amendment had not granted blacks the social status of whites, a status that the Court, for the purposes of this case, admitted was a *property* right.[27] In effect, the Court refused to take from whites the vested advantages of their whiteness, which included, in those days, the right not to associate with blacks in public facilities.

Decided only three years after *Lochner, Berea College v. Kentucky*[28] illustrated, perhaps even more strikingly than had *Plessy,* the Court's readiness to view state segregation laws as protective of, rather than a threat to, private property interests under the *Lochner* rationale. The Court in *Berea College* upheld a state statute that barred the private school from continuing its policy of integrated education. The Court reasoned that, since the state that chartered the college could revoke the charter, it could also amend it to prohibit instruction of the two races at the same time and in the same place without defeating or impairing the object of the original charter. The Court's "hands-off" attitude on segregation legislation that overrode principles of free association, occupational liberty, freedom of contract, and property rights was actually at odds with the freewheeling, laissez-faire constitutionalism of that era.[29] Focus on the corporate charter did not obscure that fact. But in a period of rampant Negrophobia, seemingly supported by Social Darwinism, few beyond the Justice Harlans and, of course, the blacks themselves were much concerned with judicial findings that state-sponsored restraints could further individual freedoms.

Justice Harlan, by the way, failed to tell us how a color-blind Constitution could be expected to provide even the most basic protection to blacks in a country where, according to his own prideful admission in the same paragraph, the "white race deems itself to be the dominant race in this country." "And so it is," Harlan continued, "in prestige, in achievements, in education, in wealth and in power. So, I doubt not, it will continue to be for all time, if it remains true to its great heritage and holds fast to the principles of constitutional liberty."[30]

For the fact is that the general belief as to which race is dominant in the society has helped motivate—and justify—the many compromises in which the interests of blacks are bartered and sometimes sacrificed to further accords between groups of whites. Over time, beliefs in white dominance, reinforced by policies that subordinate black interests to those of whites, have led—as the plaintiff in *Plessy* contended—to an unrecognized but no less viable property right in whiteness, an entitlement to those advantages gained over blacks by virtue of a white identity. As this symposium gets under way, we celebrate the thirty-third anniversary of the Court's rejection of the "separate but equal" doctrine of *Plessy*.[31] But in the late twentieth century, the passwords for gaining judicial recognition of the still-viable white property right include "higher entrance scores,"[32] "seniority,"[33] and "neighborhood schools."[34] And Justice Harlan's bold—if unrealistic—reminder that our Constitution is color-blind has become, in our time, the major argument of those who oppose all affirmative action remedies.

The Benefit to Whites of Black Freedom Efforts

The seemingly endless conflict over the pace and content of civil rights for blacks obscures the question of whether race has served functions in American law other than those involving either the subordination or the quasi liberation of black people. Even so, we do know that the ongoing agony of "the American dilemma" has a significance in American law that is deeper than the difficult-to-eradicate heritage of slavery. And the all-consuming effort by blacks to gain, through law, the entitlement of "all the civil rights that the superior race enjoy,"[35] as the *Strauder v. West Virginia* Court put it, has been of value to those involved in the increasingly inscrutable endeavor we call constitutional interpretation. Professor Arthur Kinoy raises this point when he suggests that "one of the most fascinating areas of the evolution of our constitutional law yet to be explored is the catalyzing effect of the myriad forms of struggle for Negro freedom and equality upon the development of constitutional rights and liberties applicable to all citizens—white and black alike."[36]

In support of Professor Kinoy's statement, we now have the perspective of the three-decade period in which courts and the Congress responded to black freedom demands by resurrecting and giving new vitality to the post-Reconstruction amendments. We should now be able to recognize that this long-delayed validation of black citizenship claims, like those rights conferred in the wake of the Civil War, was motivated as much by the perceived advantage that it would afford to the political and economic interests of dominant whites as by the patiently brilliant litigation efforts of civil rights lawyers. This conclusion, controversial but impressively defended by scholars who include Arthur Selwyn Miller[37] and John Nowak,[38] is supported by the constitutional experience of blacks throughout history. The stiff opposition of many whites to these gains should not mislead us. Much of the populace opposed Lincoln's signing of the Emancipation Proclamation—a policy that furthered the interests of the North far more effectively than it freed slaves.[39]

In recent years, the civil rights movement has lost momentum, despite the vast extent of its unfinished work, precisely because so many whites now view black gains as a threat rather than as a support for their status, including that property they hold in being white. Black claims that reach beyond formal quality and seek real opportunity—for racially balanced schools and affirmative action employment policies, for example—conflict rather than coincide with what whites perceive as their interest. Often, the opposition is not rational.[40] But it provides more than ample proof that a property value in whiteness exists and that unless infringements are carefully tailored—as was true in *United Steelworkers of America v. Weber* (1980) (involving Kaiser Aluminum's program of hiring and promoting black workers)[41]—it will continue to gain judicial protection and to frustrate the efforts of civil rights lawyers who seek to translate formally recognized rights into substantive remediation of past (and continuing) racial disadvantage.

Supreme Court decisions requiring hard-to-obtain evidence of overt discrimination as the prerequisite for challenging so-called racially neutral policies that are clearly disadvantageous to blacks are founded on the fear that blacks would upset any number of otherwise legitimate government policies, if relief against such policies could be based on proof of disparate impact alone. The Court has conceded as much. The issues that these cases raise are complex, but the proof standards adopted in *Washington v. Davis*[42] and *Mobile v. Bolden*,[43] for example, reflect a priority for vested property interests of whites over unfulfilled equality requests by blacks. These decisions differ from the original slavery compromises more in scope than in kind.

Here, truly, is the stuff of tragedy. But black efforts to avoid that tragedy have given a growing dimension of equality to the Constitution that extends far beyond the vision of the framers. Evidence of this equality dimension is not hard to find. Commentators, including Professors Paul Freund,[44] Arthur Kinoy,[45] and the late Harry Kalven[46] among them, have noted that while the Constitution specifically excluded blacks from its historic recognition and protection of individual rights, the major *implementation* of individual rights for *all* Americans has come through the efforts by blacks and their supporters to use the law to eliminate discrimination. One might add to this phenomenon the contributions of Jehovah's Witnesses, communists, and other minorities who, although unpopular, are adept at litigation.

To what extent are these precedents—for example, the right to fairly apportioned electoral districts,[47] the protection of freedom of speech as against powerful, public figures,[48] the elimination of invalidated criteria from civil service tests and other job qualifications,[49] the admission of college students on criteria other than grades and test scores (which are social class–related),[50] the elimination of poll taxes,[51] the protection of whites charged with crime from trial by a jury selected on a racially discriminatory basis[52]—more than happy coincidences, societally beneficial by-products of the long freedom struggle in the courts by blacks? How many have dared even to explore that question? Is it not at least worthy of debate that the injustices that so dramatically diminish the rights of blacks because of race also point up serious disadvantage suffered by many whites who lack money and power? Consider, for example, the "one person, one vote" cases.[53] For decades, the American political landscape was marked by the maintenance of voting districts that favored the powerful few over the quasi-disenfranchised many. Rural, sparsely populated areas controlled political power in far greater proportion than their votes, while the residents of major urban areas suffered serious dilution of their potential political influence. But despite frequent invitations, the Supreme Court declined to "enter this political thicket."[54]

As has happened so often, the Court was urged out of its cautious constitutional stance by the stark drama of racial discrimination that not only disenfranchised blacks but threatened to turn the whole apportionment process into a political travesty. When the Alabama legislature, fearing the growing black voter registration in the city of Tuskegee, redrew the lines so as to exclude virtually all blacks from the city, the Court was forced to act to protect basic black suffrage and, just as important, to defend the legitimacy of the electoral process.[55]

Consider also the advances in the right of due process for college students that grew out of racial cases. A long line of cases denying procedural rights to students facing disciplinary action was overturned by *Dixon v. Alabama State Board of Education*. Black students were expelled from Alabama State College without notice or hearing for engaging in a series of civil rights protest demonstrations. The court held that the students were entitled to the "rudiments of an adversary proceeding."[56] Subsequently all students have gained such rights.

Conclusion

Further examples could be cited, but the illustrations already given should help broaden recognition of the intricate relationship of race and political and social reform. Discrimination based on race provides a dramatic focus that reveals more subtle, though hardly less pernicious, disadvantage suffered by many whites. By looking carefully at black history, and the struggle for opportunity and dignity, one can also see there the history of most whites. Compulsive fascination with the difference in status between blacks and whites obscures the far more sizable gap between the status of most whites and that of the few who occupy the highest echelons of our society.

Constitutional scholars, as well as civil rights lawyers, can benefit from the tardy recognition that protection of promised constitutional rights will not necessarily result from the well-wrought legal brief, the persuasive oral argument, or the easy reliance on some intellectually satisfying neutral principle. We must supplement our advocacy skills and our analytical tools with a closer, more honest study of the history of our fundamental law. We will see that the provisions on which we rely for individual justice were intended by the framers to protect property and its owners from a too-strong government on the one side and from the masses on the other. Both were viewed as serious dangers.

The uniqueness of the Constitution is not its provisions that recognize individual rights. It is the fact that from time to time, minorities and other groups lacking economic power and political popularity have been able to avail themselves of those provisions; and that when the pressures of conscience were sufficiently strong, the provisions provided a justification for both the nation and the courts to extend a degree of relief to the powerless. Of course, those same provisions also contained mechanisms for placing limits on the remedies they sanctioned, in order to ensure that vested property interests would not be threatened or seriously undermined.

Thus, in the long effort to gain equality through integration, blacks have learned that white America will accommodate the interests of blacks and other racial minorities when and *only* when those interests converge with those of whites.[57] This means, for example, that the Fourteenth Amendment will not by itself authorize a judicial remedy providing effective racial equality for blacks, if that remedy would threaten the status of middle- and upper-class whites.[58]

Doctrine in the affirmative action field is, of course, the ideal illustration of the property-protecting nature of these remedies. As early as 1883, Justice Bradley admonished blacks that when

> a man has emerged from slavery, and by the aid of beneficent legislation has shaken off the inseparable concomitants of that state, there must be some stage in the progress of his elevation when he takes the rank of a mere citizen, and ceases to be the special favorite of the laws, and when his rights as a citizen, or a man, are to be protected in the ordinary modes by which other men's rights are protected.[59]

Most civil rights proponents, this author included, bemoan the readiness of the Court to give priority to the expectations of "innocent white workers" over minority hopes that long-awaited racial justice will prove more substantive than the principle of formal equality. In fact, the degree of protection extended to white workers is determined less by their "innocence" than by the culpability attributable to their unions or employers.[60] Again, whether intended or not, decisions grounded in the principle of neutrality protect not the innocent but rather the major property owners, except when they have, by their conduct, surrendered their entitlement to that protection.

I am suggesting that a conclusion, unavoidable in the analysis of racial cases, is applicable as well to cases of social reform in general. The availability of constitutional protection for the society's disadvantaged—

blacks, women, the poor, homosexuals, and the mentally and physically disabled—is not actually determined by the quantity of harm alleged or of liability proved. Social reform remedies, judicial and legislative, are instead the outward manifestations of unspoken and perhaps unconscious policy conclusions that the remedies, if granted, will secure, advance, or at least not harm societal interests deemed important by the middle and upper classes.

It is for this reason that racial and social justice—or the appearance thereof—may from time to time be counted among the interests deemed important by the courts and by society's policymakers. Of course, in every reform movement since abolition, there have always been those individuals for whom the principles of justice and equality were sufficient motivation. But, as with abolition, the number who will act on morality alone is insufficient to bring about the desired reform.

The constitutional formula for reform, like the original provisions protecting slavery, does not declare itself as such. Its presence must be inferred, not from the words but from the workings of a document that, for those whose economic and political interests were not represented back in Philadelphia, has so far promised more than it has delivered. This lesson—hard-learned by black people—is of no less value for their counterparts who are white. The challenge in this bicentennial year remains what it has been from the beginning of the American age: extending the meaning of liberty under the Constitution to those who lack the property prerequisites that our law has traditionally required for its full enjoyment.

Perhaps the goal may be more readily achieved if those of us teaching and writing about the Constitution begin more often to view it through the eyes of those whose only property was faith, who tried, and who continue to try, despite all the obstacles, to elevate that faith into constitutional protections of life and liberty, regardless of property, for all.

Notes

1. When the former student returned to the law school recently, I reminded her of our conversation. She told me that despite my warnings, she had become a partner in a large Washington, D.C., law firm, a position she had just left to begin teaching full time.

2. Robert Starobin, "The Negro: A Central Theme in American History," *Journal of Contemporary History* 3 (1968): 37.

3. Ulrich B. Phillips, "The Central Theme of Southern History," *American Historical Review* 34 (1929): 30. Despite its diversity, the white population of the South is described by Phillips as "a people with a common resolve indomitably maintained—that it shall be and remain a white man's country. The consciousness of a function in these premises, whether expressed with the frenzy of a demagogue or maintained with a patrician's quietude, is the cardinal test of a Southerner and the central theme of Southern history" (31).

4. Consider *McCleskey v. Kemp*, 107 S. Ct. 1756 (1987), where the Court rejected by 5–4 vote a challenge to the death penalty based on a statistical study indicating that racial factors influence the imposition of the death sentence in Georgia. In dissent, Justice Brennan reminded the nation of its racist past and warned that "we cannot pretend that in the three decades [since *Brown v. Board of Education*, 347 U.S. 483 (1954)] we have completely escaped the grip of an historical legacy spanning three centuries." By ignoring the evidence of racism in the imposition of the death penalty, Brennan warned, "we remain imprisoned by the past as long as we deny its influence in the present" (at 1794).

5. Randall Kennedy, "Race Relations Law and the Tradition of Celebration: The Case of Professor Schmidt," *Columbia Law Review* 86 (1986): 1622.

6. A happy exception is Paul Brest and Sanford Levinson, *Processes of Constitutional Decisionmaking*, 2d ed. (Boston: Little, Brown, 1983). The text breaks new ground in weaving racial cases into its historically oriented presentation of legal doctrine, and of the economic, social, and political factors likely to have affected that doctrine.

7. In 1790, the U.S. Census reported 757,363 Negroes, representing 19.3 percent of the U.S. population. Of these, 59,466 were free and 697,897 were slaves. See Peter Bergman, *The Chronological History of the Negro in America* (New York: Harper and Row, 1969), 68.

8. The best-known sections are the "three-fifths" provision in Art. I, Sec. 2; the provision that bars prohibiting the importation of slaves in Art. I, Sec. 9; and the "fugitive slave" provision of Art. IV, Sec. 2. See, for example, Staughton Lynd, *Class Conflict, Slavery, and the United States Constitution* (Indianapolis: Bobbs-Merrill, 1967).

9. Southern delegates were adamant even on the unpopular subject of importing slaves. John Rutledge from South Carolina warned: "If the Convention thinks that N.C.; S.C. & Georgia will ever agree to the plan, unless their right to import slaves be untouched, the expectation is vain. The people

of those States will never be such fools as to give up so important an interest" (Max Farrand, ed., *The Records of the Federal Convention of 1787* [New Haven: Yale University Press, 1911], 2:373).

10. The debate over the morality of slavery had raged for years, with influential Americans denouncing slavery as corrupt and morally unjustifiable. See, for example, William M. Wiecek, *The Sources of Antislavery Constitutionalism in America: 1760–1848* (Ithaca: Cornell University Press, 1977), 42–43. Slaves themselves petitioned governmental officials and legislatures to abolish slavery. See Herbert Aptheker, ed., *A Documentary History of the Negro People in the United States* (New York: Citadel, 1969–73), 1:5–12.

11. See Charles A. Beard, *An Economic Interpretation of the Constitution of the United States* (New York: Macmillan, 1913), 64–151; Pope McCorkle, "The Historian as Intellectual: Charles Beard and the Constitution Reconsidered," *American Journal of Legal History* 28 (1984): 314. McCorkle reviews the criticism of Beard's work and finds continuing validity in his thesis that the framers sought primarily to advance the property interests of the wealthy.

12. See Robert K. Faulkner, "John Locke," in *Encyclopedia of the American Constitution*, ed. Leonard W. Levy et al. (New York: Free Press; London: Collier Macmillan, 1986), 3:1175.

13. Donald L. Robinson, *Slavery in the Structure of American Politics, 1765–1820* (New York: Harcourt Brace Jovanovich, 1971), 200.

14. See my "Foreword: The Civil Rights Chronicles," *Harvard Law Review* 99 (1985): 4. There I wrote that, cloaked "in Caucasian chauvinism, the framers resolved the dilemma they faced at the nation's birth by writing into the Constitution *both* alternatives—equality and slavery—bequeathing as a principal heritage to a new nation a contradiction between their professed ideals and their established practices" (7).

15. See Edmund S. Morgan, "Slavery and Freedom: The American Paradox," *Journal of American History* 59 (1972): 5. After reviewing the critical importance to the early economy of tobacco produced with slave labor, Morgan observes that "the position of the United States in the world depended not only in 1776 but during the span of a long lifetime thereafter on slave labor. To a very large degree it may be said that Americans bought their independence with slave labor" (6).

16. Farrand, *Records*, 1:533.

17. *Dred Scott v. Sandford*, 60 U.S. (19 How.) 393 (1857).

18. Wiecek, *Sources of Antislavery Constitutionalism*, 79–80.

19. Plantation states provided a market for Northern factories, and the New England shipping industry and merchants participated in the slave trade.

The Northern states also utilized slaves in the fields, as domestics, and even as soldiers to defend against Indian raids. See Robinson, *Slavery in the Structure of American Politics*, 55–57.

20. See John E. Nowak, "Resurrecting Realist Jurisprudence: The Political Bias of Burger Court Justices," *Suffolk University Law Review* 17 (1983): 549. Nowak denies that the Court, "as an historic institution, has championed the right of racial minorities. Proving racial minorities have benefited from the existence of judicial review can be accomplished only by disregarding all Supreme Court history outside the quarter century between 1954 and 1979" (618, n. 334).

21. 198 U.S. 45 (1905).

22. 163 U.S. 537 (1896).

23. 198 U.S. 45, 69 (1905).

24. 163 U.S. 537, 560 (1896).

25. 163 U.S. 537, 559 (1896).

26. 163 U.S. 537, 544 (1896).

27. The plaintiff had argued that in any racially mixed community "the reputation of belonging to the dominant race, in this case the white race, is *property*." In conceding this to be so, the majority was at a loss to see how the segregation statute deprived the plaintiff, a black man, of any right to such property. A white person assigned to a colored coach would have an action for damages against the company for being deprived of this property. But if, the Court said, a colored man was assigned to a colored coach, "he has been deprived of no property, since he is not lawfully entitled to the reputation of being a white man" (at 549).

28. 211 U.S. 45 (1908).

29. Alexander M. Bickel and Benno C. Schmidt, *The Judiciary and Responsible Government*, vol. 9 of the *Oliver Wendell Holmes Devise History of the Supreme Court of the United States* (New York: Macmillan, 1984), 736.

30. 163 U.S. 537, 559 (1869).

31. In *Brown v. Board of Education*, 347 U.S. 483 (1954).

32. See *Regents of the University of California v. Bakke*, 438 U.S. 265 (1978).

33. See *Wygant v. Jackson Board of Education*, 476 U.S. 267 (1986).

34. See *Milliken v. Bradley*, 418 U.S. 717 (1974).

35. *Strauder v. West Virginia*, 100 U.S. 303, 306 (1880).

36. Arthur Kinoy, "The Constitutional Right of Negro Freedom," *Rutgers Law Review* 21 (1967): 389, n. 6.

37. Arthur S. Miller, "Social Justice and the Warren Court: A Preliminary Examination," *Pepperdine Law Review* 11 (1984): 473. According to Miller, the justices "perceived the problem of human needs as basic to social

stability. They were concerned with the continuity of social order over time. Stability and continuity are conservative virtues which, paradoxically, were furthered by the liberal, activist decisions of the Warren Court" (489).

38. See n. 20 above.

39. See Derrick A. Bell, Jr., *Race, Racism, and American Law,* 2d ed. (Boston: Little, Brown, 1980), sec. 1, 2.

40. See the case of *United Steelworkers of America v. Weber,* 443 U.S. 193 (1979), in which white workers opposed an apprenticeship program, which the company would not have established in the absence of civil rights pressure, because half of the openings went to blacks having lower seniority than some of the whites.

41. *United Steelworkers of America v. Weber,* 443 U.S. 193 (1980).

42. 426 U.S. 229 (1976).

43. 446 U.S. 55 (1980).

44. Paul Freund, "The Civil Rights Movement and the Frontiers of Law," in a special issue of *Daedalus* devoted to "The Negro American," ed. Talcott Parsons and Kenneth B. Clark (Boston: Beacon Press, 1966), 364.

45. Kinoy, "The Constitutional Right of Negro Freedom," 389–90.

46. See Harry Kalven, *The Negro and the First Amendment* (Columbus: Ohio State University Press, 1965).

47. *Gomillion v. Lightfoot,* 364 U.S. 339 (1960), held that a state statute adjusting city boundaries effectively deprived black citizens of their right to vote, in violation of the Fifteenth Amendment.

48. *New York Times Co. v. Sullivan,* 376 U.S. 254 (1960), established the "actual malice" standard in libel law for public officials in the context of a Northern newspaper's advertisement criticizing a Southern public official.

49. *Griggs v. Duke Power Co.,* 401 U.S. 424 (1971).

50. *Regents of the University of California v. Bakke,* 438 U.S. 265 (1978).

51. *Harper v. Virginia Board of Elections,* 383 U.S. 663 (1966).

52. *Peters v. Kiff,* 407 U.S. 493 (1972).

53. For example, *Reynolds v. Sims,* 377 U.S. 533 (1964).

54. In *Colegrove v. Green,* 328 U.S. 549 (1946), a plurality decided that judicial involvement in apportionment questions went beyond judicial competence and infringed on the powers specifically invested in Congress.

55. *Gomillion v. Lightfoot,* 364 U.S. 339 (1960).

56. 294 F.2d 150, 159 (5th Cir. 1961).

57. Derrick A. Bell, Jr., "Comment: *Brown v. Board of Education* and the Interest-Convergence Dilemma," *Harvard Law Review* 93 (1980): 518.

58. See, for example, *Milliken v. Brady,* 418 U.S. 717 (1974), which refused relief found appropriate by two lower federal courts in a school

desegregation case in which the only workable means of desegregating the predominantly black Detroit school system was to consolidate it with fifty-four suburban school districts.

59. *Civil Rights Cases*, 109 U.S. 3, 25 (1883).

60. See, for example, *Wygant v. Jackson Board of Education*, 476 U.S. 267 (1986), which denied preferential protection against layoffs for black teachers, provided for in the collective bargaining agreement, because there was no showing of prior discrimination; and *Firefighters Local Union No. 1784 v. Stotts*, 467 U.S. 561 (1984), which found that in the absence of findings of intentional discrimination, a bona fide seniority system could not be set aside to protect black workers with less seniority from layoffs. Compare those cases with *Local 28 of the Sheet Metal Workers' International Association v. EEOC*, 106 S. Ct. 3019 (1986), which approved a percentage goal for nonwhite membership because of the union's long history of discrimination; and *United States v. Paradise*, 107 S. Ct. 1053 (1987), which affirmed a one-black-for-one-white promotion quota as a temporary measure against a state police department that had refused to implement earlier consent orders.

CHAPTER 12

Constitutional Structure and the Protection of Rights

Federalism and the Separation of Powers

• • • • •

HARRY N. SCHEIBER

The Constitution was intended above all to establish a national government on a foundation of powers that would be adequate to great national purposes—yet to do so in ways "compatible with the principles of liberty."[1] The framers' approach to the protection of individual rights and liberties was in some measure prescriptive, embodied in explicit provisions of the original 1787 document that limited discretion of the states, as in the contract and ex post facto clauses. Also protective of citizens' rights in a direct sense was the guarantee in Article IV that "citizens of each State shall be entitled to all privileges and immunities of citizens in the several States." And finally, the framers in 1787 included in the same article a critically important, if highly generalized, guarantee that every state would have a republican form of government.

The Federalist leadership, in arguing for ratification, pleaded that these provisions of the Constitution were ample protections against "formidable instruments of tyranny" that history had taught Americans to fear.[2] But because the opposition focused such powerful objections to the Constitution on the absence of a more comprehensive enumeration of the people's rights and liberties, the Federalists agreed to introduce amendments as part of the political compromise that put the Constitution into effect. Hence the original document's provisions on rights were augmented by the Bill of Rights—that expansive set of prescriptive amendments that so magnificently encapsulate key elements of the political and moral tradition that the Constitution has come to represent for American law and society.

Despite the Federalist leaders' acceptance of the ten amendments, they generally agreed with James Madison that such prescriptions had all the limitations of mere "parchment barriers" against oppression. Instead, they placed their principal faith in what may be termed the iron barriers of structure. Here, in structure, was a defense of fundamental rights, a framework that would rest on the underpinnings of political dynamics (in checks and balances of power in motion) rather than on verbal prescription. Given the proper structures as defense against "omnipotent" power in any one branch, or any one locus of authority, "the force of opinion and habit, as these ally themselves with our political institutions"—as Madison put it in later years—would assure the security of republicanism and of the people's rights.[3]

The first structural element that the framers regarded, I think, as the more fundamental with regard to the defense of rights and liberties was the separation of powers. The second, no less important politically or historically but different in its origins, was federalism—that is, the federal design that retained the states, giving them the right to function as separate constitutional (not merely administrative) entities, or polities, within the larger system in which the national Constitution was supreme.[4]

In a sense, each of these two basic structural features of our system works, and was meant to work, *against* optimum efficiency in government.[5] Thus, from the founders' era to the present, critics have caviled that the states are an anachronism. To Hamilton, they represented the "political monster *imperium in imperio*," their sovereignty and parochialism the source of the nation's endless troubles, reducing it under the Articles of Confederation to "almost the last stages of national humiliation," its officers the servants of a "mimic sovereignty."[6] From Hamilton's time to the present day, critics of the federal design have argued that, where unitary structure would have provided for a smoother administration and greater political unity, the states introduced an unwarranted element of complexity. The enormous variations in size and population of the individual states, quite apart from the irrationality of the promiscuous political boundaries that in many instances define their jurisdictions, have also been regularly adduced as criticism of federal design.

In the modern economic and social context, moreover, a formal vesting of powers, however vague and protean, as part of a bundle of constitutional "rights" that belong to the states alone, is an invitation to the defeat of important national purposes. In this view, federalism is completely inconsistent with the needs of an integrated industrial or postindustrial economy, let alone a citizenry now so numerous that each of half a dozen of our metropolitan centers has a population that exceeds that of the original United States. Policy concerns that once could be sensibly designated "local" or "state" have today become truly "national" in their scope and relevance. It is difficult, in this view, to conjure up any policy issue in which the national government—and a national constituency of citizens—cannot claim a legitimate and rational interest and in which an important role for the national government would be inappropriate.[7]

So goes the critique of federalism. It has been met in recent years with spirited defense of the states' role and states' rights, sometimes from liberal and more often from conservative elements in national politics. The Reagan administration's various "New Federalism" initiatives—and certainly the particular brand of "original intent" jurisprudence that that administration has adopted as a conservative credo—have been posited, both in political discourse and in more academic styles of writing, upon a highly specified version of the federal design of 1787, the framers' intentions, and the historic meaning of federalism as a set of values. The constitutional imperatives that neoconservatives distill from their version of the history and the law are mobilized to set a clear agenda for what they declare to be the "proper" state-federal balance. That is, these critics call for both a restoration of an older type of federalism that they deem legitimate and a modification or abandonment of the system in place since the New Deal, which they view as illegitimate and unfaithful to original intent.[8]

The other basic structural feature of our constitutional order, separation of powers, has also come under frequent attack historically. And it is the subject of lively political and academic controversy today.[9] To some extent, the criticism is general and is directed to the basic issue of administrative efficiency. From one quarter, it is argued that the system is "cumbersome" (a word that appears often both in political dialogue and in Supreme Court opinions on the issue) and as such must be appraised with a view toward "streamlining" and avoiding unwarranted "excess" in the operation of checks and balances. More important, however, is the criticism leveled by Lloyd Cutler, James Mac-Gregor Burns, James L. Sundquist, and others, that the separation of powers works against the ideal of responsible government. Echoing Woodrow Wilson's famous reflections on the advantages of cabinet-style government over our system, these modern critics premise their proposals for constitutional reform upon the view that parliamentary government is both more accountable and more efficient than our own. Where executive officers are drawn from the ranks of the elected legislators and strong party discipline can be exerted, the argument runs, truly responsible government results: An unambiguous majority party (or coalition) decides on policy in a disciplined manner and can be held accountable for its decisions. The frequent division of power between the two major parties, between control of the houses of Congress, or between Congress and president, or indeed (as during 1981–85) both, means fragmentation of authority, lack of accountability, and frustration of majority will.[10]

Separation of powers is also controversial because of the very prominent concern that has surfaced periodically since the nation's founding, and which is prominent in today's politics, over checks and balances. Indeed, seldom in our history has political discourse from diverse segments of our society exhibited a higher intensity of concern over, variously, the "imperial presidency," judicial activism (both conservative and liberal in its substantive objectives), and the alleged tendencies of Congress to overstep the bounds of its prescribed constitutional authority.[11]

The United States Supreme Court has also been the scene of important debates and decisions in these areas during recent years. Thus, on the matter of federalism and the rights of the states, the Court has twice in the last two decades turned about 180 degrees on the meaning of the Tenth Amendment and inherent state authority as limitations upon the regulatory power of Congress under the commerce clause. In *National League of Cities v. Usery*, decided in 1976, the Court, for the first time in nearly forty years, found such limitations in the Constitution's structural design and explicit terms to invalidate federal regulation of public employees' hours and wages in the states. Nine years later, in the *Garcia* decision, the Court reversed itself again on the question, reinstituting what virtually amounts to a plenary congressional regulatory power, subject to the political restraints that the states may exercise through their influence in Congress. Even after the second swing-around, justices who were members of what had become once again the minority warned that the day was not far off when another 180-degree reversal could be expected.[12]

Meanwhile, the Court has had to deal with a set of federalism issues that represent matters of deep importance to contemporary economic and social policy. These include the states' authority to enact plant-closing laws with a major impact upon industrial-labor relations and upon the local and regional economies of the nation, the rights of the states with regard to natural resources within their boundaries, and the extent to which federal regulatory agencies' preemption powers should be read broadly or narrowly when restricting the authority of the states in vital areas of regulation.[13] Formal constitutional adjudication and academic exchanges on the matter of states' sovereignty have been extended, too, by the move toward exercise of "adequate and independent state grounds" in the state courts—that is, the reading of citizens' rights under the state constitutions in ways that can give a higher degree of protection than the U.S. Supreme Court is willing to deduce from similar language in the national Constitution. This fascinating development, to which I return later in this essay, has underlined the complexities (and also the vitality) of the jurisprudence of federalism in our constitutional order. While "federalism is dead" may have been the anthem of social science literature, and to some extent of legal scholarship, in the 1960s and 1970s,[14] federalism is today very much at the center of many important debates in law and politics.

It becomes important, therefore, to assess separation of powers and federalism along several lines of inquiry in light of their renewed significance. Three distinct but related questions should be explored. First, what were the origins of these two structural features of the original Constitution and what goals were they intended to serve? Second, a historical inquiry: How well has each of them worked in the actual course of governance over two centuries' time? And finally, in light of the other inquiries, how should one appraise the crossfire of conflicting interpretations, criticisms, and defenses of federal structure and separation of powers today? For the truly critical issue, to come full circle, is to discover how well these structural elements of the Constitution stand up today, in modern socioeconomic and political contexts, as mechanisms that serve to protect individual liberties and rights.

We begin with original intent (itself a vexed and complex concept) in relation to the Constitution's two major structural features.[15]

Separation of powers is much the easier case: It was incorporated into the original design as a matter of principle. "No concept of government," writes a leading commentator, "was so unanimously accepted by all the statesmen" prominent in the founding generation.[16] A major premise on which the framers operated—and also a main cautionary theme of George Washington's Farewell Address, after eight years' experience under the new Constitution—was that each branch of government would tend to operate with a "spirit of encroachment," which, lacking checks and balances, would end in a situation that would "consolidate the powers of all the departments in one"—posing the threat of "a real despotism."[17] As James Madison wrote, in setting forth his argument for separation of powers in the 51st *Federalist*, this structural feature of the Constitution was "admitted on all hands to be essential to the preservation of liberty." It was the device by which "ambition [would] be made to counteract ambition," in recognition of human nature. As Madison asked:

> What is government itself but the greatest of all reflections on human nature? If men were angels, no government would be necessary. . . . In framing a government which is to be administered by men over men, the great difficulty lies in this: you must first enable the government to control the governed; and in the next place oblige it to control itself. A dependence on the people is no doubt the primary control on the government; but experience has taught mankind the necessity of auxiliary precautions.[18]

The theoretical foundations of the state constitutions adopted in 1776 and afterward also reflected the accepted wisdom of the day, the notion that separation of powers was axiomatic as an "auxiliary precaution" for the protection of liberty. The framers did not conceptualize separation of powers as a static thing, however, but rather viewed it as part of the dynamic of politics in a republic. Checks and balances (that is, the *effect* of separation of powers) was what served as the defense against tyranny. Although they wished to make each branch "as independt. [*sic*] as possible,"[19] it was well recognized that the states themselves had not actually created "absolutely separate and distinct" structures.[20] In his lectures on law in 1790–91, James Wilson thus argued for the independence of each branch, its proceedings to be "free from the remotest influence, direct or indirect, of either of the other two powers."[21] He went on, however, to contend that "separation" and "independency" were not meant to indicate stasis: Government did not operate on the basis of insulated and compartmentalized departments. Rather, Wilson concluded, interdependency properly came into play once the deliberate proceedings of each branch had concluded and implementation of policy or law had commenced. The "dependency" of each branch on the other, he wrote, "consists in this, that the proceedings of each, when they come forth with action and are ready to affect the whole, *are liable to be examined and controlled* by one or both of the others. . . . Each part acts and is acted upon, supports and is supported, regulates and is regulated by the rest."[22] The same view, that a salutary tension among the branches of government would serve "to guard against corruption and tyranny . . . before they shall have gotten hold on us," was also expressed in Thomas Jefferson's *Notes on the State of Virginia.*[23] In sum, as Norman Dorsen has reminded us, this structural element of the Constitution's design "contemplated an element of inefficiency in preference to autocracy."[24]

I have said that when we seek to understand original intent, separation of powers is an easier case than federalism, because the separation concept was a matter of such widely shared belief as to desirability and effectiveness. One is hard-pressed to find in any of the Anti-Federalist tracts, or in other expressions of opposition during the ratification fight, any voice renouncing the theory of separation of powers. Strongly as the Anti-Federalists attacked the pro-Constitution position, their arguments centered on the issue of whether the Constitution's design met the specifications of true separation. They did not deny the desirability or importance of separation of powers; rather they denied that the Constitution's specific terms could be relied upon to trigger or channel effective checks and balances. Federalism was a very different matter. It became part of the Constitution's core structural design not because it was derived from a priori political concepts, the product of axioms in widely accepted political theory. Rather, federalism was an ingenious political accommodation. It was the child of political necessity.

In the course of the ratification debates, the champions of the Constitution shifted to a strongly assertive argument for the positive merits of the federal design. But at the outset—even as late as when the 51st *Federalist* was published—Madison, for one, presented a strikingly negative view of the federal division. He worried that "in exact proportion as the territory of the union may be formed into more circumscribed confederacies or states, oppressive combinations of a majority will be facilitated" and the security of individual rights would be proportionately endangered. In other words, he presented the perpetuation of the states, in the new federal design, as a source of potential danger for liberty—a danger that could be reduced by the system of checks and balances among the branches of the national government.

This view was indeed a dim one with regard to how liberties would fare within the states individually, relative to the protection that a strong national government in a larger republican union would provide. It was, of course, also at the heart of Madison's famous argument in the 10th *Federalist*, that to "extend the sphere" would control tyrannous majorities better than would dividing it into political units of more limited size and greater homogeneity. The "public good and private rights" were less likely to be secured against factions within a single state as within the larger federal union.

Thus Madison expressed the view, which unquestionably dominated the proceedings at the 1787 Convention, that the states and their sovereignty were the heart of the new nation's problems. It was precisely to correct the evils that had emerged within the states—the neglect of public good and private rights, the petty localism that had reduced the national government to the status of a "mimic sovereignty," as Hamilton termed it—that motivated the principal leaders of the Convention. Against this background of belief that the states and state sovereignty were the source of their young Republic's troubles, it is understandable that the federal design was the result of compromise, not the child of principle.

It was not long, however, after the document went forward for ratification that the Federalists encountered serious political problems, based on the charge that they were foisting upon the American people a "consolidated" government, with terrible implications for liberty.[25] Having incorporated the states into their new federal design, as constitutional entities and not merely administrative units, the champions of the Constitution moved to a more positive public stance on the matter of that design's virtues: They began to invest the proposal for a new federalism with the sound and substance of principle. In sum, a creative recognition of the day's political necessities—the need to accommodate the states—began as a brilliant act of political realism but ere long was invested with the grandeur of something closer to authentic principle.

Arguments for the Constitution's federal design became more and more elaborate (and also more positive) as the ratification debate went on. Ironically, these arguments borrowed heavily from the premises and contentions of the Anti-Federalists, who had all along been driving home the message that the states' positive virtues must be recognized and honored. By the time the first Congress met, what I term the "arguments for the states" had been formalized. They would very soon be given a stronger theoretical foundation in constitutional thought by the Jeffersonian response to the Alien and Sedition Acts. But in the hands of the Constitution's champions in 1786–87, they were values inseparably linked to expressly nationalistic premises. That is, the arguments for the states were given legitimacy in the context of the larger case for a powerful national government with authority sufficient to deal effectively with national problems and policies. This nationalistic context of the Federalists' arguments for the states should be kept firmly in mind, in light of today's debates on federalism. For it is often overlooked that some of today's neoconservative appeals for "restoring" the terms of an alleged original understanding much more resemble what the opponents of the Constitution believed than what the framers contended for.[26]

To be sure, federal design was described ambiguously in the *Federalist* essays and the ratification debates. Some (like Madison) stressed the strictness with which the national powers were enumerated, others (like Hamilton) gave much more weight to the advantages of a national government with "independent energy" and flexible authority. Whatever the differences among the framers and within the Federalist leadership, however, all shared the determination to create a strong central government. They insisted that independence had been won, at vast cost in blood and treasure, by the American people as a whole and not by independent states, and they placed the argument for the states in a nationalistic, juridical context when they championed the new constitutional design. The states were to be maintained and perpetuated as constitutional polities, not merely administrative entities, and the Constitution would assure their survival, together with significant prerogatives.[27] In that context, the founding generation elaborated and formalized the arguments for the states and for the federal design.

These arguments advanced three central values. The first was addressed to the defense of liberty—the idea, also embodied in separation of powers theory, that diffusion of power through federalism

HARRY N. SCHEIBER

would provide additional structural protection for rights and liberties.
The outlines of this positive argument for federalism and liberty were
first discernible in the Convention debates; as one delegate declared,
"the division of the Country into distinct States" would augment the
advantages of separation of powers, providing a further diffusion of
power.[28] Federalism, whether or not presented with an emphasis on
enumeration of powers as a strict limit on the national government, was
portrayed more and more as a structural barrier against the sort of
"plenary & Consolidated Govt." that the framers insisted they wished
above all to avoid.[29]

The second argument was directed toward the positive value of
preserving diversity. The unique mix of interests—or political cultures, as some would have it—that was represented in the thirteen
states would be perpetuated, and room would be left for them to
develop policy suitable to themselves under localized control. Not only
would the existing states be assured of their survival as constitutional
polities—each with its own constitution, its own legal system, and its
own policies and administration in matters not given over to uniform
national legislation and policy—but also the Union would be expanded, each new state being admitted on equal terms with the existing
ones. Federal structure in this sense was seen as a way of accommodat-
ing cultural and political diversities. As Hamilton argued, moreover,
the perpetuation of diversity would assure that localistic pressures from
the thirteen individual states—indeed, the "intrinsic difficulty of governing" with thirteen states involved as constitutional polities—would
"constantly *impose* on the national rulers the *necessity* of a spirit of
accommodation to the reasonable expectations of their constituents."[30]
After the passage of many years and the fighting of the young Republic's great ideological battles, James Madison developed a principled view of diversity in relation to liberty, within the federal design:
He praised the "combination of the federal with the local systems of
government, which multiplies the divisions of power, and the mutual
checks by which it is to be kept within its proper limits and direction."[31]

Finally, along with liberty and diversity, there was a third value
associated with the federal design in an argument for the states: efficiency. Few political ideas have so consistently been reiterated in American history as Madison's assertion that if the states were abolished, "the
general government would be compelled by the principle of self-

preservation, to reinstate them in their proper jurisdiction."[32] The federal design—what Madison himself termed "a novelty & a compound," and what Hamilton declared was "necessarily . . . a compromise of . . . dissimilar interests and inclinations"[33]—was founded in part on a pragmatic recognition of the need for effective administrative decentralization of some kind. That this decentralization was given a unique constitutional dimension, in the states as polities within a union, was what made the American experiment unique. But the manifest efficiency of leaving matters of local interest to the decision-making authority and administration of the state units was a goal that could be justified as a tenet of federalism either pragmatically or, instead, in principle. As the ratification debates wore on, the champions of the Constitution tended to argue less from the pragmatic ground and more for viewing state authority as the product of principle.

Concern with "original intent," however, cannot end with 1787 or the Bill of Rights, or indeed with antebellum America. Original intent must also embrace the values that sometimes were in conflict with federalism, if not with separation of powers. One such value, as we have noted, was the strident nationalism of many of the framers, as reflected, for example, in John Marshall's jurisprudence in the Republic's early years. Another, present at the foundation but given entirely new meaning by Abraham Lincoln, by the "logicians of Gettysburg,"[34] and by adoption of the Fourteenth Amendment in 1868, was the value of due process and equality before the law. In assessing basic constitutional precepts such as federalism, moreover, one must take account of more than the arguments advanced for federalism and the states in the founding period. There is also the whole of the constitutional tradition and the particulars of its long history, especially such transforming moments as Reconstruction or the adoption of amendments that provided for women's suffrage, a national income tax, or direct popular election of senators. I append this commonsense observation to the foregoing discussion, at the risk of belaboring the obvious, because so much of today's discussion of "original intent"—especially with regard to federalism and its values—neglects to take account of the constitutional tradition as a whole. Thus, the attorney general, Edwin Meese, recently implored the public to "take federalism seriously" by recognizing that "the Framers of the Constitution understood that the new national government would be a government of limited and enumerated powers only and that the states would retain the bulk of power and responsibility for governing society."[35] The attorney general's argument for a return to "first principles" is flawed because it denies out of hand the possibility that as a matter of constitutional revision other values may take precedence over the values of federalism—and as the product of legitimate changes in understanding how best to achieve the values of federalism, as opposed to the specific terms of the 1787 federalism bargain. It would be well for the former attorney general to take the Fourteenth Amendment seriously, and to take the whole of constitutional development seriously, as he recommends that we do for the original federalism of the framers.

Such were the values associated originally with the principle of separation of powers, and with that ingenious compromise that became a principled argument for a political accommodation, the federal element of the constitutional design. We need also to consider historic performance: How well have the structural bulwarks of liberty actually worked, over the two centuries of our national life?

The appraisal of federalism is necessarily complex. In the first place, it is important to recognize that the federal system as a working constitutional system—and not only with regard to doctrinal development, especially since adoption of the Fourteenth Amendment—has gone through several distinct stages, each one involving an increasing centralization of authority and policy-making responsibility.[36] The period before the Civil War was one in which Americans associated their loyalties and interests in very large measure with the states; they looked to state government for most (though certainly not all) of the rules and services they wanted from the public sector. Jefferson was incontestably right when he wrote in 1817 that the "spirit of our government" was "republican, but also federal."[37] Despite the strictures of the Marshall Court, the nation's governance remained highly decentralized. Indeed, as I have argued, the abstract concept of dual federalism—with its view that the states and the central government had distinctive "spheres," the two operating in a spirit of mutual tension—bore a close resemblance to the actual working of the American constitutional system down to 1860.[38] Without question, the original arguments for the states and the 1787 federal design were borne out in two respects: The decentralization of authority that prevailed did promote diversity in a great variety of policy areas and perhaps even in political culture; and, despite the effects of overlapping and some irrational effects of rivalistic mercantilism of the states, many of the desired efficiencies of decentralized administration were achieved.[39]

What was clearly not achieved, however, was the goal of mobilizing federalism as a structure of liberty to protect fundamental rights. I do not say "citizens' rights," because we need to consider the matter of slavery—the population left outside the perimeters and protective doctrines of citizenship. Viewed from that perspective, the most palpable and enduring "contribution" of federalism to American political life since the founding was its service as a structure for preserving slavery for seventy years. And then it served equally well for perpetuation of discrimination and Jim Crow for nearly another century. Whatever the values of federalism and the arguments for the states that we may, in our political discourse, still admire and advance, we need always to keep clearly in mind this darker side of the actual record of governance.

Also, the record of federalism in action was riddled with other problems of decentralized power and its consequence, which was the movement toward greater centralization and uniformity in the modern era. Among them is the problem of the "race to the bottom" that the federal structure has encouraged in matters of economic and social regulation.[40] Because the states are rivals for investment and enterprise in a system that allows special interests to shop for whatever legislative and judicial forums are favorable to them, it is difficult for any single state or group of states to adhere to high standards of regulation. A classic illustration of this problem was the regulation of child labor. Another was the "New Jersey haven," later the "Delaware haven," for corporations and trusts seeking more favorable treatment than they could find in other states, given differences in corporation and taxation law. In the twentieth century, the problems of regional and state wage differentials as the product of variations in tax levels, child labor laws, laws governing collective bargaining and union organizing, and the like, similarly highlighted one of the weaknesses of a federal system: the competitive pressure against measures that tend to be rejected if only a single state seeks to adopt them, yet would have a much better chance of public acceptance and legislative enactment if they were imposed uniformly in the whole nation.[41]

To remarkable degree, of course, the history of uniform national policies since the New Deal, in the areas of regulation, social welfare, and security, has been the history of ameliorating the effects of federal design and decentralized authority. The same may be said of modern Fourteenth Amendment jurisprudence. The civil rights and criminal justice decisions of the Supreme Court since the 1930s have put an end to blatant patterns of racial discrimination, to grievous malapportionment of legislatures (often in violation of the states' own explicit constitutional requirements), and to abuses of personal rights in the processes of arrest, confinement, and trial. All this has been accomplished by the Court at the expense of the values of federalism that Attorney General Meese recommended to the public with such enthusiasm, but in pursuit of other values that are also embedded in the Constitution and our constitutional jurisprudence.[42]

In sum, the record of American federalism, both before and after the Fourteenth Amendment, is a strong one in regard to promoting diversity; it is mixed, but certainly not without merit, on the matter of efficiency; and it fails tragically as a bulwark of liberty. This record has its ironies, as today it is the admirers of Warren Court jurisprudence, unhappy with the more conservative doctrines of the Burger and Rehnquist years, who are promoting the expansion of liberties and rights under terms of the state constitutions—who are promoting, in the technical phrase, the doctrine of adequate and independent state grounds. Justice William Brennan, Jr., and others have contended that in the states' bills of rights one finds a second line of defense for liberty, what many of the framers would have contended was the first line of defense, augmented by the federal document.[43] However that may be—and whatever the achievements of those who have endorsed the approach to expanding rights on state grounds—the historical record of federalism as a structural protection for liberty gives little comfort to a public admonished to restore the "original understanding" in federal-state relations.

With regard to separation of powers, the historical record is manifestly different. It is difficult to discern how respect for the doctrine has at any time in American history militated against the objective of diffusing power and thus protecting liberty—except insofar as one credits the argument that strong presidential discretion is justified and necessary in wartime (or, as some argue, in any diplomatic or intelligence matters in the context of cold war or other international tension). And on the record, it is difficult to quarrel with the proposition that when one branch of government or another heedlessly crosses the boundaries of its legitimate authority, it seriously endangers liberty. Neither the temporary suspension of constitutional guarantees by Lincoln in the Civil War years nor, certainly, the internment of the Japanese in World War II seems in retrospect to have been justified; both did serious damage, not only to the rights and interests of individuals but also to the spirit of tolerance in the society at large. The Watergate and Iran-Contra scandals bear all the marks of the classic abuses of power that the framers most clearly discerned as potential dangers and most explicitly warned against.

In sorting out the historical record on abuses of the line of separation, it seems manifest that restraints that were self-imposed or pressed from without, as a matter of constitutional principle, did serve the interests of liberty and accountability of government. The charges of imperial presidency have to be weighed against the magnitude and meaning of similar charges aimed at the federal judiciary and its alleged "activism" since the 1930s. The greatest danger to liberty does not seem to me to come from Supreme Court activism, either of the left or of the right; such decisions, though they may come down hard on particular interests or individuals in the instance, can be reversed through legislation or constitutional amendment. Nor does it come from Congress, checked by the judiciary, as well as by the presidential veto, and subject to the electoral process in any event. The greatest danger comes from executive power wielded without outside constraints. For it is in precisely the areas for which advocates of untrammeled executive power make their most compelling claims that the most damage can be done in the shortest time—damage that may easily be irreversible, may violate the most deeply held convictions of the public as to the wisdom and morality of given policies, and may affect profoundly the interests and welfare of the citizenry at large. And again, as we have learned by such episodes as Watergate and the Iran-Contra machinations of the insiders who wielded unchecked power, not only the funds and the policies of the Republic but also the probity of its most essential political processes—its republicanism—is often threatened. In light of these lessons, it is ironic that the Supreme Court has restricted one of the most benign and inventive possible instruments for maintenance of a check on the executive, the congressional veto, while failing to find in its reservoir of constitutional authority the grounds for curbing a significant range of executive claims to exclusive and unchecked authority.[44]

In closing this essay, I want to take one further look at the ironies and problems of contemporary federalism—a more complex issue, in my own view, than the issue of separation of powers that stems in so straight a line of development from principled beginnings. Nothing in the lexicon of American constitutional doctrine is more difficult to define precisely, or continues to be so productive of confusion in our political dialogue, as the phrases "states' rights" and "principles of federalism." Disagreement over the proper relationship of national to state government has vexed our politics since the founding.

What makes the issue particularly troublesome is each side's temporizing and faithlessness to real principle. The champions of decentralization and greater regard for state sovereignty, no less than the generally liberal proponents of a strong national authority, do not wait long to jettison principles of federalism doctrine when those principles conflict with cherished policy aims.

It has always been so. Thus in the 1850s the abolitionists became powerful advocates of states' rights—specifically, the right of state governments to refuse cooperation, or actively interfere with, enforcement of the national fugitive slave law. It was the Southern slave interests who were the strong nationalists on that issue, despite the fact that they wrote the book on states' rights.[45] Similarly, the advocates of segregation and discrimination after the Civil War were enthusiasts for judicial activism so long as it worked in their favor; they became critics of the Supreme Court only when the majority restored a view of the Fourteenth Amendment that upheld the rights of racial minorities to equal protection.

Similarly, in our own day, the Reagan administration put federalism back on the front pages as a leading political issue by arguing for a return of power to the states. Yet the Reagan-Meese view has not prevented the administration from attacking state sovereignty and decision-making authority in the regulatory area.[46] Despite its criticism of the Supreme Court's "activism" in applying the Fourteenth Amendment on other counts, the Reagan administration welcomes the Court-imposed restraints on state powers to regulate zoning and land use.[47] The New Federalists are also among those who call for a strong federal presence in such matters as Baby Doe and right-to-die decisions.

Similarly, abundant political and legal activity has been generated by liberal advocates of states' rights. Many who favor strong civil rights and civil liberties doctrines today contend that it is legitimate for state courts to exercise independent and separate authority in such matters. Predictably, on these issues it is conservatives who are the nationalists, deploring the lack of national uniformity of law that results from state court activism and urging the superior claims of the federal judiciary.[48] Environmentalists, who made historic advances in the 1960s and 1970s in expanding the federal judicial and legislative roles in resources protection, now demand a broad construction of legislation that gives the states control over the offshore, forest, water, and mineral resources that a business-oriented national administration wants to exploit aggressively. Hence we are constantly reminded of the notorious smoke-screen effect of federalism: It can camouflage the real agenda in virtually any legal or political confrontation.

And yet, across the whole spectrum of American politics the question of what role the state should properly play in our system is still respected. Despite the centralization that has occurred since the New Deal, we still do not have a unitary government in the United States. Significant, and not merely trivial, areas of authority remain largely under control of the states. And whether or not one agrees that the structural elements of the system—such as representation in the Senate and House and the electoral college—protect states' interests well enough to preclude the Supreme Court's having to play umpire in federalism disputes,[49] it is evident that the states continue to exercise considerable influence on the course of national affairs. Still, we continue to be vexed by the absence of a constitutionally drawn and unambiguous boundary between state and national power, of a clearly defined area, on one side of that boundary, where the states must be left alone.

As Woodrow Wilson wrote more than seventy years ago, the definition of that boundary is a question that each generation in the United States faces anew, on terms reflecting the society and the problems of its own day. As we continue to consider how best to draw or redraw that line, it is important that we retain the fundamental values of the federal design, and not the specific boundaries it inscribed for a society so vastly different from ours, two centuries ago. But whether separation of powers, still an axiom and a cherished principle of our constitutional design, ought to be treated with the same degree of flexibility is in my view quite a different question. Born as a principle, and not manufactured, it stands as a concept justifying a stricter orthodoxy and a more absolutist defense in the law.

Notes

1. Hamilton, in *The Federalist*, ed. Jacob E. Cooke (Middletown, Conn.: Wesleyan University Press, 1961), no. 17. All further references to *The Federalist* are to this edition.

2. Hamilton, *The Federalist*, no. 84.

3. Madison to John Adams, May 22, 1817, reprinted in Philip B. Kurland and Ralph Lerner, eds., *The Founders' Constitution* (Chicago: University of Chicago Press, 1987), 1:335. This vision, which was also reflected in Madison's *Federalist* essays during the ratification period (esp. nos. 47 and 51), rested, in the last analysis, not on blind faith in the people's capacity for self-government and a tolerant protection of the rights of minorities but on the hope that republican spirit—"the force of opinion and habit" of a free people—would be reinforced and given full play by the proper institutional structure. I have discussed this point more elaborately in "Federalism and the Constitution: The Original Understanding," in *American Law and the Constitutional Order*, ed. Laurence M. Friedman and Harry N. Scheiber (Cambridge: Harvard University Press, 1978), 96–98. See also George Carey, "Federalism: Historic Questions and Contemporary Meanings—A Defense of Political Processes," in *Federalism: Infinite Variety in Theory and Practice*, ed. Valerie Earle (Itasca, Ill.: F. B. Peacock, 1968), 42–61.

4. On the original understanding of federalism, see references cited in n. 3 above; on separation of powers, see also Edward H. Levi, "Some Aspects of Separation of Powers," *Columbia Law Review* 76 (1976): 371–91; Norman Dorsen, "Separation of Powers and Federalism—Two Doctrines with a Single Goal: Confirming Arbitrary Authority," in *American Law: The Third Century—The Law Bicentennial Volume*, ed. Bernard Schwartz (New York: Fred B. Rothman for the New York University School of Law, 1976), 25–44; and Gerhard Casper, "The Constitutional Organization of the Government," *William and Mary Law Review* 26 (1985): 177. The earlier developments were traced by Malcolm P. Sharp, "The Classical American Doctrine of 'The Separation of Powers,'" *University of Chicago Law Review* 2 (1935): 385.

5. Dorsen, "Separation of Powers and Federalism."

6. *The Federalist*, no. 15.

7. See, e.g., the arguments in Theodore J. Lowi and Alan Stone, eds., *Nationalizing Government: Public Policies in America* (Beverly Hills: Sage

Publications, 1978). Still valuable as a discussion of the arguments for federalism and against the juridical and political trends toward centralization is Gottfried Dietze, The Federalist: *A Classic on Federalism and Free Government* (Baltimore: Johns Hopkins University Press, 1960).

8. See the discussion of Reagan-era federalism by Daniel Elazar, "Forces Shaping the Federal System Today," in *Emerging Issues in American Federalism* (Washington, D.C.: U.S. Advisory Commission on Intergovernmental Relations, [1985]), 13–26. Professor Elazar is sympathetic with the expressed values associated with much of the Reagan-era New Federalism, and even some of the arguments for "original intent" jurisprudence (at least as seen through a neoconservative lens), but he is also robustly critical of some of the specific policies of the Reagan administration—both policies consistent with a view of federalism that wants to expand the states' role and policies manifestly in conflict with that goal. For a more skeptical view of the Reagan administration federalism initiatives, see, in the same volume, Scheiber, "Some Realism about Federalism," 41–64.

9. See, for example, the essays in Robert A. Goldwin and Art Kaufman, eds., *Separation of Powers—Does It Still Work?* (Washington, D.C.: American Enterprise Institute for Public Policy Research, 1986).

10. Lloyd N. Cutler, "To Form a Government," in *Separation of Powers,* ed. Goldwin and Kaufman, 1–17 (reprinted from *Foreign Affairs,* Fall 1980); James L. Sundquist, *Constitutional Reform and Effective Government* (Washington, D.C.: Brookings Institution, 1986); James MacGregor Burns, *The Deadlock of Democracy: Four-Party Politics in America* (Englewood Cliffs, N.J.: Prentice Hall, 1963).

11. See essays in *Separation of Powers,* ed. Goldwin and Kaufman, and the now-voluminous writings that make up the neoconservative critique of "judicial activism" (at least, liberal judicial activism), e.g., the Federalist Society pamphlet of reprinted essays and speeches by Justices Brennan and Stevens, Judge Bork, President Reagan, and Attorney General Meese, *The Great Debate: Interpreting Our Written Constitution* (Washington, D.C.: The Federalist Society, 1986).

12. *National League of Cities v. Usery,* 426 U.S. 833 (1976); *Garcia v. San Antonio Metro. Transit Authority,* 469 U.S. 528, 552 (1985), declaring that "state sovereign interests . . . are more properly protected by procedural safeguards inherent in the structure of the federal system than by judicially created limitations on federal power."

For analyses (with sharply divergent conclusions) of the *Garcia* decision and its implications, see A. E. Dick Howard, "*Garcia:* Federalism's Principles Forgotten," *Intergovernmental Perspective* (U.S. Advisory Commission on Intergovernmental Relations publication, Spring/Summer 1985), 12–14; and Jesse H. Choper, "Federalism and the Constitution, Before and After

HARRY N. SCHEIBER

Usery and *Garcia*," in *Perspectives on Federalism: Papers from the First Annual Berkeley Seminar on Federalism*, ed. Harry N. Scheiber (Berkeley: Institute of Governmental Studies, University of California, 1987), 13–24.

13. See discussion of the modern preemption questions in Susan Bartlett Foote, "Regulatory Vacuums: Federalism, Deregulation, and Judicial Review," *U.C. Davis Law Review* 19 (1985): 113–52.

14. For discussion of the "federalism is dead" argument and new concerns, see, e.g., Harry N. Scheiber, "Federalism and Legal Process: Historical and Contemporary Analysis of the American System," *Law and Society Review* 14 (1980): 663–721.

15. I do not seek to deal systematically here with the intricacies of the complex current-day debate of original intent, many aspects of which are discussed in other essays in this symposium. Apart from methodological issues, which I touch on only briefly, below, as needed to deal with some specific issues of federalism and separation, I have already written on original intention and federalism as a substantive issue in historical interpretation ("Federalism and the Constitution," *American Law and the Constitutional Order*). See Russell K. Osgood, "Governmental Functions and Constitutional Doctrine: The Historical Constitution," *Cornell Law Review* 72 (1987): 553–98.

16. Arthur T. Vanderbilt, *The Doctrine of the Separation of Powers and Its Present-Day Significance* (Lincoln: University of Nebraska Press, 1953), 4.

17. *Writings of George Washington*, ed. W. C. Ford (New York: 1892), 13:277, 306.

18. *The Federalist*, no. 51.

19. In Max Farrand, ed., *The Records of the Federal Convention of 1787* (1911; reprint, New Haven: Yale University Press, 1966), 1:86.

20. Madison, *The Federalist*, no. 47.

21. James Wilson, quoted in Sharp, "The Classical American Doctrine of 'The Separation of Powers,'" 415, n. 59. Even Montesquieu, from whom the framers departed on some major issues, especially the role and the relative importance of the judiciary, was in accord on this point because, as he was quoted in *The Federalist*, no. 47, "there can be no liberty where the legislative and executive powers are united" did not mean, for him, that "these departments ought to have no *partial agency* in, or no *control* over, the acts of each other."

22. James Wilson, quoted in Sharp, "The Classical American Doctrine of 'The Separation of Powers,'" 415, n. 59. See also Dorsen, "Separation of Powers and Federalism," 37.

23. *Notes on the State of Virginia* (1784), in Kurland and Lerner, *Founders' Constitution*, 1:318.

24. Dorsen, "Separation of Powers and Federalism," 35.

25. See Robert Rutland, *The Birth of the Bill of Rights* (Chapel Hill: University of North Carolina Press, 1955).

26. See Herbert J. Storing, *What the Anti-Federalists Were For: The Political Thought of the Opponents of the Constitution* (Chicago: University of Chicago Press, 1981). Also, on the framers' emphasis that the rhetoric of the enumerated powers concerned "objects" of policy and not only allowable means, essential background to understanding the breadth of the "necessary and proper" concept, see discussion in David F. Epstein, *The Political Theory of* The Federalist (Chicago: University of Chicago Press, 1984), 2.

27. See Alpheus T. Mason, *"The Federalist*—A Split Personality," *American Historical Review* 57 (1952): 625–43.

28. John Dickensen, in Farrand, *Records*, 1:86.

29. Madison, in Farrand, *Records*, 3:517.

30. *The Federalist*, no. 85.

31. Madison to John Adams, May 22, 1817, in Kurland and Lerner, *Founders' Constitution*, 1:335. His principled view was foreshadowed, of course, by the Virginia Resolves against the Alien and Sedition Acts, the product of Madison's own hand, and developed in the "strict constructionist" moments of his presidency.

32. *The Federalist*, no. 14.

33. Madison in Farrand, *Records*, 3:517; Hamilton, in *The Federalist*, no. 85.

34. The phrase is Charles Black's, quoted in William A. Fletcher, "The Discretionary Constitution: Institutional Remedies and Judicial Legitimacy," *Yale Law Journal* 91 (1982): 696.

35. Edwin Meese III, "Taking Federalism Seriously," *Intergovernmental Perspective*, Winter 1987, 8–10. This article relies heavily upon, and endorses, the Report of the Working Group on Federalism, White House Domestic Policy Council, *The Status of Federalism in America* (November 1986), a document notable for its grievous neglect or ignorance of a vast scholarly literature on federalism—all of that literature "taking federalism seriously" and much of it addressing precisely the issues raised in the White House study, which unfortunately presents a single-dimensional approach impoverished intellectually by its lack of concern to analyze alternative perspectives on the modern-day centralization of power in American governance.

36. I have made the case for this view in "Federalism," in *Encyclopedia of the American Constitution*, ed. Leonard W. Levy, Kenneth L. Karst, and Dennis J. Mahoney (New York: Macmillan, 1986), 2:697–704; and, earlier, in a fuller discussion in "American Federalism and the Diffusion of Power," *University of Toledo Law Review* 9 (1978): 619–74.

37. Letter of Jefferson to Spencer Roane, 1817, in Boalt Hall Library Manuscripts Collection, University of California, Berkeley, School of Law.

38. See works cited in n. 36 above.

39. I am not making the argument that the division of administrative or policy-making responsibility was rational on all counts, nor that efficiency was in any sense optimal or even reasonably acceptable in many areas of governance. But the general objective of having such matters as education, criminal justice, property law, commercial law, and the like left to localized authority was certainly achieved, as I see it, without an unacceptable loss of efficiency. The standard of reasonableness is obviously a subjective one, and there is abundant evidence in the literature of legal history that less than optimal standards in some areas deteriorated badly enough to warrant the characterization "drift and default." See, for example, Willard Hurst, *Law and Economic Growth: The Legal History of the Lumber Industry in Wisconsin, 1860–1915* (Cambridge: Belknap Press of Harvard University Press, 1964).

40. William Cary, "Federalism and Corporate Law: Reflections upon Delaware," *Yale Law Journal* 83 (1974): 663.

41. Harry N. Scheiber, "Federalism and the American Economic Order, 1789–1910," *Law and Society Review* 10 (1975): 72–100; Scheiber, "State Law and 'Industrial Policy' in American Development, 1790–1987," *California Law Review* 75 (1987): 415–44.

42. See A. E. Dick Howard, "Federalism in the Courts," in *Emerging Issues in American Federalism*, 27–39; and Archibald Cox, *The Court and the Constitution* (Boston: Houghton Mifflin, 1987), 177–321.

43. William J. Brennan, Jr., "State Constitutions and the Protection of Individual Rights," *Harvard Law Review* 90 (1977): 489–504; A. E. Dick Howard, "State Courts and Constitutional Rights in the Day of the Burger Court," *Virginia Law Review* 62 (1976): 873–944.

44. *Immigration and Naturalization Service v. Chadha*, 462 U.S. 919 (1983), is the landmark case overturning the legislative veto; *Bowsher v. Synar*, 478 U.S. 714 (1986), overturned the delegation to the Controller General of congressional control of expenditures. See *"Bowsher v. Synar,"* *Cornell Law Review* 72 (1987): 421–597. The War Powers Act of 1973 is the focus of political controversy but as yet no definitive Supreme Court rulings. See Cox, *The Court and the Constitution*, 346–47.

45. Arthur Bestor, "The American Civil War as a Constitutional Crisis," *American Historical Review* 69 (1964): 327–52.

46. Susan Bartlett Foote, "Administrative Preemption: An Experiment in Regulatory Federalism," *Virginia Law Review* 70 (1984): 1429; Martha Derthick and Paul Quirk, *The Politics of Deregulation* (Washington, D.C.: Brookings Institution, 1985).

47. Reference here is to the 1987 cases concerning California regulations of shoreline development permits and concerning the definition as a taking of a full mandated halt on development of an inland property. *First*

English Evangelical Lutheran Church v. County of Los Angeles, 107 S. Ct. 2378 (1987), *Nollan v. California Coastal Commission,* 483 U.S. 825 (1987).

48. See the symposium issue devoted to "The Emergence of State Constitutional Law," *Texas Law Review* 63 (1985): 959–1375.

49. The view implied in the landmark analysis by Herbert Wechsler, "The Political Safeguards of Federalism: The Role of the States in the Composition and Selection of the National Government," *Columbia Law Review* 54 (1954): 543, was developed as a proposal for doctrinal application by Jesse H. Choper, *Judicial Review and the National Political Process: A Functional Reconsideration of the Role of the Supreme Court* (Chicago: University of Chicago Press, 1980), and applied by the Court's majority in the *Garcia* case, 469 U.S. 528 (1985).

CHAPTER 13

Federal Judicial Power
and the "Consent"
of the Governed

·····

LAURENCE H. TRIBE

The Reagan administration, speaking through Attorney General Edwin Meese, occasionally defended an active role for the federal judiciary. It did so in its crusade against affirmative action for women and minorities, and it did so in its attacks on congressional legislation that would have restricted executive prerogatives. More often, however, that administration sought to attack an active federal judicial role. It urged that "liberal" Supreme Court decisions need not be respected: After all, it is "the Constitution," and not "constitutional law" as developed by the Supreme Court, that merits obedience. And the administration insisted that only judges committed to undoing the results of such liberalism should be appointed to the federal bench. To support these views, the administration painted a simple and sometimes appealing picture of how federal courts ought to behave. In that picture, the central feature is deference to majority rule and insistence on the consent of the governed—a deference and an insistence that leave only the most limited room for constitutional review of government action by the independent federal judiciary described in Article III of the Constitution.

Thus Attorney General Meese proclaimed the sanctity of the original Constitution of 1787, its meaning largely fixed for him by a supposed "jurisprudence of original intent." According to that jurisprudence, the more liberal decisions of the Warren era and the Burger era—and, at times, the Hughes era and even the Marshall era—are said to represent illicit lawmaking rather than legitimate interpretation. The 1787 Constitution, according to Meese, expressed the people's consent to judicial intervention in defense of certain specified rights and no others, despite the Ninth Amendment. The rights that Meese's Constitution empowers courts to protect from the masses are largely those of the propertied classes—rights that Reagan judicial nominees like San Diego professor Bernard Siegan are committed to defend, even if it means invalidating the New Deal and more.

But the reference to the "consent" of the governed is as manipulable and problematic as it is seductive. Consider how the Supreme Court relied on the Constitution's protections of "property" and of "contract" both before the Civil War, in the infamous *Dred Scott*[1] decision of 1857, and during the *Lochner*[2] era from the 1890s until 1937, when the Court read the Civil War amendments to bar social welfare legislation. Could these protections of property be defended as legitimate by simply telling the Court's critics that "We the People" had enshrined possessive individualism and rights of economic exploitation in our founding document? Hardly. The whole point that the critics sought to make was that "We the People" had done no such thing. They argued that the Court's holdings to the contrary were grounded not in sound constitutional interpretation but in sheer force and will. Yet, all the while, the defenders of the Supreme Court's property-protecting role of course insisted that theirs was the correct understanding of what the people's original consent encompassed. And academics of the law and economics persuasion, including, most prominently, Chicago's Richard Epstein, echo that view of the original consent even today.

Or consider the Supreme Court's still controversial 1973 abortion ruling in *Roe v. Wade*.[3] The Court in *Roe* interpreted the word "liberty," as it appears in both the Fifth Amendment and the Fourteenth Amendment, to include a woman's freedom to end a pregnancy she either never wanted or initially desired but no longer wants. The decision's critics insist that "We the People" never intended, when ratifying those amendments, to adopt principles of privacy—or, for that matter, of equality—powerful enough to override the claims of the unborn or strong enough to displace the power of local majorities to ban abortion. These critics, too, certainly cannot be silenced by asserting that the relevant majorities—those who ratified the Fifth and the

Fourteenth amendments—have already spoken, whatever today's local or state majorities might say.

Thus, for anyone who believes (as I do) that *Dred Scott* and *Lochner* were wrong, and that *Roe v. Wade*—like *Brown v. Board of Education*,[4] even if less clearly so—was right, pointing to the "consent" supposedly embodied in the document's ambiguous text simply cannot suffice. Exactly what was "consented" to is the very question.

But this argument about consent proves a great deal less than some suppose. For we must recognize that the *opposite* conclusions in these contested cases would be no *more* capable of being defended in terms of a supposed constitutional consent. No one ever consented, after all, to be governed by local or state majorities in all cases where the Constitution is arguably ambiguous; and what is ambiguous to some readers will seem clear as day to others.

Surely slaves did not consent to a constitutional scheme under which they could be bought and sold as property in any state that chose to regard them so. Neither did the working and unpropertied classes consent to the particular notions of property and contract that courts enforced when state and federal laws protective of laborers were struck down by the dozens in the maximum-hours and child-labor decisions, such as *Lochner v. New York* and *Hammer v. Dagenhart*.[5] Nor did black children or their parents consent to a sterile notion of "equal protection" under which racial apartheid, decreed by law, would be deemed tolerable as long as facilities for blacks and whites display formal equality. And *neither women nor the unborn* may fairly be deemed to have consented to a regime under which the fates of both would be disposed of by local majorities.

The truth, in my view, is that consent is an ultimately illusory source of legitimacy for the enterprise of constitutional interpretation. Whether the interpretation under discussion is that of unelected judges or that of elected officeholders, the legitimacy of an interpretation must depend on something beyond the always-circular claims of consent. Those claims necessarily raise the double question of whose consent *counts* and what the consent *encompassed*. The legitimacy of an interpretation must instead depend on the *function* that the interpretive enterprise as a whole plays in the evolving process of challenging and defending power in constitutional terms.

It is this function that Justice Thurgood Marshall seemed to have overlooked, in an address delivered in May 1987, when he decried the original Constitution as defective and denounced its framers as more bigoted than visionary. He stressed the founding generation's willingness to preserve and protect slavery while professing to believe in freedom and equality. Only the Civil War, Justice Marshall observed, ended that obscenity. For him, although "the Union survived [that] war, the Constitution did not."

I doubt that Thurgood Marshall meant to agree with Edwin Meese, but in a sense Justice Marshall, like Attorney General Meese, was focusing on consent. For the justice, however, "the People" who were the "We" in the 1787 Preamble illegitimately excluded blacks, women, and those without wealth or property. But just as Meese's reliance on consent provides no adequate defense for his conservative Constitution and the role it would assign to federal courts, so Justice Marshall's complaints about those who were left *out* of the "original consent" provide no decisive support for his liberal Constitution and the quite different role it would assign the federal judiciary. For without the entire Constitution of which the Civil War amendments became a part—and, in particular, without the elaborate eighteenth-century scheme of separated and divided powers—the enterprise of judicial review would have no foundation; there would be no grounding whatever for the action of federal judges in resisting today's majorities in the name of yesterday's articulation of rights and tomorrow's vision of what those rights should mean.

It is true, and it is shameful, that it took the Supreme Court nearly a century to begin giving the Civil War amendments anything like the force their text and history demanded. But the institution of judicial review through which those amendments were vindicated was put in place under the 1787 Constitution as construed by the Supreme Court over which John Marshall presided. When the Supreme Court finally started to give the Civil War amendments their due in the mid-twentieth century, it sometimes built on congressional enforcement efforts—made possible, as often as not, under the commerce power traceable to 1787. The Supreme Court sometimes moved well ahead of the other branches. Always it spoke in a voice continuous with that of chief justices like John Marshall and Charles Evans Hughes, building on structural arrangements and understandings that long preceded the Civil War.

Neither consent, then, nor gaps in consent can justify either the version of judicial review sponsored by the right or the version sponsored by the left. As we all know, the Constitution's text is silent on the role that federal courts are to play in giving life to the document over time. So, too, the assumptions of the framers and ratifiers—as evidenced most prominently by the *Federalist* papers in the late 1780s and by the congressional and state legislative debates of the 1860s and 1870s—leave unresolved the proper reach and the ultimate limits of the federal judicial function. What gives legitimacy to an active version of that function, in the end, must be the value of the role it plays in constitutional democracy, not the notion that any particular group "consented" to one or another version of that role.

The role of judicial review, our history makes clear, has been one of calling our traditional and emergent political practices to account in terms of ideals expressed in constitutional language. When the challenge to emerging practices has been ill-conceived, as was *Dred Scott*'s challenge to the Missouri Compromise, violent upheaval has at times been needed to set us back on course. But a judicial challenge cannot be dismissed as illegitimate simply because, in hindsight, the challenge is rebuffed. The *Lochner* Court's challenge to the social welfare state reflected a genuine, and not a fabricated, tension between the more conservative strands of the 1787 Constitution and governmental activism in regulating the economy and in rectifying maldistributions of wealth. So too the Court's *Roe v. Wade* challenge to the entrenched legal tradition that linked female biology to social destiny reflects a profound, and not an artificial, tension between long-standing rules governing sexuality and reproduction and the deepest premises of liberty and equality that many of us see as protected by the Civil War amendments. It is too early to say how history will ultimately evaluate that challenge. But what counts most in assessing judicial review is not which challenges succeed and which fail. What counts most is how the judiciary, *in making such challenges possible,* compels our political discourse to address issues of power in the language of constitutional principle, a language that connects our past to our aspirations as a people.

It is often remarked, quite correctly, that the other branches, too, are sworn to uphold the Constitution. But courts have a unique capacity and commitment to engage in open discourse—to explain and justify their conclusions about governmental authority in a dialogue with those who read the same Constitution even if they reach a different view.

That is a commitment that only a dialogue-engaging institution, insulated from day-to-day political accountability but correspondingly burdened with oversight by professional peers and disinterested lay critics, can be expected to maintain. The enemies of this commitment are those, both on the constitutional left and on the constitutional right, whose principal mode of argument consists in self-righteous appeals to ideas *beyond* argument, whether expressed as principles of fairness to minorities or as certitudes about original intent, whether derived from modern sensibility or from ancient tradition.

If judicial review is defensible because it supports the thread of language by which we test our practices against the Constitution's principles, then the sine qua non of judicial review must be a humility that renounces both Attorney General Meese's pretense that judges are simply the oracles of an infallible past and Justice Marshall's rejoinder that judges must become crusaders committed to a brave new future. The truth, alas, is far more complex than is dreamed of in either philosophy.

Notes

1. *Dred Scott v. Sandford*, 60 U.S. (19 How.) 393 (1857).
2. *Lochner v. New York*, 198 U.S. 45 (1905).
3. *Roe v. Wade*, 410 U.S. 113 (1973).
4. *Brown v. Board of Education*, 347 U.S. 483 (1954).
5. *Hammer v. Dagenhart*, 247 U.S. 251 (1918).

CHAPTER 14

The Founders on Families

•••••

SYLVIA A. LAW

As we celebrate two hundred years of history under our Constitution, some of the most heated interpretative controversies arising from that grand document involve conflicting versions of the family, gender, and sexuality.[1] Many influential lawyers, scholars, judges, and public officials would have us look to the "original intent" of the men who drafted and ratified the Constitution to determine its contemporary meaning.[2] My contention is that original intent fails to provide answers to today's problems, for two reasons. First, the people who crafted our Constitution themselves held conflicting ideas and values about families and the role of women in society. Second, and perhaps more important, the founders' dominant conceptions of families denied the liberty, equality, and even personhood of women. It hardly needs to be said that there exists today a wide consensus, spanning a broad political and moral spectrum, that as complete human beings, women are entitled to the full panoply of classic liberal rights that our Revolution and Constitution sought to secure for white men. The challenge today is to envision constitutional and cultural arrangements that read the words "We the People" literally and inclusively, even though that reading is not what was originally intended.

The discussion that follows is divided into three sections. The first recounts the prevailing views on women and families held by the original drafters of our Constitution. The second tells of the way in which events of the Revolutionary period refocused questions of liberty and equality. The third comments on the meaning of this history for contemporary constitutional interpretation. Each considers information from constitutional debates; the intellectual, moral, and philosophical concepts that influenced those debates; the ordinary legal context that defined formal rights and relationships; and the living context in which these political and intellectual debates were rooted. Our Constitution is, after all, a popular document reflecting the aspirations and prejudices of ordinary people, as well as the ideas of those elite white men who are conventionally credited with its parentage.

The Dominant Vision of Families and the Constitution in the Eighteenth Century

Searching for the wisdom of the founders on women and families, we are met with an almost total, and for that a very telling, silence. I have scrutinized the constitutional text, the *Federalist* papers, the historic national debates that produced the Constitution, and the ratifying debates throughout the individual colonies. Virtually nothing in the original constitutional debates directly addresses the situation of women and families or illuminates the difficult issues that we confront today. In the *Federalist* papers, for example, the only reference to women or families is a brief allegorical discussion of the dangers that the private intrigues of courtesans and mistresses pose to the safety of the state.[3]

We do, however, find these issues discussed in the private correspondence of John and Abigail Adams.[4] On March 31, 1776, on the eve of Independence, John Adams was serving in the Continental Congress in New York, while Abigail Adams—in the midst of insecurity, war, and epidemic—managed their farm, family, and household in Braintree, Massachusetts. She wrote:

> I long to hear that you have declared an independency—and by the way in the new Code of Laws which I suppose it will be necessary for you to make I desire you would Remember the Ladies, and be more generous and favourable to them than your ancestors. Do not put such unlimited powers into the hands of the Husbands. Remember all Men would be tyrants if they could. If particular care and attention is not paid to the Ladies we are determined to foment a Re-

bellion, and will not hold ourselves bound by any Laws in which we have no voice, or Representation.

That your Sex are Naturally Tyrannical is a Truth so thoroughly established as to admit of no dispute, but such of you as wish to be happy willingly give up the harsh title of Master for the more tender and endearing one of Friend. Why then, not put it out of the power of the vicious and the Lawless to use us with cruelty and indignity with impunity. Men of Sense in all Ages abhor those customs which treat us only as the vassals of your Sex. Regard us then as Beings placed by providence under your protection and in immitation [*sic*] of the Supreem [*sic*] Being make use of that power only for our happiness.[5]

John Adams's response made two things plain: He did not take her modest request seriously, and he saw any alternative to the traditional relations between men and women as a threat to the social order he knew.

As to your extraordinary Code of Laws, I cannot but laugh. We have been told that our Struggle has loosened the bonds of Government every where. That Children and Apprentices were disobedient— that schools and Colleges were grown turbulent—that Indians slighted their Guardians and Negroes grew insolent to the Masters. But your Letter was the first Intimation that another Tribe more numerous and powerful than all the rest were grown discontented.— This is rather too coarse a Compliment but you are so saucy, I wont blot it out. Depend upon it, We know better than to repeal our Masculine systems. Altho they are in full Force, you know they are little more than Theory. We dare not exert our Power in its full Latitude. We are obliged to go fair, and softly, and in Practice you know We are the subjects. We have only the Name of Masters, and rather than give up this, which would completely subject Us to the Despotism of the Peticoat, I hope General Washington, and all our brave Heroes would fight. I am sure every good Politician would plot, as long as he would against Despotism, Empire, Monarchy, Aristocracy, Oligarchy, or Ochlocracy.[6]

John Adams's confident belief that "our Masculine systems" would long endure reflected the intellectual tradition of his time. Many of the men who crafted the fundamental structures of our democracy drew upon the work of the classical and more contemporary philosophers, as well as their own experience, in creating the new American Republic.[7] For political philosophers from Plato and Aristotle to Rousseau and Locke, the function of the family and the nature of women were matters of important concern. Possibly excepting the Plato of the *Republic*, all of these philosophers assumed the necessity of the male-headed nuclear family and women's subservient role in it.[8]

In Enlightenment political theory, the male-headed family—not the individual—was the basic unit of political interaction. In the political sphere, for example, John Locke challenged absolute patriarchal rule and virtual representation of ordinary people by the elite.[9] Yet, at the same time, he thought it natural and inevitable that men dominate in the home and represent the family in politics. Where "the things of their common Interest and Property" are concerned, Locke argued, since the husband and wife may disagree, "the Rule . . . naturally falls to the Man's share, as the abler and the stronger."[10]

Our Constitution's founders also relied more directly on the contemporary political writings of the English commonwealth and radical Whig opposition. Historian Carl Degler summarizes their ideology: "Women were not then thought of as anything other than supportive assistants—necessary to be sure, but not individuals in their own right. The individual as a conception in western thought has always assumed that behind each man—that is, each individual—was a family. But the members of that family were not individuals, except the man, who was by law and custom its head."[11] This is no trivial matter. The consequence of the founders' belief is not just that women were unfairly excluded from public life. Women were assigned, on the basis of status, to perform the essential work of production, reproduction, maintenance, and acculturation in the home. Home and family— which constitute the core social unit upon which our constitutional, political, and economic arrangements are built—are constructed on the premise that women are not active citizens who are free to pursue the full range of common occupations and callings.

The ordinary law that governed the lives of our Constitution's framers assumed, along with the philosophers and political theorists, that the patriarchal family was natural and socially vital. As the American edition of Blackstone's *Commentaries* explained, when a woman married, her legal identity merged into her husband's; she was dead under civil law. She could not sue, be sued, enter into contracts, make wills, keep her own earnings, or control her own property. Her husband had the right to chastise her, restrain her freedom, and force her to engage in sexual intercourse against her will. [12] Close examination of the property rights of American women, both before and after the Revolution, reveals "above all else a picture of their enforced dependence." [13]

Because in American political theory, claims to political rights were premised on Locke's notion that only those who actually owned a stake in the community had a voice in its affairs, the married woman whose control over her property had passed by marriage to her husband had also conceded her political voice. [14] By this logic, unmarried adult women who owned property should have been allowed to vote. Yet, while unmarried women could protect their property, they were not permitted to exercise the political rights that theoretically accompanied those economic interests.

Formal legal rules do not necessarily describe ordinary daily life. While there are serious limits on our ability to understand the texture of ordinary life in the eighteenth century, it does seem clear that the families our founders knew were profoundly different from the families of today. The economic, personal, and sexual relations among family members then would seem foreign to us now. Legal, religious, and social ideology condemned any sexual relationship except procreative intercourse within marriage. The strictures on sexual behavior and the expectations of patriarchal family life were enforced by the law, the family, the churches, and the neighbors. Privacy was rare. Most people lived in small houses where all family members slept in the same room, especially during winter, when a single fireplace provided heat. Loosely constructed houses allowed neighbors and kin to observe what happened behind closed doors. [15] Churches fined or excommunicated sexual transgressors, and public opinion reinforced community values by condemning extramarital sexuality. [16] A homogeneous population, shared religious values, and geographical proximity facilitated community responsibility for upholding conventional moral standards. [17]

Custom and law strongly encouraged the formation of families, and virtually everyone lived in a family. New England colonies forbade "solitary living" to ensure that everyone would be "subject to the governance of family life." [18] Connecticut made it a crime to court a woman without her father's permission. [19] Fathers controlled their children's choice of a marital partner, basing that choice on economic factors rather than on attraction or affection.[20] But even apart from the legal rules, economic survival necessitated family living for all but a few affluent men.

The central fact of family life in the late eighteenth century was that women of all classes, once married, could expect to bear children from the time of marriage until menopause. The *average* white woman of the Revolutionary era bore more than seven children.[21] Black women, whose masters could increase their human property simply by encouraging their female slaves to have children, experienced ten to eleven pregnancies during the fertile years.[22] This pattern of constant childbearing was debilitating to women, and sometimes fatal. Pregnancy, and caring for newborns and the children who survived past infancy, were exhausting, especially when combined with the work of running a household: food preparation and preservation, sewing, candle making, soap making, and laundering in iron pots over open fires, with water carried by hand from the nearest well or stream.[23]

Understandably, many women experienced dissatisfaction with domestic life. But the point of this story is not to bemoan the difficult life of the colonial era.[24] Nor is it to suggest a view of history as ineluctable progress—"See how far we have come." Rather, this story is intended to convey how the founders' social assumptions about family and women are, by the standards of late-twentieth-century America, at once so profoundly sexist and so foreign as to preclude our taking their particular views on a discrete issue as guidance for contemporary society.

Stirrings of Liberty and Equality in Eighteenth-Century Family Life

It is possible to tell another, very different story about the founding fathers, families, and women, a story of increasing gender equality and sexual liberty. It too is a part of our constitutional legacy. In principle, the central tenet of our Constitution is that all lawful power derives from the people. The state is nothing more than the sum of its citizens. The people themselves are sovereign. Against a long religious and secular tradition in which legitimacy and power were conceived of as flowing from God and the monarch, our Constitution's founders were truly revolutionary in asserting that the people are sovereign and the state merely an artifact that serves to effect those purposes specifically assigned to it by the people. Our founders' revolutionary political theory embodies two conflicting elements. On the one hand, the state is ultimately responsible to the will of the majority. On the other hand, the power of the state is strictly limited, no matter what the will of the majority, according to the nonmajoritarian precepts of a constitutional structure.

The authors of our Revolution and Constitution rebelled against the patriarchal power of kings and the notion that political authority may legitimately rest on birth status.[25] That their culture prevented them from perceiving clearly that these antipatriarchal principles also have a direct application to women and within families does not eradicate the importance of the founders' commitment to equality and individual liberty.

In daily life, many women and families of the Revolutionary era did not fit the ideological mold ascribed to them. The traditional schoolbook narrative of the American Revolution depicts a series of pitched battles between uniformed armies. In fact, the Revolution was a civil war involving the entire population. With men away in the army, white American women assumed responsibility for maintenance of family and property. As active fighting drew near, women also needed to choose whether to attempt to flee to safety or to stay and protect their homes. Flight—with children and such provisions as could be carried—was harrowing. Those who stood firm were often required to quarter and maintain soldiers, and provide refuge to displaced friends and relatives in circumstances of utmost deprivation and danger.[26] When the active fighting subsided, women managed farms and businesses and braved epidemics of smallpox and dysentery. Historian Mary Beth Norton describes the "standard pattern" that emerges from letters of Revolutionary couples: "Initially, the absent husband instructed his wife to depend upon male friends and relatives for advice and assistance. . . . But as time went on, women learned more about the family's finances while at the same time their husbands' knowledge became increasingly outdated and remote. . . . After months and sometimes years of controlling their own affairs women tended to reply testily when their husbands persisted in assuming their subservience."[27] Of course the "standard pattern" does not describe the lives of all women in the Revolutionary period. Some, particularly those from families with fewer material resources, traveled with the army, working for wages as cooks and nurses.[28] Black women confronted a very different set of choices. The British, in an effort to decrease the labor supply, offered liberty to black slaves. Previously only single men had attempted to flee the plantations, but when the British camp lay only a few miles away, many more women and children also fled. Others remained, because they either feared the harsh conditions in the British refugee camps or were attached to the homes they knew.[29]

Women also made more direct political contributions to the Revolutionary cause. Boycott of British goods—tea, clothing, and ale—was a central tactic of both practical and symbolic importance. Revolutionary women supported the boycott and urged others to do so. Women, sometimes by the hundreds, physically attacked the property of merchants who hoarded or stocked British goods.[30] As purchasing was politicized, so too was manufacture. Patriotic women gathered together in spinning bees, saved rags for making paper and bandages, turned in lead weights from windows to be melted down for bullets, and saved family urine for saltpeter.[31]

The Revolution also generated the first women's proclamation and political organization of our nation. Little in the dominant political ideology of the time supported a direct political role for women; nonetheless, in Philadelphia in 1779 the wives and daughters of the leaders of the Revolution issued a proclamation and initiated a door-to-door campaign soliciting funds to support the army. The Philadelphia women raised more than $300,000 and inspired women in other places to mobilize such campaigns.[32] In the years following the war, scores of women's services and reform societies were organized to provide charity for widows and orphans.[33] Many of the women who became interested in politics during the Revolutionary period no longer accepted the convention that their sphere of concern was solely domestic. They continued to read the newspapers, follow public events, and express their political observations in letters and conversation.[34]

The stirrings of women's liberty and equality in the later eighteenth century were not limited to those changes generated by the exigencies of the Revolutionary War. In the economic sphere, courts of equity increasingly recognized married women's property interests, and courts of law protected the rights that some had acquired through prenuptial contracts with their prospective husbands.[35]

Our founders lived in a world in which relationships between men and women, as well as ideas about those relationships, were rapidly changing. Increased mobility, the disestablishment of the Protestant church, the growth of cities and commercial agriculture—all weakened the interlocking controls that community, family, and church had exerted over social and sexual relationships. Enlightenment ideas about the relation of the individual to society supported a new concept of marriage as serving individual happiness, not simply as enforcing the duty to procreate or to fulfill obligations to one's spouse.[36]

As changes in community, family, and church loosened constraints upon premarital sexuality, young women bore greater responsibility to preserve their chastity. The incidence of premarital pregnancy rose sharply in the late eighteenth century.[37] In some parts of New England by then, as many as one in three brides was pregnant, compared with fewer than one in ten in the seventeenth century.[38] The number of illegitimate births also rose.[39] In the years following the Revolution, both men and women were allowed greater latitude in selecting their spouses. Parents, urged to do so by republican prescriptive literature, increasingly permitted children to choose their own mates.[40]

Strong objective evidence of falling birthrates within marriage suggests that, in the 1780s, the drafting of the Constitution was accompanied by a dramatic increase in the practice of contraception.[41] Contraceptive practice represented a new willingness to make family size a matter of choice, rather than a divinely ordained fate. It also suggested that sexual pleasure, apart from reproduction, was important to married couples. No new breakthrough in contraceptive technology (such as it was) explains this decline in birthrate. Mary Beth Norton attributes the decline, and the increase in contraceptive practice inferred to explain it, to the "new egalitarianism" in marriage that arose in response to the Revolution and women's participation in it. "As long as women remained subordinate within the home, they had little to say in the determination of their childbearing futures, and men who were accustomed to wielding autocratic domestic authority had no reason to accede to their wives' desire to bear fewer children."[42] As women developed a sense of themselves as people and the culture encouraged a concept of marriage as a relation of mutuality, however, contraceptive practices that depended upon cooperation between husband and wife became possible.

Late-eighteenth-century patterns of divorce also suggest a freer, more egalitarian concept of marriage than was prevalent in pre-Revolutionary years. During the period when our Constitution was adopted, divorce laws were liberalized in some states, divorce became more common, and the number of women initiating divorce actions increased.[43] Divorce was not allowed in England, and some American revolutionaries defended the freedom to leave an intolerable marriage as a republican right. In 1773, the English Privy Council disallowed a new Pennsylvania divorce act and sent instructions to all colonial governors to withhold consent from any provincial bill of divorce. Freedom to regulate colonial marriages, like freedom to regulate colonial taxation, became a Revolutionary issue.[44]

More generally, the new responsibilities and stature that women had assumed during the Revolution did not vanish when the fighting was over. Rather, the efforts of women were redirected to the vital republican enterprise of inculcating qualities of virtue in the young. Our founders assumed that the democracy could work only if citizens were "virtuous" in their public and private lives.[45] Norton explains that the "domestic realm, which had hitherto been regarded as peripheral to public welfare, now acquired major importance. With new stress on the household as the source of virtue and stability in government, attention necessarily focused on women, the traditional directors of household activities. The transition was startling in its swiftness and intensity. Before the war, females had been viewed as having little connection with the public sphere. . . . In the 1780s and 1790s, by contrast, numerous authors proclaimed the importance of America's female citizens."[46] The generalities of republican principles and the reality of women's active participation in the war effort conflicted sharply with prevailing conceptions of their cultural subservience and legal nonexistence. The culture of our founders responded to this tension by creating the archetype of the Republican Mother. The Republican Mother was to educate her children and guide them in paths of morality and virtue. As Linda Kerber observes, the "ideology of Republican Motherhood seemed to accomplish what the Enlightenment had not by identifying the intersection of the woman's private domain and the polis. . . . Restricting women's politicization was one of a series of conservative choices that Americans made in the postwar years as they avoided the full implications of their own revolutionary radicalism."[47]

The Intent of the Framers and a Constitution for the Ages

How then does this history illuminate the meaning of our Constitution for contemporary families? Often particular positions on current constitutional controversies are defended on the basis of the intent of the founders. As a dramatic example, in 1986 the Supreme Court upheld state power to impose criminal sanctions upon two adults who engage in private, consensual sexual activity. Justice Byron White, writing for the Court, rejected arguments that important individual interests in liberty, privacy, expression, and equality were violated by such prosecution; instead, he invoked the intent of the framers. He wrote that "proscriptions against that conduct have ancient roots. . . . Sodomy was a criminal offense at common law and was forbidden by the laws of the original thirteen States when they ratified the Bill of Rights."[48]

This essay's brief examination of the framers' ideas about families suggests that history is too ambiguous and complex to allow the meaning of the Constitution to be determined today by any direct, literal appeal to "original intent." Historical intent is never singular. It points in different directions. Ideas about women and families that were held by the people who adopted our Constitution tell sharply divergent stories. Further, simplistic appeal to original intent actually proves far too much. To the extent that the framers' intent can fairly be inferred, it denied the humanity and equality of a *majority* of the American people, including women, the Native American population, and people of color.[49] As we have seen, the legal world of the framers was built upon a particular family structure. That structure was enforced by a complex, intrusive web of legal and social norms that defined women as civilly dead and required citizens to submit to the discipline of a tightly prescribed form of familial governance.

But it is a structure that is, in turn, inconsistent with the more abstract principles upon which our nation was founded. The brilliance and stability of those principles suggest that the framers did not intend for their personal expectations, purposes, and prejudices to control the future meaning of specific constitutional provisions.[50] The Constitution, like any political document, is the product of compromise and is bound by the culture of its time. It often incorporates into its structure departures from its own best principles. Both the disenfranchisement of women and the institution of slavery violated republican principles of equality and liberty of all people. The framers understood the Constitution and the Republic it shapes as an experiment, built upon the experience and theories of others but, at the same time, creating something truly unique. The founders intended the spirit of experimentation to continue and grow.

The Supreme Court participates, with the original framers, in giving meaning to the Constitution. More broadly, all of the American people participate in articulating its meaning. The Supreme Court does not act alone or of its own initiative in that endeavor. Rather, the Court responds to evolving concepts of justice and equality in giving flesh to the Constitution. We the people develop our norms of justice through public debate and political action, as well as in our intimate relationships and the ordering of our daily personal lives.

Although the use of sexist and intrusive laws to enforce particular familial relations was rooted in and sanctioned by the specific intent of our constitutional founders, the Supreme Court has correctly recognized that the allocation of rights and responsibilities on the basis of gender is inconsistent with our more general constitutional commitment to individual liberty and equality. Blatantly sexist ideas about families and women are so inconsistent with contemporary values that even Attorney General Edwin Meese, who has zealously urged adherence to the original intent of the framers, has also affirmed that discrimination on the basis of gender "offends our best principles as a nation."[51]

Professor Martha Minow suggests that we conceptualize the Constitution as a foundation, which the dictionary tells us is a "ground upon which something is built up or overlaid."[52] For two hundred years Americans have engaged in the process of constructing our social edifice upon the foundation that is our Constitution. That foundation has provided a language and a process by and within which we have engaged in passionate debates about our identities, values, and visions as a people. It is also appropriate to conceptualize families as foundations for our individual personalities and character, as well as for all other social, economic, and political institutions. For most of our history that foundation and women's central role in maintaining it have simply been assumed. The voices of women have been excluded from the debates by which our culture and law are shaped. Yet, just as plainly, women have always played a vital role in constructing our nation. A challenge for the coming century is to reconstruct the family, and the society of which it is an integral part, to promote the liberty and equality of all people.

Notes

1. For example, a series of cases beginning with *Levy v. Louisiana*, 391 U.S. 68 (1968), has limited state power to favor children of married parents. *Loving v. Virginia*, 388 U.S. 1 (1967), held that the state may not prohibit interracial marriage, but *Bowers v. Hardwick*, 478 U.S. 186 (1986), upheld a Georgia law prohibiting sexual relations between people of the same sex. *Griswold v. Connecticut*, 381 U.S. 479 (1965), held that the state may not prohibit married people from using contraceptives, but *Eisenstadt v. Baird*, 405 U.S. 438 (1972), prohibited unmarried persons from purchasing or using contraceptives. *Carey v. Population Services Int.*, 431 U.S. 678 (1977), held that the blanket prohibition of the distribution of contraceptives to minors is unconstitutional, but *Bellotti v. Baird*, 443 U.S. 622 (1979), established an exceedingly complex, cumbersome process by which the state may require parental consent for, or state judicial review of, a minor's decision to have an abortion. In *Roe v. Wade*, 410 U.S. 113 (1973), the Court held that the Fourteenth Amendment's guarantee of liberty encompasses a woman's decision to terminate a pregnancy. In *Zablocki v. Redhail*, 434 U.S. 374 (1978), the Supreme Court held that the state may not induce men to support their children by barring those who fail to do so from marrying.

2. Constitutional law "should be rooted in principles that are derived from the text and original intention of the Constitution" (address of the Honorable Edwin Meese III, Attorney General of the United States, before the American Enterprise Institute, September 6, 1986, arguing that *Roe v. Wade* should be overruled). Courts should "return to a jurisprudence of original intention—i.e., a way of constitutional thinking and litigating that begins with the text of the Constitution, as informed by the intentions of those who wrote, proposed and ratified that text" (remarks of William Bradford Reynolds, Assistant Attorney General, Civil Rights Division, at the Federal Society Symposium, Chicago, November 15, 1982). See also, for example, Raoul Berger, *Government by Judiciary: The Transformation of the Fourteenth Amendment* (Cambridge: Harvard University Press, 1977), 300–311, 363–72; Jesse H. Choper, *Judicial Review and the National Political Process: A Functional Reconsideration of the Role of the Supreme Court* (Chicago: University of Chicago Press, 1980), 241–43; Robert H. Bork, "Neutral Principles

and Some First Amendment Problems," *Indiana Law Journal* 47 (1971): 1;
William H. Rehnquist, "The Notion of a Living Constitution," *Texas Law
Review* 54 (1976): 693.

3. *The Federalist*, ed. Jacob E. Cooke (Middletown, Conn.: Wesleyan
University Press, 1961), no. 6.

4. Adams's role in crafting the Constitution is controversial. See Gordon
S. Wood, *The Creation of the American Republic, 1776–1787* (Chapel Hill:
University of North Carolina Press, 1969), chap. 14.

5. *The Adams Papers*, Series II, *Adams Family Correspondence*, ed.
L. H. Butterfield et al. (Cambridge: Belknap Press of Harvard University
Press, 1963), 370.

6. Ibid., 382.

7. Wood, *Creation of the American Republic*, 8, 14, 29, 48, 282–91,
371.

8. For an excellent discussion, see Susan Moller Okin, *Women in Western Political Thought* (Princeton: Princeton University Press, 1979). In the
Republic Plato argued that the innate qualities of women could not be known so
long as the socialization and education of the sexes were so different. As a
prescriptive matter, the *Republic* would include women in the governing class,
both for moral reasons and because confining all women to domestic seclusion
was extremely wasteful of human resources. But for Plato, including women
in the public sphere was made possible only by abolishing the family and
creating a highly hierarchical society in which essential work was done by
slaves and others who were excluded from the privileged class. Through our
history Americans have rejected this notion and affirmed the core social role of
the family. See, for example, *Parham v. J.R.*, 442 U.S. 584 (1979). Indeed,
even Plato, writing later in the *Laws*, affirmed the value of the family and
resurrected the notion of a woman's natural domesticity to preserve it.

9. Locke's *First Treatise of Government* attacks Robert Filmer's effort to
justify absolute monarchy by analogy to the patriarchal family. Filmer relied
on the biblical injunction to "honor thy father." Locke took seriously the
biblical commandment to "honor thy father and thy mother" and argued that
if family power and responsibility are to be shared by men and women,
governmental power too must be shared and limited by mutual responsibility.
For discussion, see Linda K. Kerber, *Women of the Republic: Intellect and
Ideology in Revolutionary America* (Chapel Hill: University of North Carolina
Press, 1980), 16–19.

10. John Locke, *Two Treatises of Government*, ed. Peter Laslett (Cambridge: Cambridge University Press, 1960), 2:82.

11. Carl N. Degler, *At Odds* (New York: Oxford University Press,
1980), 189.

12. See Wendy W. Williams, "The Equality Crisis: Some Reflections

on Culture, Courts, and Feminism," *Women's Rights Law Reporter* 7 (1982): 175–77.

13. Marylynn Salmon, *Women and the Law of Property in Early America* (Chapel Hill: University of North Carolina Press, 1986), xv.

14. Kerber, *Women of the Republic*, 120.

15. David H. Flaherty, *Privacy in Colonial New England* (Charlottesville: University Press of Virginia, 1972), 42–43, 76.

16. Peter Laslett, *The World We Have Lost* (London: Methuen, 1971), 155, 158.

17. The boundary between family and community was much more permeable then than it is today. See Phillippe Aries, *Centuries of Childhood: A Social History of Family Life*, trans. Robert Baldick (New York: Vintage, 1962).

18. The Massachusetts Bay Colony prohibited solitary living from early in its history. In 1669 the Plymouth Colony first compelled unmarried persons to live under regular "family government." Even when Plymouth allowed unmarried men to live alone, they were required to seek permission of local authorities to do so, and permission could be withdrawn if they deviated from accepted standards of decent behavior. Unmarried women invariably lived with a relative, either a parent or a sibling. See John Demos, *A Little Commonwealth: Family Life in Plymouth Colony* (New York: Oxford University Press, 1970).

19. Jay Fliegelman, *Prodigals and Pilgrims: The American Revolution against Patriarchal Authority, 1750–1800* (Cambridge: Cambridge University Press, 1982), 136.

20. Degler, *At Odds*, 10, 11. Paternal influence over the choice of a marriage partner was less pronounced in the Southern colonies, perhaps because there were so many more men than women there during the early history of those colonies.

21. According to Degler in *At Odds*, the average woman bore 7.04 children in 1800, and the birthrate had fallen steadily since 1750. According to Demos in *A Little Commonwealth*, birthrates in the Plymouth Colony averaged 7.8 for first-generation families, 8.6 for second-generation families, and 9.3 for third-generation families.

22. Mary Beth Norton, "The Myth of the Golden Age," in *Women of America: A History*, ed. Carol Ruth Berkin and Mary Beth Norton (Boston: Houghton Mifflin, 1979), 44. Norton points out that while blacks constituted nearly 20 percent of the American population at the time of the Revolution (a higher percentage than at any time since), historians have completely neglected the study of black women slaves during that period.

23. Ibid., 37.

24. Ibid. The whole of Norton's chapter is instructive in this regard.

25. "No Title of Nobility shall be granted by the United States." U.S. Constitution, Art. I, Sec. 9, cl. 8.

26. Mary Beth Norton, *Liberty's Daughters* (Boston: Little, Brown, and Co., 1980), 195–205.

27. Ibid., 216, 222.

28. Kerber, *Women of the Republic*, 51–52; Norton, *Liberty's Daughters*, 213. James Fenimore Cooper paints a fictional portrait of a woman who traveled with the Revolutionary army out of patriotism, as well as economic need, in *The Spy: A Tale of Neutral Ground* (London: G. and W. B. Whittaker, 1822).

29. Norton, *Liberty's Daughters*, 209–10. In general, see Ira Berlin, *Slaves without Masters: The Free Negro in the Antebellum South* (New York: Pantheon, 1974).

30. Kerber, *Women of the Republic*, 43–45.

31. Ibid., 38, 42.

32. Ibid., 99–111. Kerber points out that "historians of women in the Revolution have admired the Philadelphia project excessively. . . . Benjamin Rush, whose wife was an enthusiastic participant in the campaign, wrote, 'The women of America have at last become principals in the glorious American controversy.' But they were not principals, of course, they were fund raisers, and only for a brief time" (103). See also Norton, *Liberty's Daughters*, 177–88.

33. Kerber, *Women of the Republic*, 111.

34. Norton, *Liberty's Daughters*, 188–90.

35. On equitable actions to protect women, see Williams, "The Equality Crisis," 176, n. 4, and 177, n. 8. On prenuptial contracts, see Demos, *A Little Commonwealth*, 82–86. On women who managed businesses, see Elisabeth Anthony Dexter, *Colonial Women of Affairs* (Boston: Houghton Mifflin, 1924). See also Kerber, *Women of the Republic*, 140–41.

36. Lawrence Stone, *The Family, Sex, and Marriage in England, 1500–1800* (London: Weidenfeld and Nicolson, 1977), chap. 10; see also Fliegelman, *Prodigals and Pilgrims*, chap. 5.

37. Historians are divided on the reasons behind this phenomenon. For a comprehensive discussion, see Daniel Scott Smith and Michael S. Hindus, "Premarital Pregnancy in America: An Overview and Interpretation," *Journal of Interdisciplinary History* 5 (1975): 537. See also Joan Hoff Wilson, "The Illusion of Change: Women and the American Revolution," in *The American Revolution: Explorations in the History of American Radicalism*, ed. Alfred F. Young (DeKalb, Ill.: Northern Illinois University Press), 404.

38. Daniel Scott Smith, "The Dating of the American Sexual Revolution," in *The American Family in Social-Historical Perspective*, ed. Michael Gordon (New York: St. Martin's Press, 1973), 323.

39. Robert V. Wells, "Illegitimacy and Bridal Pregnancy in Colonial America," in *Bastardy and Its Comparative History,* ed. Peter Laslett et al. (London: Edward Arnold, 1980), 354–55.

40. See Norton, *Liberty's Daughters,* 229–30.

41. Robert V. Wells, "Family Size and Fertility Control in Eighteenth-Century America: A Study of Quaker Families," *Population Studies* 25 (1971): 76.

42. Norton, *Liberty's Daughters,* 232.

43. Nancy F. Cott, "Divorce and the Changing Status of Women in Eighteenth-Century Massachusetts," *William and Mary Quarterly,* 3d ser., 33 (1976): 592, 594, 613–14; Henry S. Cohn, "Connecticut's Divorce Mechanism, 1636–1969," *American Journal of Legal History* 14 (1970): 35. Even under the liberalized laws, divorce was available only in a narrow set of circumstances, such as desertion, adultery, or fraud, and in some states divorce was not available at all. See Kerber, *Women of the Republic,* 159–73.

44. Kerber, *Women of the Republic,* 160.

45. Wood, *Creation of the American Republic,* 65–70.

46. Norton, *Liberty's Daughters,* 243.

47. Kerber, *Women of the Republic,* 283, 287.

48. *Bowers v. Hardwick,* 478 U.S. 186, 192 (1986).

49. In relation to black people, the framers were quite conscious of the tension between the rhetoric of freedom, on the one hand, and the reality of slavery, on the other. See Bernard Bailyn, *The Ideological Origins of the American Revolution* (Cambridge: Belknap Press of Harvard University Press, 1967), 232–46.

50. See H. Jefferson Powell, "The Original Understanding of Original Intent," *Harvard Law Review* 98 (1985): 885.

51. Edwin Meese, Address to the Students and Faculty of Dickinson College, September 17, 1985. It should be noted that the attorney general asserted his opposition to gender bias while attacking affirmative action programs that would aid women in overcoming centuries of discrimination.

52. *Webster's Ninth New Collegiate Dictionary* (1983), s.v. "foundation." Professor Martha Minow pointed out this definition at New York University's Law and Society Colloquium, March 11, 1987.

CHAPTER 15

Public Law versus Public Rights

The Constitution and Strategies for Environmental Protection

•••••

FREDERICK R. ANDERSON

While preparing this paper, I received *The Enchanted Wilderness*, published by Four Corners West of Torrey, Utah. The population of Torrey could not exceed 200. The author, Ward Roylance, has been many things but never a professor of law, history, or government. Now retired, Mr. Roylance has served as foreign service officer, schoolteacher, state employee, tour leader, and photographer. He obviously loves the Colorado Plateau—his enchanted wilderness. Roylance writes: "Those who like to hike and enjoy unspoiled nature believe they have a *right* to preserve a portion of the public domain as wilderness. . . . At the very least, when development or conversion of wild areas are [*sic*] proposed, the public has a right to be fully informed and to participate in decision making."[1]

In his comments about environmental rights, Roylance expresses a grass-roots view widely held in the United States. In the American system, many feel that individual rights—judge-made qualitative norms—should protect environmental quality if other institutions fail. A vigorous tradition of volunteerism and self-expression underpins these rights. Many of their proponents share with Roylance the view that the public possesses both direct rights to environmental quality and special participatory rights if governmental decisions threaten the environment. Nor are these rights necessarily confined to those that exist in common law or that have been created by statute in recent years in the outpouring of environmental legislation. To persons like Roylance, such rights may also be constitutional, although exactly how this is so may be unclear.

In addition to this *public rights approach* to environmental protection, and often at odds with it, is the *public law approach*. Of the two, the latter is quite plainly the preferred approach, not only by the modern American administrative state but also by most other economically advanced societies. The public law approach to the protection of environmental quality operates through detailed statutes that vest authority in large agencies. Substantively, these environmental statutes are divided between the few, which are heavily skewed toward environmental protection at any cost, and the many, which require cost-benefit trade-offs. Under most of the statutes, the states are charged with implementing standards set by the federal agencies.

Critics of the public rights approach maintain that individual rights to environmental quality should not be conferred, because environmental quality is a collective responsibility, to be managed with utilitarian regard for costs and benefits, not brought about by the initiative of a few environmentalist plaintiffs. The rights-based approach would result in uneven environmental protection nationwide. Constitutional environmental rights, besides having no explicit basis in the Constitution, or in the two hundred years of its evolution, are particularly difficult to define and implement. Critics point out that, in any event, citizen participation is deeply embedded in the American public law approach. Public participation takes place through the relatively new, "administered" participatory democracy: agency hearings, written public comment, and judicial review.

Yet many citizens still firmly share Ward Roylance's rights-based perspective, although it is the messier, less efficient, more ad hoc and absolutist of the two. Consequently, it would be a grave error to dismiss the public rights view as simply moral conviction or extralegal sentimentalism, to be blended into public law and given "appropriate" weight by the environmental technocracy. Because of the nature of public concern about the environment, and the need for decisional norms to remain open and accessible in the pluralist democratic tradition, the public rights approach is not likely to fade away. The question, rather, is how to reconcile the emotive, simple, and, yes, political position of persons like Ward Roylance with the scientifically complex systems of modern administered environmental protection. The tension between the two approaches is likely to endure.

I would like to argue that the public law approach adequately addresses only some aspects of the environmental problem and to propose a reexamination of the role of judge-made environmental law under the common law and broad statutory and constitutional norms. This essay addresses the themes of technocracy, citizen action, and constitutionalism by exploring the environmental problem as a collection of paradoxical challenges. It does not address environmental federalism, preemption, the scope of the Tenth Amendment, standing, exhaustion of administrative remedies, or commerce clause regulation, all of which are widely viewed as the salient constitutional questions regarding the environment today. While acknowledging their importance, I see them as more-technical matters best left to other forums.

The Paradoxical Environmental Problem

The environmental problem makes for strange bedfellows in any system of governance. It weds technical concerns to philosophical ones, personal moral absolutes to political and economic trade-offs, technocracy to the grass roots, Romantic aesthetics to efficiency and the cost-benefit ratio. These, obviously, are shotgun marriages. Problems like atmospheric carbon dioxide or the weakening of the earth's ozone shield are literally global, but others are local. Environmental decision making may involve marginal trade-offs between economic and environmental values, but moral and aesthetic considerations also color those decisions. Should a forest be managed to optimize its combined outputs of timber, range, habitat, watershed, and recreation? Or should it be allowed to return to wilderness? Where should the new waste dump be located? What about the new McDonald's? An issue may fall in the arena of politics and policy-making but also arouse intense personal feelings and imperatives. Toxic contamination of the town water supply prompts us to invoke the social contract one moment, the need for privacy the next. In the bicentennial year of the Constitution, geothermal development threatened Old Faithful. What economic benefit, what trade-off, is worth Old Faithful? Who says this is the question to ask?

The environmental problem may involve arcane scientific causes and technological solutions. Yet the public keeps the environment at or near the top of the political agenda for rather simple reasons. The Environmental Protection Agency may rely on statistical aggregation of potential impacts to conclude that human exposure to three parts per billion of an airborne chemical may lead to ten excess cancer deaths nationwide in a year, but to the public this may mean only that the chemical kills people. Thresholds, synergism, mouse-to-person extrapolation, margins of error, and statistical mortality are slippery concepts. As political concepts, they are as explosive as they are elusive.

Regulation and the Administrative Technology: The Public Law Approach

Some believe that centrist, heavily administered regulation responding to environmental, health, and safety threats came into being ex nihilo in the 1970s. In fact, it was the experiences of the Progressive Era, the New Deal, World War II, and the Great Society that together promoted federal regulation as the corrective to corporate and market failure to allay those threats. Environmental, health, and safety legislation did reach its height in the 1970s, however. Congress added some eighty new statutes to social regulation between 1970 and 1979, doubling the thirty-five enacted in the preceding decade and dwarfing the output during any preceding decade, including the 1930s with twenty-one. Direct federal expenditures by federal agencies almost tripled over the decade, while agency staff levels more than tripled. More significant perhaps are the "off budget" private sector expenditures necessitated by regulatory agencies. Regulatory cost accounting is a very uncertain art, but annual private sector expenditures may amount to between $150 billion and $200 billion per year.[2]

Today, under the public law approach, Congress empowers the administrative technocracy to select and implement command-and-control regulations that apply prospectively to polluters, manufacturers, and employers. The process does not match a civics textbook's explanation of how a bill becomes a law, but one can plausibly maintain that more lawmaking is done today by agencies under authority delegated them by Congress than by Congress itself. After proposing their guidelines and regulations (their "rules") for written public comment, counterproposal, and perhaps a public hearing, the agencies publish final rules, with an explanation. The *Federal Register* serves the technocracy as the *Congressional Record* serves the Congress; the Code of Federal Regulations in turn parallels the U.S. Statutes-at-Large. The reliance on regulatory standards as the principal means of providing protection against the dangers of modern life constitutes the central feature of the contemporary public law approach.

The result of this proliferation of public law is that the center of most domestic policy-making is now the federal administrative process, which rivals local and state government (the constitutional home of welfare protection), the federal courts, the presidency, and Congress itself as the governmental center of attention to domestic issues. Regulatory expansion has affected not only how safe products, drugs, and workplaces are, and how clean or enriching the environment is, but also how we are governed—the federal-state balance, the separation of powers, the power of the bureaucratic state over individuals and private organizations, the techniques by which agencies (instead of Congress) legislate, the importance of administrative advocacy, and the nature of governmental responsibility for scientifically complex and dangerous technologies.

The success of the public law approach depended in large part upon its ability to appear to preserve public involvement in the actions undertaken. Congress attempted to infuse the new administrative lawmaking with safeguards appropriate to a pluralist democracy. In so doing, Congress reflected the grass-roots origins of the environmental movement. The new regulation guarantees broad rights of public participation; indeed, expansion of participatory rights, a democratic process of policy-making by accommodation of interests, has been identified as the most important development in administrative law of the 1970s.[3]

The triumph of the public law approach agitated, and changed, the federal courts. In addition to providing for the usual judicial review of the reasonableness and procedural correctness of agency action, environmental legislation typically invites "any person" concerned that a statute is not being properly enforced to sue any party (including the United States) who the plaintiff claims has failed to perform mandatory duties. The statutes also usually authorize the courts to award attorneys' and expert witnesses' fees when appropriate.

In some ways, administratively "legislated" rules are produced more pluralistically than congressional legislation. While the courts cannot review the preenactment legislative record to ensure that minorities, the uninformed, the weak, the less well organized, or the unborn are heard at congressional hearings, the courts have, by various means, responded to those and other constituencies in administrative rule making. The frequency, breadth, and depth of citizen participation in these proceedings make it a unique facet of American constitutionalism.

The federal circuit courts, particularly the D.C. Circuit—the closest court in the United States to a special administrative tribunal—responded to the tide of environmental health and safety legislation by awakening from almost half a century of lethargy to take a hard look at agency decision making. Following the Supreme Court's lead in an important 1971 case,[4] the courts' review of agencies' records and decisions became "searching and careful."[5] Judges wrote of the "long and ·fruitful collaboration" between agencies and courts in furtherance of the public interest.[6] Courts began to experiment with judge-made requirements for hearings, cross-examination, and reasoned responses to public comment, all of which fueled concern that the courts were legislating new procedures and indirectly determining pro-environmental policy outcomes. A type of judicial entrepreneurship arose to parallel legislative entrepreneurship.[7] Among D.C. Circuit judges who fundamentally shaped many environmental laws were Judge Skelly Wright (the National Environmental Policy Act), Judge David Bazelon (the pesticide control laws), and Judge Harold Leventhal (the Clean Air Act).

Yet the courts' emerging role was curtailed in the late 1970s. The courts' attempt to control the new legislation never developed into a constitutional issue, because the Supreme Court discouraged judicial activism.[8] Subsequent Supreme Court decisions have reaffirmed the administrative agencies' discretion to make policy without judicial intervention and have gone on to strengthen the agencies' lawmaking and interpretive power.[9] Finally, the penchant for constitutional formalism in recent Supreme Court decisions affecting separation of powers suggests a curbing of judicial power through a reinvigorated interpretation of executive and legislative functions.[10] The result is that the courts have now settled into a deferential role consonant with the need of the modern administrative state. Environmentalists cannot expect the courts to challenge agency hegemony if Congress has assigned the solution to the technocracy. Incidentally, from the environmentalists' point of view, it is fortunate that Congress has taken up the task assumed first by the reviewing courts in the early 1970s. Congress now legislates hearings, cross-examination, and agency obligations, even if the Supreme Court has curtailed the ability of the lower courts to do so.

The public law approach has yet to come to grips with the federal system. The state and local role under environmental statutes is one of the least-understood aspects of American federalism, even by specialists in pollution control law. The *theory* of "environmental federalism" is that the federal government sets environmental quality standards, and the states implement and enforce them. The reality, uncovered only by reading the details of the statutes and by observing implementation practices, is that the federal government also largely controls implementation and enforcement. All implementation plans and legal enforcement actions are federally reviewed; the federal government can substitute its own plan, personnel, and attorneys virtually as it wishes. The result is a complex environmental quality program centralized in all essential respects, staffed by federal and state technocracies whose frequently voiced differences of opinion are greatly outweighed by their collegiality and singleness of federal purpose. This reality is likely to be enhanced by the 1985 *Garcia*[11] decision, which undermined the states' ability under the Tenth Amendment to resist "conscript[ion] . . . into the national bureaucratic army."[12]

Inadequacies of the Public Law Approach

Critics of the prevailing public law strategy are not hard to find. The deregulation, paperwork reduction, and bureaucracy bashing of both the Carter and the Reagan administrations have created a hospitable environment for criticism. Scientists have argued that the environmental statutes were based on misconceptions about biological and physical systems. Atmospheric chemists have attacked the threshold concept and the imprecision of modeling. Engineers have criticized technology-based standards. Economists, the most outspoken of all, have condemned the statutes as inefficient. Political scientists and legal scholars have complained that the statutes lack clarity, are inequitable and ineffectual, and spawn interminable litigation.

Additional shortcomings of the prevailing strategy, however, suggest that excessive reliance on administered schemes is a mistake. Public rights strategies whose roots are deeply ingrained in the American constitutional system are available, and they might be combined with the public law approach in a unique and balanced way.

Conventional and Unconventional Environmental Problems

Complex, heavily administered environmental management schemes effectively address certain environmental problems but not others. Pollution control statutes function passably well for conventional air and water pollutants. These pollutants have reasonably clear causal impacts on health over limited geographic regions and over fairly short periods. The existing schemes for management of forests, grazing lands, parks, and wildernesses seem also to function passably well. Some schemes for regulation of toxic products and hazardous wastes seem to work, if the problem addressed has been fairly well understood.

The current public law approach functions well when its purpose is to control aesthetic and health effects, which, while serious, do not threaten life or promote genetic impairment or birth defects. The system also functions well when the values at stake include a desire for the preservation of remaining unspoiled habitat, for diversity of flora and fauna, for quiet, solitude, and emotional and psychological distance from modern civilization, for open space and pleasing urban configurations, and for wilderness and untrammeled areas. Persons who share these interests are concerned about the disruption and uncertainties that economic growth engenders. Often their desires recall the simpler, apparently more frugal values and ethics of earlier times, an older, different set of cultural and social norms. Economic trade-offs and multiple uses seem to be appropriate means to these essentially political ends.

Public law functions less well, however, where the issues entail philosophical and personal moral imperatives. Where life, health, family, and personal liberty are threatened by an environmental problem, an administrative agency seems inappropriate as the exclusive decision-making body. Fundamental conditions for human existence are threatened by the risks imposed by newer, vastly disturbing forms of pollution that promote cancer, respiratory disease, and mutagenic and teratogenic effects, among other ills. The current public law responses to these harms are weak, because it is hard to mount collective legislative responses.

Simple Politics for Complex Realities

The administration of environmental statutes is far removed from their grass-roots origins and politics. A fundamental tension exists between the straightforward, even simplistic public perception of environmental problems and the solutions adopted by the technocracy created to deal with their underlying causes.

Simplifying and moralizing the environmental problem, casting polluters as evil giants, and framing the environmental problem as a highly symbolic struggle between good and evil helped secure passage of environmental legislation. [13] But that legislation veers sharply from public expectations of how the problems it addresses will be remedied. Under the statutes, for example, polluters do not pay damages to the persons whom they harm. (An environmental "victims movement" is just now being formed.) The pollution statutes contain criminal sanctions, but these underutilized provisions are dwarfed by the rule-making activities of the agencies. Punishment or liability for specific injury to known citizens by blameworthy individuals actually plays a very minor role in the pollution laws. The reason is subtle but vital to understanding why the environmental regulatory statutes seem distant from voters' experience. Early difficulties of proof with some of the most common forms of pollution led to the use of shortcuts to simplify enforcement. Liability attached upon proof of discharge alone, not proof of harm. As pollution statutes evolved, they made even greater use of harm "surrogates," thereby foreclosing inquiry into the extent and nature of actual environmental harm. The wrongs involved today are "paper wrongs," such as failure to report or failure to abide by the conditions of a permit. These are administrative delicts, rather than direct affronts to public health. Enforcement of paper wrongs transforms the field of environmental protection.

Oversimplification

The simpler a pollution problem, the more easily obtained is the political benefit of claiming to enact a comprehensive solution. A bill's supporters must "freeze" perception of an environmental problem, much as a lawyer must argue a case based upon an established set of facts. The result is that the legislative process profoundly misstates the real nature of environmental threats and severely underestimates the magnitude and speed of changes in the scientific understanding of environmental problems. Pollution control schemes may be premised upon incorrect assumptions about the extent of the threat, its regional or global impact, the physical nature of the pollutants themselves, the nature of the processes that produce the pollution, the technologies available for its control, and even in what medium the pollutants are found.

Yet a bill's sponsors rarely seek tentative answers to narrowly defined types of emerging problems. Instead, they mandate the complete and comprehensive removal of entire classes of hazards. At first the public is pleased with the comprehensiveness that Congress claims to have achieved. Yet, paradoxically, this congressional overreaching lays the groundwork for an agency's shrinking away from specific situations, a diminution of government effort, and consequent public disappointment.

Systematic Administrative Solutions

Agencies concentrate their knowledge on systems and nationwide impacts. This is reflected in the incentives that agencies provide to their staffs. The facts to which agency regulators learn to become accustomed are abstract and generalized; regulators are not hired or promoted because they are proficient in handling real situations. The goal of the agency is to set an entire system into operation, rather than to measure accomplishment by how well it understands and addresses specific harms and control technologies. This approach leads to profound misunderstanding between the constituencies that think that they helped create the agencies in the first place and agency bureaucracies that do not believe that specific remedies should be their focus or their strength.

The obsession with systems is so complete that limited agency resources are normally apportioned out over the entire scope of a regulatory program, rather than concentrated upon the worst problems. It is hardly surprising that agency staff who have acquired specific knowledge are so frequently hired away by firms that can put their talents to better use.

Public Rights Revisited

Congress expects quick responses to environmental problems and sets deadlines to force agencies into action. But it also imposes procedures that safeguard interested parties. Due process and speed are inversely proportional; to enhance the one, the other must suffer. Turning the agencies into quasi legislatures under the interest accommodation model of administrative governance necessarily slows things down.

Overspecific statutes leave the agency vulnerable to citizen groups and industry alike when it tries to set priorities or bend the rules to fit emerging problems. The twin goals of prompt comprehensiveness and public participation expose the agency to intense, long-term pressure from interest groups—which is precisely what evenhanded congressional solutions are designed to avoid. In a prolonged process, specific polluters with a focused interest in certain pollutants have a greater likelihood of successfully lobbying for exemptions. This process can result in the skillful use of judicial review to wrest control over an agency's priorities away from the agency itself.

Against this background, one might ask for specific examples of public rights approaches that might enrich the public law approach and correct its deficiencies. Let me suggest three.

The Common Law. Historically, the common law redressed wrongs between private parties. Environmental injuries to a person or to property were remedied by money damages or injunctive relief. By the twentieth century, Anglo-American legal systems had put in place some statutory regimes to prevent environmental harm. These early statutes were almost all prospective. Under them, courts denied damages but enjoined future harms if harm was currently being sustained. The statutes also redressed public rather than private wrongs.

By the 1970s, Congress and state legislatures had enacted much broader environmental protection measures. Yet in the recent triumph of regulation, the statutory displacement of remedies for damages has occurred at a slower pace than the displacement of preventive injunctions. Legislatures have been slow to provide compensation to wronged parties, whether from the public treasury or through a government-supervised transfer of funds from the persons responsible for harm.

Even today in the late 1980s, preventive regulation still far outpaces administered compensation. For this reason, many still believe that there are distinct advantages to having common law judges decide environmental cases,[14] especially where public law is still in its formative stages and does not yet provide adequate ameliorative and compensatory awards for environmental harms *past*. But it also applies to preventive orders, especially where they fill in interstitially for the evolving public law.

Plenary Environmental Rights Conferred by Statute. Several states have attempted to overcome the limitations on common law environmental actions by enacting statutes that charge the courts to decide environmental cases. The statutes make liability and proof easier than they would otherwise be at common law. In the early 1970s Congress considered similar legislation but has so far not adopted this approach.

The Michigan Environmental Protection Act and similar legislation in at least eight other states have enabled state courts to create a state common law of the environment through case-by-case application of the public trust doctrine.[15] Courts are given both jurisdiction to determine the reasonableness of actions that impair the environment and authority to enjoin them unless no prudent alternative exists. Courts can "correct" agency standards found wanting. Every individual has the right to a judicial hearing on any environmental issue. Rebuttable presumptions are used to ease difficulties of proof at common law.[16]

Rather than obligating the courts to take the lead in environmental protection, the legislation takes the approach of broadening and encouraging the judicial role in environmental protection, while leaving primary responsibility for most environmental problems to state agencies. Admittedly, the statutes do not explicitly confer primary jurisdiction on agencies, nor do they explicitly forbid the courts to intervene until the administrative process has completely run its course. Theoretically, courts could nudge agencies aside and assume authority to set standards themselves. However, the bellwether Michigan statute makes clear that courts are intended to intervene only when all else fails, that is, when the administrative process fails to do its job properly or when gaps appear in the spectrum of needed environmental protections. This has in fact been Michigan's experience.[17] Some critics feared that a flood of litigation would occur once the statute was enacted, but the flood never materialized.[18]

Before enactment of these statutes there was doubt that the courts would accept a direct role in environmental decision making. Over the past eighteen years, that doubt has been removed by the courts, which have concluded that the statutes are not unconstitutional delegations of legislative authority to the courts, that the operative words that confer upon courts a sweeping opportunity to evolve common law based on the public trust concept are not unconstitutionally vague, and that the courts do have the experience to develop a common law of the environment.[19]

Constitutional Rights to Environmental Quality. At the beginning of the "Environmental Decade" of the 1970s, in the first flowering of environmental law, at least ten states placed environmental rights provisions in their constitutions.[20] Scholars developed theories on which courts could base a federal constitutional right to environmental quality.[21] One federal district court tentatively endorsed the concept.[22]

As the decade wore on, however, scholarly opinion on the matter became a good deal less enthusiastic.[23] Judges in environmental cases did not base relief on either federal or state constitutional rights. In commenting on a draft of this essay at the Smithsonian Institution's International Symposium on the Bicentennial of the United States Constitution in 1987, Rex Lee, former solicitor general, flatly denied any possibility of a constitutional environmental right under the federal Constitution. Yet that year the National Wildlife Federation, whose membership of 4.6 million makes it the largest of the environmental membership organizations, mounted a grass-roots campaign to secure an environmental rights amendment.[24]

The obstacles to finding a federal constitutional right to environmental quality are many: lack of any indication that the framers of the Constitution, the Bill of Rights, or the Civil War amendments intended to protect individuals' environmental rights; the resemblance between assertion of environmental rights and assertion of economic rights via substantive due process; the absence of state action on the part of the most likely defendants, especially if the defendant must be exclusively engaged in discharging a public function or if a direct causal nexus must exist between public function and the environmental harm caused; and the difficulty of making such a right self-executing if the precise content of the right and causal nexus is not spelled out in a detailed statute.

Yet one can imagine how a federal constitutional right to environmental protection might possibly evolve in the future. Proponents of such a right in the early 1970s failed to make an important distinction. Highly personal individual interests in safety, health, and life are quite different from interests in resources management, aesthetics, conservation, and recreation. The injury threatened by toxic wastes, for example, is quite different from that threatened by a water storage proposal on a free-flowing stream. The concepts of life, liberty, and property in the Fifth Amendment conceivably cover the interests threatened by carcinogens, mutagens, and teratogens. More broadly, genetic manipulation, organ transplantation, artificial insemination, surrogate motherhood, contraception, abortion, and life-prolonging drugs all redefine the fundamental concepts of life, death, parenthood, privacy, liberty, and property, and will inevitably be litigated under the Constitution in decades to come.

Erosion and invasion of safety, health, and life are just as destructive to an individual's integrity as are invasions of the marital relationship, free and private communication between individuals, one's home, or one's choice about how to handle the physiological and emotional facts of pregnancy or sterility. One's perceptions of threat to oneself, one's spouse, one's children, and even to children yet unborn, may excite the same kind of concern and unease that one would feel if confronted by a government knock at the door, electronic surveillance, or interference with a marital relationship. The environment does not only environ us; when poisoned it threatens to immobilize, diffuse, and fundamentally reduce our humanness. Further, rDNA technologies, organ transplantation, mechanical organs, and birth technologies blur the distinction between the *environment* and the individual. An environmental right based on substantive due process would be analogized by the Court to economic rights, and probably rejected, so long as all that is desired is the infusion of stronger environmental values into decision making. But when individual interests in safety, health, and life are separated from more-generalized harms to natural ecosystems, the case for fundamental constitutional protection improves markedly.

If the state causes or condones invasions of the person, it may act in ways that are at bottom very much like the actions that have been prohibited under more conventional constitutional analyses of individual liberties. Assuming no change in the Court's constricted approach to state action, state management of public buildings (where, for example, asbestos is a threat), of dumps containing toxic substances, of military facilities, and of facilities in state receivership still offers a rich context for the development of a constitutional environmental right.

Conclusion

The public law approach provides centralized, systematic, comprehensive environmental protection. The technocracy provides specialized managerial and scientific expertise. Decisions are democratic, in that they flow both from the competition of interest groups in the legislature and from the accommodation of views by the administrative agencies.

Yet, as we have seen, the public law approach may be too systematic, comprehensive, proceduralized, and technocratic, tending to become distanced from grass-roots politics. Regulatory law is complex; it punishes administrative delicts, not palpable wrongs, and citizens shy away from endless rule-making deliberations and hearings. Solutions become frozen in place under "comprehensive" statutory schemes that are soon outdated by rapidly evolving scientific understanding of environmental threats. Technocrats shrink from innovative approaches.[25] They focus on putting "programs" in place slowly and cautiously, rather than dealing first with the worst episodes of real harm. Courts feel constrained by regulatory legislation to uphold agency action unless procedures are abused or agency decisions are patently unreasonable.

Still, the public law approach does provide partial antidotes to many of these ills. A European must be strongly impressed by the extent to which participatory rights for citizens are built into American public law. This is true not only for regulatory pollution statutes but also for a wide array of planning statutes, such as the national Environmental Policy Act and the four major public land management statutes. Courts defer to agency decision makers, but they appear to take an especially hard look at decisions affecting health, safety, and the environment. The energy and skill that federal reviewing courts have invested in agency oversight of environmental decisions led Professor Richard Stewart to suggest the existence of a quasi-constitutional right to exceptionally close judicial scrutiny where environmental values are threatened,[26] although his suggestion was made before the Supreme Court curtailed the imposition of special procedural safeguards by lower federal courts.[27]

The public rights approach can help correct the deficiencies of the public law approach. It can, for example, bring a much-needed concern for equity into overadministered environmental programs. Suits brought by injured persons focus attention on special harms; they appeal to the public's sense that the injured should be directly vindicated. They cut across the grain of comprehensive programs, follow a different schedule for remediation, and flesh out facts that agencies may find inconvenient to assimilate into their programs. Using judicial inquiry rather than scientific study as a means of validating claims, they vest decision-making authority in a significantly different forum. Pressing public rights to environmental quality through the courts can counteract the disappointing metamorphoses of congressional legislation, the opacity of administrative rule making, the commitment of public solutions to an elite technocracy, and the exclusive focus on the prevention of future harms rather than on the redress of present injury.

One need not worry about insulating environmental decision making from popular preference by committing it to unelected judges. The public law approach will undoubtedly continue to dominate. But a reinvigorated public rights approach could help make public law more supple, fact-oriented, and responsive. Further, one need not anticipate wholesale conversion of environmental law to a rights-based approach, in which every environmental problem becomes an excuse to sue.[28] We have begun to see stresses within some of our social sectors, for example in education and medical care, for which excessive reliance on rights-based solutions is a symptom. Environmental policy-making still seems likely to emerge from a complex blend of education, negotiation, scientific inquiry, legislation—and public rights litigation.

Notes

1. Ward Roylance, *The Enchanted Wilderness* (Torrey: Four Corners West, 1987).

2. Frederick R. Anderson, "Human Welfare and the Administered Society: Federal Regulation in the 1970s to Protect Health, Safety, and the

Environment," in *Environmental and Occupational Medicine,* ed. William Rom (Boston: Little, Brown, 1983).

3. Richard B. Stewart, "The Reformation of American Administrative Law," *Harvard Law Review* 88 (1975): 1667.

4. *Citizens to Preserve Overton Park v. Volpe,* 401 U.S. 402 (1971).

5. 401 U.S. 402, 416 (1971).

6. *Environmental Defense Fund, Inc. v. Ruckelshaus,* 439 F.2d 584, 597 (D.C. Cir. 1971).

7. James Q. Wilson, ed., *The Politics of Regulation* (New York: Basic Books, 1980); Helen Ingram, "The Political Rationality of Innovation," in *Approaches to Controlling Air Pollution,* ed. Ann Friedlaender (Cambridge: MIT Press, 1978). See especially James Q. Wilson, "American Politics, Then and Now," *Commentary* 67, no. 3 (1979): 39.

8. *Vermont Yankee Nuclear Power Corp. v. Natural Resources Defense Council,* 435 U.S. 519 (1978).

9. For example, *Chevron U.S.A., Inc. v. Natural Resources Defense Council, Inc.,* 467 U.S. 837 (1984).

10. For example, *Immigration and Naturalization Service v. Chadha,* 462 U.S. 919 (1983); *Bowsher v. Synar,* 478 U.S. 714 (1986); *Buckley v. Valeo,* 424 U.S. 1 (1976).

11. *Garcia v. San Antonio Metro. Transit Authority,* 469 U.S. 528 (1985).

12. "Titles I and III of PURPA conscript state utility commissions into the national bureaucratic army" (Justice Sandra Day O'Connor in *F.E.R.C. v. Mississippi,* 456 U.S. 742, 775 [1982]).

I am describing, not decrying. For the large category of conventional environmental problems, "environmental federalism" is, to my mind, the correct approach. I do not agree with critics like Professor Richard Stewart, who believe that in a large and diverse country, locally different environmental policies and implementation approaches generally should be allowed to prevail (Richard Stewart, "Pyramids of Sacrifice? Problems of Federalism in Mandating State Implementation of National Environmental Policy," *Yale Law Journal* 86 [1976]: 1196). Water-quality policy may require different approaches for the eastern and western states, but two, not fifty, approaches would do: Aquatic biology is largely the same all over, industries pollute in pretty much the same way, and the standard control technologies are sold in national and international markets. Interstate effects are so numerous that his argument that local communities should be allowed to suffer greater pollution if they choose cannot withstand close scrutiny. It eludes me why, for example, the national problem of a few models of automobiles, centrally produced in Detroit or Tokyo, fouling urban air with the same few pollutants at the same time of day, should be left to the sturdy denizens of city hall, when uniform car design specifications and emissions control procedures are known to produce superior results. Those who see environmental federalism as an artifact of the mid-1960s doubt that Congress could or would ever move into the zone of state police power.

13. Wilson, "American Politics, Then and Now."

14. See Barry R. Furrow, "Governing Science: Private Risks and Private Remedies," *University of Pennsylvania Law Review* 131 (1983): 1403.

15. M.C.L.A. §691.1201 *et seq.*, M.S.A. §14.528(201) *et seq.*

16. M.S.A. §3(1). See Superfund §301(e) Study Groups, Injuries and Damages from Hazardous Wastes—Analysis and Improvement of Legal Remedies, 97th Cong., 2d Sess., Part 2 Appendices at 312 (Comm. Print 1982).

17. J. Sax and J. Di Mento, "Environmental Citizen Suits: Three Years Experience under the Michigan Environmental Protection Act," *Ecology Law Quarterly* 4 (1974): 1.

18. Ibid.

19. Ibid.

20. For citations to ten state environmental constitutional provisions, see *Environmental Law Reporter* 3 (1973): 10126. For analysis of the provisions, see Roland Frye, "Environmental Provisions in State Constitutions," *Environmental Law Reporter* 5 (1975): 50028. See also A. E. Dick Howard, "State Constitutions and the Environment," *Virginia Law Review* 58 (1972): 193.

21. Two approaches to constitutional recognition of a fundamental right to environmental quality have been discussed in recent years. Neither, however, seems likely to prevail under the current vector of Supreme Court cases in the area. The first relies upon one or all of the penumbra, substantive due process, the Ninth Amendment theories discussed in *Griswold v. Connecticut*, 381 U.S. 479 (1965). This approach would establish an independent environmental right that would take its place alongside the specifically enumerated rights of the Bill of Rights so that it could not be invaded by the federal government except under carefully defined circumstances. The second approach relies upon rather more specific constitutional guarantees, such as the Fifth Amendment's prohibition on the taking of life or liberty without due process of law, or the taking of property without due process and compensation. Under this approach plaintiffs must show that the specific guarantee of the amendment has been violated. See Frederick R. Anderson, "Fundamental Rights and Environmental Quality," in *Science for a Better Environment* (Kyoto: Science Council of Japan, 1975), 825. See also Philip Soper, "The Constitutional Framework of Environmental Law," in *Federal Environmental Law*, ed. Erica L. Dolgin and Thomas G. P. Guilbert (St. Paul: West

Publishing Co., 1974), 20–125. For further contemporaneous support for federal constitutional protection, see E. F. Roberts, "The Right to a Decent Environment, $E = MC^2$: Environment Equals Man Times Courts Redoubling Their Efforts," *Cornell Law Review* 55 (1970): 674, 686; E. F. Roberts, "The Rights to a Decent Environment: Progress along a Constitutional Avenue," in *Law and Environment*, ed. Malcolm F. Baldwin and James K. Page (New York: Walker and Co., 1970), 134–65; David Sive, "Some Thoughts of an Environmental Lawyer in the Wilderness of Administrative Law," *Columbia Law Review* 70 (1970): 612; John C. Esposito, "Air and Water Pollution: What to Do While Waiting for Washington," *Harvard Civil Rights–Civil Liberties Law Review* 5 (1970): 32; William D. Kirchick, "The Continuing Search for a Constitutionally Protected Environment," *Environmental Affairs* 4 (1975): 515; Note, "Toward a Constitutionally Protected Environment," *Virginia Law Review* 56 (1970): 458. For an international perspective, see "The Right to a Humane Environment: A Seminar," *Environmental Policy and Law* 86 (1975).

22. *Environmental Defense Fund v. Hoerner Waldorf*, 1 Environmental Reporter Cases 1640 (D. Mont. Aug. 27, 1970).

23. See Soper, "The Constitutional Framework of Environmental Law"; Richard B. Stewart, "The Development of Administrative and Quasi-Constitutional Law in Judicial Review of Environmental Decisionmaking: Lessons from the Clean Air Act," *Iowa Law Review* 62 (1977): 713.

24. Text of amendment in NWF brochure on file with the author.

25. Guido Calabresi, *A Common Law for the Age of Statutes* (Cambridge: Harvard University Press, 1982), 47.

26. See Stewart, "Development of Administrative and Quasi-Constitutional Law in Judicial Review of Environmental Decisionmaking."

27. See the *Vermont Yankee* case.

28. Richard E. Morgan, *Disabling America: The "Rights Industry" in Our Time* (New York: Basic Books, 1984).

CHAPTER 16

The Impact of Technology

•

•••••

DON K. PRICE

President Reagan's executive order that public officials in positions of sensitive responsibility be required to submit to tests in order to prove that they are not drug addicts led various cities and states, as well as federal agencies, to require that officials have samples of their urine tested by a new technical process. This has stirred up a political rebellion that raises the broad issue of the extent to which modern technology affects our constitutional rights. Police officers in many cities have refused to submit to testing. They are joined by the American Society for Public Administration, which contends that the tests violate the Fourth Amendment's constitutional prohibition against unreasonable searches and seizures. The Federal Center for Disease Control reports that the tests are technically unreliable anyway.

This trivial incident well illustrates the changing relationship of technology to our political and constitutional system. For a century or two technology was considered the foundation of economic and social improvement, as indeed it was, and it led to dreams of limitless and perpetual progress. Now it is seen as a threat to human welfare, and even possibly to the survival of human life on the planet, as indeed it may be. Whether we can maintain its advantages and control its dangers will depend not only on inspired political leadership but also on the way in which our rights may be protected by the general constitutional system. The task of restraining technology's dangers while enabling it to advance human welfare entails the protection of rights by action of the courts. But it also requires an approach far broader than the scope of federal judicial proceedings, broader even than the traditional checks and balances of the federal government's three branches.

Modern technology has created fundamental changes in the nature of our governmental system, changes that we should take into account as we think about the Constitution whose bicentennial we are celebrating. The government's attempts to keep up with advances in the speed of communications, or transportation, or the delivery of nuclear missiles, reflect one such change. Another involves the scope of the federal government, which has long since been able to convert state governments into its agents by the grant-in-aid system and is doing much the same thing with many private corporations by contracting out to them the administration of federal programs. Still another is the practical way in which the so-called branches of government function. The federal executive branch is not merely an extension of the presidency. The ties of its bureaus to congressional committees, and the dependence of their staffs on professional and technological career systems in private institutions, raise new questions of political accountability as the federal executive branch confronts the constitutional rights of private citizens.

If, therefore, we are to deal with the major issues involved in technology's impact on our government and our citizens, we must take a view of the Constitution that is broader than the one that the typical civics textbook presents. We must recognize that, along with the formal document we now celebrate, there is also an unwritten constitution—a hodgepodge of the traditions and customs and institutions that in many important ways explain and control the way the formal Constitution works. And since no one in 1787 could have imagined how technology would influence government two centuries later, we must expand our imagination to visualize the changes in our unwritten constitution that technology has brought about and to assess clearly what they have done either to threaten our rights or to renew our hope for human progress.

As we do so, we should keep two broad points in mind. First, the various fields of technology (and the several scientific disciplines by which these may be developed) are intertwined in their substance. New discoveries in physics or chemistry may, for example, become the basis for new biological knowledge, and engineering inventions may play an important part in medical technology. Such interlocking relationships often make it difficult for a business corporation or government department to arrange for cooperation among technical staff members who need to understand how their work may affect the work of others.

Second, the federal government may try to control technological development without seeking statutory authority to issue orders or regulations that would be subject to review by the courts if challenged on constitutional grounds. Since the federal government pays for the support of so large a proportion of the technological or scientific research in the country, it may regulate that research by exercising its right to withhold funds for certain types of projects—for example, those involving experiments on human subjects. It does not need to rely on the patent system to encourage the research that it can pay for directly.

If we recognize these two points, we must also recognize that those interested in the way technology affects our constitutional rights must deal not with isolated cases but with the complex political fabric of the nation as a whole, and that they must think of the federal government as a means of promoting, as well as restraining, the freedom of individuals and institutions.

An adequately detailed discussion of the impact of technology on our constitutional system—unwritten as well as written—would fill an encyclopedia. The best one can do in a brief article is to note in summary some of the ways in which the application of technology (and science) may threaten constitutional rights or be devoted to their defense. I would like in this article to look briefly at the (1) physical, (2) institutional, and (3) ethical threats posed by technology, and at the benefits that might offset them. It will then be in order to try to assess the bigger picture and to suggest some ways of improving it.

Physical Threats and Benefits

The most fundamental change in the relation of the United States to the world and of its citizens to unchecked authority has of course been brought about by advances in nuclear weapons technology. It is easier to maintain freedom in a country that is relatively immune to foreign attack. England permitted its citizens more freedom than its Continental rivals could allow their citizens because the Channel protected it against invasion, and the House of Commons, while feeling secure enough to let the king control the royal navy with long-term funds, denied appropriations for the army on more than an annual basis. After the Revolution, Americans assumed that the Atlantic was broad enough to permit strict limits on executive power.

But since long-range nuclear missiles now make possible destruction from around the world in a few hours, the original constitutional defenses are quaint relics. The control of the militias by the states means little. The two-year constitutional limit on appropriations for the army has a merely formal effect as the president and the Congress compete for control of long-term financial commitments for the development of weapons technology. The congressional monopoly over declarations of war does not keep the president from sending troops into battle without one or from conducting covert operations abroad and counterintelligence at home. As long as the "hot line" to Moscow exists, the courts and the Congress need to concede to executive discretion to a greater extent than an old-fashioned view of constitutional rights would deem safe.

When a government is sufficiently confident of technology to revoke the licenses of drivers who fail to pass "Breathalyzer" tests, it probably puts far greater faith in such technologies than their statistical reliability justifies, and it certainly fails to comply with the normal requirement of due process in a court of law prior to conviction. In a similar case, when a career military officer, later the president's national security adviser, was suspected (on the basis of *New York Times* reports) of collaboration with foreign espionage and was required to take a polygraph (lie detector) test, which he failed twice, he was cleared only after the *Times* was willing to break its normal rules and vouch for his innocence.

On the other hand, insofar as personal freedom depends on the protection of private property, some of the worst threats to it have come from a new set of highly reliable techniques on which most financial institutions and government offices now rely. If a citizen's record of bank deposits, tax payments, and medical treatments are all on record in some electronic file, they may well become available to institutions that might turn out to be his adversaries. The possibility of such a scenario was recently made apparent in Canada, where the records of all taxpayers in the nation were stolen. The Canadian government reported that modern technology had made it possible to store data on the income of every citizen on microfiche in a quantity that could be carried in a lunch bucket. That technology might well have made it possible to *protect* the privacy of citizens' financial records more effectively than could any paper files, but the extra cost of that alternative often makes it an unattractive one, at least on this side of the Atlantic. In the United States, there has been no sustained effort to follow the example of various European countries to prevent such invasions of privacy as happened in Canada. The threat of a presidential veto led the Congress to drop a proposed Privacy Protection Commission from the Privacy Act of 1974, and the Office of Management and Budget has not been sufficiently staffed for the job.

Two centuries ago, the protection of the environment did not require a coordinated national effort; fresh air and clean water were the responsibility of each state or each county. It is significant, then, that the first important bill taken up by the One-hundredth Congress was the Clean Water Bill, vetoed by the president in 1986 but enacted over his veto by an overwhelming margin. Newer developments in technology are not always to be blamed for today's environmental problems; acid rain, for example, comes from the old smokestack industries of the Middle West. Its damage to New England forests (like the damage to Scandinavian forests from industry in Great Britain) might indeed be controlled more effectively by expansion of sophisticated technologies. But these also have their risks: A federal court has had to penalize a private manufacturer heavily for releasing toxic PCBs into New Bedford harbor and other waterways of southern Massachusetts, damaging the beaches and the fisheries of the area. Leaks in gas pipelines from New Jersey to Mississippi have been found to contaminate sources of drinking water.

Institutional Threats and Benefits

Constitutional rights were relatively easily protected by three branches of the federal government when the economy was based on the independent enterprise of the individual and when state and local governments had more control over business and agriculture than they do now. That situation has changed slowly but profoundly with the movement toward "privatization." Great corporations have come to dominate industry and commerce; the system of federal grants-in-aid has weakened states' rights, and federal agencies have begun to contract the management of governmental functions out to private corporations.

We may therefore grasp our problem more directly if we move away from technology's immediate physical threats or benefits to constitutional rights and ask how changes in the institutional structure of society have affected those rights. To answer that question, we need first to consider the operation of governmental institutions, not only as they are controlled by the unwritten constitution but also as they are influenced by private institutions, such as the established professions.

The system of contracting and subcontracting illustrates some of the ways in which the participation of private institutions in governmental operations may now affect our interests. Electronic circuits, silicon chips, and magnetic materials are the basis of modern military weapons, and U.S. firms with weapons contracts have subcontracted much of their manufacture out to other countries, especially to Japan. This international dependence goes deeper than the factory level, into the institutions that produce new technological knowledge. More foreign than American students are now receiving Ph.D.s in engineering in American universities, and some of the most prestigious of these universities have developed systematic ties with major Japanese companies to raise money and develop research laboratories on a cooperative basis.

Nuclear accidents, massive oil spills, and other pollution control failures in various countries have made it more and more apparent that the protection of human welfare depends not only on American collaboration with other governments but also on the influence of technology and the sciences on legal processes and on the several professional organizations that are influential in policy issues. Protecting the rights of the citizen as they are broadly defined in the Preamble of the Constitution—maintaining a strong national defense, promoting the general welfare, and securing for each individual the blessings of liberty—requires systematic action by groups with the knowledge and expertise to deal with the social consequences of modern technology. The groups that possess the needed skills are the established professions, notably law, engineering, and medicine. Each has been involved in both complicating the enforcement of rights and seeking new ways to protect them.

Of these three, the one we have relied most heavily upon in the past to protect our constitutional rights has, of course, been the legal profession, the foundation of the judicial system. This reliance has been most useful when the interest of the citizens requires the prevention of action by governmental authority. But in dealing with the effects of complex technological developments on human welfare, it is necessary to take into account not only the legal issues but also their interaction with economic and technical problems. Technological progress has surely fostered the interdependence of the nation's various economic activities, and in the public interest it has become necessary to put stricter limits on property rights and on the freedom to initiate new forms of business without counting their costs to society as a whole. When the public interest requires private business to internalize the costs of protection of the environment or of the public health, it becomes necessary to go beyond the original system of judicial procedure and to resort to the network of administrative law within regulatory agencies and commissions.

Take as an example the issue of food safety regulation. At one time the Food and Drug Administration was prepared to prohibit saccharin, the artificial sweetener used by many adults who were trying to reduce their weight and by many children who were addicted to soft drinks. At that time a federal statute that banned carcinogens in any quantity was already in place, and improved testing procedures were able to register minuscule amounts of carcinogens that in earlier years had been undetectable. Saccharin became one of the offending substances to be taken off the supermarket shelves. But protests against such a rigid ban were led by the very scientists whose research had frightened the politicians into action. Their concern led Congress to delay the ban, while requiring a study of the problem by the National Academy of Sciences, a federally chartered private organization. The academy's report led to a more balanced judgment: The use of saccharin should not be prohibited, and the Food and Drug Administration should be allowed more flexibility and discretion in dealing with substances on which the scientific verdict is not clear-cut. In such cases, it is not always the scientists who wish to use the results of science to limit constitutional freedoms.

The saccharin case was typical of many in which the legal approach—laws enacted by Congress, interpreted by the courts, and made the basis of suits by individuals—comes to be less than satisfactory in the protection of individual rights. The compromise procedure of administrative law and regulatory agencies or commissions, which some political scientists have described as the "fourth branch" of the government, has often turned out to involve as much procrastination and fumbling as the legal approach itself.

Some scientists have suggested that the best solution would be to set up a "science court," a formal body of scientists who would identify the important issues as they arose and then deliberate among themselves to find the best way of responding to them. That idea has never been implemented, perhaps because it depends on the assumption that technical issues can be separated from other issues and decided on their own, an assumption about which politicians and administrators (and an increasing number of scientists) are deeply skeptical. To these critics, yet another piece of constitutional machinery, another locus of formal authority, would be worse than useless. Working science and technology into our system of checks and balances requires a more flexible system, outside the scope of constitutional rights as the legal profession has customarily interpreted them. If the legal profession is reluctant to adjust its approach to the impact of technology on rights, it may be because the profession itself, protected by bar examinations, law schools, and court rules, enjoys a status in society too powerful to put in jeopardy by making compromises. But if law does not adjust itself readily to deal with the problem, what about other professional groups?

Many have looked to engineering as an obvious alternative. A diverse professional group, less tightly organized than the law, it had never managed to the same degree to define its own qualifications, or to set up as clear-cut a system of training within universities. But it does supply a large share of the managers who go on to executive jobs in industrial corporations. Such leaders have traditionally been quick to observe the danger to enterprise of too much federal regulation of their corporations. This reaction, encouraged in the 1920s by Herbert Hoover, the eminent engineer and secretary of commerce, led to the organization of private institutions like the American Society of Mechanical Engineers, which defined safety standards that were made effective either by voluntary compliance or by being enacted into law by state legislatures. This decentralized approach was similar to that encouraged by the federal land-grant system for the support of agriculture and the "mechanic arts."

During World War II, engineering allied itself with the sciences as the basis of its professional identity in government as well as in the leading technological universities. Engineering research and education, thanks to Vannevar Bush and his colleagues in the Office of Scientific Research and Development, came to be suffused with the basic sciences, and to have a profound effect on the way in which the executive branch dealt with major issues in domestic as well as international affairs.

In some administrations, technological advice was rendered through a president's Science Advisory Committee, and in others through individual advisers, always with a mix from the National Academy of Sciences and from private institutions such as the Rand Corporation (many of them financed by government), to which the study of problems might be assigned. Even though engineering as a profession is not as tightly organized as the legal profession, its general influence is often considered when issues arise in which individual constitutional rights need to be balanced against the benefits of technological development.

The medical profession is as tightly organized as the law, and it has as immediate an impact as does engineering on political and social issues. In the area of public health, medicine has always worked closely with engineering; public sanitation, prevention of water pollution, and food safety require government regulation that protects the consumer and is therefore not considered a violation of the constitutional rights of business interests.

Advances in medical science, however, pose new problems. Genetic engineering has produced new forms of life that the courts have decided can be patented. Computers now control medical devices, and regulators wonder what to do, for example, about heart pacemakers that are programmable from outside the body—and not only by the patient or his physician. With more than 50,000 chemicals in common use, it has become impossible to estimate the damage done by exposure to them in small amounts over long-term use, to find ways for lawyers to bring tort actions against their manufacturers within the period of the statute of limitations, or to organize lawsuits to deal with mass disasters affecting many people to slight degrees.

New medical techniques challenge the old legal assumptions about the life span from birth to death. When doctors learned how to determine the sex of a fetus, or to identify its disabilities, or to implant sperm into a womb without sexual contact, they raised a new set of problems for biomedical ethicists, not to mention would-be parents.

At the other end of the life span, the possibility for biological functioning to outlast consciousness raises questions of how much effort and expense should be devoted to maintaining some kind of existence for a human being who will never again be aware that he or she is alive. The legal definition of death, like the legal definition of a parent or a person, is made the subject of much uneasy scrutiny in the deliberations that take place in hospitals and courts.

Along with the established professions, the press, with its constitutional guarantee of freedom, is expected to defend the rights of citizens. But today's news media play a different role from that of their predecessors. One need not idealize the small journals of the eighteenth century to believe that something has been lost by the consolidation of papers into vast chains, and even more by their replacement by television as the public's major source of news. With a mass audience, a general newspaper finds it risky to take a critical stand that may offend the sensitivity of a group of subscribers. With three great television networks dominating the news channels, and concerning themselves more with entertaining than enlightening their viewers, much of the function of criticizing public officials has been taken over by the newsletters and periodicals of business, labor, scientific, and reform groups.

Newspapers at least make an effort to distinguish between factual reporting and the expression of editorial opinion. Television, with its emotional impact on the viewer and its illusion of immediate participation in such violent events as terrorism, often fails to distinguish between facts and values in its news programs and has a less creditable role in the protection of civil and constitutional rights. The National Institute of Mental Health concluded a few years ago that there was a causal relationship between the depiction of violence on television and violent behavior in real life. Regardless of whether the behavioral sciences can prove such a connection, it seems obvious that television makes it far more difficult for the voters to delegate to their constitutional representatives adequate authority to deal with such matters as international terrorism or subversive threats. Civilian officials with authority over military forces must find it very difficult to resist the pressure put on them by the evening television news to take immediate and drastic offensive action.

Ethical Questions

The framers of the Constitution were aware that their formal legal institutions could not by themselves guarantee liberty. They could not possibly be effective if corrupted by degraded moral attitudes. James Madison, the most hardheaded inventor of the checks and balances in the Constitution, asked whether there was any virtue among us. If not, he said, no form of government could make us secure. To suppose that any kind of government would guarantee liberty or happiness without virtue in the people was a chimerical idea, as far as he was concerned. If Madison was right, and I think he was, then we need to consider not merely what protection is given to our constitutional rights by the vigilance of the courts, the established professions, or the freedom of the press, but what the prevalent moral or ethical principles are that guide their actions and our own. We cannot expect to find precise answers, but we should try at least to ask the questions.

A major purpose of the new Constitution was "to provide for the common defense." In view of the protection of the Atlantic Ocean and the outcome of the American Revolution, that seemed a feasible goal. But over the centuries that had preceded the Constitution, advancing technology had weakened the limitations on aggressive warfare: The longbow and then the rifle had made popular armies predominant over the armored feudal chivalry; later, the cannon, the battleship, and the airplane undermined the independence of the small European nations. With guided missiles and nuclear bombs, where will such threats to the common defense of the United States stop, short of participation in a new Constitution embracing the world as a whole, or at least other democracies? For the continuous threat posed by new technologies has come from beyond the influence of treaties, and it is difficult to combat by American action of the kind that involved congressional declarations of war or presidential authority over army or navy campaigns. In the light of these technological developments, what moral principles must guide the relations of the United States to the United Nations or to our allies, or the extent to which covert activities are justified, or the need to have presidential decisions checked by congressional review?

"To promote the general welfare" was another stated purpose of the new Constitution. Throughout much of the nineteenth century, economic welfare was promoted by the new technology that made greater industrial productivity possible and by the courts' support of its growth in great corporations. As the idea of "welfare" came later to demand governmental programs to protect lower-income groups, the social sciences were enlisted to help determine how best to maximize economic benefits through political action. The answers were sought through policy analysis, which undertook to calculate the combination of administrative actions, and the limits on them, that would produce the greatest good for the greatest number. But it has become increasingly clear that there are moral limitations on the efficiency approach to the general welfare—policy analysts must also take into account the rights of minority groups, the considerations of distributive justice, political freedom, and the rights of future generations.

Such ethical or moral issues were for many years not the main, or even a major, restraint on the expansion of economic productivity and the efficient distribution of national income—political manipulation by regional and minority groups had always had their effects on the proceedings of the Congress. But as time went on, the concern of more and more scientists for the protection of the environment or other aspects of the national ecology led them to engage in political action. Such protection required action from influential leaders, like the governors from the Northeast who protested acid rain or warned of the danger of radioactive contamination threatened by the newer atomic power plants.

Securing "the blessings of liberty"—another great purpose of the Constitution—depended on a compromise between moral beliefs based on religious tradition and the Enlightenment's doctrine of religious toleration, as advocated by John Locke and observed in later centuries by Montesquieu and Tocqueville. That compromise, with its wide differences among the various states, was rather shakily maintained for nearly two centuries. While most Protestant churches were split over the issue of slavery and the Civil War, the civil rights movement was furthered by the support of most churches a century later. But other fundamental moral issues, over which religious leaders are divided, have been raised by the technological developments of the past few years. The new biological technologies that have challenged our most basic understanding of human life call for a more searching moral approach to constitutional rights. Is it right to permit a new form of life to be patented? Is the abortion of a defective fetus morally warranted, now that the Supreme Court has legalized abortion, and new methods of detection of defects during early pregnancy have been discovered? And what should the courts do about euthanasia, or surrogate motherhood, or the creation of test-tube babies? Considerations of economy or immediate welfare lead families to petition the courts for more latitude than would have been tolerable a few decades ago.

But now some scientists have joined the philosophers and theologians who are beginning to ask whether the new technology does not require a new moral conception of constitutional rights, one whose ethical foundation is more stable than the mere struggle for existence. On such issues, the political views of religious groups are confusing and confused. Respected Catholic theologians express views on economic and moral issues that shock the hierarchy, and among the more populist Protestant denominations we have seen a great resurgence of fundamentalism supporting aggressive political action on every level, including the office of president.

The most conspicuous effect of technological development on international defense, economic welfare, and individual liberty over two centuries has been to increase the scale of government. In the early days of the Constitution, checks and balances were relatively simple; the government as a whole was tiny, and below the top level of each of the three branches there was no substantial independent organized force to be taken into account. Today, the tens of thousands of staff members serving the Congress, and the millions in the civil and military services of the executive branch, develop corporate wills of their own. And the system of checks and balances then becomes far more complex. Some of the most difficult issues that now arise are not between the president and the Congress, but between the executive office, with its temporary political staffs, and the subordinate executive agencies, whose career personnel are often committed to policies that are based on their own technological backgrounds and ambitions and that the president sometimes fails to understand. In such cases, it seems clear that the ethic of hierarchical accountability is hardly adequate in the American constitutional system.

Conclusion

Technology has developed so broad a range of problems that involve the federal government with the interests of local governments, private corporations, and welfare institutions that it is impossible to rely entirely on the traditional defenses of individual rights. The new intellectual interest in "privatization" is one part of the effort to construct centers of administrative independence against centralized authority. But the advocates of privatization must confront the new nature of the problem of defending individual rights; namely, that it is no longer possible to rely on formal constitutional barriers; it is necessary instead to recognize the greater effectiveness of a political and moral consensus on the general institutional structure of society as a whole.

Individual rights therefore depend less and less, year by year, on the letter of constitutional law as defined by the courts, and more and more on the unwritten constitution, as supported by the moral beliefs of the general public. By 1787, the authors of the written Constitution understood that science and technology were not the basis for a single ideology, a pervasive system of authority. Their memories of escaping from royal oppression and from the Puritan dogmatism of the previous century had inoculated them, so to speak, against the doctrines that, beginning with the French Revolution, swept the European continent eastward and (in the rhetoric of Comte and Hegel and Marx) established a scientific theory of politics that supported single-party domination.

As that experience shows, it is impossible to rely completely on the leaders of science and technology to provide the intellectual basis for an unwritten constitution that defends our rights and liberties against authoritarian ideologies. But the institutions that those leaders have organized for their support, both within their own professions and in collaboration with government, have been based on a continuous specialization of interests and an unwillingness to let any one specialty or intellectual paradigm dominate the others. Science and technology do not have the answers to our major political problems, as indispensable as they may be to the solutions to those problems. To let science and technology take over would be a great danger to the rest of society. But as checks and balances against each other, and against the systems of law and politics, they may play an important role in interpreting and defending the unwritten constitution—as long as they are in harmony with the moral sense of the general public.

That moral sense has supported the defense of constitutional rights and freedoms continuously ever since the Enlightenment leaders of our constitutional tradition, including Franklin, Jefferson, and the Adamses, played an active role in the principal scientific and intellectual organizations of their era. That tradition demands political pluralism and human freedom, and if we can defend it, it will help preserve our rights far more effectively than will the finely tuned logic of constitutional lawyers.

But in spite of the reassurance that traditions bring, technology has brought threats that could destroy our traditions, our freedoms, and our lives. The threat of nuclear war is the greatest of these threats, since it has the technical potential to destroy all human life. And the need to protect the nation against military threats, or against environmental pollution or terrorism or other dangers that technology has wrought, may lead to concentrations of political and administrative authority that would endanger human rights. Which way the balance will turn remains to be seen, and much depends on the vigilance, as well as the moral consensus, of our citizens. My final estimate is that I remain an optimist, in the terms of the classic definition of an optimist as one who holds that the future is still uncertain.

CHAPTER 17

The United States
Constitution, Public Opinion,
and the Problem
of American Exceptionalism

.....

MICHAEL KAMMEN

How distinctive is the American constitutional system? Although that question has not been altogether neglected, rarely has it been responded to in cultural rather than structural terms. It has traditionally been answered, in fact, by contrasting the operational relationships among governmental institutions or branches in the United States with those in Great Britain. Frequently the analyst then carries the comparison a step further by indicating a preference for one system rather than the other, or else by arguing that one's own arrangement would be improved by incorporating certain essential attributes of the other.[1]

I would like to explore the issue along cultural lines by looking at the role of public opinion in our constitutional setup. More specifically, I am interested in American attitudes toward the function or proper place of public opinion in a governmental system that aspires to be democratic while having an independent (and largely unelected) judiciary at its upper echelons.

It is necessary to acknowledge at the outset that we cannot comfortably generalize about public opinion in a singular way, either in a diachronic or in a synchronic sense. Why? Because we find either ambivalence or an absence of consensus at any given moment in time (whether it be the 1830s, the 1870s, or the 1980s), but also because there have been fundamental changes over time in American feelings about the proper role of public opinion in constitutional matters. More on these shifts in a moment. First, I should clarify what I mean by "exceptionalism," especially in the context of constitutional matters.

For nearly a decade now we have been sensitized to the importance of comparative analysis in order to avoid the parochialism that has caused too many historians of the United States to make contestable claims for the uniqueness or autonomy of American history.[2] It is particularly noteworthy, however, that increased attention to comparisons has caused many observers, American as well as foreign, to be more impressed by differences than by similarities. Reports that American exceptionalism is dead seem to have been premature, to say the least. If anything, that phenomenon or perspective has been rather solidly bolstered by new bodies of impressive evidence.[3]

If we look at constitutionalism in the United States through the lens of American exceptionalism, we should not be surprised to find multiple patterns arranged around a complex core of kaleidoscopic changes. James Madison, for example, along with most members of his generation, subscribed to the belief that the American people possessed their own peculiar "genius," particularly in politics, and that the federal Constitution of 1787 *had* to be a product of that genius and also to remain consistent with it. As Madison wrote in his essay on "Charters," published in the *National Gazette* early in 1792: "In Europe, charters of liberty [i.e., constitutions] have been granted by power. America has set the example . . . of charters of power granted by liberty. . . . The citizens of the United States have peculiar [i.e., distinctive] motives to support the energy of their constitutional charters."[4]

Less than a century later, however, serious students of American constitutionalism would acknowledge that in significant respects our system shared common origins with that of the British and had, moreover, become more like it with the passage of time.[5] By the middle of the twentieth century, when Perry Miller became immersed in his work *The Legal Mind in America, from Independence to the Civil War* (1962), he sought guidance from authorities at Harvard Law School. This extract from a long advisory letter written by Professor Henry M. Hart is indicative of a cosmopolitan and spreading skepticism concerning American exceptionalism: "It seems to me important to make clear that the controversy over codification was raging at the same time in Europe [the 1840s and 1850s] and with comparable intensity. I do not mean to say that this fact invalidates your thesis that the codification movement here was an expression of a significant strain in

American culture. But codification was not an American conception. The idea simply found hospitable soil here."[6]

Judicial review, by way of contrast, has frequently been touted as the most distinctive American contribution to the entire history of Western constitutionalism, and its origins are traditionally located between 1796 (*Hylton v. United States*),[7] when the Supreme Court upheld an act of Congress, and 1803 (*Marbury v. Madison*),[8] when the Court invalidated one section of the Federal Judiciary Act of 1789.

Commonly overlooked, however, is the American propensity, visible even before state constitutions first appeared in 1776, to declare unacceptable policies or actions by a government unconstitutional. Assertions of that sort were common in 1774–75 and provide one of the earliest and most striking instances of constitutionalism firmly rooted in popular opinion at the grass-roots level. In 1774, for example, the standing Committee of Correspondence in Gloucester County, Virginia, resolved "that it is the opinion of this meeting, that taxation and representation are inseparable. . . . Every attempt of [Parliament] to impose internal taxes on *America,* is arbitrary, unconstitutional, and oppressive." Echoes of that resolve could be heard in Kent County, Delaware, and Hackensack, New Jersey.[9]

Populist patriots discoursed on matters *un*constitutional even before they learned and contributed to the language of constitutionalism. From the eve of the American Revolution onward, public opinion and constitutionalism powerfully reinforced one another. They made a potent combination. Except for a brief and unsuccessful flurry in Britain during the 1780s and 1790s, they had no counterpart as a tandem anywhere else in the world. It seems fair to assert, then, that an incipient notion of popular constitutionalism preceded and helped to provide an impetus for our most creative phase of formal constitution making, 1776–87.

That truly remarkable era would stamp American constitutionalism as a distinctive phenomenon for a long time to come. Constitutions that are written, succinct, and new cannot serve as "mythical charters," which is what one finds through most of recorded history up until that time, and even well into the nineteenth century. The heroic epics of ancient Greece, transmitted by oral tradition, served as mythical charters, just as the discolored skull of a venerable chieftain, wrapped in cloth strips taken from the robes of all his successors, fulfilled the same role for certain preindustrial peoples.[10] Such "charters" were suffused with sacred stories, and hence human interest, in a way that the American constitutions of 1776–87 could not be. However much the latter enjoyed the imprimatur and legitimacy of popular sovereignty, they could not and would not embody the broad appeal of popular myths meant to explain the founding of a people or a state.

Other sorts of contrasts emerge if we examine the constitution of Renaissance Venice, which was literally displayed in the traditional ducal procession. As Edward Muir has explained:

> Besides illustrating the symbiosis of the religious and political organs of authority, the origins of Venetian independence, and the harmony of Venetian society, the [ducal] procession created a paradigmatic arrangement of the Venetian constitution and social structure. . . . More than merely reinforcing the ideology of Venice, the ducal processions helped create the ideology by serving as a conscious, visible synthesis of the parts of society: each symbol or person in the procession corresponded to a specific principle or institution; placed together and set in motion, they were the narrative outline for the myth of Venetian republicanism.[11]

Unlike the American constitutions, which combined a degree of popular sovereignty with domination by accessible elites, the Venetian constitution wrapped patrician domination in a myth of social harmony and the legitimacy of historic origins. That myth provided the Venetians with more than a modicum of constitutional flexibility. As Muir puts it: "What could be more delightful than a political paragon that was kaleidoscopic? Turned slightly this way or that, the Venetian constitution could become almost anything one wanted or needed it to be." Note well, however, that here "one" refers to patrician leaders, not to popular opinion. The constitution and political culture of republican Venice were vastly different from those of republican America.[12]

Similarly, the Constitution of Epidaurus that launched modern Greek independence in 1822 was susceptible to manipulation in various ways but did not lend itself to being applied or revised through the filters of public opinion. So also was the long-standing British notion of an "ancient constitution," as well as the symbol-laden constitution that the British bestowed upon India in Victorian times.[13] By contrast, the new American constitutions were more fixed and less flexible. Yet the force of public opinion could and did result in periodic revisions—

and even replacements. One of the most remarkable (yet unremarked) differences between most early modern constitutions and our own is that the latter were not mythical charters. They were real, written, and consequently less malleable in any immediate way. With the passage of time, however, that would change.

Although scholars have not been indifferent to the role of public opinion in American life, their attention to it has been more random, episodic, and hortatory than systematic and substantive.[14] We know that a journal called *Public Opinion* appeared in the 1890s, for instance, and that in time of war, especially, public opinion has been used as coercive pressure in order to mobilize support. During World War I, for example, a widely distributed poster displayed a woman (presumably a compound of Columbia and Miss Liberty) in classical drapery, her right fist clenched and her left hand raised in a gesture that seems to suggest the imminence of a citizen's arrest. Above her head, in very bold letters, appear the words "I AM PUBLIC OPINION," followed by this admonition:

> All men fear me!
> I declare that Uncle Sam shall not go to his knees to beg you to buy his bonds. That is no position for a fighting man. But if you have the money to buy and do not buy, I will make this No Man's Land for you!
> I will judge you not by your mad cheers as our boys march away to whatever fate may have in store for them.
> I will judge you not by the warmth of the tears you shed over the lists of the dead and the injured that come to us from time to time.
> I will judge you not by your uncovered head and solemn mien as our maimed in battle return to our shores for loving care.
> But, as wise as I am just, I will judge you by the material aid you give to the fighting men who are facing death that you may live and move and have your being in a world made safe.
> I warn you—don't talk patriotism over here unless your money is talking victory over there.
> I AM PUBLIC OPINION!
> AS I JUDGE, ALL MEN STAND OR FALL!

Directly below those stanzas the poster advised: "Buy U.S. Gov't. Bonds Fourth Liberty Loan."[15]

By the early 1920s, Walter Lippmann and Edward L. Bernays

had alerted the country, as never before, to the potential force of popular opinion in business and advertising as well as public affairs.[16] Within a decade scholars had made the scientific study of public opinion an innovative subdiscipline. Public opinion polling developed rapidly during the later 1930s and has proliferated for various purposes ever since.[17] Indeed, it is one of the most precise areas of activity within the social sciences.

To what extent, then, did the framers of the United States Constitution anticipate the swift emergence of public opinion as a prominent force in American politics? The customary response to such a query has ranged somewhere between "not at all" and "barely." I would like to suggest that they were not so naive as those answers might appear to indicate. On the one hand, they recognized that public opinion is an exceedingly elusive phenomenon. But on the other, they believed that republicanism and popular sovereignty, by their very nature, permitted public opinion to play a more influential role than in any other governmental system ever known.

There is abundant evidence that public opinion began to be taken into account as an inescapable factor by the boldest expounders of political thought in Great Britain during the last decades of the eighteenth century.[18] Their writings circulated in North America and confirmed what many there already knew: namely, that the Stamp Act crisis of 1765–66 had aroused widespread political awareness and activity. One of the most telling legacies of that crisis, in fact, may very well have been an insatiable hunger for political news—a direct result of the recognition that such news could affect behavior as well as attitudes. In 1795, for example, when St. George Tucker of Virginia asked Jeremy Belknap how Massachusetts had managed to abolish Negro slavery, Belknap replied: "The general answer is, that slavery hath been abolished here by *public opinion;* which began to be established about thirty years ago."[19]

For the delegates to the Constitutional Convention in 1787 there certainly was no "representative" position concerning the most appropriate or ideal role of public opinion in the governmental system they hoped to establish. Nevertheless, remarks made by William Paterson of New Jersey on June 9 seem to have been a reasonable summation of the sentiments shared by many. According to Paterson (as reported by James Madison): "The idea of a national Govt. as contradistinguished from a federal one, never entered into the mind of any of them [i.e., the state legislatures], and to the public mind we must accommodate ourselves. We have no power to go beyond the federal scheme, and if we had the people are not ripe for any other. We must follow the people; the people will not follow us."[20] From Paterson's perspective, the nature of the new government ought to be responsive to the "public mind," not merely in an expedient sense but as a matter of republican political ethics.

On June 18 Alexander Hamilton delivered a very long address to the Convention, a schematization of his ideal constitution that is said to have lasted for more than five hours. Half a century later, at the time of the Constitution's Golden Jubilee, John Quincy Adams found a copy of Hamilton's speech in the papers of James Madison. Although Adams admired many particular aspects of Hamilton's plan, he conceded that it would have placed too much power in the new national government and that it bore too many similarities to the British constitution. Consequently its tendencies were such "as the public opinion of that day never would have tolerated."[21]

Hamilton was not so unrealistic and oblivious to public opinion as he is customarily depicted to have been, however. He differed from most of his contemporaries only in wishing to shape and lead rather than consistently follow public opinion. In the 70th *Federalist* he positively acknowledged "the restraints of public opinion" as a safeguard "for the faithful exercise of any delegated power." And in the 84th *Federalist* he insisted that freedom of the press ultimately depended not so much upon constitutional clauses as upon "public opinion, and on the general spirit of the people and of the government."

Soon after Hamilton's strange (though apparently uninterrupted) speech on June 18, he left the Convention for a period in order to return to New York. On July 3 he explained to George Washington in a letter that during his travels and since reaching New York City he had "taken particular pains to discover the public sentiment." He then revealed that he, for one, would be content to placate whatever appeared to be the public will. "The prevailing apprehension among thinking men," he observed, "is that the Convention, from a fear of shocking the popular opinion, will not go far enough."[22]

In the 49th *Federalist*, first published on February 2, 1788, Madison offered one of the shrewdest commentaries on the fundamen-

tal character of public opinion. He followed up a very sweeping generalization with an important qualification based upon his keen understanding of human nature.

> If it be true that all governments rest on opinion, it is no less true
> that the strength of opinion in each individual, and its practical
> influence on his conduct, depend much on the number which he
> supposes to have entertained the same opinion. The reason of man,
> like man himself is timid and cautious, when left alone; and acquires
> firmness and confidence, in proportion to the number with which it
> is associated.

Early in 1792, when Madison published his essay "Charters"
[i.e., constitutions], he elaborated this theme of public opinion in the
context of republican government. "All power has been traced up to
opinion," he wrote.

> The stability of all governments and security of all rights may be
> traced to the same source. The most arbitrary government is con-
> trouled where the public opinion is fixed. . . . The most systematic
> governments are turned by the slightest impulse from their regular
> paths, where public opinion no longer holds them in it. . . . How
> devoutly is it to be wished, then, that the public opinion of the
> United States should be enlightened; that it should attach itself to
> their governments as delineated in *great charters*, derived not from
> the usurped power of kings, but from the legitimate authority of the
> people.[23]

Although Madison's positions in 1787–88 and 1792 are consistent, his tone had changed from speculative and analytical to hortatory,
if a bit apprehensive. What had happened during that four-year span to
alter his tone? We cannot know with certainty, but one expert on the
period, Professor Jack N. Rakove, has persuasively suggested that the
state ratification campaigns in 1788 had been designed to activate
public opinion and had succeeded beyond anyone's wildest imagination. Constituent impact promptly became more important than leaders
had anticipated; and by 1790 coping with the pressures of public
opinion turned out to be much more problematic for elected officials
than delegates to the Convention had anticipated in 1787.[24]

During the decades that followed, two lines of discourse emerged.
The first, and the less important in my view, celebrated in a rather
mindless (and sometimes insincere) manner the emergence of public

opinion as a sign of the progress of civilization.[25] The alternative response revealed a deepening of Madison's concern, and it cut across ideological lines. An arch-Federalist like Fisher Ames, for example, worried that public opinion would "govern rulers," and he urged that it "be purified from the dangerous errors from which it is infected."[26] Thomas Jefferson, however, the founder and figurehead of democratic republicanism, also expressed concern that "public opinion erects itself into an inquisition, and exercises its office with as much fanaticism as fans the flames of an auto da fe."[27]

When the revolutionary generation was supplanted by several sorts of successor groups during the middle third of the nineteenth century, that apprehensiveness about public opinion gave way to a determination to guide or even control it. That task was challenging enough. In 1835, for example, the executive committee of the Female Moral Reform Society determined that "public opinion must be operated upon by endeavoring to bring the virtuous to treat the guilty of both sexes alike, and exercise toward them the same feeling."[28]

The toughest tests arose, however, when Americans disagreed strenuously—when public opinion was fundamentally divided—concerning an issue that was overtly constitutional or else required constitutional resolution, such as chartering a national bank,[29] federal regulation of slavery in the territories, or a proposal from the National Liberal League in 1876 to seek a constitutional amendment for "the total separation of Church and State."[30]

An unusual (in fact, rare) response to situations of that sort has been to seek a constitutional referendum. When repeal of the Eighteenth Amendment (Prohibition) remained a bitterly contentious political issue in 1932–33, Congress wanted to utilize the constitutional process that seemed most indicative of the majority voice in public opinion. Consequently Congress required that specially elected state conventions be chosen to ratify the Twenty-first Amendment (repeal of Prohibition), rather than using the existing state legislatures.[31] So far, that has been the *only* occasion in our history when Congress chose the selection of special state conventions. The point, however, is that mechanisms do exist so that if the Constitution is altered, it can happen (as closely as possible) in accordance with the popular will.

The value of mobilizing public opinion in order to assist or impede constitutional change has not been lost on political activists. In February 1937, for example, after Franklin D. Roosevelt announced his "Court-packing" plan, a New York–based group that opposed it asked Frank Gannett, the conservative newspaper magnate, to energize and lead a public opinion crusade against the plan. As Senator William E. Borah of Idaho wrote to Gannett: "With your newspaper training and your background you can inform the people back home of the dangers of this bill."[32]

Gannett formed a National Committee to Uphold Constitutional Government. The size of his mailings increased from an initial test probe of 10,000 persons spread across all forty-eight states to nearly 15 million envelopes sent from New York City during the most crucial six months of the struggle. It was the largest mailing effort ever mounted in connection with any legislative struggle in American history. Gannett also mobilized a shrewd telegram campaign directed at key senators who appeared to be wavering. He provided carefully selected information for the writers of newspaper editorials, and his committee prepared thirteen recordings (mostly speeches) for release to radio stations. The pervasive use of public opinion to achieve political and constitutional ends was unprecedented in 1937.[33] It is difficult to imagine that process being carried out on such a scale (under non-authoritarian auspices) anywhere else in the world at that time.

Perhaps the most frequent and visible interaction between public opinion and constitutional change has involved the United States Supreme Court. The lessons of history that emerge from this nexus are, however, anything but clear-cut. Alexis de Tocqueville once remarked of the justices that "their power is immense, but it is power springing from opinion." He then added, in two sentences that are rarely quoted: "Of all powers, that of opinion is the hardest to use, for it is impossible to say exactly where its limits come. Often it is as dangerous to lay behind as to outstrip it."[34] How prophetic Tocqueville turned out to be with respect to the desegregation of public facilities, busing to achieve racial balance in the schools, affirmative action programs, abortion, capital punishment, and school prayer.

During the past generation, scholars have scarcely neglected the interaction between public opinion and the Supreme Court. Predictably, thanks to the abundance of polls on the Court in general as well as particular issues that it has decided, we know a fair amount about American attitudes toward the Court[35] (and, to a lesser degree, toward the Constitution itself[36]).

What remains neglected, however, is the "flip side" of the coin: namely, the attitudes of the justices themselves toward public opinion and its relationship—real and perceived—to their roles. This matter is of some consequence, since most of the justices have held strong views about public perceptions of their work—and about how responsive they ought to be to those perceptions. On some occasions, for example, the Court has been so concerned about the state of public opinion that it has delayed the announcement of decisions.[37] Even more important, there have been times when the Court became less activist (in 1937 and 1968, for example) in order to minimize damage to the institution's prestige.

When we look to the justices themselves, however, we swiftly find that they have been of several minds concerning the proper relationship between public opinion and Supreme Court deliberations. The earliest position, so far as I can tell, as well as the most persistent, assumes that public opinion will play a major role whether we want it to or not, but that in a democratic system, public opinion is likely to enjoy a degree of power that may be inappropriately excessive. In an 1829 address, for instance, Justice Joseph Story put it this way: "Our government is emphatically a government of the people, in all its departments. It purports to be a government of law, and not of men; and yet, beyond all others, it is subject to the control and influence of public opinion."[38] Story's apprehensive outlook, widely shared among moderates and conservatives, is notable for its emphasis upon American exceptionalism as well as its concern about the impact of public opinion upon American law and constitutionalism.

In 1837, when Story found himself a distressed dissenter in the Charles River Bridge case, he denounced the Taney Court (pro-Democrat) for placing the whims of public opinion above the obligations of law.[39] That has been the essential attitude ever since of Justices Oliver Wendell Holmes and Robert H. Jackson, and, most recently, of Chief Justice William H. Rehnquist.[40] Rehnquist presented his position with prudent restraint in 1976 and once again a decade later: "A mere change in public opinion since the adoption of the Constitution, unaccompanied by a constitutional amendment, should not change the meaning of the Constitution."[41]

Many of the justices, particularly during the past fifty years, have argued with intense feeling that the Bill of Rights, above all, ought to be insulated from the passions and prejudices of an ill-informed public. Justice Jackson epitomized this view in a major opinion written for the Court in 1943. The occasion was the second of the well-known flag salute cases involving Jehovah's Witnesses. "The very purpose of the Bill of Rights," Jackson wrote, "was to withdraw certain subjects from the vicissitudes of political controversy, to place them beyond the reach of majorities and officials and to establish them as legal principles to be applied by the courts."[42]

Although such attitudes, ranging from cautious to critical, have predominated, they have not always prevailed, and they certainly do not represent the entire spectrum of the justices' views of, or responses to, public opinion. There have been occasions when the Court has obviated a constitutional or legal response by invoking the popular will. Here is an example articulated by Justice William Johnson in 1812: "Although this question [whether the federal courts possessed a power to try offenses made criminal by English common law] is brought up now for the first time to be decided by this Court, we consider it as having been long since settled in public opinion."[43]

In a closely related approach, the Court from time to time has developed jurisprudence grounded in a historical assessment of public opinion at a critical and seemingly pertinent historical moment. To cite the most notorious instance, in 1857 Roger B. Taney's *Dred Scott* opinion for the Court relied, in part, upon his insistence that when the United States Constitution was first written, public opinion perceived blacks as "beings of an inferior order" and hence not entitled to the same legal status and rights as whites.[44]

By contrast, John Marshall Harlan utilized a similar mode of reasoning—but exactly in reverse. He insisted that judicial precedents that had been created in a climate of opinion no longer acceptable did not and could not carry constitutional weight. His famous dissent in *Plessy v. Ferguson* (1896) charged the Court's majority with invoking inappropriate references to state cases.

> Some, and the most important, of them are wholly inapplicable, because rendered prior to the adoption of the last amendments of the Constitution, when colored people had very few rights which the dominant race felt obliged to respect. Others were made at a time when public opinion was dominated by the institution of slavery; when it would not have been safe to do justice to the black man. . . .

> Those decisions cannot be guides in an era introduced by the recent amendments [Thirteenth, Fourteenth, and Fifteenth] of the supreme law.[45]

In modern times the justices have acknowledged that public opinion affects the acceptability of some of their most difficult choices, including the decision to hear a controversial case or appeal. Felix Frankfurter became exceedingly apprehensive about public perceptions of the Rosenberg spy case in 1952–53. He and Hugo Black believed that the issue of appeal and possible stay of execution might ultimately threaten or undermine the Court's moral authority.[46]

When the Court upheld the convictions of eleven prominent leaders of the Communist party in 1951, the infamous *Dennis* case, Justices Black and William O. Douglas dissented on the grounds that the Smith Act (1940) permitted unjustified invasions of free speech. Black's dissent acknowledged the role of public opinion in affecting the Court as well as popular reactions to its work.

> These petitioners were not charged with an attempt to overthrow the Government. They were not charged with overt acts of any kind designed to overthrow the Government. They were not even charged with saying anything or writing anything designed to overthrow the Government. The charge was that they agreed to assemble and to talk and publish certain ideas at a later date. . . . Public opinion being what it now is, few will protest the conviction of these Communist petitioners.[47]

It has often been said—sometimes without serious reflection—that democracy as a just and good form of government works most effectively when public opinion is aroused. The unfortunate examples of Communist witch-hunting in the years following World War II and of widespread support for the internment of Japanese-Americans during that war should give us pause and lead us to qualify that sweeping generalization.[48]

If it is valid to say, as an American did in 1948, that "only an aroused public opinion can persuade our Congress to do justice to the American Indian and redress our national guilt as exploiters and treaty breakers,"[49] it is equally true that an aroused public opinion has occasionally been responsible for some very unjust coercion. Alexis de Tocqueville anticipated this democratic dilemma 150 years ago. Can we move a step beyond what by now must seem a banal truism? I believe that we can.

Others have demonstrated in considerable detail that at least *some* constitutional issues and pressures have a persuasive effect upon public opinion. I have tried to suggest that the judiciary, in its turn, responds to public opinion in various ways, some of them more self-aware than others. What new light, if any, do these findings shed upon the problem of American exceptionalism? Paradoxically, two different sorts of conclusions seem appropriate, even though they lead us in opposite directions.

First of all, for more than a decade now some innovative scholars have been asking whether we do not have, in a very real sense, an unwritten national constitution.[50] My own view is that we do. But I would add to the aspects of an unwritten constitution already acknowledged by others[51] the powerful role played by public opinion in gradually yet continuously aerating our constitutional system.[52]

Consequently, we hold much in common with others among the established democratic political cultures in the modern world. I emphasize the contrast between earlier governmental systems and those that have achieved independence since 1945, because most of the latter are closer to the circumstances of the United States during the half century following 1789, when we expected to be governed by a blend of natural law, common law, legislative statutes, and our newly minted national Constitution.[53] With the passage of two centuries, our system has changed in ways that make a clear-cut distinction between written and unwritten constitutions untenable. We need not shift all the way to a parliamentary setup to be more like the British than we once were a century or two ago.

My second conclusion about the relationship among public opinion, constitutionalism, and American exceptionalism leads in the opposite direction. We have reason to believe that public opinion emerged throughout the Western world as a force in domestic as well as international affairs late in the eighteenth century.[54] If we look at the records of the Constitutional Convention in 1787, however, we find a sense of despair (or call it realistic frustration) about the prospects of "knowing" public opinion well enough to be properly responsive. As Gouverneur Morris declared on July 5, 1787: "Much has been said of the sentiments of the people. They were unknown. They could not be known."[55]

In 1791, however, James Madison wrote a brief editorial titled

"Public Opinion." In it he proposed a series of important distinctions that we have tended to overlook or ignore. His thoughts are so germane to the subject of this essay that I shall quote a lengthy extract:

> Public opinion sets bounds to every government, and is the real sovereign in every free one.
>
> As there are cases where the public opinion must be obeyed by the government; so there are cases, where not being fixed, it may be influenced by the government. This distinction, if kept in view, would prevent or decide many debates on the respect due from the government to the sentiments of the people.
>
> In proportion as government is influenced by opinion, it must be so, by whatever influences opinion. This decides the question concerning a Constitutional Declaration of Rights, which requires an influence on government, by becoming a part of public opinion.
>
> The larger a country, the less easy for its real opinion to be ascertained, and the less difficult to be counterfeited; when ascertained or presumed, the more respectable it is in the eyes of individuals.—This is favorable to the authority of government. For the same reason, the more extensive a country, the more insignificant is each individual in his own eyes.—This may be unfavorable to liberty.[56]

The passage of time and the experience of just a few years under the new government enabled Madison to offer insights more complex and, in certain respects, less agnostic than those of Gouverneur Morris.

The United States was then, and has remained, a large and diverse country. Public opinion regarding constitutional issues is not easy to ascertain, least of all when the issues at hand are controversial.[57] Consequently, there are cases where government may seek to influence public opinion—influence in the sense of inform and reorient—as was the case with racial desegregation (1954–55) or one person, one vote (1962–64). In other instances, where the nature of public opinion is less ambiguous, such as broad national approval of New Deal measures for economic recovery (the later 1930s) or anxiety about the expansion of protection for the rights of suspected criminals (the later 1960s), public opinion has, as Madison suggested, helped to redefine the scope of acceptable government policy or decision making by the judiciary.

Enter (or reenter) American distinctiveness, if not outright exceptionalism. Two points must be made—one having to do with origins, the other with ongoing developments. When Madison wrote his intriguing essay "Public Opinion" in 1791, it was unexceptionable in a very real sense. It may have been unusually astute, but in a new Republic where everyone, irrespective of partisan affiliation, paid lip service to popular sovereignty, few—if any—would dispute Madison's emphasis upon and concessions to public opinion.

In Great Britain, by contrast, even though theirs was the closest political culture to our own, the recognition that PUBLIC OPINION (it often appeared in capitals during the 1790s in order to acknowledge the relative novelty of the concept) had recently become a potent force elicited a very substantial body of literature. These pamphlets, tracts, and newspaper essays called for governmental restraint or resistance in responding to public opinion, particularly where calls for constitutional reform were concerned.[58]

The historical legacy of this fundamental divergence between American and European political cultures (c. 1790–1832) provides the core of my second contention. Public opinion emerged and mattered elsewhere, but only in the United States was there a growing consensus that it was *appropriate* for it to matter; and only in the United States was its impact upon the judiciary (and hence upon questions requiring constitutional interpretation) so palpable. Lord Bryce summarized the situation toward the close of the nineteenth century:

> The Supreme Court feels the touch of public opinion. Opinion is stronger in America than anywhere else in the world, and judges are only men. To yield a little may be prudent, for the tree that cannot bend to the blast may be broken. There is, moreover, this ground at least for presuming public opinion to be right, that through it the progressive judgment of the world is expressed. Of course, whenever the law is clear, because the words of the Constitution are plain or the cases interpreting them decisive on the point raised, the court must look solely to those words and cases, and cannot permit any other consideration to affect its mind. But when the terms of the Constitution admit of more than one construction, and when previous decisions have left the true construction so far open that the point in question may be deemed new, is a court to be blamed if it prefers the construction which the bulk of the people deem suited to the needs of the time? A court is sometimes so swayed consciously, more often unconsciously, because the pervasive sympathy of numbers is irresistible even by elderly lawyers.[59]

Bryce returned to this theme with some frequency throughout *The American Commonwealth* and never diminished his insistence upon the distinctively potent and central role of public opinion in American political culture.[60] Other observers have composed variations on his theme ever since.

Over the past two centuries, needless to say, the American press and other media have played an increasingly important role in shaping public opinion on a broad range of constitutional questions. It all started with "Publius" and the *Federalist* papers, perhaps, and was perpetuated by newspaper editorials, by the droll craft of political cartoons, and now by investigative journalism that is undertaken with a competitive intensity previously unknown in American history. Most Americans do not read either the Constitution or the texts of Supreme Court decisions. They do, however, notice cartoons that depict justices as baby-killers (in abortion decisions) or as hangmen (capital punishment). Most likely those caricatures reinforce existing attitudes rather than form them de novo. Nevertheless, they imprint images and unquestionably influence or perpetuate attitudes.[61]

Public opinion has clearly played a complex role in shaping the character of American constitutionalism. We must never forget, however, that public opinion in a large, diverse, and free society is not a monolith. The implications of that unexceptionable assertion are important. Perhaps I can best explain why by comparing two national mottoes. Bhinneka Tunggal Ika, the Indonesian national motto, is customarily translated as Unity in Diversity. Consequently, it is sometimes viewed as a rough equivalent to the American motto, E Pluribus Unum. There are, however, differences. The American motto is understood to mean a process of unification out of (and despite) divergent elements, whereas the Indonesian motto suggests the inseparability of unity and diversity.[62]

Given the range of diversity in American society and public opinion on constitutional issues, and yet viewing that diversity in the context of our truly remarkable history of stability under a single Constitution, I cannot help wondering whether Bhinneka Tunggal Ika would not be closer to the bull's eye as the American national motto. Unity and diversity inseparable: That may sound, at first, like an oxymoron. It is, nevertheless, an accurate summation of our paradoxical historical experience with constitutionalism and public opinion.

Notes

1. See Michael Kammen, *A Machine That Would Go of Itself: The Constitution in American Culture* (New York: Knopf, 1986), chap. 6; Donald L. Robinson, ed., *Reforming American Government: The Bicentennial Papers of the Committee on the Constitutional System* (Boulder: Westview, 1985), esp. 11–29, 50–58, 131–54, 191–208, 299–306.

2. For the most succinct assessments, see Laurence Veysey, "The Autonomy of American History Reconsidered," *American Quarterly* 31 (Fall 1979): 455–77, and Carl Degler, "In Pursuit of an American History," *American Historical Review* 92 (February 1987): 1–12.

3. See, for example, Alfred D. Chandler, Jr., *The Visible Hand: The Managerial Revolution in American Business* (Cambridge: Belknap Press of Harvard University Press, 1977), 64, 93, 205; Wyn Wachhorst, *Thomas Alva Edison: An American Myth* (Cambridge: MIT Press, 1981), 120; Sean Wilentz, *Chants Democratic: New York City and the Rise of the American Working Class, 1788–1850* (New York: Oxford University Press, 1985); and Rebecca Scott, "Comparing Emancipations: A Review Essay," *Journal of Social History* 20 (Spring 1987): 565–83, esp. 574, 576.

4. "Charters," in *The Writings of James Madison*, ed. Gaillard Hunt (New York: G. P. Putnam's Sons, 1906), 6:83–84; Joyce Appleby, *Capitalism and a New Social Order: The Republican Vision of the 1790s* (New York: New York University Press, 1984), 80.

5. Kammen, *A Machine That Would Go of Itself*, 166–70.

6. Hart to Miller, Hart Papers, box 5, fol. 6, Harvard Law School Library, Langdell Hall, Cambridge.

7. 3 U.S. (3 Dallas) 171 (1796).

8. 5 U.S. (1 Cranch) 137 (1803).

9. Peter Force, ed., *American Archives*, 4th ser. (Washington, D.C.: Government Printing Office, 1837–53), 1:539, 635; 2:130–31.

10. See M. I. Finley, *The Use and Abuse of History* (New York: Viking Press, 1975), 26; Bronislaw Malinowski, *Magic, Science and Religion and Other Essays* (Garden City, N.Y.: Doubleday, 1954), 117; Jan Vansina, "History in the Field," in *Anthropologists in the Field*, ed. D. G. Jongmans and P. C. W. Gutkind (Assen: Van Gorcum and Co., 1967), 107.

11. Edward Muir, *Civic Ritual in Renaissance Venice* (Princeton: Princeton University Press, 1986), 211. See also Felix Gilbert, "The Venetian Constitution in Florentine Political Thought," in *History: Choice and Commitment*, ed. Felix Gilbert (Cambridge: Belknap Press of Harvard University Press, 1977), 179–214.

12. Muir, *Civic Ritual*, 49, 189–90. For the promulgation of a re-

markably comparable constitution in 1889, see Carol Gluck, *Japan's Modern Myths: Ideology in the Late Meiji Period* (Princeton: Princeton University Press, 1985), 42–49.

13. See Michael Herzfeld, *Ours Once More: Folklore, Ideology, and the Making of Modern Greece* (Austin: University of Texas Press, 1982), 6; J. G. A. Pocock, *Politics, Language, and Time: Essays on Political Thought and History* (New York: Atheneum, 1971), 209; Bernard S. Cohn, "Representing Authority in Victorian India," in *The Invention of Tradition*, ed. Eric Hobsbawm and Terence Ranger (Cambridge: Cambridge University Press, 1983), 179–83, 190, 197–98.

14. See Melvin Small, ed., *Public Opinion and Historians: Interdisciplinary Perspectives* (Detroit: Wayne State University Press, 1970); Lee Benson, "An Approach to the Scientific Study of Past Public Opinion," in *Toward the Scientific Study of History: Selected Essays*, ed. Lee Benson (Philadelphia: Lippincott, 1972), 105–59; Joseph R. Strayer, "The Historian's Concept of Public Opinion," in *Common Frontiers of the Social Sciences*, ed. Mirra Komarovsky (Glencoe, Ill.: Free Press, 1957), 263–68.

15. Stephen Vaughn, *Holding Fast the Inner Lines: Democracy, Nationalism, and the Committee on Public Information* (Chapel Hill: University of North Carolina Press, 1980), 164.

16. Walter Lippmann, *Public Opinion* (New York: Penguin, 1922); Edward L. Bernays, *Crystallizing Public Opinion* (New York: Boni and Liveright, 1923). See also A. Lawrence Lowell, *Public Opinion and Popular Government* (New York: Longmans, Green, 1914).

17. See *The Gallup Poll: Public Opinion, 1935–1971*, 3 vols. (Wilmington, Del.: Scholarly Resources, 1972); Hans Speier, "Historical Development of Public Opinion," *American Journal of Sociology* 55 (January 1950): 376–88.

18. J. A. W. Gunn, *Beyond Liberty and Property: The Process of Self-Recognition in Eighteenth-Century Political Thought* (Kingston and Montreal: McGill-Queen's University Press, 1983), chap. 7; H. T. Dickinson, *Liberty and Property: Political Ideology in Eighteenth-Century Britain* (New York: Holmes and Meier, 1978), 188–92, 195, 209–15, 219–21. See also Paul A. Palmer, "The Concept of Public Opinion in Political Theory," in *Essays in History and Political Theory in Honor of Charles Howard McIlwain* (Cambridge: Harvard University Press, 1936), 230–57.

19. *Collections of the Massachusetts Historical Society for the Year 1795* (Boston, 1795), 1st ser., 4:201. The italics are Belknap's.

20. Max Farrand, ed., *The Records of the Federal Convention of 1787*, rev. ed. (New Haven: Yale University Press, 1937), 1:178. For a similar position taken by Madison respecting the most sensible manner of selecting

U.S. senators, see *The Federalist*, ed. Jacob E. Cooke (Middletown, Conn.: Wesleyan University Press, 1961), no. 62. My references to the *Federalist* papers are to this edition.

21. Quoted in Catherine Drinker Bowen, *Miracle at Philadelphia: The Story of the Constitutional Convention, May to September 1787* (Boston: Little, Brown, 1966), 114.

22. Hamilton to Washington, July 3, 1787, in *The Papers of Alexander Hamilton*, ed. Harold C. Syrett (New York: Columbia University Press, 1962), 4:223–24.

23. *Writings of Madison*, 6:85. The italics are Madison's.

24. Jack N. Rakove, "The Structure of Politics at the Accession of George Washington," in *Beyond Confederation: Origins of the Constitution and American National Identity*, ed. Richard Beeman et al. (Chapel Hill: University of North Carolina Press, 1987), 290–91, 293.

25. See Edward Everett, "The History of Liberty," an oration delivered at Charlestown, Massachusetts, July 4, 1828, in *Orations and Speeches on Various Occasions*, 9th ed., ed. Edward Everett (Boston: Little, Brown, 1878), 1:168–69. Cf. Thomas Jefferson to Joseph Priestly, March 21, 1801, in *The Works of Thomas Jefferson*, ed. Paul L. Ford (New York: G. P. Putnam's Sons, 1905), 9:218: "This whole chapter in the history of man is new. . . . The mighty wave of public opinion which has rolled over [the republic] is new."

26. *Works of Fisher Ames*, ed. Seth Ames (Boston: Little, Brown, 1854), 1:310, 400; 2:82.

27. Quoted in Anson Phelps Stokes and Leo Pfeffer, *Church and State in the United States*, rev. ed. (Westport, Conn.: Greenwood Press, 1975), 244. Compare those sentiments with ones that Jefferson articulated thirty-three years earlier in a letter that explicitly anticipated the imminent inevitability of constitutional change: "The want of power in the federal head was early perceived, and foreseen to be the flaw in our constitution which might endanger its destruction. I have the pleasure to inform you that when I left America in July the people were becoming universally sensible of this, and a spirit to enlarge the powers of Congress was becoming general. . . . The happiness of governments like ours, wherein the people are truly the mainspring, is that they are never to be despaired of. When an evil becomes so glaring as to strike them generally, they arouse themselves, and it is redressed" (Jefferson to Richard Price, February 1, 1785, in *The Papers of Thomas Jefferson*, ed. Julian P. Boyd [Princeton: Princeton University Press, 1953], 7:630–31).

28. Quoted in Carroll Smith-Rosenberg, *Disorderly Conduct: Visions of Gender in Victorian America* (New York: Knopf, 1985), 117.

29. For the national bank issue, so volatile throughout the 1830s, see

Martin Van Buren's Message to a special session of Congress, September 4, 1837: "It cannot be concealed that there exists in our community [i.e., the nation] opinions and feelings on this subject in direct opposition to each other" (*A Compilation of the Messages and Papers of the Presidents, 1787–1897*, ed. James D. Richardson [New York: Bureau of National Literature, 1914], 3:330).

30. See William M. Wiecek, *The Sources of Antislavery Constitutionalism in America, 1760–1848* (Ithaca: Cornell University Press, 1977); S. Cushing Strout, "Jeffersonian Religious Liberty and American Pluralism," in *The Virginia Statute for Religious Freedom*, ed. Merrill D. Peterson and Robert C. Vaughan (New York: Cambridge University Press, 1988).

31. See Robinson, *Reforming American Government*, 267.

32. Samuel T. Williamson, *Frank Gannett: A Biography* (New York: Duell, Sloan, and Pearce, 1940), 177–80.

33. Ibid., 182–85, 188–89, 191–92, 196–98.

34. J. P. Mayer, ed., *Democracy in America* (Garden City, N.Y.: Doubleday, 1969), 150. In support of Tocqueville's observations, note this comment made by Justice Samuel T. Miller in his 1873 opinion for the Court in the *Slaughter-House Cases*: "In the early history of the organization of the government, its statesmen seem to have divided on the line which should separate the powers of the National government from those of the State government, and though this line has never been very well defined in public opinion, such a division has continued from that day to this" (83 U.S. [16 Wallace] 81–82 [1873]).

35. See David G. Barnum, "The Supreme Court and Public Opinion: Judicial Decision Making in the Post–New Deal Period," *Journal of Politics* 47 (May 1985): 652–66; Walter F. Murphy and Joseph Tanerhaus, "Public Opinion and Supreme Court: The Goldwater Campaign," *Public Opinion Quarterly* 32 (Spring 1968): 31–50. The second essay, based upon a long-term survey of public opinion in relation to the judiciary, is particularly sophisticated and informative.

36. Kammen, *A Machine That Would Go of Itself*, chaps. 11–13, passim; Adam Clymer, "Opinion Narrows over High Court," *New York Times*, July 13, 1986, sec. A, p. 15.

37. The Court's decision in *Georgia v. Stanton*, 73 U.S. (6 Wallace) 50 (1867), was announced on May 13, 1867, but was not read until February 10, 1868, in part because of the intensity of public opinion concerning aspects of Reconstruction at that time. See Carl Brent Swisher, *Stephen J. Field: Craftsman of the Law* (Washington, D.C.: Brookings Institution, 1930), 158.

38. Quoted in R. Kent Newmyer, *Supreme Court Justice Joseph Story: Statesman of the Old Republic* (Chapel Hill: University of North Carolina Press, 1985), 247.

39. Stanley I. Kutler, *Privilege and Creative Destruction: The Charles River Bridge Case* (New York: Norton, 1978), 121.

40. Edmund Wilson, *Patriotic Gore: Studies in the Literature of the American Civil War* (New York: Oxford University Press, 1962), 784–91; Richard Kluger, *Simple Justice: The History of Brown v. Board of Education and Black America's Struggle for Equality* (New York: Random House, 1975), 690.

41. William H. Rehnquist, "The Notion of a Living Constitution," *Texas Law Review* 54 (May 1976): 696–97; "Constitutional Law and Public Opinion," address delivered at the Suffolk University School of Law, Boston, April 10, 1986 (41-page unpublished typescript, courtesy of Chief Justice Rehnquist).

42. *West Virginia State Board of Education v. Barnette,* 319 U.S. 624, 638 (1943).

43. *United States v. Hudson and Goodwin,* 11 U.S. (7 Cranch) 32 (1812), quoted in Robert H. Jackson, *The Supreme Court in the American System of Government* (Cambridge: Harvard University Press, 1955), 31. See also Leon Friedman and Fred L. Israel, eds., *The Justices of the United States Supreme Court 1789–1978: Their Lives and Major Opinions* (New York: Chelsea House, 1980), 1:362–63.

44. See *Dred Scott v. Sandford,* 60 U.S. (19 How.) 393, 407 (1857), and Judith A. Baer, *Equality under the Constitution: Reclaiming the Fourteenth Amendment* (Ithaca: Cornell University Press, 1983), 70. Taney began the central contention of his opinion with this sentence: "It is difficult at this day to realize the state of public opinion in relation to that unfortunate race, which prevailed in the civilized and enlightened portions of the world at the time of the Declaration of Independence, and when the Constitution of the United States was framed and adopted."

45. *Plessy v. Ferguson,* 163 U.S. 537, 563 (1896). For a fine example of public opinion affecting constitutional policy and behavior during the 1890s, see Kluger, *Simple Justice,* 73.

46. Michael E. Parrish, "Cold War Justice: The Supreme Court and the Rosenbergs," *American Historical Review* 82 (October 1977): 805–42.

47. *Dennis v. United States,* 341 U.S. 494, 579–81 (1951). See also William O. Douglas, *The Right of the People* (Garden City, N.Y.: Doubleday, 1958): "What we have witnessed during the last decade is not a new but a recurring problem. Each generation must deal with it. The only protection is an enlightened public opinion forged by men who will stand against the mob. . . . The remedy is in making public opinion everybody's business and in encouraging debate and discourse on public issues" (84).

48. See Mark Silverstein, *Constitutional Faiths: Felix Frankfurter, Hugo Black, and the Process of Judicial Decision Making* (Ithaca: Cornell University

Press, 1984), 195–202; Peter Irons, *Justice at War: The Inside Story of the Japanese American Internment Cases* (New York: Oxford University Press, 1983), 43.

49. Oliver LaFarge to James Truslow Adams, March 15, 1948, Adams Papers, Butler Library, Columbia University, New York City.

50. See Thomas C. Grey, "Do We Have an Unwritten Constitution?" *Stanford Law Review* 27 (February 1975): 703–18; David A. J. Richards, "Sexual Autonomy and the Constitutional Right to Privacy: A Case Study in Human Rights and the Unwritten Constitution," *Hastings Law Journal* 30 (March 1979): 957–1018.

51. Consider, for example, the increased national attention given during the past decade to state constitutions and state constitutional law. The complexity and creativity of what has been called "horizontal federalism" may very well cause our system to function in a manner that is less distinctive than Madison and his contemporaries envisioned. See, for example, A. E. Dick Howard, "State Courts and Constitutional Rights in the Day of the Burger Court," *Virginia Law Review* 62 (1976): 873–944; William J. Brennan, Jr., "State Constitutions and the Protection of Individual Rights," *Harvard Law Review* 90 (1977): 489–504; *Texas Law Review* 63 (1985) (a symposium issue on state constitutional law).

52. See the interesting letter written by Logan Hay, member of a law firm in Springfield, Illinois, to Andrew C. McLaughlin, December 3, 1935, McLaughlin Papers, box 2, Regenstein Library, University of Chicago. McLaughlin had just published his 800-page synthesis titled *A Constitutional History of the United States* (New York: Appleton-Century, 1935). "We have in the constitutional history," Hay wrote, "the story of the building of the framework of a democracy institutionalizing that framework in a written constitution. . . . All this, however, is mere framework and machinery. After all, the motive force is the force of public sentiment, almost necessarily slow moving in a constitutional democracy and yet at times running with a strong and rapid current and subjecting the machinery to violent strains and breaks."

53. See Seymour Martin Lipset, *The First New Nation: The United States in Historical and Comparative Perspective* (New York: Norton, 1977); Clifford Geertz, "After the Revolution: The Fate of Nationalism in the New States," in *The Interpretation of Cultures: Selected Essays*, ed. Clifford Geertz (New York: Basic Books, 1973), 234–54; Edward Shils, "Intellectuals, Public Opinion, and Economic Development," in *The Intellectuals and the Powers and Other Essays*, ed. Edward Shils (Chicago: University of Chicago Press, 1972), 424–44.

54. See Richard Buel, *Securing the Revolution: Ideology in American Politics, 1789–1815* (Ithaca: Cornell University Press, 1972), pt. 3; Speier, "Historical Development of Public Opinion."

55. Farrand, *Records*, 1:529.

56. "Public Opinion," first printed in *The National Gazette*, December 19, 1791; reprinted in *Writings of Madison*, 4:70.

57. See, for example, Edward J. Larson, *Trial and Error: The American Controversy over Creation and Evolution* (New York: Oxford University Press, 1985); Eva R. Rubin, *Abortion, Politics, and the Courts: Roe v. Wade and Its Aftermath* (Westport, Conn.: Greenwood, 1982).

58. See Gunn, *Beyond Liberty and Property*, 287, 289–90, 292. For France and Germany during the same period, see Palmer, "The Concept of Public Opinion in Political Theory," 239–43, 247–49.

59. James Bryce, *The American Commonwealth*, 2d ed. (London: Macmillan, 1891), 1:267.

60. Ibid., esp. 1:6, 376, 437; 2:239–40, 243, 248–49, 251–53, 257, and chap. 78, passim. Cf. A. V. Dicey, *Lectures on the Relation between Law and Public Opinion in England during the Nineteenth Century*, 2d ed. (London: Macmillan, 1914).

61. For some prime examples, see Jim Berryman, "Another Deserter!" *Washington Evening Star*, July 20, 1935, p. 1; Harold M. T. Talburt, "Widen the Road or Else!" *Washington Daily News*, June 3, 1935, p. 16; and the Herblock cartoon "We Were Told They Were 'Strict Constructionists,'" discussed in Bob Woodward and Scott Armstrong, *The Brethren: Inside the Supreme Court* (New York: Simon and Schuster, 1979), 505.

62. See Ben R. O. Anderson, "The Idea of Power in Javanese Culture," in *Culture and Politics in Indonesia*, ed. Claire Holt (Ithaca: Cornell University Press, 1972), 15.

CHAPTER 18

Enlivening the Text

Interpreting (or Inventing) the Constitution

· · · · ·

SANFORD LEVINSON

"The Constitution," says James Boyd White, "is by its very nature lifeless and inert unless it is put to work in the world by the citizens who live under it."[1] It is in making use of the Constitution that we breathe life into it. White's metaphor of constitutional genesis has an overtone suggesting in effect that *we* create a "living Constitution" by continually resuscitating a document always threatened by the death-dealing plague of inattention.

Such a notion of an enlivened text, if you will, obviously raises for many onlookers an immediate problem: What is the relationship between the potentially dying text and its putative life-givers? More particularly, does the enlivening partake of an *invention* of ever-new worlds, brave or not? Or can we instead delimit *some* creations as those truly authorized by the constitutional dust, while others perhaps are more aptly described as Frankenstein's monsters created by demented judges? (Or might we decide that the opposition between interpretation and invention is a false one? Perhaps the task before us is to construct a more useful description rather than to choose between unsatisfactory alternatives.)

The idea of a living Constitution—especially when coupled with developmental or evolutionary notions—is one of our central metaphors, not to say clichés. I daresay that few speakers during this bicentennial season have resisted the temptation to use it as a way of praising the Constitution. It is hard to find anyone who is truly willing to reject it, given that the alternative seems to be a *dead* Constitution, an option that, so far as I know, has no explicit supporters.

Still, as Chief Justice Rehnquist once said, "the phrase 'living Constitution' has about it a teasing imprecision that makes it a coat of many colors."[2] He was happy, however, or at least willing, to quote Justice Holmes's famous comment from *Missouri v. Holland* about the framers' having performed "a constituent act," calling into life "a being the developments of which could not have been foreseen completely by the most gifted of its begetters."[3] The "organism" that was "created" in Philadelphia thus took on a life of its own. What the chief justice presumably objects to is not the fact of organic development as such, but rather the de facto creation of a new organism on the basis of the earlier one's having turned out to have defective genes. Similarly, even one willing to use developmental metaphors might nonetheless profess to be able to distinguish between development that, however unexpected, is implied by the organism's structure and outright mutation generated by exogenous causes.

As lawyers know (or at least believe), abstractions take on new meaning when viewed within the context of concrete cases, and this is true as well of notions like the living Constitution. Indeed, James White makes the remark with which I began in the course of an extended consideration of the rhetorical performance of John Marshall in *McCulloch v. Maryland*.[4] For me that is a happy coincidence: I want as well to discuss *McCulloch*, though I prefer to describe my remarks as a tale of (at least) two Virginians. What could be more suitable, given the beginning of the Smithsonian symposium at the University of Virginia in Charlottesville, than a meditation on the tangled debate between James Madison and John Marshall that took place surrounding what is perhaps the most majestic single case in all American judicial history?

Paul Brest and I begin our casebook in constitutional law not with *Marbury v. Madison* but with a marvelously rich speech by James Madison to the 1791 House of Representatives. Part of the reason is to make the all-important point that judges do not have a monopoly on either the duty or the performance of the task of constitutional interpretation, a point all too likely to be lost in the standard rush toward *Marbury*. But that is certainly not the only reason, for the Madison speech, not to mention the response to it at the time, raises some of the most complex issues in all constitutional theory.

In that speech the representative from Virginia explains why he rejects as unconstitutional Alexander Hamilton's proposal to charter a Bank of the United States. He begins his explanation by recalling "that a power to grant charters of incorporation has been proposed in the general convention and rejected."[5] That is, the man often designated as the father of the Constitution reminds his audience that he was present at the creation, in Philadelphia, where he himself had proposed that Congress be authorized "to grant charters of incorporation where the interest of the U.S. might require."[6] Because of its clearly controversial nature, Madison's proposal never even came to a vote. The Convention did vote on a motion authorizing Congress to charter corporations for the construction of canals, which was defeated 8–3.

In any case, Madison clearly lays out his reasons for believing that the Constitution of enumerated powers does not authorize the bank. Indeed, he specifically warns his listeners against accepting the kind of reasoning exhibited by Hamilton, with its generous notion of acceptable means conducive to attaining the limited ends. "The essential characteristic of the Government, as composed of limited and enumerated powers, would be destroyed: If instead of direct and incidental means, any means could be used"[7] that are deemed merely convenient, rather than genuinely necessary, to the attainment of a legislatively authorized end. In a remarkably prescient description of the actual development of American constitutional interpretation in the twentieth century, Madison notes that the linkage of Hamiltonian implication will allow the formation of "a chain . . . that will reach every object of legislation, every object within the whole compass of political economy."[8] What is for Madison a reductio ad absurdum designed to strike terror into the hearts of his audience is for us today the common sense of the matter, what every schoolchild (or at least law student) knows. In any event, Congress clearly paid little heed to Madison's analysis. The Senate appears to have given its unanimous approval to the bank, the House following along by a vote of 39–20. It may be worth pointing out that fully half of the Senate's twenty members had been in Philadelphia; only seven representatives had been so occupied in the summer of 1787. They split 4–3, in favor of the bill.

Although my primary tale concerns Madison and Marshall, it is only appropriate, given the Charlottesville venue, to note that Mr. Jefferson was not without views on the matter.[9] He read the newly adopted Tenth Amendment as "the foundation of the Constitution," establishing a principle of narrow construction of national power. Like Madison, he read the word "necessary" as a limitation, limiting the new government "to those means without which the grant of power would be nugatory." Like Madison, of course, he failed in his immediate purpose, which was to persuade President Washington to veto the bill so warmly supported by his secretary of the treasury. Instead, the president signed the measure, thus presumably endorsing its propriety under the Constitution over whose creation, of course, he had presided in Philadelphia.

McCulloch technically concerned the constitutionality of the Second Bank of the United States, yet I think it fair to say that it also serves as an advisory opinion that the First Bank was perfectly constitutional as well. Marshall, of course, takes the occasion to spell out his overarching theory of national power, culminating in a practical assignment of basically plenary authority to Congress. I will not rehearse all of what is probably familiar to most readers, including the functional elimination of the Tenth Amendment and the necessary and proper clause as meaningful limits on the federal government. I cannot resist, though, quoting one of the single most famous sentences of the opinion, where Marshall emphasizes that he is expounding "a constitution intended to endure for ages to come, and, consequently, to be adapted to the various *crises* of human affairs."[10] Interestingly enough, the word Marshall emphasizes is "crises." I prefer, on the other hand, to put a bit more stress on the word "adapted."

It is time, however, to return to Madison, who wrote yet another Virginian, Chief Justice Spencer Roane of the Virginia Supreme Court. He referred to the bitter struggles over ratification some thirty years before, where "friends of the Constitution" only narrowly prevailed over an Anti-Federalist opposition that had been condemned as unfair for fearfully suggesting that the necessary and proper clause would be interpreted in precisely the way that later gained Marshall immortality. Madison wondered what would have been the consequence had the supporters of the new Constitution frankly articulated "a rule of construction . . . as broad and pliant as what has occurred." He could not "easily be persuaded that the avowal of such a rule [at the state ratifying conventions] would not have prevented its ratification."[11] Jefferson was characteristically restrained, referring to the judiciary as a "corps of sappers and miners, steadily working to undermine the independent rights of the States, and to consolidate all power in the heads of that government in which they have so important a freehold estate."[12]

Of Marshall's opinion in that case, James White writes that it "seems to be less an interpretation of the Constitution than an amendment to it, the overruling of which is unimaginable."[13] What I find intriguing is that White does not appear to be leveling a criticism against either the opinion or Marshall, even as he offers a kind of support to Madison's and Jefferson's skepticism about the provenance of Marshall's opinion. He comes truly to praise Marshall rather than to criticize him. But if White is correct—that is, if we share both his perception and his willingness to commend Marshall's performance in *McCulloch*—then we need to recast much of the contemporary debate about constitutional interpretation. This debate in substantial measure concerns the limits to the authority of constitutional interpreters, be they judges or others. Presumably the "best" judges are the ones who recognize such limits and stay within them. But what do we do with Marshall in terms of the conventional debate?

The principal alternative to recasting the debate is the almost equally unimaginable casting out of John Marshall from the ranks of commendable judges, moving if not for his retroactive impeachment then at least for his removal from the pantheon he has tended to occupy within the American legal consciousness. Perhaps that is less unthinkable than one might suppose: A recent article by the conservative Robert Bork quite strikingly omits Marshall from a list of nineteenth-century constitutional theorists worth emulating. Marshall is mentioned only as having (illegitimately) suggested that courts have the "extra-constitutional" power to invoke "natural justice" to strike down offensive legislative enactments even in the absence of specific textual limitation on the legislature in the Constitution. Bork does not recommend impeachment, but it is clear nonetheless that he views Marshall as far less worthy a guide to constitutional interpretation than his models of Joseph Story, James Kent, James Bradley Thayer, and Thomas Cooley.[14]

Bork is one of the major proponents of what Attorney General Edwin Meese has labeled "the jurisprudence of original intent," the view that the Constitution can legitimately be given only the meaning "intended" by its authors. We can ask, therefore, what moral might be drawn from our story by those committed to such a view, given the repudiation of Madison's views by Marshall (and, of course, by many others as well). Moreover, even Marshall, in *Marbury v. Madison*, had defined the importance of a written constitution—the "greatest improvement on political institutions" put forth by the new American nation—as consisting in the specification of powers (and limits) of the government: "The powers of the legislature are defined and limited; and that those limits may not be mistaken, or forgotten, the Constitution is written. To what purpose are powers limited, and to what purpose is that limitation committed to writing, if these limits may, at any time, be passed by those intended to be restrained?"[15] The problem, of course, is how we decide disputes about what the "writing" actually means.

More particularly, our tale leads us to ask about James Madison's status as a reliable guide to constitutional meaning. One might read the story I have described as demonstrating a widespread belief, shared by Congress, president, and Court alike, that he is a most unreliable guide. Indeed, there is a way of reading Madison himself as accepting such a conclusion, for as president he signed the bill establishing the Second Bank of the United States, referring to "repeated recognitions, under varied circumstances, of the validity of such an institution."[16] He thus bowed to the weight of contrary opinion and accepted the apparent consensus, though I think it important that he never specifically repudiated his declaration of unconstitutionality some twenty-five years earlier. Rather, what was hitherto unconstitutional had become, through a complex process, constitutional. Indeed, Madison's own acquiescence to the 1816 rechartering helps to explain the unanimity of the Court's decision, for there were relatively few among the national political elites who continued to attack the bank on constitutional grounds.

The last thing I would want to argue is that Madison's views are definitive for constitutional meaning. I am not an "originalist," that is, a person committed to the view that the Constitution should be interpreted in a way likely to accord with the specific understandings of those who drafted or ratified it. Even if I were, however, I would resist giving any priority to the Philadelphia Convention, let alone any individual within it, as against the determinations of the ratifying conventions. Still, there must be *some* significance to James Madison's 1791 views on the Constitution's meaning vis-à-vis banks. After all, one of the standard practices of many who interpret the Constitution is to put forth the *Federalist* papers, written substantially by Madison and Hamilton, as an especially authoritative guide to its meaning. If we accept this practice as legitimate, why not accord the same status to Madison's speech to the Congress? Did Madison suddenly lose his authority as a constitutional explicator between the time he authored those papers and his 1791 speech? Is the reasoning of the papers demonstrably better than that of the speech? (How would any such "demonstration" take place?)

In any case, we are left with Marshall's rejection of the views articulated in that speech and to our own appellation for his exercise in constitutional interpretation in *McCulloch*. Marshall's own word to describe *McCulloch* is "adaptation"; White's is "amendment"; Jefferson's (and perhaps Madison's) might well be "usurpation." Can we hope to achieve a principled (and is this the same thing as saying "disinterested" or "nonpolitical"?) resolution of the dispute about proper description? If, as I believe, the answer is no, what might that tell us about the existence of a generally recognized boundary line between interpretation and invention?

As Stanley Fish would be the first to point out, incidentally, each of us at every moment is quite able to construct—and even believe in—such a line so far as our own analyses are concerned. That is not the question of greatest public concern, though. Instead, I think that we must necessarily wonder if there is sufficiently *shared* perception of the line, so that we in fact can agree most of the time when it has been crossed.

There are a variety of ways that we might seek the answer to the question before us concerning the boundary between interpretation and invention. The direction I wish to explore in this essay, though, takes us on a somewhat indirect route that asks another question: What sorts of change would *require* a constitutional amendment? Why might such a question be helpful in achieving our principal task? The answer, I submit, is that by definition, assertion of such a requirement would entail a belief that one could not justify a particular change—or "adaptation"—through "interpretation" of the existing, nonamended Constitution. From this perspective, amendments are inventions, to be treated as such and requiring the special process laid out in Article V of the Constitution.

Let me suggest some possibilities:

1. Would amendment be necessary in order to deprive states of their equal representation in the Senate, as one might think from a reading of Article V? (Indeed, Article V appears to require a "super-amendment," inasmuch as it treats amending representation in the Senate wholly differently from ordinary amendment.) The answer is clearly no, at least if one looks at the so-called Reconstruction Congress of 1866, which rejected both senators and representatives "elected" to Congress by the Southern states. Although we are reliably informed that Virginia remained throughout its history part of "an indestructible Union of indestructible States" (though what about West Virginia?), it nonetheless shared the fate of its confederated compatriots so far as representation was concerned, without any clarifying amendment being thought necessary.

To be sure, the events of 1861–68 were special. One solution to my citation of them is simply to say that the Constitution was not amended so much as suspended during that period, though that raises a variety of exquisite problems that cannot be fully developed here. One of them, though, concerns the legitimacy of the so-called Civil War amendments, about which Bruce Ackerman is currently engaged in a fascinating project that certainly tests the bounds of what counts as constitutional orthodoxy in regard to the mechanics of the amending process as set out by Article V of the Constitution.

(It is also relevant in this context to address the theme often sounded in this bicentennial season—that the Constitution has lasted two hundred years. Indeed, one of the Washington speakers wore a button proclaiming "Still working after 200 years." As Joyce Appleby has aptly pointed out, the Constitution was "in the shop" for several of those years. To put it mildly, most constitutional analysts have not begun to confront the problems posed for constitutional theory—including the crucial problem of continuous identity—by the events of 1861–68.)

2. What about impairments of contract or abridgments of speech? After all, the Constitution, at least to the naive reader, might be read as stating that "No State shall . . . pass any . . . Law impairing the Obligation of Contracts" and that "Congress shall make no law . . . abridging the freedom of speech." Many of us are old enough to remember a distinguished judge named Hugo Black—indeed, Dick Howard and Walter Dellinger clerked for him—who used to say that

"no law" meant "no law"; but who today believes that, even in the absence of any amendment? Instead, most contemporary analysts "know" (and teach) that the "proper" reading of the first statement above is that states shall not pass laws *unreasonably* impairing the obligation of contracts. The second statement is more complicated; the state can punish at least political speech only by presenting such extremely cogent reasoning as to meet the so-called compelling-interest test, which is far more stringent than mere reasonableness. Still, whatever the technical words of legal art, both of these interpretations by definition allow impairments and the making of laws that literalists would perceive to be banned by the "unequivocal" words of the text. (The free speech clause of the First Amendment also presents special problems in regard to the multifarious kinds of speech that come within its ambit. Thus the regulation of commercial speech like advertising requires a less stringent showing of reasons by the state than would be the case if the speech concerned politics.)

In regard to both contracts and speech, moreover, the rhetoric of decision making has affinities with that offered in regard to the wartime events alluded to above. Thus the *Blaisdell* case,[17] which crucially interpreted the contract clause to mean less than the categorical prohibition that the "naive" reader might have thought it required, occurred within the context of the Great Depression; Chief Justice Hughes's opinion is suffused with reference to the "emergency" facing the nation, though he blandly insisted that "emergency does not create power" but provides only the "conditions" for exercising otherwise legitimate power. Similarly, opinions supporting the ability of Congress to restrict free speech rights recurrently evoke images of national and international crisis in which one is almost ubiquitously faced with clear and present dangers to security. In any event, the Court has not required amendment; interpretation has sufficed.

Lest I be misunderstood, I am not arguing that there is in fact no agreement at all within contemporary lawyerdom as to what would require amendment. It would be quite "off the wall," for example, to suggest at the present time that a thirty-year-old man or woman born of French parents in France was eligible to become a United States president without the passage of at least two constitutional amendments. Whether it is literally inconceivable that eligibility could occur without amendment is another matter, and there I am more skeptical. But I accept the notion that we are at all times embedded within interpretive structures that license certain interpretations even as they assure that others will expose their authors to ridicule and censure. Stanley Fish is famous for his assertion that interpretation is the only game in town, which is correct as against the assertion that a possible alternative to interpretation is an unmediated grasping of reality as it is or the text as it really means to speak. This issue provides one of the major debates in contemporary legal and literary theory. It is important, though, not to confuse that debate and its central opposition—interpretation and un- mediated perception—with a second, much less metatheoretical, de- bate that also uses the word "interpretation" as one of its central terms. This paper concerns the second debate: Can we distinguish between plausible (or "on-the-wall") interpretations (which we honor by calling them "interpretations") and implausible, off-the-wall ones (which we condemn by labeling them "inventions")? From the perspective of the metatheorist engaged in the first debate, both indeed are interpreta- tions, but that is irrelevant when we shift our attention to the second debate. I do not understand myself to be quarreling with Fish; I am in fact borrowing the language of "on the wall" and "off the wall" from his own 1980 analysis in *Is There a Text in This Class?* Still, all of these concessions and stipulations do not make any easier the development of a satisfactory theory explaining how to locate the boundary line between legitimate interpretation and such newfangled invention as would re- quire amendment.

One might believe that an answer to my question about the neces- sity of amendment might at least come from the amendments them- selves. Surely their very existence is presumptive evidence that amend- ment was thought to be required? Well, yes and no. They are evidence that *someone* might have thought they were required, but the question is whether *we* think they were required.

This issue of the necessity of amendment was present at the very beginning of the Constitution whose writing (and ratification) we are discussing (and, some of us, celebrating). After all, the principal impediment to ratification was the failure of the Convention to include a Bill of Rights. The supporters of the Constitution insisted that no such bill was necessary, for the federal Constitution, unlike its state counterparts, was adopted under a theory of "assigned powers." That is, the national government was not plenary, lacking only that power specifically excluded by its foundation document. Instead, it had only those powers that text specifically granted. Alexander Hamilton made that point the crux of his argument in the 84th *Federalist:* How could anyone seriously believe that Congress could have the power to regulate the press, given that it was nowhere assigned any such power? "The Constitution ought not to be charged with the absurdity of providing against the abuse of an authority which was not given."[18] James Wilson had made a similar argument in an address to Pennsylvania ratifiers. One problem with this analysis, of course, was the existence of Article I, Section 9, which specifically prevents the Congress from, among other things, passing bills of attainder or creating titles of nobility. Indeed, Hamilton specifically emphasizes the importance of Section 9 as providing basic protection; he does not, however, address the point that if Section 9 is in fact "necessary" in order to prevent such legislation, then the Wilson-Hamilton argument fails. Many opponents of the Constitution were not so restrained, gleefully pointing out the tension between Section 9 and the argument that the Constitution should be construed only as a grant of explicitly assigned powers. Still, Hamilton's argument, if accepted, renders wholly "unnecessary" the First Amendment. It may be a nice thing to have a clear specification of the inability of Congress to regulate the press or establish a religion, but that is more a stylistic than a legal insight, for according to this view, nothing would be lost by its absence.

It may be jarring to suggest that the First Amendment contributes nothing, strictly speaking, to the Constitution. That may be evidence, however, only of the distance we have traveled from the original understanding of the Constitution as creating only a limited government of assigned powers.

One may wonder about other amendments and equally doubt their legal necessity. Take, for example, the Thirteenth Amendment, abolishing slavery. If today we believe that the Thirteenth Amendment is required in order to abolish slavery, then I suggest we must be dubious about practically every important commerce clause decision since 1937. Can it conceivably be the case, for example, that a Congress authorized to tell the Darby Lumber Company that it must pay a minimum wage to its laborers is without the power to transform chattel slavery? If we accept the legitimacy of decisions like *United States v. Darby, NLRB v. Friedman-Harry Marks Clothing Co.* (the companion case to the more famous *NLRB v. Jones & Laughlin Steel Corp.* decision), and *Wickard v. Filburn*,[19] then we simply cannot believe that the Thirteenth Amendment is of more than symbolic importance. (I do not berate symbolism: That was a good enough reason to support the Equal Rights Amendment, but there is an obvious difference between praising it as a symbolic artifact and asserting that it would have transformed legal possibility.)

Similarly, I doubt that many contemporary analysts believe that the Fifteenth and Nineteenth amendments are "necessary," given contemporary interpretations of the Fourteenth Amendment in regard to race, gender, and fundamental rights. And, if the Supreme Court was correct in *Harper v. Virginia Board of Elections*,[20] which found Virginia's poll tax for state elections unconstitutional, then surely the Twenty-fourth Amendment, which two years before barred a poll tax in federal elections, is wholly unnecessary. Only if one agrees with Justice Harlan's considerably less generous reading of the Fourteenth Amendment would it be the case that we would lose something legally significant were the Fifteenth, Nineteenth, and Twenty-fourth amendments suddenly to disappear from the text of the Constitution. Indeed, ironically (but fittingly) enough, there were some supporters of the Fourteenth Amendment who nonetheless argued that it was not at all necessary because it simply spelled out what a correct interpretation of the Constitution already required.[21] Let me quickly concede once more that an accurate historical portrayal of the background of all of those amendments would take into account the perception of the best constitutional analysts of the day that they were indeed necessary. But that is only to highlight one of the central mysteries of what I call constitutional faith: the process by which "best constitutional analysis" is subtly transformed in the passage of time so that A becomes not-A, without amendment ever being deemed necessary. We do well to consider in this context Ronald Dworkin's recent statement that "questions considered easy during one period become hard before they again become easy questions—with the opposite answers."[22]

"The idea of a written Constitution," to quote the title of this panel, surely includes the hope that writing is a source of closure. That hope is chimerical. As Bray Hammond put it so well, in a statement regarding banking but in fact generalizable to all significant matters of constitutional politics, "the Constitution had not displaced rival principles or reconciled them but had become their dialectical arena."[23] As such, it becomes the central province of dialecticians, of whom perhaps the greatest in our history was John Marshall. But the reference to dialectic raises the ancient debate between Socrates and the Sophists and the moral and epistemological status of the dialectical acrobatics presented to the audience seeking edification. Those topics, I am happy to say, lie well beyond the mandate given me by the organizers of this symposium.

It is enough for now to return to our Virginians and the debate that ensued among them. As an exercise in constitutional interpretation, is *McCulloch* a model to be venerated or a travesty to be condemned? If that is a false dichotomy, then what is the true one? I do not deny, incidentally, that upholding the bank is easily defensible if one adopts an interpretive principle of allowing Congress to prevail whenever the constitutional text admits of more than one "on the wall" reading. The obvious problem with that principle is that it would quite effectively negate the possibility of judicial invalidation, for there is no case in our history—or at least among the litigated cases that are featured in our casebooks, beginning most certainly with *Marbury*— that presents the Court with a suitably unambiguous text. In any event, the question is not what *we* could have written about the bank, but rather what our reaction is to what Marshall wrote.

We can, of course, take a more Olympian perspective and assert that our task is neither to commend *nor* to condemn. I have certain sympathies with that view. The question then becomes how wide the sweep of any such principle turns out to be: Are we as willing to profess agnosticism about *Dred Scott* and *Lochner, Brown* and *Roe v. Wade?*[24] Indeed, are we willing to be equally detached from the Constitution itself, so that we avoid celebrating (or condemning) *it* with the same scrupulousness that we present ourselves in regard to *McCulloch?*

Surely there must be *something* we wish to say about *McCulloch* before racing to the ostensibly sheltering embrace of such consensus as exists concerning the two-thirds requirement for overriding a veto or the inability of Charles Robb to choose his spouse as his running mate should he be nominated for the presidency.[25] But what is it, and what light does it throw on the ideas we have of a written Constitution and of the process by which we breathe life into it? To be able to give a confident answer to that question, one that would in turn be accepted by the general community of those who style themselves constitutional interpreters, would be no small feat. *Not* to be able to do so, or to perceive no consensus among the receiving audience, provides its own illumination about the state of contemporary constitutional theory.

Notes

1. James Boyd White, *When Words Lose Their Meaning* (Chicago: University of Chicago Press, 1984), 247.

2. William H. Rehnquist, "The Notion of a Living Constitution," *Texas Law Review* 54 (1976): 693.

3. Justice Holmes in *Missouri v. Holland*, 52 U.S. 416, 433 (1920), quoted in Rehnquist, "Living Constitution," 694.

4. 17 U.S. (4 Wheat.) 316 (1819).

5. As reported by the *Gazette of the United States*, February 23, 1791; reprinted in *The Papers of James Madison*, ed. Robert A. Rutland et al., 15 vols. (vols. 1–10 at Chicago: University of Chicago Press, 1962–77; vols. 11–15 at Charlottesville: University Press of Virginia, 1977–85), 13:374.

6. Max Farrand, ed., *The Records of the Federal Convention of 1787* (New Haven: Yale University Press, 1937), 2:615.

7. *Gazette of the United States*, February 23, 1791; *Papers of James Madison*, 13:376.

8. *Papers of James Madison*, 13:378.

9. See Paul Brest and Sanford Levinson, *Processes of Constitutional Decisionmaking*, 2d ed. (Boston: Little, Brown, 1983), 14.

10. 17 U.S. (4 Wheat.) 316, 415 (1819).

11. Ferrand, *Records*, 3:435.

12. Jefferson, "Autobiography," chap. 24 in *The Complete Jefferson*, ed. Saul K. Padover (New York: Duell, Sloan, and Pearce, Inc., 1943), 1173.

13. White, *When Words Lose Their Meaning*, 263.

14. Robert H. Bork, "Styles in Constitutional Theory," *South Texas Law Journal* 26 (1985): 384.

15. 5 U.S. (1 Cranch) 137, 176 (1803).

16. Brest and Levinson, *Processes of Constitutional Decisionmaking*, 18.

17. *Home Building & Loan Association v. Blaisdell*, 290 U.S. 398 (1933).

18. *The Federalist*, ed. Jacob E. Cooke (Middletown, Conn.: Wesleyan University Press, 1961), no. 84.

19. *United States v. Darby*, 312 U.S. 100 (1941); *NLRB v. Friedman-Harry Marks Clothing Co.*, 301 U.S. 58 (1937); *NLRB v. Jones & Laughlin Steel Corp.*, 301 U.S. 1 (1937); *Wickard v. Filburn*, 317 U.S. 111 (1942).

20. 383 U.S. 663 (1966).

21. See, e.g., Michael Kent Curtis, *No State Shall Abridge: The Fourteenth Amendment and the Bill of Rights* (Durham, N.C.: Duke University Press, 1986), 90–91.

22. Ronald Dworkin, *Law's Empire* (Cambridge: Belknap Press of Harvard University Press, 1986), 354.

23. Bray Hammond, *Banks and Politics in America from the Revolution to the Civil War* (Princeton: Princeton University Press, 1957), 120.

24. *Dred Scott v. Sandford*, 60 U.S. (19 How.) 393 (1857); *Lochner v. New York*, 198 U.S. 45 (1905); *Brown v. Board of Education*, 347 U.S. 483 (1954); *Roe v. Wade*, 410 U.S. 113 (1973).

25. Interestingly, neither Robert nor Elizabeth Dole would be similarly confined should either of them ever win the Republican nomination. On this latter example, see the Twelfth Amendment.

PART 3

Responsibilities: Citizenship under the Constitution

CHAPTER 19

What Is a Citizen?

•••••

FRANÇOIS BOURRICAUD

TRANSLATED BY MARY STELLA DEEN

Without entering into the classic sociologists' quarrel over the relative importance of consensus and division in political life, we can grant that in our Occidental societies there is a somewhat general agreement about the role of the citizen, and about the rights and duties that this role entails. As for the nature of that agreement—its extent, its *basis*—opinions differ. What makes examination of these opinions so difficult is that they arise from very different interests and inspirations, and they are defended and argued about with more or less conviction and rigor. Everyone has "his" opinion about what the average citizen has the right to demand in the way of respect from other citizens, civil servants, and political leaders. We also take for granted that we owe "something" to the state—even if we would often be hard-pressed to say what the "something" consists of: dying for one's country, paying one's taxes, respecting the laws?

Philosophers, for their part, have reflected on these questions since the beginning of time. But can common sense and philosophy support one another in this sphere? In any case, our idea of the modern citizen is largely borrowed from conceptions elaborated in the past by men and in circumstances that our contemporaries have nearly forgotten, while at the same time this idea is continually illuminated by a more or less methodical consideration of contemporary problems.

Instead of trying to find a completely coherent notion of what the citizen is, it is more prudent to look for the principal dimensions of modern citizenship and to establish their connection to the successive contributions that have constituted "citizenship." This task is what we will attempt in the following pages, using for support the diverse opposing views to which the formulation "citizen" claims to respond. This exercise will give us the opportunity to be more specific about what we formerly referred to as "ideological tinkering about."[1]

First it is necessary to emphasize that the notion of citizen is a historical category. In his essay "La Nation" (1920?), Marcel Mauss distinguishes among several forms of political organization. Mauss's classifications bear the stamp of the evolutionism evident in his uncle Émile Durkheim's teaching in *The Division of Labor* (1893) and more specifically in the chapter "Rules of the Sociological Method." At the least-differentiated level of human societies, political functions are absorbed by domestic functions. Moreover, the obligations to which the members of primitive societies submitted are of a customary nature, and the authority that clothes them is at base religious. The clan characterizes this first form of organization. The tribe may be distinguished from the clan insofar as a first differentiation allows us to identify in the tribe specialized titulars in the role of authorities, who receive and transmit their roles and their status by inheritance. At these first two levels, human societies are groups few in number, lacking well-defined connections to the territory in which they move about. Along with empires appear concentrations of population, territory, and power unlike any observable in clannish or tribal organizations. The empires rest on a differentiation between governing and governed and on a centralization in the hands of the governing, who concentrate the means of constraint that assure them the obedience of the governed. But this concentration is not sufficient to ensure an authentic integration of imperial societies. Not only are the latter stratified into groups of very unequal power and prestige but also they place at the disposal of the governing a medley of conquered people who have nothing in common besides their obedience to the same masters. The city, as it is formed in Greece, for example, may be distinguished from clans and tribes, but also from empires. In contrast to the first two forms of organization, here the truly political functions are clearly differentiated. In a city there are governing and governed—as in an empire. Similarly, the governing exercise their power in this case over a well-defined territory. But in contrast to what happens in the empires, the cities are not juxtapositions of different ethnic groups subject to a single despot. They are communities. Historians find at the origin of Greek cities a founding act, imputed to a more or less mythical legislator (Lycurgus or Solon), that causes the qualities peculiar to the ethnic groups making up Athens or Sparta to merge. The political community rests on the cult of a single set of gods, the respecting of a single set of laws, and the inculcation of what Montesquieu will call "the general spirit of a nation."

What the city brings that is new is the conscience of a singularity, a particularized universal, Hegel would say, that assures the collective independence of its members by their participation in a common spirit. It is from the city of antiquity that modern civic-mindedness originates. But a peripeteia struck the ancient city with a perhaps irreparable caducity, and with it the virtues that were developing there. With Alexander, and then with Caesar, the imperial idea rediscovered protagonists worthy of it; Rome is not a copy of Babylon any more than Alexander's plan was a retake of Darius's plan. But the citizen of antiquity, ready to defend, weapons in hand, the liberty of his country—his own liberty—belonged to a community that was small, unified, and closed. Drowned in the immensity of an empire of universal aspirations, does the Gaul, the Numidian, the Greek, or the Roman himself belong to a single political and spiritual community? With the triumph of imperialism, which for several centuries stretched its commanding power over the entire earth, as much and more than the authority of its laws, didn't the *citizen* become again a *subject*?

Benjamin Constant, who set the democracy of the moderns against that of the ancients, was undoubtedly right to denounce the utopia of those French revolutionaries who believed themselves able to bring back to life Lycurgus's "beautiful city," where there was no virtue higher than civic-mindedness—without suspecting that in our commercial and industrial societies, the Reign of Terror would be the precondition, both bloody and vain, of an impossible "regeneration." But what Benjamin Constant did not see as clearly was that civic-mindedness had lost its hold well before the modern era, even well before the appearance of the Christianity that Rousseau accuses of turning us away from the celestial city to fix and keep our attention on the sole terrestrial city. Everyone will agree that the problems of civic-mindedness are very differently manifested in nineteenth-century French society than in Lycurgus's Sparta. But beyond this idea, rather banal at bottom, a more interesting idea may be delineated: There are cycles of civic-mindedness, and it is possible and profitable to isolate the conditions of their appearance.

But if the imperial form, after more or less prolonged eclipses, is reborn periodically from its own ashes, then from the classification outlined by Mauss emerge other lessons equally essential to the understanding of modern citizenship. First is the distinction between governing and governed, manifest as early as the appearance of the tribal form of political organization. The modern citizen lives this distinction within himself. As an elector he is governor, or at least has some part in the government. As taxpayer and individual subject to court action, he is subject to a law that applies to him, even if he judges it contrary to his preferences and interests. But the enigmatic nature of the civil obligation that the moderns tried to find a "basis" for—with more patience, it would seem, than success—had already struck Aristotle. The authority of the political chief—of Pericles, for example— is different from the authority that the father of a family exercises over his wife, his children, or the people (freemen or slaves) who work in his house. It rests on a common good that is the object of an often confused apperception of governing and governed. The head of the city is neither father nor despot. He is a citizen like others, and he has command over others only because in certain relationships those he commands are his equals. In order for that to be so, there must be present certain conditions, which have to do with the size of the society, the degree of cooperation or of conflict among its members, the relations between governing and governed, and the strength and solidity of the "general spirit" that animates the city. Today, Mauss's readers would be struck by what would appear to them perhaps to be naïveté. For the French sociologist writing in 1920, at the end of World War I, there is no doubt that these conditions can be realized only in the democratic nation-state. The solution to the political problem that the ancients perceived is certainly not applicable to modern societies, notably because of progress in the division of labor. But does their conception of a law that is not simply the will of the governing but, beyond opinions and interests, is based on a common reason, retain in our stratified societies, voluminous and complicated, a validity sufficient for civic-mindedness and citizen to be other than historical categories?

Let us put aside evolutionist speculations, which always affect to some degree the most original analyses of Durkheimian sociology.

Does citizenship, as its model emerges in the democratic nation-states and which finds its best expression, for Mauss, in the Third French Republic, constitute the perfect form of all political organization, destined for universal diffusion? In any case, the comparative-historic overview that Mauss suggests has for us an undeniable appeal. Calling attention to certain contrasts, whether capable of resolution in a stable equilibrium or, on the contrary, susceptible to degeneration in insoluble tensions, Mauss isolated the conditions that favor the formation of modern citizenship and that, in spite of a thousand difficulties, have ensured until today the persistence and the survival of this institution and the values associated with it.

There is a minimal condition for being a *citizen*. It is not to be a *subject*. Here Montesquieu can serve as our guide. What does despotism consist of for him but government without citizens? *Fear* is necessary in a despotic government.[2] Montesquieu does not say terror, but fear. It is true that the word "terror," in the revolutionary sense, had not yet been invented. But the objective of terrorists like Robespierre or Saint-Just has nothing to do with the objectives of the Shah of Iran or the Great Turk of whom Montesquieu is thinking. The Mountain dreams of a society where Virtue reigns, that is to say, as Montesquieu says: "moral virtue . . . directed to the public good"; or again: "love of the republic."[3] The Reign of Terror, for the Mountain, is nothing more than the way to reduce the "uncivilized" to silence, to take away their capacity to warn, or even to exterminate them. The despot has not the least civic notion. He acknowledges no obligation toward his subjects. If such obligation flitted across his mind, he would detect in it a risk of subversion. The despot wants only the obedience of the subjects. He thinks he can obtain it by instilling fear in them, not necessarily a horrible and relentless fear but a vague fear. For the despot not to feel threatened, it is not sufficient for himself and his close guard to instill fear. Most important is for the subject to be made to feel vaguely and constantly watched, to feel that he does not have a will of his own, and at all times and without remedy to know himself to be subject to the whim of the despot and his henchmen. Moreover, the latter are not less exposed than the most lowly subjects. "When a despotic prince . . . can not instantly demolish those whom he has entrusted with the first employments, all is over."[4]

A citizen is first of all an individual sure of his rights.[5] This security concerns his relations with the other private individuals, notably those relations that are contractually defined. But it also rests on the individual's relations with the administrative and political authorities. I must be able to count on the tax agent not to claim the same taxes from me twice, to know that he will set my dues not according to his caprice but according to criteria established by legislation and regulation currently in force. With respect to the agents of public administration, my security depends as a last recourse on my ability to appeal their decisions, either to hierarchical authorities of superior rank, who would bring the capricious civil servant back to order, or to the judicial authorities themselves.

But a given individual does not want only to protect himself against the encroachments of the administration. He also expects to cover himself from the abuses of the prince. The despot means to appropriate for himself all the resources of the people, either for the exclusive use of his house or to finance public services like the army, whose administration he intends to reserve for himself or for his people. In order to ensure control over their own goods, the people are led to control the authorities' use of the resources obtained by taxation.

The parallel between the subject and the citizen runs, however, into difficulty. The diverse procedures by which the prerogatives of individuals can be acknowledged lead to a limitation of the despot's aims. Even if he proclaims himself absolute—autocrat, as the czars say—the monarch is led to concede a sphere that, if not completely autonomous, at least is reserved to the competence of his officers and his clerks. The king of France, even at the summit of his power, will be almost constantly obliged to take account of judges and parliaments. Symbolically he is their chief. Among his attributes is the hand of justice, and its ancestor, Saint Louis, distributed justice under the oak of Vincennes. But his magistrates make him pay dearly, by refusing to record his edicts or by holding out so many reservations at their recording that the obedience of parliament, summoned in the name of justice, is often equivalent to a public censure of the crown. Therefore Montesquieu, although he sees the absolutist drift begun by Richelieu and Louis XIV, recognizes that the French monarchy is not an oriental despotism and situates it among moderate regimes.

But can the given individual, covered by the double movement of bureaucratic and judicial action that protects him against the infringements of the king and his people, publicly express in all safety his religious and philosophical convictions? It is hard for us to admit today that an individual prevented from practicing the cult of his choice, obliged to profess faiths that he finds absurd, can be taken for a citizen in whole—even if his goods, his ability to enter into contracts, to employ himself, or to hire others, to live a life of leisure within the limits of his means, to marry or to remain single, to have as many children as he and his wife (or his companion) judge suitable—are all reasonably guaranteed. One of the guarantees, that is to say, according to the equivalence proposed by Montesquieu one of the essential *freedoms* of modern man, is the free expression of his opinions in all matters, even religious. But this liberty has as a necessary condition tolerance at least, and at best the neutrality of political authorities in delicate matters.

Even once Christian churches had more or less sincerely, more or less completely renounced the effective control that they had so jealously and for so long exerted as a monopoly over the public mind, once they resigned themselves to exert only moral magistracy, two difficulties remained that even today affect the liberty of the modern citizen. Doesn't the expression of criticism by ordinary people risk leading to sedition? One must expect that with every proposal the governing activate this risk of subversion. For their part, subversives and activists will shoot for their own concerns, will try to take up their position for ambush in the sanctuary of the laws. A perfectly tolerant society does not only risk giving itself over unarmed to its enemies. It demobilizes ordinary citizens in leaving them without a fixed principle. It leaves them to fight each for his own interest. Can an absolutely tolerant society maintain the minimum unity without which its survival is threatened?

Is emancipation from a despot who is not accountable to anyone sufficient to transform the subject into citizen? In truth, this mutation is not harmless. In effect, the enfranchisement is only one face—the most manifest—of the process from which the modern citizen emerges. The other face of the same process is the recognition of an obligation that he cannot legitimately shrink from: the one that is imposed on him by law. At the same time, the problem of tolerance changes. Pilate asked, "What is Truth?" Modern skepticism has never stopped asking, "What is Law?" It is no longer a question of eluding the dictates of a despot. One must submit to the maxims of a common reason, common at least to all the members of a single political community, if not to all people. The citizen, ceasing to be a subject, is confronted with new problems: his relationship to the law, his relationship to reason, and the relationship of his city's law to universal reason.

A reading of Hegel and Marx, to my mind much too perfunctory, gave substance to one of the worst commonplaces with which we continue to live. It supposes the bourgeois and his rights on one side and, on the other, the citizen and his. It marks the division between one domain and the other so well that the second becomes merely the reflection or the epiphenomenon of the first. Or rather, the rights of the citizen come to have only the function of guaranteeing those of the bourgeois.

We still say that the bourgeois is the man of civil society. But what is meant by civil society? In French at least, the term "civil" has a multitude of usages. I will skip over the civil-military contrast—although we must come back to it, scarcely modified, a little later. French jurists are in the habit of contrasting civil law and public law. Essentially, the first comprehends rules applying to contracts for the exchange of goods, for buying and selling them, for services and the remuneration of services, for marriages, for filiation, and for inheritances. We reserve "public law" to name rules fixing the interaction among the different powers of the state, the functioning of public services, the relations between states. But it would be pushing things too far to oppose civil law and public law by characterizing the former as nonpolitical, by the absence of state control, while the latter exclusively would take care of the state, of the sources and modes of its power of command, and of the manner in which it carries out that power within and outside the territory in which it exercises it. It is true that the obligations, at least those dealt with by the civil code, are derived from past agreements between the parties and that these agreements are binding only to the extent that the parties behave as autonomous wills. But the autonomy of these wills is subject to several restrictions. To produce legal effects, they can come into play only over lawful subjects. Their autonomy might itself have occasion to be evaluated by judicial authorities. The validity of the contract might be subjected to the evaluation of the judge. Finally, the latter might have cause to intervene in order to ensure the execution of the contract. It is thus only with great caution that one can call the obligations of civil law "private." They are private in the sense that they come into being separately from the administration and the governing. But can we say that they would be all they could be if the state were not there?

In a more philosophic than juridical sense, "civil" is the opposite of "natural." We can describe as natural the prohibition against killing and lying and the obligation to help someone whose survival depends on our help. Supposing that these obligations and prohibitions can be adequately and concretely defined, they can be natural in that they would impose themselves upon us in the absence of a civil authority that had ways of making us respect them. Let us leave aside the question of their "basis." Whether they rest on the dignity of the human being, which we would have to respect in others as in ourselves, or inhere in the interest or compassion or sympathy that makes us feel as if others' pain and joy were ours, these obligations do not require the sanction of civil authorities. The sign that we take them seriously is that we would conform to what they prescribe even in the absence of all sanction. Civil society is distinguished from natural society by at least two characteristics. First, it can decree obligations that we judge arbitrary or even frankly unjust—whereas the maxims "one must not lie," "one must not steal," and "one must not kill," even if one doubts their effectiveness, will be recognized as indisputable in themselves. The second trait of civil society is that it has at its disposal an instrument of constraint by which it makes its prescriptions respected.

The absence of all state constraint would also characterize one of the domains of social life that, since the eighteenth century, has been frequently designated by the term "civil society," the one in which the "bourgeois" is master at home. Furthermore, this conception of society reduced to only its economic activities is not clear. In Hegel's *Philosophy of Right*, 1821, the "*burgerliche Gesellschaft*" concerns not only the relationship between production and consumption. It also includes domestic relations. In fact, civil society in Hegel entails the cohesiveness between the activities of production and consumption in households, tending to satisfy socially and culturally defined needs. The "bourgeois" can be "satisfied" (*befriedigt*) with his professional, familial, and communal life only if it is given to him to live in a reasonably organized state.

It is true that economic liberalism insistently demanded the free circulation of goods, services, and capital, and, consequently, that of the man who chose to produce and consume them. Laissez-faire proposes a program of disarmament in customs, administration, and regulation that obviously reduces the scope of the competence and aspirations of this first sketch of the welfare state, which was the society of orders and of states of the European ancien régime. But in its purest, most Manchesterian form, nineteenth-century liberalism never pretended to create the economy of a state able to guarantee contracts and assure the functioning, or at least the control, of public services. No one ever believed that civil society works all by itself. It is no more "autonomous" with respect to the state than the latter is "autonomous" with respect to it. The "bourgeois" can dream of a retired life in the bosom of "little societies" (to use Tocqueville's language), where along with his close friends, associates, and neighbors, he will pass peaceful and studious days far from the forum. His security, in the face of enemies perhaps come from a foreign country, or in the face of violent types who could seize his person and his goods, cannot be fully assured by himself alone.

The relations between civil society and political society on the one hand, and civil society and natural society on the other, are thus far from being as clear as they might at first seem. Pascal had a thought that allows a negative response: Force without law is unjust, law without force is impotent. Of course, it is necessary to agree on the meaning of terms like "law" and "injustice." Leaving aside the question of the origins of law, whether one sees in it the translation of divine wisdom for use by men or pictures it from a secular perspective as the sum of the rights and duties necessarily linking men together because of their belonging to a *common* nature, law institutes among men the relations that should exist if these relations were not perverted by extortion and exploitation. The law, even if its prescriptions conform to God's commandments or to the evidence of reason, risks being nothing more than a pious wish or a "vain form" as long as the violations of its orders remain unpunished. The law supposes an organized recourse to a secular arm, but it is not confined to this recourse. It does constitute a system of sanctions that can be instigated against offenders. But one must also think of it—perhaps above all—as a process that recognizes certain of the claims we make on one another as lawful or legitimate, while it eliminates others as unfounded. The law is thus not limited to the constraint of the judge backed up by the force of the gendarme. How can we imagine the authority that allows us to distinguish between a pseudolaw, which is merely an abuse of justice, and a law at once just and effective, which can count on both the legitimacy and the effectiveness of its dictates?

Obviously this question concerns the citizen of modern democracies. If the instructions we conform to did nothing more than ratify in a more or less dissimulated manner the interests of our governors, would the administrative and jurisdictional guarantees that we flatter ourselves for achieving be anything other than illusion? In most respects, we would have nothing to envy the subjects of the Great Turk. In order to give the instructions of the governing an incontestable basis, one solution would be to affirm that nature (as created by God or as its evidence is revealed to human reason) constitutes the authority or the reference in whose name society articulates the laws that it takes upon itself to see executed. The citizen may be thus authentically distinguished from the subject, since he is not exposed to the arbitrary and self-interested constraint of the governing. According to the constant lesson of the classics, it is the existence of law that enables the citizen to evade despotism.

Obedience to law is civic-mindedness, which constitutes the "virtue" of the citizen. In analyzing the notion of civic-mindedness, we will not fail to elucidate that of law, in the sense that the classics take it. Montesquieu writes, apropos of virtue, "it is a love of the republic; it is a sensation, and not a consequence of acquired knowledge."[6] Virtue requires the abdication of individual interests, what Rousseau will call a "denaturation." This conversion is to a great extent the effect of education. But in no case, according to Montesquieu, should we see in it the result of reasoning. No argument can persuade us to sacrifice our lives to the state. Virtue, that is to say love of the Republic, can only be a feeling. But it is a feeling fed by the citizen's beliefs about those who govern and about his own fellow citizens. In the first place, the governing, those who give orders in the name of the law, must not be enemies. Why would I obey someone who is indifferent to my welfare or, worse, who wishes me harm? Undoubtedly I can give in to violence. Perhaps it is in line with my interest to bow down in order to avoid the worst. But my obedience is nothing more than the submission of one defeated. A despot who treats his subjects as though they were slaves treats them in fact as though they were strangers. Political domination is merely a result of conquest.

Different from that of the slave, different also from that of the subject, the obedience of the citizen must be characterized in terms of the law. The law is not just any command. It cannot be reduced to the contest of two wills, one superior and effective, the other passive and subordinate. What characterizes law is the community it establishes, not only among those to whom it applies but also among them and those who decree it and become strong to make it respected. The result is that the status of the governor is of necessity different in republics from what it is in despotic regimes. The governor exercises his power only within the limits of the law and in the name of the law. His power is by nature delegated, even if this delegation, the terms of which are fixed by charter or by constitution, in no way constitutes a representation in the sense that in private law a contractual representative "represents" his principal. What counts is perhaps not so much the delegation process (election, drawing lots, co-optation, et cetera) as the intrinsically delegated nature of the power that the governor is led to exercise.

There is no citizenship if the delegated nature of the power is not recognized beforehand. This question was obscured by the classic opposition between direct and indirect democracy. Benjamin Constant brought attention to the fact that the moderns, in contrast to the Greeks or the Romans, have neither the time nor the taste to conduct for themselves the business of their own city. The complexity of affairs, the preference that the moderns give to their private interests, the necessity they discover (in contrast to the ancients, who had slaves) of working to ensure their subsistence and that of their families, easily explains why they voluntarily leave it up to representatives. Montesquieu was already congratulating himself with this arrangement: The "people are extremely well qualified for choosing those whom they are to intrust with a part of their authority. . . . But are they capable of conducting an intricate affair, of seizing and improving the opportunity and critical moment of action? No; this surpasses their abilities."[7] Rousseau sees in this displacement of the citizen at the hands of his representatives a renouncement that returns the citizen to the condition of subject. But Rousseau's criticism does not resolve the problem presented—or, rather, masked—by the existence of representatives. Suppose that the latter, as Rousseau hopes, are held on such short rein by the body of citizens that they are merely its commissioners.[8] The difficulty presented in the case of the representatives will present itself with respect to the citizens. There would be grounds to fear that the representatives would abuse their mandate because they could be tempted to decide according to their individual interest and not according to the interest of their constituents. When citizens vote, they are exposed to the same temptation. Will they not decide according to their personal, professional, familial, and regional interests? The "represented" are in the same situation as their prospective representatives. In order for one and the other to make up their minds according to interests other than their own, they must be supposed capable of reaching a decision according to the imperatives of a common, if not a universal, law. The possibility of the bourgeois becoming a citizen is suspended upon this condition.

But this condition is neither very clear nor easily achieved. To get some idea of it, we will say that this common law is nothing other than putting into operation the laws of nature, either as they are revealed to us by God himself or as a more or less mysterious authority, conscience, succeeds in making us feel it. Here we glimpse the boundaries of politics and ill-defined domains of which political men acknowledge the existence without much resistance, but which they are wary of exploring. The common law that the citizen must obey at the same time constitutes the only law he can obey without ceasing to be a citizen. Granted. But who has been entrusted with it? A church? And if so, which one? And, failing some church, would the precious trust fall to the political community itself? Rousseau chooses this second solution. Professor Robert Bellah looks for the religious sources in which American civic behavior grounds itself.[9] The American style of "civic religion" is different from that which might have been dreamed of by a reader like Robespierre. The problem of tolerance did not present itself in the same terms for the founders of the American Republic as for the French of the Lights, resolved to shatter the secular monopoly of Rome and borne forward at the same time by their obsession with ancient-style "virtue" to make of the state a "Re-total" rather than a "Republic," to borrow from Sieyes this very illuminating word play. The nature of this common law would be no further illuminated when at the beginning of the Third Republic the founders of modern democracy in France—the Ferrys, the Gambettas, the Waldeck Rousseaus— would look for it in the default of the religious Catholic tradition, which repulsed them as obscurantist or retrograde, either in the way of the "good old morality of our fathers" or along the lines of a Kantian-inspired ethic.[10]

Whatever the obscurities of the thought process we have just outlined, it limits the scope of a common law, since it makes the common law depend on a nonwritten source. In certain cases the citizen will be able to arm himself with this "nonwritten" (or at least not written by the legislator) law against the laws of the state. He will invoke against the latter the precepts of religion or morality. But modern political thought is seeking not only a law worthy of the citizen's obedience. It wants also to found an effective political order, from which factious rebellions—concurrent attempts by particular groups or individuals to give a universal scope to their interests and wills—are absent. By letting the laws of the city subsist next to the "nonwritten" laws or, to an even greater extent, by subordinating the first to the second, one risks ruining the very notion of common law. This is undoubtedly why Rousseau, affirming the necessity of a civic religion but fearing that it could be invoked to limit the sovereignty of the democratic state, as good as entrusts the torch to the citizens themselves, who are invited to form themselves into a people of priests.

Is the citizen effectively protected against the risks of despotism by the existence of a common law conforming to the demands of God, or reason, or nature? This is what a first democratic tradition, which we can call idealist and which is fed by various "natural law" doctrines, affirms. We can set against this first conception of the citizen a second, which we will call voluntarist. Common law is nothing more than the general will. Law has neither its seat nor its origin in divine wisdom, in a transcendent reason, or in universal necessities common to humanity. It merely expresses the will of the body politic. Nominalist philosophers teach the adage "*verum, factum.*" For them, what is true is what has been made by the human mind. Or in other words, the mind understands only what it is author of. This artificialist conception of truth is transposed in the domain of the law. But the will from which law derives is not just any will. It is said to be general, and to be so in at least two senses. First, it involves citizens taken as a body, and we will see that this strictly necessary condition is difficult to achieve. Second, it can focus only on questions of interest to individuals, not as people with particular interests but as citizens.

The first condition concerns majority rule. Failing a unanimous vote, the majority is invested with the capacity to decide in the name of the body politic as a whole. Is the citizen on the side of the minority still a citizen? Or is he as much as the citizen belonging to the majority? To settle these classic difficulties, can the voluntarist tradition have recourse only to its principles? Is it not rather going to be led to answers that borrow a great deal from the idealist tradition? Is it only because of the "generality" attached to its own will that the majority will not oppress the minority? In order to have its own rights acknowledged as inviolable and sacred, is not the latter going to invoke against the sovereign majority the rights granted to man and to the citizen in the American and the French Declarations of Rights? One might even doubt that the tenets of the voluntarist thesis could save the notion of representation. Rousseau, it is true, affirms that no will can be the objective of a delegation. For a specific purpose or for a specific period, I can give to a proxy the power to represent me, but it is not my power to will that I delegate to him. Nevertheless, what is the role of the minority with respect to the majority? One can say, along with Rousseau, that at bottom the minority wants what the majority wants. But it is Rousseau who gives himself the right to distinguish between an illusory appearance (what the minority thinks it wants but that at bottom it does not want) and what, without knowing it, it cannot *not* want. Rather than resorting to this distinction, do we not have the more difficult task of seeing in the majority the part of the body politic that represents the sum of the citizens, that speaks in their name, and that performs under their control a certain number of tasks that are entrusted to it by this mandate?

What constitutes the modern citizen is his relationship to the law. But this relationship remains ambiguous. We might even have to say that by nature it cannot be, since the law is opposed or is susceptible of opposition to our passions or to our individual interests. But it is not only because the law constrains us that it bothers or inconveniences us. According to a conception that we could describe as absolutist or radical, law may be understood as the expression of a sovereign will. In thinking of this idea, Tocqueville speaks of the "tyranny of the majority." On the contrary, according to another conception that we will describe as liberal, positive law cannot dictate anything at all. It is limited by the nonwritten laws of morality and of religion, unless it is limited by the "fundamental laws of the Kingdom," to use the language of the French jurisconsults of the ancien régime, which the king himself could not "touch except with a trembling hand," according to Montesquieu. Here we reach the heart of the conflict between the tenets of liberal democracy and the tenets of radical democracy.

This conflict is not always perceived in all its rigor and intensity. In French history several attempts at eclectic reconciliation of these two traditions took place in the course of the nineteenth century. The one that had the more lasting consequences, and that overflowed the domain of political theory to reach the very foundations of French political life, was led by the exceptionally brilliant generation of the founders of the Third Republic. The transformation of administrative law, the consolidation of public freedoms in the way of press and association, the development of a limited but real local autonomy thanks to the municipal law of 1884—these gave to the French a reasonably effective protection against bureaucratic infringements and the arrogance of the "self-importants" at the same time that it assured a significant proportion of them the enjoyment of public welfares such as health and education and a minimal participation in the functioning of the administration. The French were certainly no longer subjects. But had they become authentic citizens?

If one sticks to the strictest conception of citizenship—that of the radical voluntarists, which is the most dangerous and at the same time the most unstable—no individual is completely worthy of the name of citizen. But this paradoxical conclusion carries with it a positive lesson, which is completely in line with the views of the classics. There is in the citizen something—even if this something is unfinished—that goes beyond the bourgeois. By his participation in domestic, professional, and economic activities, the bourgeois, according to Hegel, knows only "particularized universals." Thus he cannot, as a bourgeois, participate in the life of the state. Now let us evoke the remarkable developments that Weber devotes to the city.[11] The banding together of bourgeois is born of a *contractual* agreement or of a granted charter, defining a right to be autonomous and autocephalic. The Weberian bourgeois—or rather the bourgeois that Weber believes he sees in the municipal movement of medieval Europe—is distinguished from the Hegelian bourgeois because the autonomous and autocephalic urban association rests on an act of socialization (*Vergesellschaftung*) and is founded on a *compromise* (*Ausgleich*) of rationally motivated interests or on a coordination (*Verbindung*) of (similarly motivated) interests. Thus, according to Weber, there is at the origin of the civic life of Occidental cities a mutual involvement (*Gegenseitige Zusage*) whose universality surpasses the sector-based, corporative interests of the Hegelian bourgeois.

There is thus in the citizen something more than in the bourgeois in the Hegelian or Marxist sense. But does the something derive from the universal or from the abstract? By "universal" I mean the biggest possible set of activities and of concrete people. In the social order, there would be no universal apart from humanity. But the difficulty of imagining humanity as effective organization, as a concrete corpus, is sufficient to reveal the insufficiencies, the dissatisfying nature of the demands of universality implicitly contained in the idea of citizenship, an idea that is doubly thwarted and limited. On the one hand, the universality of the citizen as a member of the state is limited by the particularity of his interests, needs, and passions. On the other hand, the universality of each state is limited by the existence of a plurality of other states. The citizen as bourgeois (in the Hegelian sense) participates only incompletely in the life of the state. And even if he participated completely in the life of such state, he would participate only incompletely in the life of humanity.

Citizenship does not completely achieve the universality that civic-mindedness carries. The general will that citizens obey is general only with respect to particular citizens. A state, if it is a universal, is never more than a particularized universal. As for humanity, neither—or not yet—is it a universal. It is either the collection of all human individuals or a plan to be realized for the good of all men. Is not the citizen, unable to achieve his universality in civic-mindedness, nothing more than an abstraction? This is the suspicion that conservative thinkers have applied themselves to elicit with more or less success. Around the status of the citizen they denounce various fictions such as that of representation and general will. But a fiction is not necessarily a *flatus vocis*. It is a way of "rescuing freaks" and of resolving insoluble difficulties. Neither the fiction of general will nor that of representation supplies us with an adequate notion of the political process. Each proliferates in baroque sophisms that depend on begging questions or simple redundancies. But fiction can also be considered articulation of a demand or an ideal, in its relation to the bringing into play—to the construction—of the conditions that could effect the realization of this demand. Thus envisioned, citizenship constitutes the process that strives to ensure the participation of individuals deriving from a single authority in a single normative system that surpasses the immediacy of their needs and their activities without, however, jeopardizing the existence of the "sociation" they were led to form.

Notes

1. François Bourricaud, *Le Bricolage Idéologigue* (Paris: Presse Universitaire Française, 1980).

2. *De l'esprit des lois* (1748). English translation, *The Spirit of the Laws*, trans. Thomas Nugent, 2 vols. (New York and London: D. Appleton, 1912), 1.3.9.

3. Ibid., 1.3.5, n. 10, and 1.5.2.

4. Ibid., 1.3.9.

5. "Political liberty (distinguished by Montesquieu from philosophical liberty) consists in securing, or, at least, in the opinion that we enjoy security" (*Spirit of the Laws*, 1.12.2).

6. Montesquieu, *Spirit of the Laws*, 1.5.2.

7. Ibid., 1.2.2.

8. Rousseau, *The Social Contract* (1762).

9. Robert Bellah, *The Broken Covenant* (1975).

10. Claude Nicolet, *L'idée republicaine en France* (1982).

11. Max Weber, *Die Stadt*, excerpted from *Wirtschaft und Gesellschaft*, 3d ed. (Tubingen: J. C. B. Mohr, 1947). French translation, *La ville* (Paris: Aubier Montaigne, 1982).

CHAPTER 20

From Town Meeting to Nuclear Power

The Changing Nature of Citizenship and Democracy in the United States

•••••

JON D. MILLER

It is entirely appropriate that on the occasion of a celebration of the adoption of the Constitution, we should examine the changing nature of citizenship in the United States and the impact of those changes on the practice of democracy. The relationship between a formal constitution and the political behavior of citizens—which I will refer to as citizenship—is both intimate and reciprocal. A constitution defines the boundaries within which citizens may seek to influence the acts of government, but it is the spirit and vigor of that citizenship that breathes life into a constitution.

Recently, much attention has been focused on the structure of American government, and on its evolution toward what Robert Dahl has termed polyarchy[1]—the optimal form of representative government possible in mass societies. To a large extent, attention has been directed to the scope of suffrage and not to the prerequisites or responsibilities of citizenship, or what might be called the quality of citizenship. Too often, citizenship has been viewed as an essential constant, perhaps enhanced or made easier by the revolutions in transportation and communications. I would suggest that citizenship has not been a constant in our system, but rather that it is the lifeblood of that system and that it has been one of the major factors in the persistence and success of the American Constitution that we celebrate today.

Citizenship in 1787 and the Early Nineteenth Century

To understand the evolution of the idea of citizenship in the United States, it is essential to begin by looking at citizenship at the time of the adoption of the new Constitution and in the first decades thereafter. From that perspective, we can then gauge the magnitude and importance of the changes that have occurred in the two centuries since 1787.

Citizenship in the first decades under the new Constitution continued to focus primarily on local affairs, usually those of the township. Tocqueville argued that New England township government became the ideal or model that fueled the democratic surge of the Jacksonian period and of the frontier. State legislative issues commanded some attention; there was little awareness of or concern about federal legislative programs or policies.

Tocqueville understood that local government, more than any other, stimulates a sense of civic pride and inspires participation in public affairs. Municipal institutions, he wrote, "constitute the strength of free nations. Town meetings are to liberty what primary schools are to science; they bring it within the people's reach, they teach men how to use and how to enjoy it. A nation may establish a free government, but without municipal institutions it cannot have the spirit of liberty."[2]

The town meeting was direct democracy in its purest form. One day each year, a substantial majority of the eligible electors would gather to review township affairs and to adopt a program for the next year. The issues were local and practical—the repair and construction of roads and bridges, the levying of taxes, the adoption of ordinances to address local problems, and the selection of one or two persons to supervise the work and enforce the ordinances. There were no committees. Every elector was expected to be able to understand the issues and to cast his vote accordingly.

The skills one needed to participate in a town meeting were basic—the ability to listen to and comprehend arguments about the cost of roads, or the advisability of requiring certain animals to be kept in fenced areas, for example. The issues were cut from the fabric of everyday life, and virtually all of the electors brought personal experience to the discussion. Moreover, the discussions were oral and did not require skill in either reading or writing. Common sense and some commitment to the common good were the minimal requirements for political participation, and virtually all of the eligible electors held these skills.

Given the immigration patterns to the areas north of the Hudson,[3] the eligible electors reflected a homogeneous and middling level of literacy. Tocqueville observed that there was no other "country in the world where, in proportion to the population, there are so few ignorant and at the same time so few learned individuals. Primary instruction is within the reach of everybody; superior instruction is scarcely obtained by any."[4]

Finally, it is important to note the slower pace of public affairs in the early years of the new Republic. The agenda of policy disputes was short. Townships were able to govern themselves adequately with one day of intense participation each year. The other 364 days were available for discussion, debate, and thinking. In the absence of radio, television, and automobiles, the majority of Americans lived in rural settings and spent their evenings in discussions with their families and other small groups. Talking around the fire or on a porch was the major form of recreation, and talking is, of course, an essential component of the political process. The details of previous town meetings would have been discussed extensively, and the absence of reading or writing skills would not have been a significant barrier to participation.

In summary, citizenship in the early years of the new Constitution was focused primarily on local affairs, and the skill requirements for participation were minimal. The ability to read a newspaper may have enhanced an individual's ability to present ideas or debate an issue, but since most of the township issues were rooted in everyday life, most citizens were able to engage in meaningful discussion about most of them. Of course, the right to participate in town meetings was limited to free males, but within that segment of the population, virtually all took part.

The Effects of Two Centuries of Modernization

Since 1787, major changes have occurred in American society that have had a substantial impact on the nature of the requirements for effective citizenship. The revolutions in transportation and communication are well documented, and their impact on the creation of a national political community and agenda are widely recognized. We need not recite that evidence. Belief in Manifest Destiny and the settlement of the West generated a sense of national competence. It allowed many Americans to put aside the experience of the Civil War and begin anew. Population of the new Western territories that eventually became states reflected the homogeneity of New England. Two world wars and a continuing cold war have generated a strong sense of nationalism, helping to unify the immigrant base of a significant portion of American society. The revolutions in transportation and communication have effectively changed the patterns of socialization, so that young people in the United States identify themselves as Americans before they develop a comparable identity with city or state.[5] Interestingly, there is little evidence to suggest that extensive media coverage of people and events from other parts of the planet has helped us to overcome the "we-they" feeling inherent in nationalism.

Finally, the experience of the Great Depression established a continuing linkage between national economic policy and personal well-being. The New England farmer in the early nineteenth century would have associated his economic well-being with his own productivity, the local weather, and the availability and condition of the roads to a market. Today's farmer is more likely to associate his economic well-being with the policies of the Department of Agriculture and the weather in the Soviet Union or Brazil. Concerns about interstate trade have become concerns about international trade, moving the issue to the federal agenda.

Citizenship Today

Although the legal scope of suffrage is now almost universal, the skills needed for effective participation are not universally shared. The dramatic changes that citizenship has undergone since 1787 have created new demands on participants.

First, the focus of political life has shifted from local to national issues for most Americans. The provision of local government services has become routinized, and most Americans do not know the names of their local officials. Few Americans ever attend a meeting of their city council or county board. And even fewer Americans know the names or views of their state legislators. In contrast, almost every child and adult in the United States knows the name, and some of the views, of the president, as well as the names of the president's spouse, their children, even their pets.

Second, the national political agenda has become so broad and complex that no one person can hope to be competent in all areas. No citizen can hope to remain continuously informed about economic, foreign, and domestic policy, and about the myriad of issues at the state and local levels. The substance of today's issues—nuclear power, genetic engineering, the value of the dollar in international trade—is far more complex than the construction or repair of local roads, and judgments about them can rarely be made on the basis of personal experience.

Further, for any given issue—economic policy, agricultural policy, science policy—more information is needed to be well informed today than would have been needed forty or fifty years ago. Economic policy is an excellent example. A few decades ago, the citizen who was attentive to economic issues needed to understand the concepts of supply and demand and something about the money supply; a lot of Keynes and a little Marshall would do. Now, to participate in the economic policy debate, an attentive citizen would need to understand, say, the competing econometric models—125-by-125 input matrices with process assumptions—for both the domestic economy and the international economy. So while the level of accuracy and professional understanding of a given issue may have increased, each step forward in sophistication increases the information threshold for the citizen, and it also reduces the number of citizens who are able or willing to allocate the time and resources needed to become and stay informed about that issue. Moreover, political concerns face strong opponents in the competition for citizens' available time. In contrast to our rural ancestors, who spent long evenings around their fire discussing every available topic, today's citizen may choose on any given evening from among live entertainment, professional and collegiate sports events, indoor recreation like swimming or tennis, dozens of motion pictures in theaters, thousands of motion pictures available for home viewing, and forty to fifty channels of television. The inevitable result of the intensity of this competition for time has been a process of political specialization.

Political specialization[6] involves two primary decisions by the

citizen. First, each citizen must decide whether he or she wishes to
follow public affairs at all. Electoral and other data from the last three
decades suggest that approximately half of all American adults do not
attempt to stay informed about politics and do not participate in the
system. The last three presidential elections, for example, have attract-
ed just over 50 per cent of the eligible electors. Most state and local
elections attract far fewer.

The American adults who do attempt to follow public affairs must
select a limited number of issues about which to remain informed and
in which to take an active role. A series of national studies over the last
decade have shown that most Americans who follow politics at all are
attentive to two or three issues. About 10 percent appear to follow a
single issue, and very few are able to attend to four or more major issue
areas. In contrast to our New England ancestors, who attended to all of
the issues in one day, the modern citizen must struggle to stay informed
about two or three major issue areas through the year.

The issue specialization process has had a major impact on the
methods and kinds of political participation. Given the small proportion of the electorate that follow any given issue, only a few issues
command a sufficiently broad audience to become electoral issues that
are debated and decided in traditional political campaigns. Indeed, the
art of politics has become the weaving together of strands of special
interests into an electoral majority. Today, most issues are decided
outside the electoral process through legislative and executive branch
lobbying. Political support on any given issue is now measured most
often by the number of letters and telephone calls that a legislator
receives from politically active citizens in his or her district or state.[7]

What, then, has been the impact of these changes on the skill
requirements for effective citizenship? I would argue that the impact
has been massive and has changed the character of our political system
in significant ways. First, and most important, effective citizenship
now requires a relatively high level of basic literacy to understand the
system and to participate in it effectively. Most of the information on
any given issue is provided in written form, usually in newspapers and
magazines. Interest groups write pamphlets and letters to argue their
case. Television, with its self-imposed two-minute limit on network
news stories, serves as a useful electronic index to breaking political
and social events, but it does not provide the substance necessary to fuel
meaningful citizen participation in a specialized political system.

Citizens who are uncomfortable with printed materials, or who have difficulty expressing their views in writing, are severely handicapped in such a system.

Second, many issue areas demand a level of specialized knowledge for meaningful participation. Economic policy is one excellent example; science policy is another. An increasing proportion of the issues dealt with by Congress require a significant level of scientific or technological competence. Benjamin Shen has estimated that fully half of the issues before a recent Congress had a scientific or technical component.[8] It is difficult to see how a citizen without some degree of scientific literacy could be expected to follow the substantive debates about issues like nuclear power, genetic engineering, or the relative competitiveness of American science and technology in the world. How many Americans could write a reasoned letter to a legislator to argue against or in favor of the federal government's spending $6 billion on a superconducting supercollider? The point is clear. There are large areas of public policy that are open only to those citizens with specialized knowledge.

Finally, the pace and complexity of the decision-making process have increased significantly. Reflecting the specialization of issues, the work of Congress is handled in subcommittees made up of subject-matter specialists. On any given day, hundreds of persons testify at dozens of hearings on specific pieces of legislation. A small industry has developed in the Washington area to keep track of these hearings and provide early warnings to interested groups and individuals. To stay abreast of current policy developments, a citizen would need to join one or more organizations or groups having a Washington staff. On most issues, the citizen who waits for the next election to make his or her views known will have long ago missed the boat.

The Future of Citizenship

Given the changes in the skill requirements for citizens since 1787, what are the implications for the future of citizenship in the United States? Are the democratic traditions rooted in the New England town meeting in danger? Can there be meaningful democratic participation in specialized issues like nuclear power or genetic engineering?

In my view, the democratic traditions that stem from the New

England town meeting are indeed in serious trouble. I concur with Dahl and others who have noted that the very size of our country makes direct democracy of the town meeting type impossible. A delegate, or republican, form of government is inevitable, though not inherently inconsistent with democratic principles. Dahl has suggested that highly participatory republican systems be termed polyarchies and be conceptualized as falling between pure democracy and oligarchy, but closer to democracy. A polyarchy should have broad suffrage, extensive freedom of press and speech, and regular elections, all of which we find in the United States today. But, ironically, in the decades during which the last barriers to universal suffrage were removed, significant new barriers seem to have arisen. Several studies have suggested that perhaps as many as one-third of American adults are deficient in basic literacy skills. Television can stimulate interest in issues or problems, but it cannot substitute for the ability to read substantive, in-depth material in a newspaper or magazine. The expression of one's views to a decision maker requires either the ability to write a coherent letter on an issue or the self-confidence to make a personal or telephone contact, and persons lacking basic literacy skills are unlikely to enter comfortably into either kind of communication. In short, at the same time that the laws requiring literacy of voters were repealed, the de facto requirements of the political system placed a significant new emphasis on basic skills.

Beyond basic literacy, the process of issue specialization often requires an additional level of literacy in a substantive area. Citizens who follow even core issues like economic policy need an increasing level of background knowledge to form judgments about the arguments and programs. More-specialized areas like nuclear energy policy demand a relatively advanced level of scientific literacy from interested followers. And even areas like agriculture policy, which were traditionally accessible to citizens on the basis of personal experience alone, now require some knowledge of international trade and monetary systems.

In his sage observations of the young Republic, Tocqueville pointed to the unimodal character of American society north of the Hudson as the prerequisite to effective democratic participation. There, the concerns flowed from everyday life, and the skills necessary for participation in the government process were shared by nearly all. Tocqueville recognized that there would be differences among individuals in speaking and reasoning skills, but he observed that these differences fell within a reasonably narrow range.

In contrast, the American political system today requires a much higher level of both basic and specialized literacy. Most issues are not accessible through personal experience, but require specialized information, the resources to obtain it, and the ability to use it. The *Wall Street Journal* may be the "daily diary" of American economic policy, but it is not free, and its contents may not be comprehensible to citizens who have difficulty reading complex material or who have no formal training in economics or business. We have become a multidimensional bimodal society.

Are we on a one-way road to a technocratic oligarchy, or is it still possible to have meaningful citizen participation in a highly specialized society and political system? I believe that a participatory republican form of government—Dahl's polyarchy—is still viable under conditions of high issue specialization. It will be necessary for us to understand that decisions in specific policy areas may be made by a minority of citizens in the normal operation of the political system. At the same time, if policies adopted in a specific policy area become sufficiently well known to the larger political system, and if those policies are unpopular, the structure of the Constitution provides a final veto by the general electorate. In both the Korean and the Vietnam wars, those policies became sufficiently visible and unpopular that the control of foreign policy was taken away from the foreign policy leaders and put into the general electoral arena, giving the full electorate an opportunity to voice its opinions about them. Currently, the growing controversy over our international trade policy suggests that this issue may move from the control of specialists to the general electoral arena.

The key to effective participatory controls in specialized policy areas is an attentive public in each issue area sufficiently large to reflect the major segments of society, although not necessarily in their exact proportions. Public participation in science policy illustrates both the potential and the problems of stimulating and supporting an effective, attentive public. On the basis of a decade of national studies, it appears that about one in five Americans is attentive to science and technology policy issues. That is, one in five reports a high level of interest in those issues and feels well informed about them. The attentive public for science policy includes about 34 million Americans. While this group is disproportionately male, and better educated than the general

335

public, it includes millions of citizens from all educational levels and from all backgrounds. It is not elitist but simply specialized. This group follows science and technology policy issues in the news, holds reasonably strong and stable views on those issues, and reads material on science and technology generally. When an issue or controversy emerges in this area, it is this group that provides the letters and telephone calls to Congress and the White House and that contributes the funds for special educational and lobbying efforts.

While the attentive-public model appears to offer some hope for the preservation of participatory governance in an era of specialization, problems remain. Looking still at the 20 percent of Americans who form the attentive public for science and technology policy, it appears that many in this group have low levels of scientific literacy. Recent studies suggest that only a third of this 20 percent actually qualify as scientifically literate, by a very lenient standard. It is not clear how many of these citizens could be mobilized for actual participation on complex issues like nuclear power and genetic engineering. Further, the serious erosion of science education in the United States in the last two decades is producing new generations of young Americans who are even less scientifically literate than their parents. Without a substantial improvement in the quality and distribution of science education, it is likely that the size of the attentive public for science and technology policy will decline in the decades ahead. And a significant decrease in the size of this attentive public would further restrict its republican or participatory character.

While I am better informed about the structure of public participation in science and technology policy than in other areas, my reading of recent studies on young Americans' awareness of the other inhabitants of this planet suggests a similar crisis in what is sometimes called global education. Relatively few young Americans can speak or read a foreign language, and only a small proportion appear to know very much about other nations and peoples. I suspect that the secondary education crisis in this country has an adverse impact on many specialized policy areas.

What, then, can and should be done to preserve the maximum level of participatory or polyarchical government in the United States? Let me argue two courses of action.

First, it is essential that our precollegiate educational system provide young Americans with strong basic literacy skills and some specialized skills. I personally believe that it is possible for every high school graduate to be made scientifically literate and globally literate at levels substantially above those found in the adult population today. To achieve this goal will require a massive overhaul of our educational system and a major infusion of leadership and resources. It may take decades, but it is a task that we must get under way if we are serious about preserving effective citizenship in the United States.

Second, in teaching our young people about their government and their ability to influence policy, we need to be realistic and deal with the specialization process that is operative today. Virtually all of the pre-collegiate social studies tests in the United States continue to depict the all-purpose citizen who is interested in all issues and capable of informed participation in any policy area. It is an unrealistic portrait, and the students know it. Because social studies teachers are nervous about teaching on local issues, too many tests and courses focus primarily on world peace and world hunger, two topics guaranteed to reduce anyone's sense of what one citizen can accomplish. But effective citizenship is still possible. Washington is full of people and organizations that understand how the system works and that function effectively in a highly specialized political system. We must begin to teach our young people how our system *really* works and how they can be effective in it. The New England town meeting is now an almost-vanished artifact, but issues like nuclear power and genetic engineering will shape the world for centuries to come, and we must prepare our young people to live successfully in that world.

Notes

1. Robert A. Dahl, *Polyarchy* (New Haven: Yale University Press, 1971).
2. Alexis de Tocqueville, *Democracy in America* (1835), trans. Francis Bowen (New York: Vintage Books, 1945), 63.
3. Tocqueville distinguished the kind of democracy practiced south of the Hudson from the kind practiced in the north. The latter, he argued, provided the model for settlements in the West. The more aristocratic model of the states south of the Hudson was limited to that area and was not emulated elsewhere.
4. Tocqueville, *Democracy in America*, 54.

5. See Fred I. Greenstein, *Children and Politics* (New Haven: Yale University Press, 1965); Robert D. Hess and Judith V. Torrey, *The Development of Political Attitudes in Children* (Chicago: Aldine, 1967).

6. For a more complete discussion of this process, see Jon D. Miller, *The American People and Science Policy* (New York: Pergamon Press, 1983).

7. James Rosenau has labeled this process "Citizenship between elections" in his book of that name (New York: Free Press, 1974).

8. Benjamin S. J. Shen, "Scientific Literacy and the Public Understanding of Science," in *Communication of Scientific Information*, ed. S. Day (Basel: Karger, 1975).

CHAPTER 21

The Individual as Citizen

·····

RALPH NADER

To citizens, the federal Constitution, justly noted for its economy of language, sends a very brief message: Liberty is rooted in law, but duty is rooted in conscience. Civic duty is not simply what we do when we possess a civic right. The exercise of civic duty is necessary to give protective roots to rights, when challenged by adversaries, and to expand these rights when they are found wanting. Clearly, the history of constitutional litigation has contributed to deeper understanding of rights, very often because individual citizens—I think of *Gideon*'s celebrated trumpet[1]—exercised committed duty. Indigents, after *Gideon*, have a constitutional right to counsel, by appointment, when they are charged with a felony. Citizen Wesberry exercised duty when he took his governor to court and eventually won before the U.S. Supreme Court the decision declaring unconstitutional a system of unequal voting representation for equal numbers of eligible voters.[2]

The United States Constitution is remarkably silent on matters of duty. Rather than exhortations, it gives us assurances that we will be free to exercise liberties and free from the arbitrary power of government. The Bill of Rights demonstrates this emphasis and specificity. The First Amendment reads: "Congress shall make no law respecting an establishment of religion, or prohibiting the free exercise thereof; or abridging the freedom of speech, or of the press; or the right of the people peaceably to assemble, and to petition the Government for a redress of grievances."

The Constitution did not impose a duty to vote, as did the Australian national constitution earlier in this century. Nor did our Constitution of 1787 impose a duty on citizens *not* to own other human beings or require the states to accord women the franchise. A "more perfect union" was paid for dearly in the currency of its charter's imperfections.

Duties were left to statutes, which in turn exhibit their own imperfections. There is military conscription, which led to major riots in New York City during the Civil War. There is jury duty, albeit with numerous escape clauses. And there have been numerous duties, many repealed, on potential voters that impeded their voting rights in ways desired by certain holders and brokers of power in the states.

Mandatory civic duties provoke healthy skepticism in our society. Staying at home on election day is viewed as a form of dissent or rejection; it happens to be very easy as well. The right to remain silent and the right to privacy are now constitutionally rooted and nourish this inclination to be free to opt out. Carried to extremes, the exercise of this privilege undermines other important values, from those associated with the principle of commonwealth to the practical preconditions of a functioning society. The boat does not move if few or none pick up the oars.

Herein lies a contradiction. The intensity of a national crisis determines the mandate it generates. In wartime the law can send us to fight and die for our country's defense. But laws that would require us to enter the civic arena to anticipate and avert national crises are perceived as either inappropriate or unworkable. We give those tasks over to a government that we license to pass laws and rules for us, rules about how we are to interact in the workplace, the marketplace, and the environment, about how public resources are used, about who wins contracts, leaseholds, and licenses. We delegate our civic duties and obey the work, and often the whims, of our delegates.

Representative democracy does have a general advantage over direct democracy. Delegating our civic responsibilities takes less time than organizing initiatives, referendums, recalls, or plebiscites. It does not require our attendance at meetings. Yet direct democracy needs to stand by, as an alternative and, where necessary, a corrective to the actions of elected officials. The roots of public justice transcend the bedrock of constitutional protections and freedoms. They lie where Judge Learned Hand observed them—in the citizenry, and with those citizens who voluntarily assume a variety of causes.

Those Americans who do appreciate the primacy of the office of citizenship have had much to say about the obstacles to exercising that office. There is the matter of corporations, never mentioned in the Constitution yet entitled to the constitutional status of "person," with most of the same rights as are accorded real people. But corporations are different from you and me; they have privileges and immunities reflecting their artificial status. Corporations are uniquely capable of accumulating power, wealth, resources, and influence far more easily than can the real persons with whom they contend under equal protection of the laws. Can equal protection of the laws obtain where there is such a structurally *unequal* amassing of power and immunity? Can we really give such artificial persons equal status with real persons (for example, under the Fourteenth Amendment) and still be true to our constitutional respect for human beings? The question, which has from time to time occupied the divided attentions and opinions of Supreme Court justices, is worthy of more public debate in these times of eminent domain extensions, patentable genetic engineering, exclusive media licenses, and growing concentrations of corporate industrial, financial, and commercial power over our political economy.

Consider two contemporary instances where both rights and duties of citizenship face assault or interposition. The Seventh Amendment to the federal Constitution preserves the right of trial by jury "in suits at common law." In recent years, that amendment has extended some remarkable benefits to the public. It was a worker sickened by asbestos who began the massive litigation that exposed that product's health risks as well as the lengthy and very extensive cover-up of those risks by certain of its manufacturers. In this case one man succeeded in humbling a large corporation into disclosing its illegal practices and compensating its victims. Also alerted into action and precaution were the long-indifferent regulatory agencies and the society at large. But this litigant would not have had a chance had he been unable to secure his right to jury trial. Juries are instruments of law that reduce the disparity of power between the haves and the have-nots. At present, a mounting attack on juries and the jury system in civil liability cases is being waged by insurance companies, trade associations, and other corporations. Recently one of their lobbies offered legislation to Congress that would preempt or limit various decisions made by juries in state courts. This lobby is testing the waters, for it has a long history of favoring replacement of the jury system with compensation boards operated by political appointees. The code word they use is "predictability"; the real word is "controllability."

How many people in our country know and understand the role of civil juries in the process of self-government, the transmission of deterrence, the reflection of contemporary values attached to life and health? Certainly, many former jurors know how seriously they started and completed their task in the institution least vulnerable to the political fix and the intimidating pressures of raw power. Perhaps what is needed is a National Association of Jurors to defend this historic institution of real people against the burgeoning attack. As a start, in preparing students for the duties of citizenship, such an association might persuade schools to include in their civics curricula the early British history of the jury and its role as bastion against tyranny.

The second of the two instances is the extension of First Amendment rights to artificial persons called corporations, in instances where these collide with the First Amendment rights of real persons. Consider, for example, the licensed power of broadcasting corporations to control the public airwaves. In the famous *Red Lion Broadcasting* case, the Supreme Court insisted that "it is the right of the viewers and listeners, not the right of the broadcasters, which is paramount."[3] This principle has not been carried out beyond enforcement of the fairness doctrine and the right of reply to personal attacks in programming. A broadcasting corporation's power to exclude remains impressive, the exclusivity of its license remains intact and free of charge, and an industry drive continues to press for what amounts to perpetual and unchallengeable licensing tenures.

The inability or unwillingness of lawmakers to recognize the crucial difference between the use of public airwaves and the use of private presses is shared by some commentators in the print media. How dare some congressmen, they declare, ask the executives of the broadcast networks to testify at public hearings in the House of Representatives? It seems to have escaped them that under the 1934 Communications Act, Congress does have some constitutionally sanctioned duties. There is the duty to uphold the public interest, necessity, and convenience standard, for example. There is the licensing function. There are antitrust questions. Our national legislators have a federal mandate as well as a duty to exercise dominion over corporations given a temporary license to decide who says what on the airwaves and to exclude anyone else who wishes to use that medium or that part of the spectrum. If electronic media are to enjoy exclusive license to portions of the airwave spectrum, they need to be held to a very different standard of accountability to citizens than the one to which the written press adheres.

Since broadcasting began in our country, it has been in the interest of networks and advertisers to deny their audience the opportunity to become electronically literate and communicative. That the same corporate elites control a larger number of stations in recent years does not change the basic exclusionary hold over the spectrum. To restore an equitable balance of power between citizens and broadcasters, Congress ought to revert an allotment of time on all television and radio stations to a publicly chartered audience network open to membership by viewers and listeners. These viewers and listeners would become the electorate for the network's directors, who would oversee the studios and their producers, programmers, and reporters.

These examples are just two of many possible ways to remind ourselves of the need to pay attention to how democracy is facilitated, and to create better ways of sustaining the institutions that promote the civic rights and civic duties that ensure a more just society. Tocqueville observed a century and a half ago that civic associations extend individual citizenship. Today, we need better access to a greater number of such associations in order more knowingly to make the exercise of democracy more feasible.

Notes

1. *Gideon v. Wainwright,* 372 U.S. 335 (1965). See Anthony Lewis, *Gideon's Trumpet* (New York: Random House, 1964).
2. *Wesberry v. Sanders,* 376 U.S. 1 (1964).
3. *Red Lion Broadcasting Co. v. FCC,* 395 U.S. 367, 390 (1969).

CHAPTER 22

The Corporation as Citizen

·····

DAVID F. LINOWES

Although many observers are inclined to think of corporations as inventions of the twentieth century, the concept of an institution as an artificial person to live beyond the lifetime of one or more individuals can be identified at least as far back as the thirteenth century, when corporations were established primarily as religious institutions or military units. Some scholars even trace the genesis of today's corporation to ancient civilizations of Asia Minor and to the Greek city-states and Roman societies.

The modern joint-stock corporation began in fourteenth-century Florence, where the Medici banking family expanded its operations to other parts of Europe.[1] In England a corporation called A Treasurer and Company of Adventurers and Planters of the City of London for the First Colony in Virginia was organized early in the 1600s to underwrite settlements in the New World. This initial effort was followed by the Hudson Bay Company in 1670, which remains an active corporation to this day. About the same time, other European nations also established corporations to develop East India trade.

The rate of incorporation during the 1700s and 1800s was slow. Most joint-stock companies were conducted as partnerships, even though the number of partners was large. The Banking Company of Aberdeen, for example, had 446 partners. During the eighteenth century, England chartered only about half a dozen manufacturing corporations and very few in any other area of business. In 1807, however, France became a model for other countries by enacting the Code de Commerce, which covered commercial associations. Despite that legislation, the increase of corporations in that country was only gradual.[2]

In 1897 the creation of corporations in England was stimulated when a court held that the legal existence of a corporation depended not upon the activities of its members but upon the legal act that created it and that the corporation was "an independent personality in the eyes of the law."[3]

The History of Corporations in the United States

The corporate form of business organization was not popular in early America. Merchants at that time had limited need for the advantages of incorporation, preferring more immediate and exclusive control of their businesses. As new enterprises requiring larger amounts of capital appeared, however, the rate of incorporation increased. Ventures like railroad and canal building were highly speculative and capital-intensive. Through incorporation, companies could obtain their needed capital while limiting potential losses to investors. Incorporation provided two additional incentives: Investors did not have to participate in management of the corporation, and they could sell out at any time.

Charters, however, were at that time difficult to obtain. They were granted by legislative acts that usually required lobbying, political favoritism, or gift-giving to officials. By the 1850s, laws eliminating the need for legislative action to establish a corporation became rather common. Thereafter, the corporate form of business organization began to grow rapidly.[4]

Although railroad development to open the West gave the movement impetus, it was not until the rights embodied in the Fourteenth Amendment were applied to the corporation by the courts that it was off and running.[5] The Fourteenth Amendment states that no "person" may be deprived of life, liberty, or property without "due process of law." This decision by the courts was critical to the corporation for purposes of preventing discriminatory taxation by the states. It served to stimulate the development of a corporate personality. By 1890 the Supreme Court held that a corporation could seek protection of liberty in the freedom to transact business, and of property in guarding assets against discriminatory state laws.[6]

Over time, courts came to look to the Constitution as an important source from which a corporation's rights and responsibilities were to be drawn. Constitutional protections to freedom of speech, press, and petition extended to corporate bodies.[7] As a result, the corporation became the principal entity for large business operations. By the middle of the twentieth century, more than half of the gross national product (57 percent) of the United States was produced through corporate activity.

Characteristics of the Corporation

Once the characteristics of the corporation had been clarified by laws and the courts, the corporate form as a business entity became widespread. The limited liability of its owners, its unlimited life, the ease with which new owners became a part of the enterprise and former owners disposed of their shares—all were important inducements. But it was much more than that.

"The corporation has a sharp legal image," John Kenneth Galbraith writes. "Its purpose is to do business as an individual would but with the added ability to assemble and use the capital of several or numerous persons. . . . The corporate charter, however, accords the corporation a large area of independent action in the conduct of its affairs. And this freedom is defended as a sacred right."[8] Although it is common to view a corporation solely as a collection of material things, its true substance is the collective effort of individuals. It is essentially a human or social organization. It is the personal component, more than the material component, that is the key to a corporation's existence. As a collective of individuals—both employees and shareholders—each corporation develops its own policies, customs, and reputation, all of which tend to mold the entire unit into a culture of its own. In the early days of the United States, the corporation was even regarded as a kind of folk hero symbolizing achievement.

As each corporation evolved its own identifiable character, it increasingly established its existence apart from each of the people who composed it and became recognized as distinctively different from other corporations. Courts gave it persona by repeatedly supporting the view of the corporation as a person, often with as many rights and responsibilities as a natural person.[9]

Changing Social Contract

As the corporation's rights and responsibilities were subjected to judicial refinements, the nature of the corporation itself changed. Although retaining the same name, the corporation in recent decades is being viewed as, and is evolving into, a different kind of organization. Professor Keith Davis of Arizona State University points out that business decisions have social consequences and cannot be regarded solely as economic acts. Business is obliged to act in ways that will protect the interests of society. Corporations that ignore the responsibility their social power entails run the risk of losing whatever power they have. As citizens, business institutions have a responsibility to become involved in areas where social needs exist. Thus, business must bear its share of the costs of citizenship, and, of course, it is entitled to benefit from the better society that results from its responsible exercise of that citizenship. Society has entrusted many of its resources to business, and it expects proper trusteeship in return. Similarly, social responsibility applies to all people regardless of their life roles.[10]

The mandate for rebalancing the relationships between corporations and society is to a large extent driven by pressure from labor unions, consumer groups, and government regulatory bodies. Not to be overlooked is the enlightened self-interest of policy-making executives who are integral parts of the corporate structure. They are—many of them—well-educated, loyal American citizens who are concerned about the welfare of our nation and its future, and they imbue their corporate entities with the same sensitivities.

Corporations benefit from numerous opportunities in this country because they function in an open and free society with only limited regulation. Some argue that it is these opportunities that have resulted in the remarkable successes that American corporations have achieved. We are justified, therefore, in expecting to receive in exchange a recognition by corporations of a duty to act for the common good. The corporation is asked to give back to society—over and above its industrial productivity—a fair share for what it receives. A full set of reciprocals is being called for in the rearticulation of the corporate social contract.

Natural Citizen and Corporate Citizen

Increasingly, the evolving corporate social contract is approaching one similar to that between a natural citizen and society. There is no exclusivity to being a good citizen. If in the immediate past the corporation had not been considered by scholars as having duties and rights of citizenship, that need not be the case today. All persons, corporate and natural, are integral parts of good government in a democracy.

Corporations are being looked to for citizen initiatives. All citizens owe allegiance to the state and are entitled to its protection. They have a right to hold and transfer property and to enjoy the protection of the Constitution and the laws. Corporations, like natural persons, develop their loyalty to their government by being afforded opportunities to achieve their goals and to influence the political process.

Citizens are expected to pay taxes, obey the laws, participate in military service to the nation when called upon—whether that service be as a foot soldier or as a productive corporate entity—and take an active part in political affairs. In each element of citizenship, the corporation shares equally with the natural citizen. In political affairs in recent years, the corporation's participation has become increasingly pronounced through the development of political action committees, whereby corporations collect funds from their employees and then allocate those funds to candidates for political office. Through lobbying activities, corporations have always assumed significant roles in the political process.

Although these lobbying activities frequently serve the self-interest of the corporation, that is not necessarily all bad. Adam Smith, writing about individual actions in his *Wealth of Nations*, convincingly showed that "although [the individual] intends only his own gain he is in this . . . led by an invisible hand to promote an end which was no part of his intention. . . . By pursuing his own interest he frequently promotes that of the society more effectually than when he really intends to promote it."[11] This is no less true for the corporation.

Corporations also take part in the political process through advocacy advertising, designed to communicate the company's position on public and social issues. Such activity is sometimes an effective form of citizen initiative. Mobil Oil Company spends $3 to $4 million per year on advocacy advertising; Atlantic Richfield, United Technology, and now Aetna Life Insurance Company are also well-known sponsors of advocacy advertising. The Supreme Court supported advocacy advertising in 1978 by ruling that corporation participation in this activity is guaranteed by the First Amendment.[12] By exercising their First Amendment rights, corporations can and do influence public opinion and thereby the political process. Recently, the Opinion Research Corporation found that "90 percent of the public have read or heard issue advertisements and 57 percent had changed opinions on an issue as a result of reading or hearing issue ads."[13]

Distinctive among the privileges and responsibilities of citizenship that the individual alone, as opposed to the corporation, may exercise are voting and holding political office. Yet since the corporation is a collective of natural individuals and acts directly and indirectly to influence its human components, it can be argued that the corporation shares in the right to vote and to hold political office. The voter and the political representative carry a bit of the corporate culture into the exercise of their respective offices.

The corporation that employs a person seeking political office has as much influence on the thinking and actions of that person as does a colleague, friend, campaign official, or relative who does not aspire to a political office but contents himself or herself with being associated with an officeholder.

Professor Peter French affirms that corporations are members of the moral community, holding moral standing comparable to that of human beings. They can be recognized as full-fledged moral persons having whatever privileges, rights, and duties are normally accorded to moral persons. It is a fact that corporations act with a view toward realizing their established corporate goals, irrespective of the self-interest of directors and managers. It is proper that corporate entities be held accountable for what they do, since some of their activities reflect the intentions of the corporations themselves. In this sense, biological existence is not essentially associated with the concept of being a person.[14] "Concepts and functions normally attributed to persons can also be attributed to organizations made up of persons," argue Kenneth E. Goodpaster and John B. Mathews, Jr., of Harvard University, who suggest that we should require of the organizations in our society the same moral accountability that we demand of ourselves.[15]

Constitutional Democracy and the Corporation

Our democratic society and the Constitution on which it is based could not have survived industrialization without the modern corporation. By promoting economic well-being for the people, and thus furnishing the leisure and the means for education, the corporation contributes to the creation of an informed electorate. People who are hungry have been known to eschew education and democratic principles. As Irving Kristol suggests, "[T]he Constitution is inextricably intertwined with the idea of economic progress. It has always been perceived to be so. Up until the Great Depression, it was routine for orators to link American prosperity to the Constitution, as effect to cause. Even today our new immigrants, as they take their oath of citizenship, clearly have this connection very much in mind."[16]

Big business (that is, the corporation) "is a superior economic tool by which to provide those things that constitute the physical basis of living," holds David E. Lilienthal. "In Bigness we have the material foundation of a society which can further the highest values known to men, values we describe as 'spiritual.'"[17]

The corporation was the vehicle of the Industrial Revolution. It planned, organized, and operated the new massive technology. Without the Industrial Revolution, economic historian T. S. Ashton argues, Europe could not have provided adequate living standards for its people. Europe, therefore, would have had the same deprived living conditions that exist in Asia, which suffers from overpopulation and lack of industrialization.[18] Needless to say, freedom and democracy could not have taken hold and flourished.

Corporations and the Democratic Nation

The established corporation, by its own power, and in its own interest, helps to monitor the federal government's reach. Because the corporation cannot survive without the guarantees of freedom of speech, free-

dom of assembly, and protection from unreasonable searches and seizures, it aggressively protects these rights in the courts and in public
opinion. With its human and financial resources and ready access to
power centers, the corporation challenges overreaching authorities and
lends corrective balance to unstable societies. Might we be seeing the
evolution of a Fifth Estate of government by the corporation, somewhat akin to the Fourth Estate of government by the press? In an
address before the New England Newspaper Association, Governor
Madeleine Kunin of Vermont observed that "in their state of coexistence the press and government assume that a healthy tension not only
keeps them alert, but assures the vitality of the democratic process. A
fat and lazy press, one that didn't ask lean and mean questions, could
soon lead to complacency, inertia, and closed-mindedness in government. That, in turn, would slacken the fibers of democracy."[19] In the
same way, it can be argued that the healthy tension that exists between
corporations and the government assures the vitality of the democratic
process.

At times it is the industrial corporate infrastructure that keeps
societies from collapsing when political hierarchies topple. People keep
their jobs, food and shelter continue to be provided, thanks to the
interlocking forces of the corporate environment that stabilize the
nation's economic base until the structure of government corrects itself.
For example, note the myriad changes of government in Italy—forty-
six cabinet changes since the end of World War II. Here we have
interdependent business corporations (supplemented by a strong family
culture) giving the nation its ongoing stability, serving the people's
needs as governments crumble one after the other.

The Future of the Corporation

Society's demands for accountability and better citizenship from businesses have been gaining momentum as the awareness of the importance of corporate social responsibility has increased. Many courts have
gone on record supporting this development. More than thirty years
ago, a New Jersey court held that "conditions require that corporations
acknowledge and discharge social as well as private responsibilities."[20]
Profit and growth as criteria of business success are inadequate. The

business firm is a servant of society. It is chartered by the state to provide for the needs of citizens. It is not an autonomous institution. Organizations exist to serve the needs of the larger society, not vice versa. Professor of management Gerald F. Cavanagh insists that "the legitimacy of any institution depends on the extent to which that institution can justify to its constituency and the larger society its right to exist."[21] Thomas Donaldson argues that a corporation is "composed of natural human beings and reflects the natural tendency of humans to form organizations; but at the same time it is an artifact in the sense that it is a product of human intention, and has a humanly malleable character. . . . The moral issue is the same for corporations as it is for persons." Corporations should therefore divulge information even if it is contrary to their interests.[22] Further emphasizing the desirability of disclosure policies and social audits, Donaldson points out that "if corporations were to take upon themselves, or be required to take on, the task of disclosing information relevant to other interest groups, then corporate morality would be enhanced. If corporations were required to disclose information about their actions affecting these interest groups, then pressure would mount to justify those acts."[23]

A number of years ago, James Heard and William Bolce, of the U.S. Department of Commerce, suggested that "the current interest in regulatory reform presents a golden opportunity for the business community to regain some measure of freedom from regulation by demonstrating convincingly to a skeptical public that it is prepared to respond more constructively to public expectations than it has in the past." By disclosing their citizenship activities through special reports, companies can capitalize on this "golden opportunity."[24] Perhaps more important, companies should produce such reports because society has the right to this information. So argue economics professor Rob Gray of the University College of North Wales in Bangor and management professor Bob Perks of Queens University, Belfast. Just as stockholders and government have a stake in a company's financial activity, society is affected by a company's activities and therefore has a right to information. Such disclosures can be viewed as an essential part of a free and fair economic system.[25]

Lord Wedderburn of the London School of Economics goes so far as to argue that multinational or "transnational" enterprise competes on equal terms with the modern state. While states are limited in their jurisdiction by territoriality, supranationality gives corporate enterprises freedom from responsibility. Law should no longer view profit maximization as the only criterion for the justification of corporate existence.[26] It is ironic that while the basic ingredient of the corporation is people, the traditional criterion for evaluating how it carries out its responsibilities in society is money, how wealthy it is as reflected in its financial statements. Obviously, a business corporation must make profits to be financially stable or it cannot survive, just as a person cannot survive without adequate financial support. But although statements of income and financial condition are valuable measurements of a corporation's health, by themselves they are inadequate. A third criterion should also be regularly applied to give visibility to how well it is carrying out its responsibilities.

A social report could be the answer. I attach as an appendix to this paper a proposal for such a report. It is called a Socioeconomic Operating Statement and sets forth social actions by a corporation that are voluntary, that is, not required to be undertaken by law or contract. Charged against these positive social expenditures are those actions or inactions by a corporation that tend to have negative impact on society.[27] Such a mechanism could help society to assess a corporation's fulfillment of its responsibilities as it continues to earn (or to fall short of earning) fuller citizenship status.

To conclude, I have tried in this essay to show that the corporation and our economic democracy are inextricably linked. Both depend on the Constitution for support, and both support the Constitution.

The genesis of the corporation was as an institution to serve the society from which it was created. As the twentieth century approached, the corporation was increasingly becoming an instrument of private moneymaking. But the pressures of judges, labor unions, consumer groups, and governmental bodies, in combination with the enlightened self-interest of policy-making executives, all contributed to the corporation's increasing efforts to undertake social actions for the good of all society, along with producing goods, jobs, and profits.

Now a rearticulated social contract is being written, providing for a full set of reciprocal actions between society and the corporation. The corporation is given the full protections of the Constitution and our laws, much as is the natural person, and society has a right to expect full reciprocal actions in return. From many indications, most corporate managements agree.

APPENDIX

Jones Corporation
Socioeconomic Operating Statement
For the year ended December 31, 1986

I. *Relations with People*
  A. Improvements
    1. Training program for handicapped workers $ 10,000
    2. Contribution to black college   4,000
    3. Extra turnover costs because of minority hiring   5,000
    4. Cost of nursery school for employees, voluntary   11,000
    Total Improvements $ 30,000
  B. Less Detriments
    1. Postponed installing new safety devices on cutting machines (cost of device)   14,000
  C. Net Improvements in People Actions for the Year $ 16,000

II. *Relations with Environment*
  A. Improvements
    1. Cost of reclaiming and landscaping old dump on company property $ 70,000
    2. Cost of installing pollution-control devices on Plant A smokestacks   4,000
    3. Cost of detoxifying waste from finishing process this year   9,000
    Total Improvements $ 83,000
  B. Less Detriments
    1. Cost that would have been incurred to relandscape strip mining site used this year $ 80,000

2. Estimated cost to have
purification process
installed to neutralize
poisonous liquid being
dumped into stream   100,000

                                                      $180,000

C. Net Deficit in Environment
Actions for the Year   ($ 97,000)

III. *Relations with Product*
  A. Improvements
    1. Salary of V.P. while
      serving on government
      Product Safety
      Commission $ 25,000
    2. Cost of substituting
      lead-free paint for
      previously used
      poisonous lead paint   9,000
    Total Improvements $ 34,000
  B. Less Detriments
    1. Safety devices
      recommended but not
      added to product   22,000
  C. Net Improvements in
    Product Actions for the
    Year $ 12,000

Total Socioeconomic Deficit for the Year   ($ 69,000)

Add Net Cumulative Socioeconomic
Improvements as of January 1, 1986 $249,000

Grand Total Net Socioeconomic Actions
to December 31, 1986 $180,000

Suggested principles for preparation of a Socioeconomic Operating Statement (SEOS) follow:

    1. If a socially beneficial action is required by enforceable law, it would not qualify for SEOS inclusion.

    2. If a socially beneficial action is required by law but is ignored, the

cost of such an item would be charged as a detriment for the year. The same treatment would be given to an item if postponed, even with government approval.

3. A pro rata portion of salaries and related expenses of personnel spending company time in socially beneficial activities or with social causes would be designated under "Improvements."

4. Cash and product contributions to social institutions and social causes would be designated under "Improvements."

5. The cost of setting up facilities for the general good of employees or the public—without union or government requirement—would be included.

6. Expenditures made voluntarily for the installation of safety devices on the premises or innovations that reduce product hazards would be included if not required by contract or law.

7. Neglecting to install safety devices that are available at reasonable cost would be a detriment.

8. Community improvements, such as the cost of voluntarily building a playground or nursery school for employees for area residents, would reflect positively on the statement. Operating costs of the facility on a year-to-year basis could also be included.

9. The cost of relandscaping strip mining sites or other environmental eyesores, if not required by law, would be displayed as an improvement on the SEOS exhibit.

10. The "aesthetic" costs of activities undertaken for the purpose of enhancing the business environment, as opposed to a purely functional goal, would be included. The dollar amount reflected under "Improvements" would be the difference between the ordinary business or functional cost and the cost of the beauty additive.

Notes

1. James S. Coleman, "Responsibility in Corporation Action: A Sociologist's View," in *Corporate Governance and Directors' Liabilities*, ed. Klaus J. Hopt and Gunther Teubner (New York: Walter de Gruyter, 1985), 72.

2. Oscar Handlin and Mary F. Handlin, "Origins of the American Business," in *Enterprise and Secular Change*, ed. Frederic Lane and Jelle Riemersma (Homewood, Ill.: Richard D. Irwin, Inc., 1953), 104–5.

3. In the case of *Salomon v. Salomon and Co.*, A.C. 22 (1897), it was also decided that the company, Salomon, Ltd., "was a person at law distinct from its individual members, with whom it would contract in the same manner as with persons in no way connected with the company" (quoted by Frederick Hallis in *Corporate Personality* [London: Scientia Verlag Aalen, 1978], xliii).

4. E. A. Johnson and Herman Krooss, *The American Economy: Its Origins, Development, and Transformation* (Englewood Cliffs, N.J.: Prentice Hall, 1960), 239–40.

5. In *Santa Clara County v. Southern Pacific Railroad*, 18 U.S. 394 (1886), the Court ruled that the term "person" in the Fourteenth Amendment could include a corporation.

6. *Chicago, Milwaukee & St. Paul Railway Co. v. Minnesota*, 134 U.S. 418 (1890).

7. *Grosjean v. American Press Co.*, 297 U.S. 233 (1936); and *Joseph Burstyn, Inc. v. Wilson*, 343 U.S. 495 (1952).

8. John Kenneth Galbraith, *The New Industrial State* (Boston: Houghton Mifflin, 1967), 72, 77.

9. In *Louisville, Cincinnati and Charleston Railroad Co. v. Letson*, 43 U.S. (2 How.) 497 (1844), the Court held that "a corporation . . . is to be deemed to all intents and purposes as a person, although an artificial person. . . . It is substantially, within the meaning of the law, a citizen of the state which created it" (at 558).

10. Keith Davis, "An Expanded View of the Social Responsibility of Business," in *Ethical Theory and Business*, ed. Tom L. Beauchamp and Norman E. Bowie (Englewood Cliffs, N.J.: Prentice-Hall, 1983), 95–96.

11. Adam Smith, *The Wealth of Nations* (London: Oxford University Press, 1976), 456.

12. In *First National Bank of Boston v. Bellotti*, 435 U.S. 765 (1978), the Court held that "the First Amendment guarantees corporate managers the right to use not only their personal funds, but also those of the corporation to circulate fact and opinion" (at 803).

13. Cited by Robert Heath and William Douglas, "Issues Advertising and Its Effect on Public Opinion Recall," *Public Relations Review* 12 (Summer 1986): 48.

14. Peter A. French, "The Corporation as Moral Person," *American Philosophical Quarterly* 16 (July 1979): 207–15.

15. Kenneth E. Goodpaster and John B. Mathews, Jr., "Can a Corporation Have a Conscience?" in *Business Ethics*, ed. W. Michael Hoffman and Jennifer Mills Moore (New York: McGraw-Hill, 1984), 157.

16. Irving Kristol, "The Spirit of '87," *The Public Interest* 86 (Winter 1987): 8.

17. David E. Lilienthal, *Big Business: A New Era* (New York: Arno Press, 1973), 190.

18. T. S. Ashton, *The Industrial Revolution 1760–1830* (London: Oxford University Press, 1969), 110–11.

19. Madeleine Kunin, "The Press and Government," *Editor and Publisher* 118 (April 6, 1985): 72.

20. *A. P. Smith Mfg. Co. v. Barlow,* 13 N.J. 145, 154, N.E.2d (1953).

21. Gerald F. Cavanagh, "Corporate Values for the Future," in *Business Ethics,* 519.

22. Thomas Donaldson, *Corporations and Morality* (Englewood Cliffs, N.J.: Prentice-Hall, 1982), 14–15.

23. Ibid., 204.

24. James E. Heard and William Bolce, "The Political Significance of Corporate Social Reporting in the United States of America," *Accounting, Organization, and Society* 6, no. 3 (1981): 248–49.

25. Rob Gray and Bob Perks, "How Desirable Is Social Accounting?" *Accountancy* 93 (April 1982): 102.

26. Lord Wedderburn, "The Legal Development of Corporate Responsibility," in *Corporate Governance and Directors' Liabilities,* 40–44.

27. For a full description of the Socioeconomic Operating Statement, see David F. Linowes, *Strategies for Survival* (New York: AMACOM, 1973), 169–77.

CHAPTER 23

The People, the Press, and the American Constitution

•••••

ROBERT F. ERBURU

Our press was not always free. Before the Revolutionary War and the adoption of the Constitution and Bill of Rights, the American press was restrained for many of the same reasons it is criticized today. In 1662 an act of Parliament restricted printers in Britain and in all the king's dominions. It opened with some majestic invective in the form of an enormously long sentence which I here amend but slightly:

> The well-government and regulating of Printers and Printing Presses is a matter of Public care and of great concern. By the general licentiousness of the late times, many evil disposed persons have been encouraged to print and sell heretical, schismatical, blasphemous, seditious, and treasonable Bookes, Pamphlets, and Papers. They still do continue theire unlawfull and exorbitant practice to the high dishonor of Almighty God, the endangering the peace of these Kingdomes, and raising a disaffection to His most Excellent Majesty and his Government. For prevention whereof no surer meanes can be advised than by reducing and limiting the number of Printing Presses and by ordering and setling the said Art or Mystery of Printing by Act of Parliament.[1]

Today, those of us who practice the "art and mystery of printing," certainly including journalism, are familiar enough with these sentiments. The charges that the press is licentious, heretical, schismatical, blasphemous, seditious, and treasonable still ring in the late twentieth century. What stands between the press and powerful animosities is the Constitution of the United States.

Recent developments illustrate the continuing debate about the press. An old superstition says that unusual events happen in groups of three. I think that superstition picked up some new believers in 1987, at least among those of us who work in the press. In only a few days' time, and in the space of only a few city blocks, three highly unusual events took place, all involving the press. First, a House subcommittee summoned the news executives of NBC, ABC, and CBS to a hearing on network news budgets and practices. Second, the *Miami Herald* staked out the townhouse of presidential candidate Gary Hart and alleged that Hart had spent the night with an attractive young woman who happened not to be his wife. And third, Congress began hearings on the Iran-Contra affair, a scandal that the press had devoted enormous resources to covering.

One could sense that the American people had conflicting emotions about the press's role in these three almost simultaneous events. Most Americans were probably confused about all the talk of news budget cutbacks by the three networks and not even quite sure what Congress was investigating. On the reporting of the Iran-Contra affair, polls have shown that most people think the press did a pretty good job. And other polls have shown that a majority of the American people have serious reservations about the ethics of the press's placing Senator Hart under surveillance. Three unusual events. Three major roles played by the press. Three conflicting emotions expressed by the American people. The end result: controversy and confusion.

So the press is back in a pretty familiar situation—winning some praise, catching some heat, and stirring up a lot of ambivalent feelings in the American people. When people praise the press, it is usually for playing its muckraking role of trying to keep the government honest, in the Watergate affair, for example, and then in covering Iran-Contra. The list of reasons for attacking the press is usually far longer and far more specific. Many press criticisms ultimately come back to basic constitutional questions over the role the press should play in our society.

An uneasy tension among the press, the government, and the people has been making itself felt since the earliest days of our country. That tension has sometimes culminated in major constitutional battles, like *Near v. Minnesota*[2] and the Pentagon Papers case.[3]

A few years ago, we at Times Mirror began to think not only about the two-hundredth anniversary of the Constitution but also about the seeming ambivalence with which so many Americans regard the press. That ambivalence can be stated this way: Americans seem to believe what the press is reporting while simultaneously expressing hostility toward its practices. They appear to hold strong beliefs about the press, while knowing relatively little about its workings or its relationship to the Constitution.

Times Mirror wanted to get some definitive answers about what Americans really think about the press, and why. So we turned to the recognized leader in public opinion research, the Gallup Organization, and we launched one of the most comprehensive opinion research programs in our nation's history. In a continuing series of surveys, Gallup interviewed nearly eight thousand Americans over two years. There has never been a richer or more detailed set of information about the way Americans think and feel about the press. And since we asked so many questions about freedom of the press, Times Mirror also now has an enormous collection of data on people's knowledge and beliefs about the First Amendment.

In this essay I want to discuss a few of the things we learned from those data about Americans' perceptions of the press. Let me first take a moment to put the current situation in perspective by offering some reflections on the historic tension among the press, the government, and the people.

Thomas Jefferson said that were "it left to decide whether we should have a government without newspapers, or newspapers without government, I should not hesitate to prefer the latter."[4] Most beginning journalism students have memorized that quote. But it is important to note that Jefferson made that statement *before* he became president. Journalism schools seldom teach that, after Jefferson became president, he wrote that "nothing can now be believed which is seen in a newspaper. . . . The man who never looks into a newspaper is better informed than he who reads them, inasmuch as he who knows nothing is closer to the truth than he whose mind is filled with falsehoods and errors."[5]

Jefferson's polar extremes neatly enclose the spectrum of early American feelings about the press. Its freedom was guaranteed by the First Amendment, but James Madison's careful minutes of the Constitutional Convention reveal virtually no impassioned discussion about freedom of the press. It was, in a sense, simply taken for granted. And yet, only a few years later, freedom of the press was under heavy attack in the Alien and Sedition Acts of 1798. Newspapers were so closely allied with the opposing political parties that not only objectivity but also freedom of the press itself was caught in the crossfire.

During the Civil War, Abraham Lincoln was the target of some of the bitterest press attacks that any president has had to endure. And this was from *Union* newspapers. Lincoln was regularly accused of being a drunk, of taking his pay in gold bars while his soldiers were paid in deflated greenbacks, and of sending his troops to be slaughtered because of his blood lust for victory. Lincoln received those attacks without responding in kind. When General William Tecumseh Sherman arrested one of Horace Greeley's correspondents for the *New York Herald* and charged him with spying, Lincoln refused the general's request to have the reporter shot. Later, upon hearing that three other Union war correspondents were killed by artillery fire, Sherman is said to have remarked: "Good, now we shall have some news from hell before breakfast." By comparison, Spiro Agnew's reference to "nattering nabobs of negativism" sounds like a compliment.

Whether it was George Washington decrying his own newspaper's reports on Revolutionary troop movements, John Kennedy trying to keep plans for the Bay of Pigs invasion out of the *New York Times,* or the Department of Defense refusing to allow reporters to accompany the Grenada invasion, there has always been a tension among press, government, and people. The press thinks it looks out for the public good. The government thinks it does. The public trusts neither of them completely.

People *do* trust the informal checks and balances that function between press and government, much like the formal checks among the three branches of government itself.

What do the American people really think of this unique relationship? The bottom line of the Times Mirror surveys is this: The press's supporters in America outnumber its critics by a margin of two to one. For those of us in journalism, that is the good news. The bad news is that the critics generally display greater knowledge about the press, greater interest in press issues, and a greater likelihood of expressing themselves about the press.

We found that the public maintains a favorable disposition toward the press, despite serious criticism of journalistic practices, in part because it appreciates the press's watchdog role, and also because it values and enjoys the news. The reservoir of public support, however, is broad but not deep. Knowledge about the press is meager, and even basic terminology is often misunderstood. Moreover, the press does not attract as much public attention as it believes it does. Large elements of the population are indifferent to it. For example, most people do *not* know that the First Amendment guarantees freedom of the press. Still, the public values the ideas that government should stay out of the newsroom and that the press should play an energetic watchdog role.

While most Americans think that the press has adequate freedom to cover national security issues, they are sharply divided about the consequences of news leaks for national security. For every four Americans who feel that news leaks rarely threaten national security, three believe the threat is serious. But only one person in five favors mandatory lie detector tests for all senior officials to help stop leaks. One in three would favor a special White House investigative unit set up for that purpose. Almost half would permit the Justice Department to block publication of information that would threaten national security.

One of the themes of this symposium is citizen participation. As national issues become steadily more complex, the need for knowledge and participation increases. But the Times Mirror surveys raise troubling questions about people's knowledge of the press and of the Constitution that protects its freedom. As I see it, the surveys also raise another disturbing issue: the press's overestimation of its importance in people's daily lives.

Let me give you an example. Because topics like the layoffs at CBS, Sam Donaldson's aggressiveness, Jane Pauley's twins, and Dan Rather's sweaters receive so much attention, you would think that a majority of the American public would be able to recognize at least the leading television journalists. But according to our in-person interviews, only one television journalist was recognized by a majority of the American people: Barbara Walters. Three-quarters of the American people recognized her picture. But I even suspect that many of them know her from her entertainment specials, not her journalism.

The next-best-known television journalist was Dan Rather, whose picture was recognized by 47 percent of the sample. The most-recognized print reporter was George Will. Despite his weekly appearances on the Brinkley show, his *Newsweek* column, and his syndicated column in four hundred papers, George Will was recognized by only

12 percent of the American people. In comparison, twice as many people recognized Caspar Weinberger.

There are other graphic examples of the public's ignorance of information that we in journalism take for granted:

- Only 27 percent know that *Time* and *Newsweek* are owned by different companies
- At least one American in four thinks the White House press secretary is employed by the news media
- 45 percent do not know what the term "news leak" means
- 30 percent believe that a newspaper reporter outranks either the editor or the publisher.

These survey results illustrate the general level of *information* the public has about the press. But the Times Mirror surveys also looked beyond the public's knowledge of surface details to uncover the *values* that define our society and the role that our institutions, like the press, can and should play.

With all the journalistic discussion of freedom of the press, we sometimes forget that our Constitution is not exactly loquacious on the subject. The First Amendment says, "Congress shall pass no laws abridging the freedom of the press." Period. But as Chief Justice John Marshall once observed, the Constitution is a living document. Freedom of the press is not defined by just those few words in the Constitution. Freedom of the press is defined by the millions of words in judicial opinions interpreting the Constitution. And judicial opinions are ultimately a reflection of the prevailing beliefs of the American people.

Our surveys found that although Americans are vague about the First Amendment, they do have much more definite opinions about the *value* of freedom of the press. But that value is very much related to the question of who pays its cost. When the issues involve the rights of news organizations versus the rights of government, the public usually sides *with* the press. But when the issues involve the rights of the press versus the rights of individuals or the rights of the community, the public regularly goes *against* the press.

One thing is clear. The American people believe in libel laws. Ninety percent believe that freedom of the press does not give news organizations the right to say anything about a person, whether true or false, without the possibility of facing a libel suit. The public believes so thoroughly in libel law, the rights of private citizens to sue news organizations for damages, that it rejects the notion embedded in constitutional doctrine that public officials should face a tougher standard of proof than anyone else.

When asked what "freedom of the press means to you," 61 percent say it means "the public has a right to hear all points of view." Only 23 percent hold that it means "the press can cover and report what it chooses." The public values its collective rights over the press's right to speak. National security issues fall between the prerogatives of political leaders and the rights of the community. So, not surprisingly, on questions of national security the public is almost evenly split between two alternatives. Half the respondents consider it "more important that the government be able to censor news stories it feels threaten national security." The other half feel that the news media should be able "to report stories they feel are in the national interest."

This issue of government censorship stands at the center of press freedom and worth. By more than two to one, Americans think it "good policy" to make it "very difficult to block publication" of "almost any type" of news. When given the facts of the Pentagon Papers case, 66 percent said they would allow publication of the papers, while 21 percent said they would not. This was a somewhat wider margin than the Supreme Court's 6–3 decision to allow publication. People were given these basic facts about the more recent case involving the journal *The Progressive:* A magazine wanted to publish an article about building a nuclear weapon; the information to be reported was already available in published material, much of it in the encyclopedia; the government argued that the law provides for blocking any communication about nuclear weaponry that "might harm the United States." Given these facts, people sided with the government to block publication by a margin of 52 percent to 35 percent. In the real world of press law, the *Progressive* case never reached the Supreme Court. The federal judge in Wisconsin who made the original determination sided with the government.[6]

The public grants press freedom grudgingly when it comes at cost to citizens. But the public is much more supportive of free press when the trade-off comes at the expense of political leaders. And when the press is defined in terms of the watchdog role, the public shows enthusiastic support. By a 67 percent to 17 percent margin, the public agrees that the press's criticism keeps leaders from doing things that should not be done.

Appreciation of the press's watchdog function probably explains another important finding. On what might be called the acid test of public attitudes toward free press, 54 percent of our respondents believe that news organizations protect the democratic process. Twenty-three percent argue that the press hurts the process. When forced to make what may be an ultimate evaluation of worth, the public at large sees the press as beneficial to the political process. The belief that the press helps democracy more than it hurts cuts across every demographic group in our survey—men and women, rich and poor, old and young, black and white, Democrats and Republicans. The public clearly believes that, despite all its flaws, the press *is* playing the role our Constitution intended for it, and playing it well.

Rather than offer my own conclusion, I would like to let the American people speak for themselves. After each Times Mirror survey was completed, we ran advertisements to highlight some of the issues raised by the data and to invite public comment. To date I have received more than eight thousand letters, cards, essays, poems, drawings, phone calls, and artifacts from all fifty states, several foreign countries, and one aircraft carrier. My youngest correspondent was ten years old; my oldest, ninety-three. The pithiest message consisted of one five-word sentence, the most expansive ran to seven typewritten pages. A Vermont correspondent ended her very thoughtful letter with an invitation to "come in for coffee and pie if you're ever in the area." Some of the letters were not very serious. One man from California wrote: "Your ad says tell us what you think. I think you're not being very smart. You have not hired my son James, a very good worker, as a sports reporter. That's what I think." Another Californian wrote: "Get a grip on yourself, guys, and do the best job you can, but don't suffer an identity crisis while doing it. Just try to spell the names right, get your facts straight and never forget that today's big story is tomorrow's birdcage carpet."

But most of the letters were very thoughtful. One read: "Freedom without responsibility is anarchy. The press should be free, but it must also be responsible." A Massachusetts woman wrote: "Editors are lucky that there is a population out here that defends their right to free speech all the way, and I am in it. It is regrettable that this protection covers so much editorial fraud. The phrase 'necessary evil,' with equal emphasis on both sides of the equation, is especially apt for the press." And finally, a Connecticut man says: "A free press is the strength of America. I love it and I'm grateful for it, but I do regret its excesses and do wish for a shade more self-restraint. But I am opposed to government restraint or government-imposed censorship. And so I am resigned to the fact that we must 'swallow' the excesses because the freedom we all cherish is worth it."

Those are good words with which to close this essay. The freedom we all cherish is worth it.

Notes

1. The complete text of this statute may be found in Danby Pickering, *The Statutes at Large* (Cambridge: Joseph Bentham for Charles Bathurst, 1763), 8:137 ff.

2. 283 U.S. 697 (1931).

3. *New York Times Co. v. United States*, 403 U.S. 610 (1971).

4. Thomas Jefferson, letter to Edward Carrington, January 6, 1787, in *The Writings of Thomas Jefferson*, ed. Andrew A. Lipscomb et al. (Washington, D.C.: Thomas Jefferson Memorial Association, 1905), 6:57–58.

5. Jefferson, letter to John Norvell, June 11, 1807, in *Writings of Thomas Jefferson*, 11:223–34.

6. *United States v. Progressive, Inc.*, 467 F. Supp. 990 (W.D. Wis. 1979).

CHAPTER 24

Schooling and Civic Education

·····

ERNEST L. BOYER

In 1972, reading the student newspaper from Stanford University, I was struck by a headline announcing that the faculty at Stanford planned to introduce a required course in Western civilization after having abolished all requirements just three years before. The students at Stanford were mightily offended by the faculty's brashness and, in a front-page editorial, declared a required course at Stanford to be "an illiberal act." The editorial concluded by asking, "How dare they impose uniform standards on non-uniform people?" The issue remains very much alive. Core curricula, distribution requirements, and canon formation are still hot issues, at Stanford as elsewhere, as faculty negotiate the often conflicting demands of promoting cultural literacy while respecting cultural diversity.

This, of course, is no easy task. But I was and am startled that some of America's most gifted students, after fourteen or more years of formal education, still have not learned the simple truth that while we are not "uniform," we do share many things in common. While we are each of us individuals, we also engage in activities together. The Stanford protesters in 1972 were unable to see that while we are all unique human beings with our own aptitudes and interests, we are, at the same time, deeply dependent on one another. Schools should prepare students to live independent, self-sufficient lives so they can be economically and socially empowered. But schools also must help students

371

move beyond their private interests and put their own lives in historical, social, and ethical perspective. Discovering our connectedness is the key to civic understanding.

We are connected through our use of shared symbols. The first priority of civic education must be to empower all students in the written and the spoken word. Of the five thousand faculty members who were surveyed for the Carnegie Foundation report *College: The Undergraduate Experience in America*,[1] more than 60 percent said their students were not prepared to do academic work, and lack of proficiency in English was identified as the primary reason.

In the report, we stress that it is through learning to write clearly that one learns to think clearly. We suggest that students in both high school and college be asked to write a senior thesis to demonstrate their capacity to explore a consequential topic and to integrate ideas.

Students should also learn that good communication means not just clear thinking but integrity as well. Several centuries ago, the Quakers would risk imprisonment and even death because they refused in court to repeat the oath "to tell the truth, the whole truth, and nothing but the truth so help me God." The problem, for the Quakers, was not simply that they objected to swearing. More objectionable was the implication that, outside the courtroom, truth might be optional. Students must understand that truth is the obligation they assume when they are empowered with the use of shared symbols, including written and spoken language.

To be civically prepared, *all* students must also discover their connections to the institutions that consequentially shape their lives. At the heart of such study is that old-fashioned academic course called civics. As early as 1922, Walter Lippmann warned that public ignorance was democracy's greatest challenge. He said that the issues facing the electorate had become enormously complex, while government appeared increasingly remote.

Civics used to be a mainstay in the high school curriculum, but recently its role has diminished. And unless we find better ways to stem the spread of civic illiteracy, we run the risk of drifting unwittingly into a new kind of Dark Age, in which specialists will control knowledge and citizens will make critical decisions not on the basis of what they know but on the basis of blind faith in one or another set of self-appointed experts.

In the Carnegie report *High School* we propose a one-year course on American government for all students. In such a course students would be introduced to classic political thinkers, from Plato and Locke to John Adams and James Madison. Students would study the Declaration of Independence, the Constitution, and *The Federalist* papers. Equally important, students would study government today and how it works. For example, each student might take one contested issue that is currently before Congress, a state legislature, or a community governmental body and report in depth on the history of the issue, points of conflict, and plausible resolutions.

Further, for students to be civically well prepared, they must see a connection between what they learn and how they live. During the Carnegie Foundation study of the American high school, I became convinced that we have in this nation not just a "school problem" but a "youth problem" as well. Students feel isolated, unneeded, and unconnected to the larger world. The epistemological gap between the lessons in the classroom and the realities of life outside its walls is alarmingly vast for most teenagers today, who, perhaps understandably, can see little connection between the school curriculum and their own communities. Moreover, they see little relationship between their own needs and the needs of those around them.

These high school students are never asked to spend time with older people, to clean up litter on the street, or to tutor children who have not yet learned to read. Too many young people do not understand that their energy must be directed positively and productively—that we are not just receivers, we are givers as well.

This gap in civic understanding is reinforced by some of the materials used in the schools. In a critique of civics textbooks issued by People for the American Way, James Carroll of the Brookings Institution concluded: "Many of the books are largely disembodied expositions of principles and facts, lacking the passion of the conflicts that infuse politics and government with meaning and significance. The student is asked only to master knowledge of the subject rather than to put this knowledge to use. Thus, the participatory side, the side that requires the individual to analyze democratic values, processes, and choices, is largely ignored."

Carroll continues by saying, "Students will learn the necessity and value of public involvement by becoming involved. Passive learning alone will not engage them. A work-study or internship element should be a basic component of American government courses. Students should be able to 'practice' responsible citizenship and observe first-hand the workings of politics and government."[2]

Vachel Lindsay wrote on one occasion, "It is the world's one crime its babes grow dull. . . . Not that they sow but that they seldom reap, not that they serve but that they have no gods to serve; not that they die but that they die like sheep."[3] The tragedy of life is not death. The tragedy is to die with commitments undefined, convictions undeclared, and service unfulfilled. In *High School* we propose a new Carnegie unit for all high school students, a term of voluntary service in hospitals, nursing homes, or art galleries, or as tutors to other children in the neighborhood or at school. Students urgently need a sense of mission.

Civic education is discovering connections: through the empowerment of language; through an understanding of social and civic institutions; and, in the end, through integrating what we learn with how we live.

Notes

1. Ernest L. Boyer, Carnegie Foundation for the Advancement of Teaching, *College: The Undergraduate Experience in America* (New York: Harper and Row, 1987).

2. James Carroll, *We the People: A Review of U.S. Government and Civics Textbooks* (Washington, D.C.: People for the American Way, 1987).

3. Vachel Lindsay, "The Leaden-Eyed," in *Collected Poems of Vachel Lindsay* (New York: Macmillan, 1969), 69.

CHAPTER 25

How the Young Learn
Responsibility

·····

ROBERT COLES

The word "responsibility," like other words in the old-fashioned moral lexicon of our past, has various connotative meanings and usages. Often children, in their unpretentious, informal, and anecdotal way, manage quite well to indicate what the dictionary more pointedly summarizes about the manner in which such a word gets used. This became apparent to me in January 1987, when I asked a young neighbor of ours, a ten-year-old boy whom my wife and I have known since his earliest weeks of life, about the significance of responsibility to him. "It means you should know how to take care of yourself and be on time," he told me without the slightest hesitation—but then he felt a need to amplify. My condensation of an impromptu discussion that lasted just under an hour will, perhaps, help us to understand how children make sense of language, not to mention their manner of fashioning a moral life for themselves:

> You have to be responsible, or you'll fall behind, and your work will be there, waiting for you, and there will be trouble, because your teacher will find out—or your parents. My dad tells me that if you're not responsible for yourself, then no one else will be. But he says he thinks about us when he's in his office, and he knows he's got to teach us to do our chores, and take care of things, and so he's responsible for us, until we've grown up, and then we will be on our own.

If a person is in trouble [we had shifted our talk somewhat] then you should try to help him. According to the Bible, you should think of others, not just yourself. You shouldn't walk down a street and ignore someone who has got into a bad jam, and needs some money, or a ride to the hospital. You have a responsibility to others, not just to yourself. The teacher tells us of all our responsibilities, and she means everything you should do: There's a lot of our duties. But in Sunday school they'll tell you that you shouldn't only be obedient; you should have a big heart—and one teacher said if you get yourself all tied up with looking at the trees, you'll lose sight of the whole forest, and that's why you shouldn't just be patting yourself on the back all the time, and telling everyone how good your track record is; you should be trying to lend a hand to the folks nearby, because they may be in a real big mess, and you can't just turn your eyes away: That's not being responsible, I don't think.

So here we have an interesting and edifying effort on the part of a young late-twentieth-century American citizen to reconcile two not altogether similar lines of interpretation with respect to the notion of responsibility. We have all urged children to show responsibility, to be responsible; we have in mind, no doubt, the execution of certain duties and obligations: a psychology of self-control and self-discipline upon which the society must place great store, lest we all be irresponsible in a profoundly disturbing way. That is to say, we cannot take one another's social behavior for granted in the most elementary respects. We have to take care, lest we all do as we please, or try to do so, and abuse all sorts of laws, from traffic regulations to building codes to the ordinances that regulate our behavior in public buildings, not to mention the lives and property of others.

On the other hand, as that child was quietly and with no rhetorical intent trying to suggest, the word "responsibility" also can suggest a duty not only to oneself, or to the society as a whole, but to specific others. These are those who, ironically, may for one reason or another not be fully responsible human beings, in the sense that they are vulnerable enough, hurt enough, weak enough to be unable to carry out, say, the ordinary routines of daily life that many of us take for granted and assume that others we know and like and trust do too. A college student of mine, more sophisticated verbally than that boy, but not necessarily more subtle morally, was struggling with the same matter when he pointed this out to me one day during my office hours:

I hear people say: You have a responsibility to do this, to do that. They mean: Shape up and do your duty! I wish I'd hear some of those same people tell me I should have lots of responsibility—to others, who are in a real bad way. "You ought to be responsible by now," my uncle said to me the other day, meaning I should put my nose to the grindstone and be the kind of person he is—a big shot tax lawyer! He's not exactly worried that if Jesus came here and watched him for a day he might not call the life my uncle and his partners are living a "responsible" one— you know [I had asked] living up to the sense of Jewish and Christian responsibility that the Gospels proclaim.

What those two citizens, one well under twenty and the other fast approaching that age, are obviously struggling to comprehend is what children (and their parents) all over the world also try to fathom—the moral contours, so to speak, of a word like "responsibility." Responsibility toward whom and toward what, and with which (secular or divine) justification or sanction? As I have watched children grow up in different parts of this country and in other countries, I have begun to realize how sensitive they are to such questions, how interested they are in defining for themselves, again and again, the ethical side of things—the moral assumptions, for instance, that a word such as "responsibility" can have for them, for their friends, not to mention their parents and teachers. Here, for instance, is an eleven-year-old girl, a bright and articulate student attending a ghetto school in Boston:

I would like to go to college. The teachers say I can get there, if I just keep doing my work and stay in school and don't get into the wrong crowd. One says: Just ignore "them"; they're bad news. She's right. You have a responsibility to yourself, and if you forget that, you'll be in real bad shape. My mother says the same thing—that you'll drown if you worry about others, especially since they're drowning. My daddy—he's drowning! He can't find a good job; he can't find any job—so he starts with one beer, and the next you know, it's two, three, and four of them. At least he won't touch drugs. He means well. He's a good man. He's smart. If he'd been born white, I think he'd be working for some good company.

When I worry about him, I can't study. Then my mother gets on my case; and so does my teacher. I feel like I'm being called bad and dumb, because I'm upset about my daddy and I can't forget him, and I think of some of my friends—the kids I grew up with—who are getting into drugs and heavy sex. Is it wrong to let others bother you like that? [I had asked her the question.] No, I don't think so. But you have to figure out your priorities. That's what growing up means—the teacher says. She's big on obeying the rules, and getting ahead; and I'm with her. I'd like to get out of here. I'd like to live like they do in the white world, in the suburbs. But I'd hate to leave my friends behind, and my daddy. Don't you have a responsibility to others, too? I've asked my mamma that question dozens of times, and she says yes, but she doesn't really think so, not compared to the responsibility she thinks I should have for myself. She said to me once: "Honey, I'll stay here and take care of your father; you go ahead and stay in school, and go further, and move out of here, and that'll be the greatest victory our family has ever had, and no one here will begrudge you what you've won." The only problem is *I* might begrudge me what I've won—what I've done. That's what I think sometimes when I've got a spare minute, and I'll be staring out the window in school, or when I'm home, and just thinking about life.

This is a poignant and compelling moral reflection on the part of a child who is struggling to learn the breadth and depth of what the word "responsibility" ought to encompass. I found it all too easy, at times, to echo the sentiments of her mother, or her schoolteacher. Not that they were not, in certain respects, right on target. This girl most certainly did have a responsibility to herself and, as was suggested by her minister, to her people; but she had a responsibility, as well, to more than her people in general—to those among them who had stumbled or fallen. Her conscience, I think it fair to say, was worthy of the Hebrew prophets—the sharply ethical exhortations of Isaiah and Jeremiah and Amos, and of the itinerant teacher who walked Galilee almost two thousand years ago, worrying long and hard (as this child has) about the rebuked and the scorned, the exiled and the outcast, the lame and the halt and the blind, the imprisoned and the unpopular.

It can be all too easy for us to let what in the Bible are called "principalities and powers" become the exclusive custodians of that word "responsibility." To be sure, we owe our commitment, our loyalty, to our communities, small and large. Children learn even before starting school, and certainly later on, the importance of such commitments and loyalties—a lesson that they absorb from parents, relatives, teachers, and indeed, from one another. (I think we tend to underestimate the amount of learning that takes place when children play, or simply hang out in a particular neighborhood.) But there are other obligations our children need to learn—how to reach out to this or that person, caught in one or another situation of jeopardy, even when the larger society has shown no great interest in or concern for such persons. Indeed, as Dietrich Bonhoeffer and others reminded us (I think of someone in my own profession, the psychiatrist Dr. Koryagin, who has just been expelled from the Soviet Union for condemning the way doctors are used in that country to help run the Gulag's concentration camps), there are moments when our moral responsibilities require that we *not* be law-abiding citizens. Rather, our responsibilities—to conscience, to God—require us to stand up in dissent, even at the price of being branded criminals, traitors. So it has gone for all sorts of martyrs whom we now (years or generations later) safely admire. So, one assumes, one hopes and prays, it will go in future times for those who are willing to think about responsibility in its fullest and boldest and ethically most-searching, most-penetrating sense—the imperative to stand up for what one believes to be right, honorable, decent, no matter the political, social, economic, or legal hazards. Our forefathers interpreted responsibility in that way when they broke with established authority and started a revolution. We can only hope that the rest of us, who have followed them in time—children of one generation after another—will not forget their example and will prove worthy of it.

CHAPTER 26

Citizenship and State Constitutions

· · · · ·

HANS A. LINDE

In 1976 Americans celebrated two hundred years of independence—
and not only Americans, because many other nations joined in honor-
ing that event. Celebrating the Constitution is more difficult. We fix a
single date for the nation's birthday, Independence Day, and remain
confidently within no more than a two-day margin of error.[1] It is less
clear when to begin to set off the fireworks for the Constitution, or
when to stop. We have chosen the earliest opportunity, the anniversary
of 1787, the year of the Convention. But the great design might have
been stillborn; it was not ratified until June 21, 1788, and did not go
into effect until March 4, 1789.

Moreover, it has never been finished. Much of this year's celebration focuses prematurely on the Bill of Rights, which the Convention
thought unnecessary and which became part of the Constitution only in
1791. Many Americans have reason to date their Constitution only
from the end of slavery and the adoption of the Thirteenth, Fourteenth, and Fifteenth amendments between 1865 and 1870. Many
others feel that the Constitution reached maturity only in 1920, when
the Nineteenth Amendment guaranteed women the same right to vote
that men had.

The great achievement of 1787, the innovation that fascinated
political theorists and practitioners throughout the world, was not the
Bill of Rights. It was not the system of checks and balances in the

381

national government. It was federalism. The daring experiment was to create not a standing conference of state governments that might speak for the new nation abroad and demand support from the member states but a new federal government that would tax and regulate individuals directly for national purposes while leaving intact the power of the states to act for most other purposes. It was to create a system in which neither level of government acted as the other's delegate, neither the Union as the delegate of its member states nor the states by delegation from the nation, but each on its own authority. The novelty that seemed almost self-contradictory was not the separation of powers but divided sovereignty.

My topic today is, What became of the states? More specifically, What significance do the states retain for the meaning of citizenship?

The Constitution now tells us: "All persons born or naturalized in the United States and subject to the jurisdiction thereof, are citizens of the United States and of the state wherein they reside." This is the first sentence of the Fourteenth Amendment. It was placed in the Constitution only after eighty years of ambiguity about citizenship, years of bitter controversy and ultimately of civil war. To understand that sentence we must look back to a time when the meaning of citizenship could not be taken for granted as it widely is today.

History

American citizenship came with Independence. The former colonies fought for Independence together and negotiated the peace together. The nation and the states were born at the same time, and with them the ambiguities of citizenship. The ambiguities themselves were not new. Before Independence, in an age of monarchies, Americans were not citizens but British subjects, a status with its own long history of ambiguity. When King James of Scotland was made James I of England, for instance, his chief justice, Sir Edward Coke, held that his Scottish subjects owed allegiance to the Crown but not to the English Parliament, although Parliament had authority over the people of Ireland, who had become subjects by conquest.[2] One hundred and fifty years later, the question of parliamentary authority over King George's American subjects was disputed within Parliament as well as in the colonies. By that time too the colonies had assumed the right to admit foreigners to membership in a colony, that is to say, to naturalize them as Virginians or Pennsylvanians, although this would not make them New Yorkers or Englishmen.[3]

Of course, different colonies had different views about who was fit to be admitted to membership in the community, particularly by the religious tests that had played so central a role in English and colonial history. At the same time, local views toward admitting newcomers were influenced, as one would expect, by a desire for new immigrants on the one hand, and by fear of competition and of foreign subversion on the other. Some things have not changed much in two hundred years. Moreover, after Independence, the new states had to deal with the status and property of those Americans who had opposed the Revolution or at least had not joined in it. During the years between Independence and the Constitution, some states spelled out tests for new citizens in their constitutions, some states authorized their legislatures to set those tests by law, and some made such laws without provisions in their constitutions.[4]

The Articles of Confederation attempted in 1781 to give Americans some rights throughout the country, but without defining citizenship, in these words: "The free inhabitants of each of these States, paupers, vagabonds, and fugitives from justice excepted, shall be entitled to all privileges and immunities of free citizens in the several States; and the people of each State shall have free ingress and regress to and from any other State, and shall enjoy therein all the privileges of trade and commerce . . . as the inhabitants thereof."[5] But, as James Madison noted, the choice of the word "inhabitants" meant that one who was an inhabitant of a state but not a citizen might have greater rights in another state than he had in his own.[6]

In short, Independence had created a nation of Americans, but at the time of the Convention, American citizenship was a very confused affair.

The Constitution of 1787

The opening words of the Convention's proposed new charter asserted, "We the People of the United States . . . ordain and establish this Constitution." But whom did the Constitution mean by "We the People"? And what did it say about citizenship? The Constitution answered some questions but, by express design and by silent assumption, it left the difficult basic issues unresolved.

Recall that the Constitution was proposed as a framework for government, not as a charter of personal rights. Personal rights had since 1776 been guaranteed in the separate constitution of almost every state. To be sure, the Constitution gave Congress the power to prescribe a uniform rule of naturalization (Article I, Section 8). It strengthened the earlier provision giving the citizens of each state the privileges and immunities of citizens in the several states (Article IV, Section 2). It gave federal courts jurisdiction over controversies between citizens of one state and other American or foreign states or the citizens thereof (Article III, Section 2). But it did not define who was a citizen of a state, and it assigned no political or substantive rights to that status. The few guarantees in the Constitution of 1787—jury trial and writ of habeas corpus, protection for contracts and against bills of attainder and ex post facto laws—applied regardless of citizenship.

The idea most closely linked with citizenship is participation in a political community. The Constitution's design of a federal government built participation on the political communities of the states. This still remains the central importance of states for the meaning of citizenship, though much has changed.

Representatives in the Congress were the only directly elected federal officials. Elected by whom? By whoever was permitted to vote for the most numerous house of the state legislatures (Article I, Section 2). Senators were chosen by state legislatures until 1913 (Seventeenth Amendment). To this day it is each separate state, not the Constitution, that lets its citizens vote for president, and each state, not the Constitution, decides that the state's electors should all go to its voters' favored candidate (Article II, Section 1; Twelfth Amendment).[7] In fact, voters need not be citizens; some states allowed aliens to vote well into this century.[8] On the other hand, states could and did require a knowledge of English, literacy, and property ownership. The Constitution left the people's most basic political act to the states.

Who were the People? Whom would the representatives represent? The Convention also was forced to compromise the nation's central dilemma: the political status of Americans born or imported into slavery. It apportioned representatives and direct taxes according to the number of each state's free persons, excluding untaxed Native

Americans, and three-fifths of all other persons, as counted by a census every ten years (Article I, Section 2). Whether one was free and counted as a whole person or unfree and counted as three-fifths of a person again was left to the states.

In the 1820 Missouri Compromise, Congress drew a boundary for containing the spread of slavery to future states. But the compromise could not last; in Lincoln's words, the nation could not survive half slave and half free. In 1857, the Constitution's uneasy ambiguity collapsed in the Supreme Court's *Dred Scott* decision.

Scott was a slave who had spent some years in territory where slavery was forbidden before he was taken back to Missouri, and he brought suit for his freedom in a federal court. To get into the federal court, he had to allege that he was a citizen of a different state from his owner; in Scott's case, the state of Missouri. In ruling against Scott, the Supreme Court held, in a disastrous opinion by Chief Justice Roger Taney, that people of African ancestry, even if free, could not be citizens within the meaning of the Constitution. The "people of the United States" and "citizens," Taney wrote, meant the same thing. "They both describe the political body who, according to our republican institutions, form the sovereignty, and who hold the power and conduct the government through their representatives." And he maintained, over contrary arguments by the dissenters, that when the Constitution was written even free blacks were not considered part of "the people" and therefore also not citizens of their states.[9] Several state courts in fact had held that free blacks were citizens in their states.[10] But on Taney's theory, states that had never allowed slavery could not make black people citizens under the federal Constitution.

Ten years later, after the Civil War, the need to overrule that theory gave us the first sentence of the Fourteenth Amendment, which I quoted earlier, making all persons born or naturalized in the United States citizens of the United States and of the state in which they reside.

Federalism after 1868

The Fourteenth Amendment settled the question of citizenship, but, beyond that, it radically changed the legal balance of federalism. The amendment forbade states to abridge the privileges and immunities of citizens of the United States, an obscure phrase without a clear antecedent, and also forbade them to deprive any person—not a citizen, but any person—of life, liberty, or property without due process of law or to deny to any person the equal protection of the laws. Most of the Supreme Court's case law in this century rests, or sometimes teeters, on those phrases.

The political balance of federalism changed even more vastly during the New Deal when Congress began exercising its power over interstate commerce and the power to tax and spend for the common defense and the general welfare (Article I, Section 8), particularly when it began to impose federal conditions on state programs as the price of federal financial support. The income tax authorized by the Sixteenth Amendment in 1913, the vast costs of the defense establishment after 1941, national highway construction, unemployment compensation, and agricultural and welfare programs centralized American government more than any legal change did. Add to this list the nationalizing effect of radio and television in concentrating daily news and public attention on the national capital, indeed, on the president personally. Still, the reports of political pundits who have pronounced the demise of the states since the 1930s remain premature.

Consider that state, not national, laws govern our most important social relationships. Marriage, divorce, and parenthood are matters of state law. State courts applying state law decide deeply human and moral disputes—whether a hospital may discontinue life support for a hopelessly ill patient or force treatment for a child over the parent's religious objections, for example, or whether a child should live with a father or with a surrogate mother who has changed her mind about her surrogate status—issues of personal rights more meaningful to many people than freedom of the press or the Fifth Amendment protections against self-incrimination or double jeopardy. Property ownership, inheritance, and the use of land are governed by state law. So are buying and selling, employment, and other contracts. So is compensation for personal injuries. Workers' compensation laws were enacted by state legislatures, and battles over tort liability and insurance coverage are won and lost there as well. The states, not Congress, decide who may practice law or medicine, be a plumber or a hairdresser, drive a car or buy a drink.

The mass of conventional crimes are defined by state laws, and the overwhelming majority of criminal cases are investigated by local police officers and prosecuted by states' attorneys in state courts. Decentralized police power and the limited functions and small number of federal law enforcement officials are crucial protections of liberty in a federal system. Consider also that, second only to law enforcement, our most important and largest social service, education, is provided by state and local schools and colleges or governed by state laws. By a simple quantitative measure, state and local governments collect and spend more than $500 billion a year, mostly without enjoying the indulgence of deficit spending.[11]

All of these essential laws and policies are made and administered under the state constitutions by officials who are politically accountable only to their own state and local citizens. Predictably, the role of the federal Constitution, besides forming a national government, has been to restrain what state officials could do to serve the parochial self-interest or the prejudices of their constituents. The list is too long to include here; it forms most of the standard law school courses in constitutional law. Our particular interest at the moment concerns citizenship in the states, and a few examples will show the range of issues.

In the nineteenth century some new states, including my own, tried to control admission to the state, for instance by provisions excluding free persons of Asian and African descent.[12] The citizenship clause of the Fourteenth Amendment made that a dead letter. During the Depression, California attempted by law to stem the flow of poor migrants looking for work or welfare. The Supreme Court struck down the law as an interference with interstate commerce, though four justices preferred to hold that movement from state to state was a privilege of citizenship under the Fourteenth Amendment.[13]

If states were not allowed to favor their own citizens in commerce, that did not halt their efforts at such favoritism in other fields, with mixed success. For a while, it seemed that states could limit hunting and fishing to their citizens on the theory that citizens collectively owned wild game, but that theory did not last.[14] The familiar differential survives for out-of-state residents in public university admission and tuition at least until state residency is established.[15] States excluded aliens from various occupations, from public employment or contracts, and from social services on the theory that taxpayers' funds should be reserved for the state's own people. But the United States Supreme Court has invalidated most such laws, either as invasions of the exclu sive federal power over the admission of aliens or as denials of the equal protection of the laws.[16] Even aliens not legally admitted to the United States could not be excluded from free education in a state's schools.[17]

To repeat, in most respects the constitutional guarantees of liberty, equality, and fair procedure protect persons regardless of citizenship. In 1973 Professor Alexander Bickel concluded that the United States Constitution itself gave citizenship only external, international, but not internal importance. Its irreducible legal significance, he said, is that citizens have a constitutional right to be here and to return if they go abroad. Aliens do not.[18]

Federalism, however, preserves two important roles for the state constitution, one political and one legal.

Political Citizenship

Let us look again at the political importance of citizenship in the states. The main idea linked with citizenship, as I have said, is participation in a political community. Our words began as Latin and Greek words for the same thing, *civitas* and *polis*. The Fourteenth Amendment defines whom a state must recognize as its citizen, but the state defines the rules of political participation, as long as it does not discriminate by race, sex, age above eighteen years, or payment of a tax, or in drawing the lines of legislative districts.

This arrangement still leaves to each state the choice of what kinds of decisions its citizens may participate in, and how. The range of differences is wide. First, states fill different offices by election. Besides governors, many elect lieutenant governors, secretaries of state, treasurers, attorneys general, commissioners of various executive agencies, and various combinations of these. Many states elect judges, others do not. Many states elect prosecutors and sheriffs, others do not. Many elect school boards and commissioners of various utility and service districts, others appoint them. Cities are governed by many different combinations of elected and appointed leadership. More than these differences in the election of officials, the quality of services most important to many people depends on drawing boundaries around responsibilities and taxation. Not a single federal office is filled by majority vote of a national constituency; election of federal judges or

Cabinet officers beyond the president would, on reflection, strike most of us as absurd.

Second, state laws shape the political nature of elections by prescribing the form of the ballot. States cannot prevent the formation of political parties or other factions, but they can and do decide whether candidates are chosen and identified by party on the ballot. The role of parties differs widely in the political traditions of the states. Most states, but not all, elect legislators and state executive officials on partisan ballots. Some still have partisan elections of judges. Elections of city, county, and district officials are fierce partisan battles in some states, nonpartisan in others. The composition of legislatures and city councils and the fate of constituencies as well as that of individual politicians depend much on whether the state employs single-member or multimember districts, or perhaps proportional representation. They depend even more on whether candidates reach the ballot after nomination by voters in a primary election or by party conventions. All these are matters of state law, as long as federal guarantees are not violated.

Most people doubtless think of political parties as national parties, because we choose between a Republican and a Democratic candidate for president, and only the presidency holds most people's attention. But that impression is false. Such national party leadership as there is between presidential elections has no voice in choosing candidates. Each house of Congress organizes itself into a majority and a minority party, but, again, their respective partisan campaign committees have no power beyond collecting and distributing campaign funds to candidates nominated in each state and district. And there is little contact among state parties. The national political establishment inside the Beltway is at the mercy of loose coalitions of diverse political systems and traditions in the states, except insofar as each is at the mercy of the insatiable money-hunger of commercial television and the attendant fundraising organizations. We, the people, may be citizens of the United States, but apart from paying our federal taxes and making national campaign contributions, we act politically as citizens of our states and under their law.

Third, the states shape our political participation by allowing or denying direct plebiscites on state and local issues. Seventeen states have some form of popular initiative or referendum.[19] Invented as a progressive reform and safeguard against corrupt, overbearing, or hidebound legislatures, the initiative process has been extended to amending the states' constitutions, often in ways that are anything but reforms of those charters. California's record furnishes the most spectacular examples.[20] Again, for better or worse, this aspect of citizenship is left to the people of each state. Although the United States Constitution guarantees to each state what the founders called a republican form of government, the United States Supreme Court has held that the limits of that form are not for it to decide, and the Congress is unlikely to do so.[21] Nor is it likely that Congress will heed occasional suggestions to put some national issue to decision by a popular plebiscite, or that such a decision would be constitutional.

Individual Rights under the State Constitutions

This brings us to our final point, the role of state constitutions as sources of individual rights. As I said at the outset, 1991 seems the appropriate year to celebrate the ten amendments of 1791 that we call the Bill of Rights. But that does not mean that until 1791 Americans had no constitutional rights. To the contrary, most of the states had placed declarations of rights at the beginning of their separate constitutions; others had entrenched such guarantees in different articles of their charters. It was the demand in the state ratification debates for similar guarantees that persuaded James Madison and the first Congress to send a federal Bill of Rights to the states.

Those amendments did nothing to protect Americans against the governments that make and administer the bulk of the laws, their own states. As John Marshall wrote for the Supreme Court in 1833, Congress did not mean to add federal protections to rights that the people of the states had or could put into their own constitutions.[22] This was not done until the Fourteenth Amendment was passed in 1868.

Many familiar clauses were found and later copied throughout the state constitutions, particularly guarantees of fair trial procedures, search warrants, compensation for property taken for public use, and other aspects of due process of law. They continue in the declarations of rights that begin almost all state constitutions today. So do other early additions, freedom of speech and religion, and equality of privileges and immunities. But state courts played no great role in their protection beyond those clauses that dealt with judicial procedures and private property. State judges indeed were a greater threat to freedom of the press than legislatures; an Anti-Federalist Philadelphia printer was jailed for contempt in 1788 because he published an appeal for the protection of jurors against the Federalist-minded court.[23] Much later, a Denver publisher and former U.S. senator was similarly held in contempt for publishing political accusations against Colorado's supreme court, a fate confirmed by the federal Court in an opinion by Justice Holmes.[24]

Moreover, eighteenth-century state constitutions gave various forms of preference to Christian faiths, and nineteenth-century states were openly and unapologetically racist; before the Civil War, the future spread of slavery and of nonwhite people were unavoidable issues. As to abuses by law enforcement officers, few state courts let these affect the conviction of defendants on unlawfully obtained evidence until after the United States Supreme Court in 1914 held such evidence inadmissible in federal trials;[25] many states continued until the Court made exclusion part of due process under the Fourteenth Amendment in 1961.[26]

Thus, federal courts developed the meaning of most guarantees in the Bill of Rights before there were interpretations of the state clauses on which the federal amendments were based. State courts then copied judicial doctrine as well as results under state law from Supreme Court opinions under the federal amendments. Once the Court after 1940 incorporated First Amendment rights and fair procedures into the Fourteenth Amendment protection of liberty against state invasions,[27] several generations of lawyers and judges stopped looking at their states' bills of rights.

This situation has changed in recent years. Many state courts now give independent attention to their state constitutions.[28] Justice William Brennan, himself a former justice of New Jersey's supreme court, devoted a James Madison lecture, quite appropriately, to the subject: "The Bill of Rights and the States: The Revival of State Constitutions as Guardians of Individual Rights."[29] We deal with the revival differently in different states. Some courts first examine what the Supreme Court would do and decide whether to do something else under the state constitution. On the Oregon court, we decide first under Oregon's own law and turn to Supreme Court cases only for any federal claims that remain.[30]

Majoritarian Constitutions and Minority Rights

The coexistence of state and federal bills of rights creates legal intricacies beyond our theme today. For our present discussion, the essential points are two.

Our first protection against abuse by our state and local officials was the constitutions and laws of our several states in 1776, and it is the constitutions and laws of our several states today. We need the guarantees of the federal Bill of Rights against federal abuses, but we need them against our own states only when, and only to the extent that, our state officials, state laws, and state courts do not meet the standards of liberty, equality, and fair procedures that the federal Constitution sets for the whole nation.

But unfortunately, people in fact need those federal guarantees more often than they should. For the second essential point is that we are more directly responsible for our own constitutional liberties as citizens of our respective states than we are for the Constitution of the United States. And this is where the two important aspects of citizenship in the states—political participation and individual rights—intersect. Indeed, they not only intersect but often collide, because rights are based in constitutions to put them beyond the reach of majorities, and most state constitutions are readily amended by majority vote.

The initiative amendment, adopted as an instrument of progress against legislative partisanship, favoritism, and corruption, has proved to be a two-edged sword. In 1922, Oregon voters amended their constitution by popular initiative to require that all children attend public schools, a move directed against Catholic schools. The United States Supreme Court held the Oregon law invalid under the federal due process clause.[31] After the Supreme Court ruled against school segregation, some states amended their constitutions to close any public school that was ordered to integrate.[32] In a move just as racist, if less overtly so, California voters initiated a constitutional ban on open-housing laws, an action that, in turn, was held to violate the Fourteenth

Amendment.[33] Now, tides of immigration trigger demands to enshrine the English language in state constitutions.[34]

The men who drafted the constitutions in the early years of Independence feared official power to seize and to search their persons, houses, papers, and effects, to hold persons without bail, and to compel them to give evidence against themselves. Their bills of rights, and ours, mostly concern abuses in criminal and civil procedure. Today majorities in some states, fearful of and outraged by crime, initiate amendments to sacrifice those protections of their state constitution, as well as the guarantees that their courts have applied to set aside death sentences.[35] Of course, sponsors of those amendments tell the voters that their rights remain protected by the federal Constitution and the decisions of the Supreme Court, and that anything beyond this is unneeded and excessive.

By that logic, the states' bills of rights are superfluous, and we are wholly dependent for protection against our state officials on federal law. That position represents a 180-degree turn away from John Marshall's view that it would be strange to look to Washington for guarantees that the people in each state can provide for themselves. But experience has shown that politically powerless groups cannot provide their own guarantees in state constitutions; hence the Fourteenth Amendment. Recent developments show that the existence of state constitutions, important as they are, does not justify relaxing the standards that the federal Constitution sets for the whole nation. It is interesting to observe that Great Britain and the other democracies joining in the European Covenant on Human Rights now face the same situation of having two sets of rights, one under their own laws and the other under the supranational laws, and that the English, for instance, lacking an entrenched bill of rights of their own, turn to their courts for enforcement of the European standards to which their nation has subscribed.[36]

In sum, after two hundred years, federalism is remarkably healthy. The states are far from dead; there is too much to be done to do without them. American politics remains state politics, though endangered by the costs of media campaigns. Most practicing politicians as well as ordinary citizens learn about government in their separate states and cities. Americans today, more perhaps than in other years, enjoy the protection of their own state constitutions, if they want it. But if not, we can be thankful that the two-hundred-year-old genius of federalism provides the safeguards along with the energy of the national Constitution.

Notes

1. The Continental Congress resolved on July 2, 1776, that "these colonies are, and of right ought to be Free and Independent States." Accordingly, the day on which final separation was officially voted was July 2, although July 4, the day on which the Declaration of Independence was adopted, has always been celebrated in the United States as the national holiday.

2. *Calvin's Case,* 77 Eng. Rep. 377 (1608).

3. James H. Kettner, *The Development of American Citizenship, 1608–1870* (Chapel Hill: University of North Carolina Press, 1978), 65, 90–105.

4. Ibid., 213–19.

5. Articles of Confederation, Art. IV (1781).

6. *The Federalist,* ed. Jacob E. Cooke (Middletown, Conn.: Wesleyan University Press, 1961), no. 42.

7. See Herbert Wechsler, "The Political Safeguards of Federalism: The Role of the States in the Composition and Selection of the National Government," in *Principles, Politics, and Fundamental Law,* ed. Herbert Wechsler (Cambridge: Harvard University Press, 1961), 49, 54–56.

8. South Dakota Constitution, Art. VII, Sec. 1, "Historical Note," *South Dakota Codified Laws* 1: 408–9.

9. *Dred Scott v. Sandford,* 60 U.S. (19 How.) 393, 404–5 (1857).

10. Kettner, *Development of American Citizenship,* 311–22, and cases cited therein.

11. U.S. Bureau of the Census, *Statistical Abstract of the United States: 1987,* 107th ed. (Washington, D.C.: Government Printing Office, 1986), 258.

12. See, e.g., California Constitution, Art. XIX (1879); Oregon Constitution, Art. XVIII, Sec. 4; *The Oregon Constitution and Proceedings and Debates of the Constitutional Convention of 1857,* ed. Charles H. Carey (Salem, Oregon: State Printing Department, 1926), 24, 30–34, 359, 361–62, 381–85.

13. *Edwards v. California,* 314 U.S. 160 (1941).

14. Compare *McCready v. Virginia,* 94 U.S. 391 (1876), and *Geer v. Connecticut,* 161 U.S. 519 (1896), with *Toomer v. Witsell,* 334 U.S. 385 (1948), and *Hughes v. Oklahoma,* 441 U.S. 322 (1979).

15. The practice of charging nonresidents higher state university tuition has been accepted since the inception of the public school system. The difficulty arises in determining who is a resident. See *Vlandis v. Kline*, 412 U.S. 441 (1973); *Starns v. Malkerson*, 401 U.S. 985 (1971) (mem.), affirming 326 F. Supp. 234 (D. Minn. 1970).

16. See, e.g., *Graham v. Richardson*, 403 U.S. 365 (1971) (invalidating state statutes denying welfare benefits to resident aliens); *Sugarman v. Dougall*, 413 U.S. 634 (1973) (invalidating statutory prohibitions making aliens ineligible for permanent positions in state civil service). The Burger Court backed off in *Ambach v. Norwick*, 441 U.S. 68 (1979) (upholding state law limiting public-school teaching certificates to aliens intending to apply for citizenship), and *Foley v. Connelie*, 435 U.S. 291 (1978) (upholding requirement that all state police officers be United States citizens). But cf. *Bernal v. Fainter*, 467 U.S. 216 (1984) (invalidating citizenship requirement for notaries public).

17. *Phyler v. Doe*, 457 U.S. 202 (1982).

18. Alexander Bickel, "Citizenship in the American Constitution," *Arizona Law Review* 15 (1973): 369–87.

19. See David Magleby, *Direct Legislation* (Baltimore: Johns Hopkins University Press, 1984), 38–40; *Book of the States 1983–1984* (Chicago: Council of State Governments, 1984), 137.

20. See, e.g., Jonathan Kirsch, "Initiatives: Cutting Up the Constitution?" *California Lawyer* 4 (November 1984): 34–39, 75.

21. *Pacific States Telephone & Telegraph Co. v. Oregon*, 223 U.S. 118 (1912).

22. *Barron v. Baltimore*, 32 U.S. (7 Pet.) 243 (1833).

23. *Respublica v. Oswald*, 1 U.S. (1 Dall.) 319 (Pa. 1788).

24. *Patterson v. Colorado*, 205 U.S. 454 (1907).

25. *Weeks v. United States*, 232 U.S. 383 (1914).

26. *Mapp v. Ohio*, 367 U.S. 643 (1961).

27. Some First Amendment freedoms had been found to apply to the states through the Fourteenth Amendment before 1940, for example, freedom of speech (*Fiske v. Kansas*, 274 U.S. 380 [1927]), freedom of press (*Near v. Minnesota*, 283 U.S. 697 [1931]), and freedom of assembly (*DeJonge v. Oregon*, 299 U.S. 353 [1937]). After 1940, the Court continued deciding cases that selectively "incorporated" various First Amendment freedoms and fair procedures guaranteed by the Bill of Rights. The list includes *Cantwell v. Connecticut*, 310 U.S. 296 (1940) (free exercise of religion), *Everson v. Board of Education*, 330 U.S. 1 (1947) (nonestablishment of religion), *In re Oliver*, 333 U.S. 257 (1948) (right to public trial), *Wolf v. Colorado*, 338 U.S. 25 (1949) (freedom from unusual search and seizure), *Mapp v. Ohio*, 367 U.S. 643 (1961) (exclusion from criminal trials of illegally seized evidence), *Gi-*

deon v. Wainwright, 372 U.S. 355 (1963) (right to counsel), *Klopfer v. North Carolina,* 386 U.S. 213 (1967) (right to speedy trial), and *Duncan v. Louisiana,* 391 U.S. 145 (1968) (right to jury trial).

28. See A. E. Dick Howard, "State Courts and Constitutional Rights in the Day of the Burger Court," *Virginia Law Review* 62 (1976): 873–944; Ronald K. L. Collins, Peter J. Galie, and John Kincaid, "State High Courts and Individual Rights Litigation Since 1980: A Judicial Survey," *Hastings Constitutional Law Quarterly* 13 (1986): 599–623.

29. William Brennan, "The Bill of Rights and the States: The Revival of State Constitutions as Guardians of Individual Rights," *New York University Law Review* 61 (1986): 535–53.

30. See *State v. Kennedy,* 295 Or. 260, 666 P.2d 1316 (1983), and cases cited therein.

31. *Pierce v. Society of Sisters,* 268 U.S. 510 (1925).

32. See generally Robert B. McKay, "With All Deliberate Speed: Legislative Reaction and Judicial Development 1956–1957," *Virginia Law Review* 43 (1957): 1205–45.

33. *Reitman v. Mulkey,* 387 U.S. 369 (1967).

34. See California Constitution, Art. III, Sec. 6.

35. See, e.g., Florida Constitution, Art. I, Sec. 12 (amended 1982); Oregon Constitution, Art. I, Sec. 40 (adopted 1984). See also Donald E. Wilkes, "First Things Last: Amendomania and State Bills of Rights," *Mississippi Law Journal* 54 (1984): 223–59.

36. See "Implementing the European Convention on Human Rights in the United Kingdom," *Stanford Journal of International Law* 18 (1982): 147–70.

Contributors

WILLI PAUL ADAMS is professor of North American history, John F. Kennedy Institute of North American Studies, Free University of Berlin.

FREDERICK R. ANDERSON is Ann Loeb Bronsman Professor of Law, Washington College of Law, American University, and counsel to Cadwalader, Wickersham and Taft.

JOYCE APPLEBY is professor of history at the University of California, Los Angeles. She is the author of *Economic Thought and Ideology in Seventeenth-Century England* and *Capitalism and a New Social Order: The Republican Vision of the 1790s.*

DERRICK A. BELL, JR., is Weld Professor of Law at Harvard Law School. He is the author of *Race, Racism, and American Law; Shades of Brown: New Perspectives on School Desegregation;* and *We Are Not Saved.*

FRANÇOIS BOURRICAUD was a professor at the University of Paris, Sorbonne (Paris IV).

ERNEST L. BOYER is president of the Carnegie Foundation for the Advancement of Teaching, a senior fellow of the Woodrow Wilson School at Princeton University, and an education columnist for the *London Times.* He has also served as the United States Commissioner of Education and as the chancellor of the State University of New York.

WARREN BURGER, Chief Justice of the United States from 1969 to 1986, chaired the Commission on the Bicentennial of the United States Constitution.

ROBERT COLES is a child psychiatrist who teaches at Harvard University and the author of the series *Children of Crisis*, volumes of which have won the Pulitzer Prize.

ROBERT F. ERBURU is chairman of the board and chief executive officer of the Times Mirror Company.

JACK P. GREENE is Andrew W. Mellon Professor in the Humanities, Johns Hopkins University. He is the author of *Peripheries and Center: Constitutional Development in the Extended Politics of the British Empire and the United States, 1607–1788* and *Pursuits of Happiness: The Social Development of Early Modern British Colonies and the Formation of American Culture*.

LORD HAILSHAM OF ST. MARYLEBONE was Lord High Chancellor of Great Britain, 1970–74 and 1979–87.

LADONNA HARRIS is the founder, president, and executive director of Americans for Indian Opportunity, a national Native American advocacy organization that assists tribes in matters of self-determination and self-sufficiency.

A. E. DICK HOWARD is White Burkett Miller Professor of Law and Public Affairs at the University of Virginia. His books include *The Road from Runnymede: Magna Carta and Constitutionalism in America* and *Commentaries on the Constitution of Virginia*. He has been consulted by drafters of other countries' constitutions, especially in Central and Eastern Europe.

MICHAEL KAMMEN is Newton C. Farr Professor of American History and Culture at Cornell University. His books include *A Machine That Would Go of Itself: The Constitution in American Culture* and *Sovereignty and Liberty: Constitutional Discourse in American Culture*.

SYLVIA LAW is professor of law, New York University School of Law, and director of the Arthur Garfield Hayes Civil Liberties Program.

SANFORD LEVINSON is Garwood Regents Professor of Law, University of Texas Law School. He is the author of *Constitutional Faith*.

Contributors

HANS A. LINDE, a former Justice of the Supreme Court of Oregon, is a member of the American Academy of Arts and Sciences and the author of several works on constitutional theory.

DAVID F. LINOWES is Boeschenstein Professor Emeritus of Public Economy and Public Policy at the University of Illinois at Urbana-Champaign. The author of several books, including *Strategies for Survival, The Corporate Conscience,* and *Privacy in America,* Professor Linowes has served as chairman of the President's Commission on Privatization and the United States Privacy Protection Commission.

NEIL MACCORMICK is Regius Professor of Public Law and the Law of Nature and Nations at the University of Edinburgh, where he has also served two terms as dean of the Faculty of Law. A fellow of both the Royal Society of Edinburgh and the British Academy, he is the author of several works in the philosophy of law and in Scottish legal thought.

JON D. MILLER is professor of political science and director of the Public Opinion Laboratory at Northern Illinois University.

RALPH NADER is a lawyer, author, and consumer advocate.

BURT NEUBORNE is professor of law at the New York University School of Law, an active civil liberties lawyer, and the former national legal director of the American Civil Liberties Union. He is the coauthor of *Political and Civil Rights in the United States.*

ROBERT R. PALMER, professor emeritus of history at Yale University, is affiliated with the Institute for Advanced Study at Princeton, New Jersey, where he now lives and where he was for many years a member of the faculty at Princeton University. A former president of the American Historical Association, he is the author of numerous books on the French Revolution and (with Joel Colton) of *A History of the Modern World,* a college text now in its seventh edition.

MERRILL D. PETERSON is Jefferson Foundation Professor Emeritus of History at the University of Virginia. His many books include *The Jefferson Image in the American Mind* and *Thomas Jefferson and the New Nation.*

DON K. PRICE is Weatherhead Professor of Public Management Emeritus at the John F. Kennedy School of Government, Harvard University.

HARRY N. SCHEIBER is Stefan Riesenfeld Professor of Law at the Boalt Hall School of Law, University of California, Berkeley. Twice a Guggenheim Fellow, he has written extensively on the history of American law.

JUDITH SHKLAR is John Cowles Professor of Government at Harvard University and has been the Pitt Professor of American Institutions and History at Cambridge University. A former MacArthur Fellow, she is the author of numerous works in the fields of European and American intellectual history, law, and political philosophy.

LAURENCE H. TRIBE is Tyler Professor of Constitutional Law at Harvard Law School and a frequent oral advocate before the Supreme Court. The second edition of his treatise, *American Constitutional Law,* was published in 1988.

Acknowledgments

The Ninth International Smithsonian Symposium, "Constitutional Roots, Rights, and Responsibilities," was held May 18–23, 1987, in Charlottesville, Virginia, and Washington, D.C. With nearly ninety constitutional experts from ten countries on the program, the symposium was organized in cooperation with the University of Virginia and the American Bar Association.

Advice and support came generously from a great many quarters in the United States and abroad, and in a variety of forms; they were most welcome and always greatly appreciated. Those primarily responsible for the planning and presentation of the symposium deserve special mention and the deepest appreciation.

Wilton S. Dillon, at the Smithsonian Institution, was director of the symposium. He also was director of the Institution's Office of Interdisciplinary Studies, the symposium's nucleus, where Neil G. Kotler served as coordinator of the symposium and Carla M. Borden as publications coordinator.

At the University of Virginia, a number of faculty members consulted with the symposium chairman, A. E. Dick Howard, in planning the program: William W. Abbot, Henry J. Abraham, Matthew Holden, Jr., David C. Jordan, David M. O'Brien, Merrill D. Peterson, Robert A. Rutland, G. Edward White, and James S. Young. Then president of the university, Robert M. O'Neil was an active participant in the process as well, as was Daniel P. Jordan, director of the Thomas Jefferson Memorial Foundation in Charlottesville.

At the American Bar Association, the staff of the Commission on Public Understanding about the Law, and in particular Robert S. Peck, at the time staff director, helped to make the symposium, and then this volume, possible.